WORKING SUBJECTS IN
EARLY MODERN ENGLISH DRAMA

Studies in Performance and Early Modern Drama

General Editor's Preface
Helen Ostovich, McMaster University

Performance assumes a string of creative, analytical, and collaborative acts that, in defiance of theatrical ephemerality, live on through records, manuscripts, and printed books. The monographs and essay collections in this series offer original research which addresses theatre histories and performance histories in the context of the sixteenth and seventeenth century life. Of especial interest are studies in which women's activities are a central feature of discussion as financial or technical supporters (patrons, musicians, dancers, seamstresses, wigmakers, or 'gatherers'), if not authors or performers per se. Welcome too are critiques of early modern drama that not only take into account the production values of the plays, but also speculate on how intellectual advances or popular culture affect the theatre.

The series logo, selected by my colleague Mary V. Silcox, derives from Thomas Combe's duodecimo volume, *The Theater of Fine Devices* (London, 1592), Emblem VI, sig. B. The emblem of four masks has a verse which makes claims for the increasing complexity of early modern experience, a complexity that makes interpretation difficult. Hence the corresponding perhaps uneasy rise in sophistication:

> Masks will be more hereafter in request,
> And grow more deare than they did heretofore.

No longer simply signs of performance 'in play and jest', the mask has become the 'double face' worn 'in earnest' even by 'the best' of people, in order to manipulate or profit from the world around them. The books stamped with this design attempt to understand the complications of performance produced on stage and interpreted by the audience, whose experiences outside the theatre may reflect the emblem's argument:

> Most men do use some colour'd shift
> For to conceal their craftie drift.

Centuries after their first presentations, the possible performance choices and meanings they engender still stir the imaginations of actors, audiences, and readers of early plays. The products of scholarly creativity in this series, I hope, will also stir imaginations to new ways of thinking about performance.

Working Subjects in
Early Modern English Drama

Edited by
MICHELLE M. DOWD
University of North Carolina – Greensboro, USA

and

NATASHA KORDA
Wesleyan University, USA

LONDON AND NEW YORK

First published 2011 by Ashgate Publishing

2 Park Square, Milton Park, Abingdon, Oxon OX14 4RN
711 Third Avenue, New York, NY 10017, USA

Routledge is an imprint of the Taylor & Francis Group, an informa business

First issued in paperback 2016

British Library Cataloguing in Publication Data
Working subjects in early modern English drama. – (Studies in performance and early modern drama)
   1. English drama – Early modern and Elizabethan, 1500–1600 – History and criticism.
   2. Working class in literature. 3. Labor in literature. 4. Work in literature. 5. Literature and society – England – History – 16th century. 6. Literature and society – England – History – 17th century.
   I. Series II. Dowd, Michelle M., 1975– III. Korda, Natasha.
   822.3'093553-dc22

Library of Congress Cataloging-in-Publication Data
   Working subjects in early modern English drama / edited by Michelle M. Dowd and
      Natasha Korda.
      p. cm. — (Studies in performance and early modern drama)
   Includes bibliographical references and index.
   ISBN 978-1-4094-1077-5 (hardback: alk. paper)
   1. English drama—Early modern and Elizabethan, 1500–1600—History and criticism.
2. English drama—17th century—History and criticism. 3. Work in literature. 4. Labor in literature. 5. Capitalism in literature. 6. Capitalism and literature—England—History—16th century. 7. Capitalism and literature—England—History—17th century. 8. Theater—England—History—16th century. 9. Theater—England—History—17th century. 10. Theater and society—England—History. I. Dowd, Michelle M., 1975– II. Korda, Natasha.
   PR658.W65W67 2010
   820.9'355—dc22

                                                                          2010027223

ISBN: 978-1-4094-1077-5 (hbk)
ISBN: 978-1-138-24925-7 (pbk)

"Der Schellenmacher," from Hans Sachs's *Eygentliche Beschreibung aller Stände auff Erden* (1568), C57.b25, Uii. © The British Library Board.

Contents

List of Figures

Notes on Contributors

Ronda Arab is Assistant Professor of English at Simon Fraser University. Her work has appeared in *Medieval and Renaissance Drama in England*, the *Journal for Early Modern Cultural Studies* and *Renaissance Quarterly*. Her book, *Manly Mechanicals on the Early Modern English Stage*, is forthcoming from Susquehanna University Press.

John Michael Archer is Professor of English at New York University. He co-edited the anthology *Enclosure Acts: Sexuality, Property and Culture in Early Modern England* (Cornell University Press, 1994) and is author of *Sovereignty and Intelligence: Spying and Court Culture in the English Renaissance* (Stanford University Press, 1993), *Old Worlds: Egypt, Southwest Asia, India, and Russia in Early Modern English Writing* (Stanford University Press, 2001), and *Citizen Shakespeare: Freemen and Aliens in the Language of the Plays* (Palgrave, 2005), which explores how the London citizen and the immigrant city-dweller figure in the action and verbal texture of Shakespeare's drama.

Amanda Bailey is Assistant Professor of English at University of Connecticut, Storrs. She is the author of *Flaunting: Style and the Subversive Male Body in Renaissance England* (University of Toronto Press, 2007), and co-editor of *Masculinity the Metropolis of Vice, 1550–1650* (New York: Palgrave Macmillan, 2010). Her essays have appeared or are forthcoming in such journals as *Criticism*, *Renaissance Drama*, *English Literary Renaissance*, and *Shakespeare Quarterly*. She is currently completing a book entitled *Of Bondage: Debt and Dramatic Economies in Early Modern England*.

Crystal Bartolovich is Associate Professor of English at Syracuse University. She edits the journal *Early Modern Culture* and has published on a variety of Renaissance topics and on Marxist theory in venues such as *Renaissance Drama*, *Journal of Medieval and Renaissance Studies*, *New Formations*, *Cultural Critique* and *Angelaki*.

Michelle M. Dowd is Associate Professor of English at the University of North Carolina, Greensboro. She is the author of *Women's Work in Early Modern English Literature and Culture* (Palgrave, 2009), which won the Sara A. Whaley Book Award from the National Women's Studies Association. She is also the co-editor of *Genre and Women's Life Writing in Early Modern England* (Ashgate, 2007) and of *Early Modern Women on the Fall: An Anthology* (MRTS, forthcoming). Her essays have appeared or are forthcoming in such journals as *English Literary Renaissance, Modern Philology*, and *Medieval and Renaissance Drama in England*.

Holly Dugan is Assistant Professor of English at George Washington University. Her essay, "Scent of a Woman: Performing the Politics of Smell in Late Medieval and Early Modern England," recently appeared in *The Journal of Medieval and Early Modern Studies*. Her book, *The Ephemeral History of Perfume: Scent and Sense in Early Modern England*, is forthcoming from Johns Hopkins University Press.

Valerie Forman is Associate Professor at the Gallatin School of Individualized Study at New York University. She is author of *Tragicomic Redemptions: Global Economics and the Early Modern English Stage* (University of Pennsylvania Press, 2008), and has published essays in *The Journal of Medieval and Early Modern Studies*, *Renaissance Quarterly*, and the collection *Money and the Age of Shakespeare* (Palgrave, 2003). She is currently at work on a new project, entitled "Developing New Worlds: Property, Freedom and the Economics of Representation in Early Modern England and the English Caribbean."

Molly Hand completed her dissertation, *"That Inimitable Art": Magic in Early Modern English Culture*, and received her PhD from Florida State University in 2009. Her article, "'Now is hell landed here upon the earth': Renaissance Poverty and Witchcraft in Middleton's *The Black Book*" appears in *Renaissance and Reformation* 31.1 (Winter 2008). She also contributed to the textual companion to *The Oxford Middleton* (2007).

David Hawkes is Associate Professor of English at Arizona State University. He is the author of three books, *Idols of the Marketplace: Idolatry and Commodity Fetishism in English Literature, 1580–1680* (Palgrave, 2001), *Ideology* (Routledge [2nd edition], 2003), and *The Faust Myth: Religion and the Rise of Representation* (Palgrave, 2007), and has edited John Milton's *Paradise Lost* (Barnes and Noble, 2004) and John Bunyan's *The Pilgrim's Progress* (Barnes and Noble, 2005). His work has appeared in such journals as *The Nation*, the *Times Literary Supplement*, the *Journal of the History of Ideas*, the *Huntington Library Quarterly*, and *Studies in English Literature*, as well as on National Public Radio.

Jean E. Howard is George Delacorte Professor in the Humanities at Columbia University and Chair of the Department of English and Comparative Literature. An editor of *The Norton Shakespeare* (2nd edition, 2008), she is author of many articles and books, the latest being *Theater of a City: The Places of London Comedy 1598–1642* (University of Pennsylvania Press, 2007), which in 2008 won the Barnard Hewitt Award for outstanding research in theater history from the American Society for Theater Research. She is now completing a book on the contemporary feminist dramatist, Caryl Churchill.

Natasha Korda is Professor of English at Wesleyan University. She is author of *Shakespeare's Domestic Economies: Gender and Property in Early Modern England* (University of Pennsylvania Press, 2002), and co-editor of *Staged*

Properties in Early Modern English Drama (Cambridge University Press, 2002). She has recently completed a book entitled *Labors Lost: Women's Work and the Early Modern English Stage*, which will be published by the University of Pennsylvania Press in 2011.

Sara Mueller has taught at Queen's University, Wilfrid Laurier University, and currently teaches at the University of Saskatchewan. Her articles include "Touring, Women, and the Professional Stage" in *Early Theatre* and "Early Modern Banquet Receipts and Women's Theatre," which is forthcoming in *Medieval and Renaissance Drama in England*. She is working on a book on women's domestic performances in early modern England.

Elizabeth Rivlin is Assistant Professor of English at Clemson University. She is editor of *The Upstart Crow: A Shakespeare Journal* and has published essays in *English Literary History* and *English Literary Renaissance*. Her book, *The Aesthetics of Service in Early Modern England*, is forthcoming from Northwestern University Press.

Tom Rutter is a Principal Lecturer in English at Sheffield Hallam University. His articles have appeared in publications including *Studies in English Literature* and *Medieval and Renaissance Drama in England*, and his book *Work and Play on the Shakespearean Stage* was published by Cambridge University Press in 2008.

Daniel Vitkus is Associate Professor of English at Florida State University. He is editor of *Three Turk Plays from Early Modern England* (Columbia University Press, 2000) and *Piracy, Slavery and Redemption: Barbary Captivity Narratives from Early Modern England* (Columbia University Press, 2001) and author of *Turning Turk: English Theater and the Multicultural Mediterranean, 1570–1630* (Palgrave, 2003). He is currently co-editing the Bedford Texts and Contexts edition of Shakespeare's *Antony and Cleopatra* and writing a book entitled *Islam, England, and Early Modernity*.

Acknowledgments

This book first began as the seminar "Working Subjects in Early Modern Drama" at the 2008 meeting of the Shakespeare Association of America in Dallas. We are grateful to all of the participants in that seminar for their engaging papers and discussion, which helped to shape the scope and direction of the current volume. Our thanks also go to our editor at Ashgate, Erika Gaffney, and series editor Helen Ostovich, for their interest in the project and their support in seeing it through to publication. Emily Benton and Anna Smith at the University of North Carolina at Greensboro assisted with copy-editing and bibliographic work in the final stages of the project and we are very grateful for their meticulous and timely assistance. We also wish to thank Wesleyan University for their financial support in the form of a collaborative project grant.

The cover image and frontispiece are reproduced by permission of the British Library Board. Figure 14.1 is reproduced by permission of the Folger Shakespeare Library.

Note on Text

When quoting from early modern manuscripts and printed texts in original or facsimile editions, we have retained original orthography except for silently expanding contractions, changing long s to short, and modernizing the letters i, j u and v where necessary.

Introduction
Working Subjects

Michelle M. Dowd and Natasha Korda

Early modern England witnessed a series of remarkable economic changes that transformed the landscape of labor and the working subjects who populated it. In addition to dramatic population growth and substantial expansion in global trade and consumerism, as the economy shifted from feudal to wage labor the hegemony of the guilds began to give way to labor contracts and more casual economic arrangements. In the midst of this dynamic, proto-capitalist economy stood London's public theaters, a cultural institution indebted both to traditional guild structures and to the innovations of a burgeoning consumer society. As a result, the plays performed in early modern London's first purpose-built theaters by its recently professionalized playing companies were uniquely positioned to interrogate the shifting boundaries of England's labor economy. Early modern drama actively participated in this changing economic landscape by staging England's heterogeneous workforce and exploring the subject of work itself. The cast of characters who labored on the stage was diverse indeed, incorporating not only masters who worked in the formal economy regulated by the guilds or twelve great livery companies (and a host of new companies incorporated during the Elizabethan and Jacobean period), their wives, journeymen and apprentices, but also a growing population of masterless men and women, foreigners, and aliens, who migrated to London seeking work in its rapidly expanding informal economy. Merchants, usurers, clothworkers, cooks, confectioners, shopkeepers, shoemakers, sheepshearers, shipbuilders, sailors, perfumers, players, prostitutes, magicians, witches, servants and slaves are among the many working subjects examined in this collection whose lives and labors were transformed by England's shifting economic climate.

Working Subjects sets out to investigate the ways in which work became a subject of inquiry on the early modern stage and the processes by which the drama began to forge new connections between labor and subjectivity. The public theaters brought into heightened visibility a newly diverse range of occupational roles––including the hitherto unknown occupation of the "professional player"—and provided a platform upon which the contours and legitimacy of these roles might be investigated and their social implications played out. The visible forms of these roles shaped and were shaped by the material culture of the stage, including its costumes (such as the characteristic flat-caps of citizens, livery of servants, and so forth), properties (designating the tools and products of various trades), and stage-furniture (indicating the shop-stalls and workshops where workers plied their trades), while their inner contours were forged and plumbed by the poetic tools of the playwright.

When Othello bids farewell to his occupation, his lament evokes both its external and internal dimensions:

> O now, for ever
> Farewell the tranquil mind! Farewell content!
> Farewell the plumed troops and the big wars
> That makes ambition virtue! O, farewell!
> Farewell the neighing steed and the shrill trump,
> The spirit-stirring drum, th' ear-piercing fife,
> The royal banner, and all quality,
> Pride, pomp, and circumstance of glorious war!
> And O you mortal engines, whose rude throats
> Th' immortal Jove's dread clamors counterfeit,
> Farewell! Othello's occupation's gone. (3.3.347–57)[1]

Othello's lamented loss of self suggests that his peace of mind and the "content" of his character are inextricably bound to his occupation, war, in its most material manifestations or circumstances: plumed troops, royal banners, mortal engines, drums, fifes, trumpets and all. Indeed, the shrill, ear-piercing quality of these implements of war breaches the boundary between external and internal. The rude, clamorous labor of battle penetrates the body of the soldier, stirring his spirit to pride, virtue and ambition, a subjective state the good soldier experiences as contentment and tranquility. Othello's lament is but one example of the way in which work was defined in the drama of the period as constitutive of subjectivity, yet it gives eloquent voice to the manner in which working life in post-Reformation England had come to be associated with a "positive sense of vocation" that was crucially linked to social credit.[2] Reputation and social identity were not solely interiorized or ephemeral concepts, but were intimately connected to the ever-changing economic and material conditions and cultural discourses that shaped or interpellated working subjects.[3]

As the example of Othello reminds us, the connection between labor and subjectivity was not always an empowering one, but was often constructed through tropes of displacement, poverty, failure, and deprivation. It is significant that Othello's homage to the virtues of his occupation is occasioned by the advent of its perceived loss. The subjective experience of losing one's occupation was

---

[1]   William Shakespeare, The *Riverside Shakespeare*, (eds.) G. Blakemore Evans et al. (Boston and New York: Houghton Mifflin, 1997). All further references to Shakespeare in this chapter are to the Riverside edition.

[2]   Alexandra Shepard, "Manhood, Credit and Patriarchy in Early Modern England c.1580–1640," *Past and Present* 167.1 (2000): 92.

[3]   On the concept of "interpellation," see Louis Althusser, "Ideology and Ideological State Apparatuses," in *Lenin and Philosophy, and Other Essays*, trans. Ben Brewster (London: New Left Books, 1971), 121–76.

one that many early modern playgoers would have known firsthand, particularly during the economic "crisis" of the 1590s. Yet the form in which such subjective loss was voiced onstage, and the dramatic actions taken in response to it, varied greatly in accordance with the dictates of genre. Othello's tragic lament stands in stark contrast, for example, to the occupational flexibility and ingenuity manifested by the working subjects who appear in comedies. Faced with a rather more advantageous change of occupation, Christopher Sly in *The Taming of the Shrew* boasts of his former vocational versatility: "Am not I Christopher Sly, old Sly's son of Burton-heath, by birth a pedlar, by education a card-maker, by transmutation a bear-heard, and now by present profession a tinker?" (Ind., 2.17–21). The subject positions that work produces in dramatic literature were thus conditioned as much by generic and formal structures as by the economic conditions of early modern society at large.

The essays assembled in this collection investigate the interface between changing or historically emergent modalities of work and the forms of subjectivity to which they gave rise in a broad range of dramatic genres, including chronicle and "citizen" history plays, comedies, tragedies, tragicomedies, travel plays, progress entertainments and civic pageants, demonstrating the vibrant and significant role dramatic literature played in responding to England's changing labor economy and helping to define the cultural meanings of work. Deploying a diverse range of methodologies, they are nonetheless all grounded in a concept of working subjectivity located at the nexus between individual or communal forms of agency and the larger social structures that shape and are shaped by them. The collection as a whole reveals that work was a culturally resonant topic that profoundly shaped the plots, themes, generic structures, poetic forms, and ideological frameworks of the period's drama, as well as the material culture of the stage, including its costumes, props, and stage-furniture, which were themselves constructed by laboring hands. Individual essays consider texts as disparate as William Haughton's *Englishmen for My Money*, Will Kempe's *Nine Daies Wonder*, and William Shakespeare's *The Tempest*, and focus on a range of topics, including the labor networks associated with the public theaters, acting as labor, women's work, labor and citizenship, global networks of trade, indentured servitude and slavery. Taken together, they offer compelling new readings of both canonical and lesser-known plays and a clearer understanding of the complex ways in which the stage reimagined England's labor economy and its own place within that economy.

The plays performed in early modern London's first purpose-built theaters by its professional playing companies were well positioned to interrogate the shifting boundaries between different definitional categories of work because the playing companies were themselves transitional economic formations. Situated on the cusp of residual and emergent modes of production, they retained aspects of the guild and patronage systems, while in other respects assuming the innovative form of joint-stock, proto-capitalist ventures. As such, they were open to attack by civic and religious authorities who refused to recognize the legitimacy of playing as a skilled, and sometimes lucrative, vocation. In the eyes of city officials and Puritan prelates, playing was not a proper calling—indeed, it was the very antithesis of work. Players were classed among the idle parasites or "Caterpillers of a Comonwelth," who sought "a more idle and easier kinde of Trade of livinge … [than] manuall Labours and Trades did or coulde bringe them."[4] The commercial theater was, according to Stephen Gosson, a "nurserie of idelness" that lured apprentices away from their legitimate trades:

> Most of the Players have bene eyther men of occupations, which they have forsaken to lyve by playing … or trayned up from theire childehoode to this abhominable exercise & have now no other way to gete theire livinge. We are commaunded by God to abide in the same calling wheirein we were called, which is our ordinary vocation in a commonweale. This is the standing, which as faithfull souldiers we ought to kepe, till the Lord himselfe do call us from it. … If we grudge at the wisedome of our maker, and disdaine the calling he hath placed us in, aspyring somewhat higher then we shoulde, … if privat men be suffered to forsake theire calling because they desire to walke gentleman like in sattine & velvet, with a buckler at theire heeles, proportion is so broken, unitie dissolved, [and] harmony confounded. … Wherefore I hope the wise will accompt it necessarie, that such as have lefte theire occupations … be turned to the same againe, … aske God forgivenes for the time so evill spent, and apply them selves speedely to live within the compasse of a common weale. Let them not looke to live by playes, the litle thrift that followeth theire great gaine, is a manifest token that God hath cursed it.[5]

Unlike Othello, a faithful soldier who fetches his very life and being from his occupation and deeply laments its perceived loss, the professional actors were accused of blithely forsaking their God-given callings "to lyve by playing," rather than honest work. Their occupational flexibility and social mobility as described by Gosson recall the rapid ascent of Christopher Sly, who is one minute a mere "rogue," and the next "gentleman like in sattine & velvet." In Gosson's view, players threaten the proportion, unity and harmony of the social hierarchy, and earn their living at the expense of the commonwealth (rather than, like the faithful soldier, serving to protect it). The professionalization of playing thus required that playwrights actively engage in contemporary debates surrounding the subject of work, and that they defend the status of players as *working* subjects. Unlike Gosson, Othello does not view his own occupation in opposition to that of the professional player. To the contrary, he defends the former by drawing on the vocabulary of the latter: "Were it my cue to fight, I should have known it / Without a prompter" (1.2.83–4), he says, suggesting that the occupation of the soldier and

---

4   Stephen Gosson, *The Schoole of Abuse. Conteining a Pleasaunt Invective Against Poets, Pipers, Plaiers, Jesters and Such Like Caterpillers of a Comonwelth* (London, 1579); see also *Statutes of the Realm*, (ed.) John Raithby (London: G. Eyre and A. Strahan, 1819), 4: 1038–9.

5   Gosson, *Playes Confuted in Five Actions* (London, 1582), G6v–G7v.

the player share common skills. In such instances, play-texts subtly cued audiences to the players' claim to occupational legitimacy.

Previous scholarship has demonstrated the importance of reading early modern English dramatic literature with and against the vibrant economic and material culture of which it was a part.[6] Attending to the complexities of England's nascent capitalist economy, including the networks of credit and debt it fostered, the systems of literary patronage it enabled, and the poverty and displacement it produced, has helped to foster a critical practice that illuminates the material conditions in which texts are produced as shaped by historical pressures of the period. *Working Subjects* contributes to this body of scholarship, while extending it in significant new directions. Older scholarship such as Louis B. Wright's *Middle-Class Culture in Elizabethan England* (1935) and L.C. Knights's *Drama and Society in the Age of Jonson* (1937), while foundational texts for thinking about early modern dramatic literature in relation to its economic contexts, tended to focus on citizen culture (and the figure of the "new man") as depicted in citizen and city comedies.[7] These works paved the way for numerous studies of city comedy in particular,[8] a genre that as Jean Howard has shown attempts to make sense of a rapidly changing and expanding city increasingly populated by *non*-citizen subjects, such as foreigners, aliens and women.[9] The essays in this volume likewise attend to this diverse population

---

[6] Some recent examples include Linda Woodbridge (ed.), *Money and the Age of Shakespeare: Essays in New Economic Criticism* (New York: Palgrave, 2003); Jonathan Gil Harris, *Sick Economies: Drama, Mercantilism, and Disease in Shakespeare's England* (Philadelphia: University of Pennsylvania Press, 2003); Jonathan Gil Harris and Natasha Korda (eds.), *Staged Properties in Early Modern English Drama* (Cambridge: Cambridge University Press, 2002); and Patricia Fumerton, *Unsettled: The Culture of Mobility and the Working Poor in Early Modern England* (Chicago: University of Chicago Press, 2006).

[7] Wright's study focuses on "the average citizen's reading and thinking, his intellectual habits and cultural tastes" (vii), and devotes only a few pages to the depiction of working subjects onstage (626–31). Knights focuses on the rise of capitalism and the figure of the "new man" (esp. 88–95) as depicted in citizen and city comedies. See Louis B. Wright, *Middle-Class Culture in Elizabethan England* (Chapel Hill: University of North Carolina Press, 1935) and L.C. Knights, *Drama and Society in the Age of Jonson* (London: Chatto and Windus, 1937).

[8] See for example Alexander Leggatt, *Citizen Comedy in the Age of Shakespeare* (Toronto: University of Toronto Press, 1973); Brian Gibbons, *Jacobean City Comedy: A Study of Satiric Plays by Jonson, Marston and Middleton* (New York: Methuen, 1980); Gail Kern Paster, *The Idea of the City in the Age of Shakespeare* (Athens: University of Georgia Press, 1985); Theodore Leinwand, *The City Staged: Jacobean City Comedy, 1603–1613* (Madison: University of Wisconsin Press, 1986); Douglas Bruster, *Drama and the Market in the Age of Shakespeare* (Cambridge: Cambridge University Press, 1992); Lawrence Manley, *Literature and Culture in Early Modern London* (Cambridge: Cambridge University Press, 1995); and Jean E. Howard, *Theater of a City: The Places of London Comedy, 1598–1642* (Philadelphia: University of Pennsylvania Press, 2007).

[9] Howard, *Theater of a City*, 22.

of working subjects, while demonstrating that both they and the subject of work itself were taken up in a broad array of genres that includes but is not limited to citizen and city comedy.

Much of the recent economic and materialist criticism of early modern culture has been focused on consumption rather than production. Studies such as Lisa Jardine's *Worldly Goods: A New History of the Renaissance* and John Brewer and Roy Porter's edited collection *Consumption and the World of Goods* have contributed in important ways to our understanding of early modern material culture, and the ways in which manufactured wares functioned as signifiers of social distinction and differentiation.[10] Yet such scholarship has often had little to say about the working subjects who labored to produce the expanding "world of goods." A collection of essays entitled *Materialist Shakespeare: A History*, for example, while providing an overview of two decades of materialist scholarship on the stage in Shakespeare's time, contains not a single index entry under "work" or "labor."[11] By focusing on the manner in which early modern subjects and objects were inscribed within social relations of production as well as consumption, *Working Subjects* broadens the interpretive possibilities of materialist and economic criticism, opening up fresh scholarly conversations about the ideological underpinnings, material practices, laboring bodies, shifting attitudes, and new technologies that gave rise to early modern England's consumer culture.[12]

Moving away from the tendency of recent criticism to focus narrowly, and at times almost fetishistically, on the stuff of consumer culture, this volume adopts a broadened perspective that considers the national and transnational, as well as local, networks of trade in which commodities were produced and exchanged, while also attending to the forces of historical change. In so doing, it takes up the subject of work in relation to a range of issues of concern to traditional Marxist thought—e.g., the processes of commodification, workings of capital,

---

[10]   Jardine, *Worldly Goods: A New History of the Renaissance* (New York: Talese, 1996); and Brewer and Porter (eds.), *Consumption and the World of Goods* (London and New York: Routledge, 1993). See also Chandra Mukerji, *From Graven Images: Patterns of Modern Materialism* (New York: Columbia University Press, 1983) and Simon Schama, *The Embarrassment of Riches: An Interpretation of Dutch Culture in the Golden Age* (New York: Knopf, 1987).

[11]   Ivo Kamps (ed.), *Materialist Shakespeare: A History* (London and New York: Verso, 1995).

[12]   Several recent studies have likewise focused on shifting conceptions of work in early modern English culture. This important body of scholarship has brought much-needed critical attention to the subject of labor as both a literary and an economic construct in the period. See John Michael Archer, *Citizen Shakespeare: Freemen and Aliens in the Language of the Plays* (New York: Palgrave, 2005); Michelle Dowd, *Women's Work in Early Modern English Literature and Culture* (New York: Palgrave, 2009); Valerie Forman, *Tragicomic Redemptions: Global Economics and the Early Modern English Stage* (Philadelphia: University of Pennsylvania Press, 2008); and Tom Rutter, *Work and Play on the Shakespearean Stage* (Cambridge: Cambridge University Press, 2008).

changing modes of production, divisions of labor and social hierarchies and forms of oppression they produce—while approaching them from a variety of critical perspectives influenced by post-Marxist thought. A number of the essays find useful, while seeking to develop and engage critically with, Marx's analysis of the economic forces that led to the transition from feudalism to capitalism in early modern England, and in particular his account of the "primitive accumulation" or amassing of private property through land enclosures and consequent creation of a landless "proletariat" or wage-laboring class. Crystal Bartolovich, for example, offers a more nuanced account of the alliances formed between old (landed) and new (monied) elites over and against the interests of labor in *The Shoemaker's Holiday*. Amanda Bailey points to contradictions in Marx's analysis of the colonial system and the role played by slave labor in the rise of capitalism and demonstrates how this account is complicated by the hybrid institution of indentured servitude in the New World, which combined elements of domestic service with chattel slavery.

A number of contributors attend to the ways in which early modern cultural and economic discourses sought to account for the historical processes that transformed the landscape of labor and, in the process, gave rise to the profession of playing. In his analysis of contemporary ways of understanding autonomous financial representation, for example, David Hawkes links the practice and discourse of usury to the rise of the credit-dependant commercial theaters. The rise of the professional stage relied on the availability of large-scale credit made possible by the 1571 usury statute, and theater people, including Shakespeare and Philip Henslowe, supplemented their incomes by lending money at interest. It is therefore not surprising that the plots of so many plays pivot on the vicissitudes of credit relations and instruments such as bonds. Another vein of contemporary economic thought that influenced theatrical representation, as Valerie Forman demonstrates, was the discourse of mercantilism, which laid the ideological groundwork for the joint-stock companies upon which the professional playing companies were in certain respects modeled.

These and other essays in the collection help to illuminate the ways in which economic processes may bear on cultural production, albeit in more complex ways than the classical Marxist "base / superstructure" model maintains. As noted above, the playing companies were transitional economic formations that retained certain aspects of a feudal-patronage and guild-system while embracing emergent capitalist methods. As such they were hybrid entities that represented diverse, and sometimes competing, economic interests. It was the tension between these competing interests that shaped the theater's diverse depictions of working subjects and gave rise to new and hybrid generic forms. Such forms include, for example, the genre of "citizen history," which as Crystal Bartolovich maintains, held "the mirror up to labor in order to refuse that image as its own," the hybrid genre of tragicomedy, which as Valerie Forman demonstrates, represented the "high costs of conducting long-distance overseas trade" as recuperated by a Christian and economic "logic of redemption," and the genre of the travel play, in which as Daniel Vitkus shows, acknowledgment of the travail associated with travel gradually gave way to a fantasy of labor-free global commerce.

Other essays in this collection that build on, while moving beyond, a strictly Marxist analysis of labor by drawing on affiliated modes of inquiry are those that incorporate materialist feminist insights into the analysis of gendered divisions of labor and interarticulations of gender with other axes of social differentiation and oppression. Along these lines, Michelle Dowd examines female domestic service, while Ronda Arab looks at emergent forms of working masculinity, as performed by the professional players. Natasha Korda and Sara Mueller examine the gendered division of theatrical labor itself, looking beyond the all-male professional theater to consider "amateur" female performers who participated in the staging of various types of work coded as female in progress entertainments at Bisham and Harefield and civic pageants at Norwich and London, and at the ways in which these performances were influenced by changing modes of economic production.

The single play that has perhaps attracted greatest attention by previous scholarship for its representation of laboring bodies onstage is Thomas Dekker's *The Shoemaker's Holiday*. The first two essays in *Working Subjects* contribute to the critical dialogue on this play, while also challenging it to move in new directions. In "Mythos of Labor: *The Shoemaker's Holiday* and the Origin of Citizen History," Crystal Bartolovich examines the representation of labor in *Shoemaker* and its relation to the generic conventions of history plays, which have not traditionally been read as concerning themselves with work at all. For this reason, *Shoemaker* is typically included among the city comedies, although the Simon Eyre plot is clearly "historical." Bartolovich argues that Dekker both makes visible and effaces labor by displaying it as part of a distant past. As a kind of "counter-factual" history, the play depicts the rise of Simon Eyre by way of his craft in a narrative that deviates considerably not only from known facts, but from plausibility. Marking a shift from chronicle to "citizen history," she argues, the cultural work performed by the play takes precedence over historical narrative. The play works first to indicate that tensions between old money and new were resolved long before, and, second, to suggest that the upward mobility of the nation, as of the individual, requires severing the link between labor and money, even as the expansion of the market and waged labor are intensifying the relation between the two. Like the terrain rendered laborless in country house poems, she maintains, *Shoemaker's Holiday* is keen to divert, recode and efface the labor it supposedly admires. History, in this sense, does for the city what pastoral does for the country.

John Michael Archer likewise examines the changing parameters of citizen-subjectivity as constituted in relation (or opposition) to labor and to non-citizen subjects in his essay, "Citizens and Aliens as Working Subjects in Dekker's *The Shoemaker's Holiday*." Archer focuses on the play's representation of the troubling figure of the "Dutch" or Flemish immigrant, who, although inherited from medieval times, caused new anxieties about labor for sixteenth-century London citizens. The Flemish shared a common "northerness" with their civic hosts: from the north of Europe, commonly thought of as "fair" and hearty, they were also Protestant opponents of Hapsburg Spain who had left behind citizen identities based on guild membership. At the same time, now aliens in London, the Flemish appeared radically different to their hosts. Sudden competitors for labor in the cloth trades and shoemaking, they also confounded north and south, for they came from the impoverished ten southern provinces that remained under Hapsburg rule. The seven northern provinces, including Holland, had meanwhile risen to rival the English at sea, trading with southern parts and the Moluccas. The word "Dutch," then, confused north with south, industry with imposed idleness, and wealth with poverty in Londoners' commercial, and theatrical, vocabulary. Archer takes up two mid-sixteenth century interludes, *Wealth and Health* and Ulpian Fulwell's *Like Will to Like*, as well as Dekker's 1590s comedy, to show how these contradictions generated an ethnic type out of antagonisms over work and trade. Lacy's disguise as Hans the shoemaker perpetuates earlier Dutch or Flemish stereotypes, and borrows directly from Tudor moralities that carried urban motifs from the Middle Ages into court culture and its pressing concern with international politics. With Dekker's play, the Dutch type returns to the popular sphere, this time as a performative strategy. In his revisiting of this familiar comedy, Archer demonstrates how closely engaged it is with the terms of guild or livery company identity, and also how it manages class differences inside and outside companies through an ethnic typing generated out of perceived competition over work. Commonness and competition created rather than dispelled anxieties about identity. London citizens averted their gaze from the presumed enjoyment of the oddly similar others among them because it embodied their own industrious, northern way of life to excess.

Like Archer's essay, Natasha Korda's "Staging Alien Women's Work in Civic Pageants" contributes to recent scholarship detailing the cultural impact of the massive numbers of Dutch- and French-speaking Protestant refugees who migrated to England during the Dutch Revolt and French Wars of Religion. Although it is well known that many of these religious refugees were skilled artisans in the luxury textile and clothing trades, and that their importation of new skills and technologies of manufacture had a huge impact on this sector of the economy, there has been no study of the ways in which the revolution in textile manufacture effected by alien workers influenced theatrical production, in light of the theaters' dependence on the clothing market, or how it may have shaped contemporary dramatic depictions of aliens. Korda sets out to investigate this area of inquiry, and discovers that attending to the material culture of the stage from the vantage of production, rather than consumption, illuminates important aspects of its hitherto obscured gendered division of labor. For the luxury attires manufactured by alien craftswomen from the Low Countries, she argues, played a vital role in the civic pageant staged by Norwich weavers of the "New Draperies" for Queen Elizabeth in 1578 and the Dutch triumphal arch staged by London's Netherlandish community as part of King James's coronation pageant of 1603–1604. The immigrant communities of Norwich and London sought to defend their status as working subjects (rather than idle parasites) and contributors to the commonwealth by staging their imported skills in textile manufacture in civic pageants in which female artisans feature prominently.

Holly Dugan's "Osmologies of Luxury and Labor: Entertaining Perfumers in Early English Drama" likewise attends to the ways in which the gendered labor of aliens was re-presented (and absented) onstage, focusing in particular on the ephemeral work of the perfumer. As Dugan demonstrates, the occupational identity of the perfumer shifted dramatically with the increasing demand for luxury goods in the late sixteenth and early seventeenth centuries, becoming a focal point for cultural anxieties surrounding working women and aliens in London's expanding informal economy. Dugan's essay pivots on Borachio's theatrical performance as a perfumer in *Much Ado About Nothing*. Reading this and other theatrical representations of perfumers in relation to their economic histories, Dugan reveals the extraordinary labor or "much ado" of alien perfumers that stood behind the insubstantial "nothing" of the ephemeral commodity, perfume. Dugan, like Korda, demonstrates the ways in which the staging of purportedly insubstantial, luxury commodities, such as perfume or lace, may point to offstage histories of a highly-skilled immigrant labor force that vitally contributed to the English economy while at the same time being denied the prerogatives of citizen-laborers or "freemen." In so doing, both authors contribute to our understanding of the contingent, discursive categories or divisions of labor that determine which categories of work and worker are defined as legitimate or illegitimate in a given historical time and place.

Tom Rutter, in "*Englishmen for My Money*: Work and Social Conflict?," analyzes the way in which the discursive category of the "alien" was articulated in relation to another crucial category through which labor was divided and hierarchized: social status or "class." Rutter is particularly interested in the way in which status defined the labor of particular playing companies, and in turn, the ways in which these companies represented work onstage. Critics such as Andrew Gurr and Robert Weimann have seen the revival of the companies of child actors in 1599–1600 as heralding a split between popular and elite theatrical cultures. This is reflected in the contrasting uses different playing companies made of the idea of work: dramatists writing for the children represented their playhouses as spaces from which workers were absent, while the Admiral's Men (in particular) asserted the dignity of manual labor in plays like *The Shoemaker's Holiday* and *Patient Grissil*. By contrast, the 1590s are often represented as a period when the adult companies produced plays that appealed to, and identified with, a "homogenous, all-inclusive social range."[13] Rutter questions whether this social inclusiveness, too, was reflected in the dramatic treatment of work, focusing in particular on William Haughton's *Englishmen for My Money*, a play that seems to unite workers of diverse types with idle gentlemen against a demonized foreigner or alien.

---

[13]   See Andrew Gurr, *Playgoing in Shakespeare's London*, 2nd ed. (Cambridge: Cambridge University Press, 1996), 158.

Ronda Arab's "Will Kempe's Work: Performing the Player's Masculinity in *Kempe's Nine Daies Wonder*" likewise takes the division of laboring bodies in accordance with social status as a central category of analysis, focusing on its relationship to the gendered division of labor, and in particular, its construction of what she calls "working-class" masculinity. Gender, she argues, cannot be understood outside of its intersection with social status. In 1600, Will Kempe, the son of a printer or a gentleman's servant, and former actor and clown for the Lord Chamberlain's Men, danced a morris dance from London to Norwich over a period of nine days in order to raise money for himself from sponsors of his activity. Shortly afterwards, he published an account of that dance entitled *Kempe's Nine Daies Wonder*, a text that carefully mediates discourses of masculinity, labor, and the professional player. Arab examines the intersection of Kempe's self-construction with ideas about working men that circulated in his day. Sixteenth- and seventeenth-century masculinities were often seen in terms of the body and through its descriptions of his dancing, Kempe's text foregrounds the significance of the physicality of the male working body. Ideal masculinity, according to dominant discourses, was achieved through outward signs of bodily strength and refinement and also through controlling passions and desires that were understood to originate from the body—any excess of sorrow, anger, vengefulness, appetite, lust, etc., could be considered unmanly behavior. Existing scholarship on the social identity of laboring and low-born men has called attention to the way these ideas about bodily refinement were used *against* them, by representing working male bodies as open and out of control, and thereby reinforcing social hierarchy. Kempe challenges this paradigm by celebrating the power and strength of the working man's body, a power and strength that results from his involvement in the vigorous, manual activity of work. At the same time, Kempe's narrative constructs the professional player as a skilled working man in order to counter accusations of idleness leveled at theater workers in the period. The professionalization of playing, as both Arab and Rutter show, required that players and playwrights actively engage in contemporary debates surrounding the subject or work, and that they defend their status as working subjects.

The division of laboring bodies in accordance with social status is further explored in Elizabeth Rivlin's essay, "The Rogues' Paradox: Redefining Work in *The Alchemist*," which examines the occupational flexibility and ingenuity manifested by working subjects in comedy as reflective of the way in which hierarchies of labor are at once foundational to and destabilized by a market economy. When Master Lovewit leaves his house in plague-ridden London in the care of his household retainer in Jonson's play, the servant and his confederates implement a variety of illicit schemes that seemingly allow them to redefine work as a capitalist venture that would avoid the conventional strictures of hierarchical service and labor. Rivlin argues, however, that in *The Alchemist*, Jonson's rogues are trapped by the recursive logic of labor, which continually reasserts itself as the only means that these workers have to enter an emerging market economy. One implication of this ironic turn is that subjects subsisting in a metamorphosing society are empowered but also restricted by their marginal positions. In an environment where profit is seen as widely accessible and social distinctions as insubstantial, obligatory and laborsome forms of work exert a renewed claim on those who are already at the bottom of social, economic, and occupational hierarchies. While perceptions of work were undeniably in flux in early modern England, *The Alchemist* suggests that the effects of change were unevenly distributed across the social landscape.

Rivlin's focus on the figure of the servant is shared by Michelle Dowd's "Desiring Subjects: Staging the Female Servant in Early Modern Tragedy," although Dowd, as her title suggests, is interested not only in the way feudal forms of service were defined in England's nascent market economy but in the gendering of the servant trade both in early modern culture at large and in the dramatic genre of tragedy. Looking primarily at Dekker, Ford and Rowley's *The Witch of Edmonton* and Middleton and Rowley's *The Changeling*, she examines how early modern tragedies dramatize the work of female domestic service. Dowd is especially interested in how tragic form both elides and makes possible specific narratives of women's service during this transitional period in English economic history. Domestic service was by far the most common occupation for early modern Englishwomen between the ages of fifteen and twenty-four, and women were increasingly replacing men as servants in middling and wealthy households. Removed from their birth homes and direct parental supervision, female servants were often viewed as transient, sexually vulnerable, and potentially disorderly single women. Furthermore, despite the general cultural expectation that women would get married immediately after leaving positions in service, many women experienced a significant gap between the end of their service in their early to mid-twenties and their marriages in their late twenties. Indeed, demographic and economic realities prevented many female servants from ever marrying. The notion of a seamless trajectory for female servants leading from work to marriage was thus more social fantasy than reality. Dowd argues that Jacobean tragedies such as *The Witch of Edmonton* and *The Changeling* stage the sexual vulnerability of the female servant in part as a cautionary narrative about domestic order and the changing parameters of the service economy. Yet the plots in which these female servants find themselves are also heavily indebted to cultural fantasies of marriage and domestic harmony, formal trajectories that seem antithetical to the genre of tragedy. Looking at the structural features of these plays and the (often oddly romanticized) narratives of service that subtend them, Dowd explores how these tragedies conceptualize the sexualized subject positions of female servants as part of a process of narrative displacement whereby fictions of desire replace both real sexual coercion and the economic imperatives that attended England's commercial labor market.

Gender and the domestic economy are similarly at the center of Sara Mueller's study, "Domestic Work in Progress Entertainments." Mueller examines the entertainments staged for Queen Elizabeth by Lady Elizabeth Russell at Bisham in 1592 and by Lord Thomas Egerton and Lady Alice Egerton, Dowager Countess of Derby, at Harefield in 1602, both of which foregrounded women's performances of domestic work. Because new economic conditions took aristocratic men away from their country estates, women became increasingly powerful on these estates. These changes created a representational crisis in the aristocracy, since noble legitimacy had previously been demonstrated by patriarchal presence, control, and management on the estate. Bisham and Harefield respond to this representational crisis in two crucial and distinct ways. First, the focus on women's domestic work in the entertainments functioned synecdochally to demonstrate the commitment of the host to the proper governance and care over the estate as a whole, presenting it as a place of unchanging noble values and patriarchal authority. However, the entertainments by their very focus on women's domestic labor—and not men's— resist an uncomplicated endorsement of nostalgic, noble ideals. Instead, they acknowledge women's active labor within the new realities of country life in a changing economy. Alongside Bisham and Harefield's obligatory assertion of traditional, patriarchal, and noble legitimacy, both entertainments register a very timely recognition of women's importance and changing roles on country estates, a recognition that stages—with radical implications—the material and symbolic contributions of women to their estates.

If the staging of domestic work in progress entertainments reveals a great deal about the gendered division of labor in early modern England, so too does the staging of witches, as Meredith Molly Hand demonstrates in "'You take no labour': Women Workers of Magic in Early Modern England." Hand explores early modern representations of women's magical practices as work. Focusing primarily on two texts, Fletcher and Massinger's play *The Prophetess* and Edmond Bower's pamphlet *Doctor Lamb Revived, or, Witchcraft Condemn'd in Anne Bodenham*, she examines the ways in which the eponymous characters of both texts are depicted both as magicians (as opposed to witches) and as workers. Delphia of *The Prophetess* for example, is both a working woman and a magician so capable that she clearly upstages her literary predecessors, Faustus and Prospero. The master/apprentice relationship between Doctor Lambe and Anne Bodenham, which Bodenham seeks to recreate with a younger woman—the ostensible "victim" of her witchcraft—highlights the way in which Bodenham imagines herself as a professional who would pass along her knowledge and skills. By appropriating (or being imbued with) characteristics more typically ascribed to male magicians, Hand argues, Delphia and Anne Bodenham resist and respond to satirical and demonizing treatments of women workers of magic.

The relationship between magic, theatricality and work is equally central to David Hawkes's "Raising Mephistopheles: Performative Representation and Alienated Labor in *The Tempest*." Dr. Faustus's question to Mephistopheles, "Did not my conjuring speeches raise thee?" recurs in various guises throughout the English drama of the sixteenth and seventeenth centuries. It asks whether magic is efficacious: can the signs and rituals employed by magicians achieve practical, objective effects in the real world? Mephistopheles's reply: "That was the cause, but yet *per accidens*" gives some idea of the issue's complexity. Magic does indeed make things happen, but only as the material expression of a deeper, ultimate causal factor. Hawkes's essay identifies that factor as alienated human labor which, in the early modern period, was in the process of displacing traditional magic as the main supernatural influence on the lives of English people. The decades between 1580 and 1640 laid the ideological groundwork for financial capitalism. The financial signs that represented alienated labor were becoming autonomous and self-generating. With the relaxation of the usury laws, they were acquiring the power to reproduce. Their influence, invisible yet clearly powerful, was insinuating itself into every crevice of experience. In the first stages of this process, according to Hawkes, people understood the independent force of alienated labor as a phenomenon similar in kind to the spiritual powers manipulated by magicians. The Tudor and Stuart theater offered a vehicle for studying the transmutation of labor into symbolic form. If *Doctor Faustus* demands that the audience consider the causal relation between the sorcerer's spells and the demonic labor performed by his familiar, Hawkes maintains, *The Tempest* externalizes Prospero's magical power in Ariel and Caliban, who carry out his will through both natural and supernatural work. In Hawkes's view, the popular drama of the early modern period attempts to teach its audience that money is more benign than magic, and our current impression of money as a neutral, even natural, and decidedly unmagical, power is testimony to that enterprise's success.

The final three essays in the volume make clear that the subject of work in early modern English drama cannot be fully understood in isolation from the global networks of trade in which England was embedded. Amanda Bailey's "Custom, Debt, and the Valuation of Service Within and Without Early Modern England" builds on recent scholarship on the dynamics of colonial labor, which challenges long held assumptions about early seventeenth-century England's geopolitical standing. While England was on the fringes of a trading network centered in the Mediterranean, larger shifts in commerce transformed it from a nation on the European margins to one positioned to take advantage of new opportunities to the West. It was in this period that London came "to dominate the servant trade," making indentured men "the most liquid form of capital in the New World." Bailey's essay explores a nation poised between worlds old and new in order to show how the period's drama forged a framework for New World mastery in the crucible of Old World slavery. While in theory indentured servitude was not slavery, in practice labor predicated on economic obligation blurred the line between the two. Indenture was always a labor contract *and* a promissory note; the promise to repay the cost of transport and room and board, for instance, was waged against the security on the loan and that security was the person of the borrower. Young, single, unskilled men, bound by the chains of debt, were ever in arrears to their masters, who in turn were under no obligation to teach them a trade, provide livery, or pay wages. Moreover, what began as a limited economic relation all too often slid into lifelong subordination sustained by extra-economic factors. Terms of labor were modified and extended, and in the end there was little guarantee that these men would receive their "freedom due" of £10 or a small plot of land. In those cases in which an indentured servant died before satisfying his debt, his children were obligated to perform compulsory labor. The indentured man had the status of neither slave nor servant, yet the mechanism by which he secured his voyage rendered him the property of those to whom he was indebted. Bailey focuses her analysis on the way Fletcher and Massinger's *The Custom of the Country* represents compulsory service, and how the English imagination of indenture complicated notions of slavery and service both at home and abroad. By casting the familiar dynamics of credit and debt in an international context, she argues, *Custom* offers a window onto the transnational implications of local economies.

Valerie Forman offers a different perspective on the global ramifications of domestic economic structures in her essay, "The Comic-Tragedy of Labor: A Global Story." Like Bailey, Forman focuses on the representation of labor in tragicomedy in particular, the seventeenth century's most popular stage genre. Both tragicomedy and theories of early modern economic practices, especially those related to global trade, she argues, reimagine initial losses as expenditures that produce more prosperous futures. Yet neither the plays nor the economic theories ever fully illuminate the precise sources or catalysts for the transformations from potentially tragic loss to prosperity: these sources remain mysterious and often some form of the magical takes their place. Forman seeks to account for those elisions by exploring how the surplus value that enables losses to transform into profits depends on labor and especially un(der)paid labor. Reading early modern economic texts alongside Fletcher's *The Island Princess* and Shakespeare's *The Winter's Tale*, she analyzes how the valuing or devaluing of labor corresponds both to the generic movements in the plays and to the potential to imagine prosperity as the result of global trade.

The concluding essay in the volume, Daniel Vitkus's "Labor and Travel on the Early Modern Stage: Representing the Travail of Travel in Dekker's *Old Fortunatus* and Shakespeare's *Pericles*," takes as its point of departure the observation that while in our own time, the word "travel" tends to be associated with leisure and pleasure, in early modern parlance it was not distinguished from what later came to be called "travail," so the various spellings of "travel/travail" signified the labor, trouble, hardship, and pain associated with travel. Vitkus focuses on the theatrical representation of overseas, long-distance travel, as a dangerous, uncomfortable, and labor-intensive. In a variety of plays, travel was staged by means of the audience's imaginative participation, and various stage devices were employed to indicate the time, labor, and expense necessary to make a long-distance voyage. While the early modern theater often produces a pleasing fantasy of instant, effortless mobility, it sometimes acknowledges the reliance of travelers on a transcultural, global network of labor. Vitkus draws upon a variety of examples to explore the tension between theatrical fantasies that concealed the exploitation of maritime laborers, on the one hand, and those moments in the plays that reveal the travail of mariners or the dependence of travelers on the labor of others. He is particularly interested in the dramatic representation of storms and shipwrecks—events that often bring out the contradictions present in the staging of travel's labor. In these moments, and in the encounter with foreigners, the dependency of the traveler on a matrix of maritime workers becomes apparent and reveals the challenge to English identity that is posed by this kind of dependency, exchange, and interaction in faraway places. With reference to these texts, Vitkus argues that what we see happening during the Elizabethan and Jacobean periods is a movement away from the notion of travel as labor or "travail" and toward the emergence of a modern conception of travel's purpose as knowledge acquisition, corresponding to a shift from a literary-fantastic vision toward more "scientific" or imperial purposes. It is not that the labor and suffering of travel becomes less necessary; it is just that it becomes more thoroughly repressed or unevenly distributed in imperial or colonial accounts of travel. Over time, the mercantile traveler's comfort increases at the expense of the lower-classes, slaves and foreigners.

In her Afterword, Jean E. Howard draws attention to three analytic categories— genres, structures of feeling, and the means of representation—that shape the essays in this volume as they explore the intersection between dramatic texts and the working world of early modern England.

Each of the essays in this volume seeks to interrogate the strategies by which early modern drama brought working subjects into being on stage, and in so doing, addresses hitherto unexplored questions raised by the subject of labor as it was taken up in the drama of the period: How were laboring bodies and the goods they produced, marketed and consumed represented onstage through speech, action, gesture, costumes and properties? How did plays participate in shaping the identities that situated laboring subjects within the social hierarchy? In what ways did the drama engage with contemporary social, political, economic, and religious discourses that defined the cultural meanings of work? How did players and playwrights define their own status with respect to the shifting boundaries between legitimate and illegitimate, profitable and unprofitable, male and female, free and bound, and paid and unpaid forms of labor? In addressing these questions, *Working Subjects* seeks to illuminate both the broad historical and cultural parameters of work as staged in early modern England and the local, textual nuances that animate these dramatic renderings.

Chapter 1
Mythos of Labor:
The Shoemaker's Holiday and the Origin of Citizen History[1]

Crystal Bartolovich

History plays, like utopias, emerge from the peculiar social disruptions and dislocations of the early modern condition; they have no direct classical precedent. Their prevalence and popularity in late sixteenth-century London, despite their manifest novelty, are striking evidence that off-the-rack genres cannot fit all situations. This does not mean that every early modern history play works in the same way. To the contrary, the variations and contradictions among—and within—English history plays at the moment of their emergence are a symptom that "history" was unsettled, the condition that largely accounts for the appearance of the genre in the first place. Reformation mistrust of the "popish" monopoly on history writing in England prior to the 1530s provoked a revisionist impulse that proliferated into secular subjects with the expansion of print and the establishment of the public playhouses.

This is worth underscoring because the canonical dominance of Shakespeare is so strong that it has discouraged critics from recognizing alternatives to the "dynastic" model for history plays that he made so successful in the 1590s. Yet it is manifestly the case that the concept of "history" was not only used in a wide variety of ways at this time, but also *contested*—a state of affairs that could hardly be imagined to elude the playhouses. We might question, then, the putative waning of "history" on the English stage after 1600, as well as the exclusivity of the "dynastic" or "chronicle" model.[2] To view Thomas Dekker's *Shoemaker's Holiday* as a challenge to this model, for example, is particularly illuminating, not only for our interpretation of the play, but also for our understanding of historical struggle

---

[1]   Earlier versions of this essay were presented at MLA and the Medieval-Renaissance Group at the University of Pennsylvania. I am particularly grateful to David Wallace, Margreta de Grazia, Peter Stallybrass, Rita Copeland and their wonderful graduate students for helpful comments. I am also indebted to Natasha Korda for encouraging me to develop the paper for this volume, as well as for her sage revision advice—and patience.

[2]   For trends in this direction see the interesting collection of essays *English Historical Drama, 1500–1660: Forms Outside the Canon*, (eds.) Teresa Grant and Barbara Ravelhofer (New York: Palgrave, 2008).

as manifested in literary form.[3] I argue here that this play attempts, by way of what I will be calling mythic counterfactualism, to elicit recognition of *elite* London citizens as capable—alongside traditional aristocratic and royal agents—of making history, while at the same time naturalizing a status hierarchy within the urban social order based on merchant transcendence of labor through the acquisition of wealth whose origins are mystified. Crucially, labor is not *historically* significant for Dekker—though it is socially significant: labor is displayed and affirmed, but makers of things are nonetheless disqualified from the recognized making of history. "The potter and tynker," Thomas Elyot matter-of-factly observes in the 1530s, "onely perfecte in theyr crafte, shal littell do in the ministration of Justice."[4] At the end of the century, Dekker's play, despite the artisanal emphasis that gives it a dissident relation to "chronicle," does not so much counter this conservative observation as confirm it. In this way, it participates in a transformation of chronicle into *citizen* history, helping to redefine what "history" means as a new hegemony is in formation while capitalism struggles to be born. By offering a counterfactual account of the rise to prominence of a "real" fifteenth-century London mayor, it demands that elite citizens be recognized as makers of history.

The concept of the "counterfactual" I am deploying here has entered historical debate in recent years largely through the work of Niall Ferguson, who uses it to undermine "determinism"—by which Ferguson mostly means Marxism. As he puts it, "the world is not divinely ordered, nor governed by Reason, the class struggle or any other deterministic 'law.' All we can say for sure is that it is condemned to increasing disorder by entropy." Methodologically, this means that "the most historians can do is to make tentative statements about causation with reference to plausible counterfactuals."[5] The political usefulness of such a strategy is evident not only in the narratives produced (though these are, of course, telling), but more important, in the notion that history is *accidental*—the conflict between oppressor and oppressed is not its motor.[6] Here I refute Ferguson's position by considering the ideological implications of Dekker's purposeful counterfactualization of history at the moment of capitalism's emergence—that is, his telling a story of wealth's origins by way of an expressly mythic counterfactual—"myth" here

---

   [3]   See Raymond Williams, *Marxism and Literature* (Oxford: Oxford University Press, 1977), 186–91.

   [4]   Elyot, *The Boke Named the Governour* (London, 1537), 5v.

   [5]   Ferguson, "Virtual History: Towards a 'Chaotic' Theory of the Past," in *Virtual History: Alternatives and Counterfactuals*, (ed.) Niall Ferguson (New York: Basic Books, 1997), 89.

   [6]   Fredric Jameson's *Political Unconscious: Narrative as a Socially Symbolic Act* (Ithaca: Cornell University Press, 1981) compellingly answered these sorts of critiques of Marxist "determinism" long ago. See also my "History after the End of History: Critical Counterfactualism and Revolution," *New Formations* 59 (2006): 63–80.

being a means, as Claude Lévi-Strauss proposed, to provide imaginary solutions to real social contradictions.[7]

Chronicle to Citizen History: Wealth, Labor and the Crisis of Status

By 1599, when Dekker's play was likely first performed, "history" was already a familiar dramatic presence in England, though of recent invention, like the public playhouses in which it became standard fare early on.[8] Its incipient form, chronicle history, as Jean Howard and Phyllis Rackin have observed, was devoted to performing "the necessary function of creating and disseminating myths of origin to authorize a new national entity and to deal with the anxieties and contradictions that threatened to undermine the nation-building project."[9] During the restive sixteenth century, such plays typically emphasized challenges to dynastic authority—usurpation, courtier intrigue, civil war, inter-state power struggles—set in earlier moments, presenting early modern problems in Medieval dress. Great men *act*, and there are consequences, not just for them, but for the state. Such plays are most prominent in the latter half of the century, following the lead of John Bale's *Kynge Johan*, with its urgent Reformation, anti-papal thrust, but were largely replaced in the new millennium by other novel dramatic forms, such as London comedy, which critics such as L.C. Knights have seen as the "natural" progeny of chronicle history.[10] Specifically, Knights suggests that the dense topographical references of the histories made them direct forerunners of the place-specifying city comedies, but I will be exploring the other side of this coin: that the city comedies also inherit from the chronicle plays assumptions

---

[7]   "The purpose of myth is to provide a logical model capable of overcoming a contradiction (an impossible achievement if … the contradiction is real)." "The Structural Study of Myth," in *Myth: A Symposium*, (ed.) Thomas A. Sebeok (Philadelphia: American Folklore Society, 1955), 65. David Kastan's "Workshop and/as Playhouse" in *Staging the Renaissance: Reinterpretations of Elizabethan and Jacobean Drama*, (eds.) David Kastan and Peter Stallybrass (New York: Routledge, 1991), also calls attention to Dekker's propensity to smooth over social contradictions.

[8]   Because the compilers of Shakespeare's First Folio separate out his chronicle plays as "histories" in the table of contents, such plays appear to have formed a distinct generic group in period understanding, although "history" could designate any "story" in its early modern usage. At the same time "history" was also manifestly deployed in the modern, more specific, sense of a putatively faithful account of past events as, for example, in Philip Sidney's separation of history from poesy in the *Defence of Poesie* (London, 1595). For a survey of period understandings of history writing, see Arthur Ferguson, *Clio Unbound: Perception of the Social and Cultural Past in Renaissance England* (Durham: Duke University Press, 1979).

[9]   Howard and Rackin, *Engendering a Nation: A Feminist Account of Shakespeare's English Histories* (London: Routledge, 1997), 14.

[10]   "The historical plays were recognized as containing direct topical references, and they led naturally to such plays as … *The Shoemaker's Holiday*," *Drama and Society in the Age of Jonson* (Harmondsworth: Peregrine, 1962 [1937]), 206.

about historical agency that they transfer to the wealthy and powerful, but non-aristocratic, Londoners who had gotten short shrift in earlier accounts. Thus they sometimes explicitly cast a historical role for merchant-elites within the larger nationalist agenda the chronicle drama had established, even to adopting their strategy of exporting current problems to a distant time. Like chronicle histories, then, *Shoemaker's Holiday* is obsessed with "myths of origin"—most immediately concerning the source of Simon Eyre's great wealth that underwrites his putative rise from shoemaker to Lord Mayor of London, but also concerning the origin of a new understanding of wealth and its relation to history in general. Unlike chronicles, however, it asserts that history was not made by titled subjects alone and thus transforms the emergent genre to accommodate a citizen agenda.

Although the main source text for Dekker's play, Thomas Deloney's *The Gentle Craft* (a collection of tales featuring the exploits of "princely" shoemakers) opens its Eyre story with the claim that "Our English chronicles doe make mention, that sometime there was in the honorable City of *London* a worthy Mayor, known by name of Sir *Simon Eyre*," it was evident to period readers that Deloney's narratives were actually doing something strikingly new.[11] Will Kempe's *Nine Daies Wonder*, for example, observes that Deloney's tales chronicle the lives of "honest men *omitted*" by Stow, Hollinshed, Grafton, Hal, froysart and the rest" even as he mocks the tendencies of Deloney's writing, especially his ballads, to exaggeration and over-attention to the ostensibly trivial and ephemeral.[12] Actually, Kempe is here exaggerating himself, since Stow does "make mention" of Eyre, a habit of the urban antiquaries derided by Thomas Nashe and others.[13] Yet Deloney, and afterwards, Dekker, not only flesh out these scanty references considerably, but insert them into accounts that are as concerned with the affirmation of the nation as are the chronicle histories—though they have a different take on what makes it thrive. Above all, Dekker invests national-historical importance in merchant-citizens, and inculcates the view that wealth on its own, as well as birth, can properly underwrite status or "name."

The political thrust of such a gesture is manifest when we remember that as late as the eighteenth century anxious defenses of merchants were still being penned, since their benefit to the nation was not self-evident. To the contrary, merchants had long been viewed with suspicion. Throughout the sixteenth century one can find frequent denunciations of them, saturated with status anxiety, such as the lawyer's

---

[11] Deloney, *The Gentle Craft* (London, 1637), F3r. For a discussion of Dekker's use of Deloney, see the introduction to the Revels edition of the play, (eds.) R.L. Smallwood and Stanley Wells (Manchester: Manchester University Press, 1999 [1979]), 17–26. All references to the play are from this edition and will appear parenthetically in the essay.

[12] Kempe, *Nine Daies Wonder* (London, 1600), D3v.

[13] Scoffing at the supposed lack of "choise words" in books such as Stow's, and asserting the superiority of the (university trained) "poet" to the "citizen," Nashe warns "Noblemen or Gentlemen" readers of *Pierce Penilesse* (London, 1592): "it is not your lay Chronigraphers, that write of nothing but mayors and sheriefs and the deare yeere and the Great Frost, that can endowe your names with never dated glory" (D3v–D4r).

protest to a merchant in Robert Greene's *Scottish Historie*: "Hob your sonne, and Sib your nutbrowne childe, / Are Gentle folks, and Gentles are beguiled."[14] Against such characterizations, however, a counter-discourse was emerging, which appreciated the contributions of merchants to *national*, rather than merely individual, wealth, and celebrated merchants for creating jobs, expanding the reach of the English empire, circulating goods and enriching the state. Richard Hakluyt's massive collections of trade and colonization narratives, which portrayed merchants as heroic and nation-affirming, were a telling symptom of this enterprise, but in the seventeenth century an extensive literature would appear on these issues, beginning with John Wheeler's well-known defense of the Merchant Adventurers.[15] Citizen history was an early—literary—entrant onto these lists.

At a time in which the national allegiance of merchants was often still in doubt, the rise of admirable English merchant figures in literature is by no means neutral. Simon Eyre's story is particularly interesting in this regard, since he is an accidental merchant, having come into wealth from the ranks of artisan householders, but not through laboring in his trade. In his case—exceptional in Deloney's collection, which mostly features princes and nobles disguising themselves as lowly shoemakers—an ordinary artisan, from a non-elite guild (neither Cordwainers nor Cobblers were among the twelve principle guilds from which the city's ruling hierarchy usually derived), becomes a princely citizen via a fortuitous investment of merchant capital.[16] Wealth is emphatically Eyre's claim to status, not labor, nor blood. Dekker's choice to stage *this* story gives rise to a historical drama concerned not only with the birth of the nation, but of wealth.

Accordingly, *Shoemaker's Holiday* engages a double gesture: it asserts status parity of merchants with traditional landed elites (who by definition were exempt from labor) while at the same time distinguishing merchants, as citizens, from artisans (who *do*, necessarily, labor). Heretofore, even when the significance of the historicizing thrust of the play has been recognized, critics have assumed it to be concerned with affirming the "middling sort" in general, so that the full complexity of the historicizing gesture remains obscure.[17] Dekker's play does not

---

[14] *Plays and Poems of Robert Greene*, vol. 2, (ed.) J. Churton Collins (Oxford: Clarendon, 1905), 5.4.2119–20.

[15] On Hakluyt, see Richard Helgerson, *Forms of Nationhood: The Elizabethan Writing of England* (Chicago: University of Chicago Press, 1992), 149–91. On the emergent trade debates, see Joyce Oldham Appleby, *Economic Thought and Ideology in Seventeenth Century England* (Princeton: Princeton University Press, 1978).

[16] For a discussion of urban guild organization, hierarchy and functioning, see Steve Rappaport, *Worlds Within Worlds: Structures of Life in Sixteenth-Century London* (Cambridge: Cambridge University Press, 2002), though I am not convinced, as he is, at the success of these structures in addressing (as opposed to repressing) social tensions.

[17] Brian Walsh's interesting "Performing Historicity in Dekker's *Shoemaker's Holiday*," *SEL* 46.2 (2006): 323–48, recognizes that a term such as "middling sort" is problematic, but he insists that it is appropriate for his purposes to describe the "technical designation conferred on members of guilds, and more generally to describe the merchant-tradesmen milieu," while I tease these latter groups apart (343, n.2). Indeed, my argument

claim history for all commoners, however, but rather displays merchant-citizens as making history—that is, being its recognized agents—alongside traditional aristocratic elites.

To understand how the play works, it is crucial to recognize the fluid and disorienting status situation of incipient capitalism. The description of England accompanying Holinshed's *Chronicles* observes that by the middle sixteenth century, merchants "often change estate with gentlemen, as gentlemen doo with them, by a mutuall conversion of the one into the other."[18] The reason for this "mutuall conversion" was not only the limits imposed on the aristocracy by primogeniture, which sent younger sons of traditional landed elites in search of alternative routes to livelihood, but the substantial—and increasing—economic power of merchants, which could put them in means, if not in rank, above Peers. Merchant wealth tapped by marriage, mutual investment, or loans, could bolster the concentrated or flagging fortunes of traditional elites to mutual benefit, however ambivalently experienced, while also generating tensions among those excluded from this dynamic as wealth and power continue to concentrate among a very few. Although there was no clear-cut struggle, then, between a static, landed "feudal" class and a dynamic, bourgeois "commercial" class in the transition to capitalism, as an earlier group of Marxist scholars had claimed, we can nevertheless track the transformation of an increasing proportion of elites, both rural and urban, into proto-capitalists, a process that engendered multiple, relatively distinct, spheres of conflict—among traditional and emergent elites for position, and between these elites and the subordinated.[19] To solve these conflicts, *Shoemaker's Holiday* proposes an *alliance* of old and new elites over and against labor (from which both courtiers and citizens are depicted as having properly freed themselves), and (counterfactually) depicts a highly unlikely figure—a shoemaker—rising into the urban elite, as if any lowly artisan might do the same. The play then anxiously tempers its own mythmaking with "holiday" exceptionality, acknowledging that such trajectories are uncommon without quite conceding that they are impossible. In the process, it introduces another counterfactual gesture: subordinated subjects and elites cohabit in a London evacuated of tension between elite citizens and the rest.

---

provides a direct counterpoint to his claim that "*The Shoemaker's Holiday* helps to reveal that the presentation of aristocratic centered national histories is also driven by middling-sort *labor*—both imaginative and bodily" (348, n.53, emphasis mine). To the contrary, both sorts of history plays do their best to exclude labor as such from history altogether. Ronda Arab's "Work, Bodies and Gender in *The Shoemaker's Holiday*" provides a more nuanced account of the role of "work" in the play, *Medieval and Renaissance Drama in England* 13 (2001): 182–212.

[18]   Raphael Holinshed, *Chronicles* (London, 1587), 163. For a discussion of status mobility, see Keith Wrightson, *Earthly Necessities: Economic Lives in Early Modern Britain* (New Haven: Yale University Press, 2002).

[19]   See Robert Brenner's "Postscript" to *Merchants and Revolution: Commercial Change, Political Conflict, and London's Overseas Traders, 1550–1653* (London: Verso, 2003), 638–716.

In actuality, London's ruling elites eyed with concern the threatening acts of apprentices, ordinary artisans and other deprivileged urbanites in the restive 1590s, and meted out severe punishments when disturbances arose.[20] Into this situation comes Dekker's play with its express thematizing of status conflict, albeit narrowed and simplified, for the most part, to mutual mistrust between an older generation of merchants and landed elites, represented by the Lord Mayor of London, Roger Oatley, and the Earl of Lincoln. Their younger relatives (Oatley's daughter, Rose, and Lincoln's nephew, Lacy) are in love, however, and ultimately overcome the impedimentary prejudice of their elders by way of two shoemakers: the Dutch journeyman, "Hans," whom Lacy impersonates to stay in London near Rose after he is issued a military commission for service in France, and the "merry" Simon Eyre, whose meteoric rise is facilitated by "Hans" after he is employed in Eyre's workshop and lends him "earnest-penny"—originary merchant capital—to enable his master's purchase of a Dutch ship's lucrative cargo. In the end, Eyre not only repays this loan "an hundred for twenty," but also helps bring Lacy and Rose together in marriage and smoothes over the resulting social crisis by interceding with the king from his new position of authority as Lord Mayor.

Eyre's rise shares crucial attributes with another widely-circulated, rags-to-riches story in the period, the "legend of Whittington" (mocked as a "Citizen" favorite in the *Knight of the Burning Pestle*). Richard ("Dick") Whittington purportedly arrived destitute to the city where he was taken in as a kitchen boy by a merchant. But he attains great wealth by way of the lucky investment of sending a cat, his sole alienable possession, on his master's trading ship, whence it is purchased at a great price by an Eastern potentate whose (catless) realm is plagued by rats.[21] The key point here is that Eyre's career, like Whittington's, seems to offer a route to fame and fortune to anyone, while proposing that *labor has nothing to do with it*. Instead of attempting to augment the prestige of labor by associating it with the highest levels of success, the earliest prominent merchant-citizen myths assert that the wealth that underwrites upward mobility is only contingently obtained; any labor that Eyre or Whittington perform is rendered accidental, rather than necessary, to their rise. As Laura Stevenson matter-of-factly puts it, the view that "making oneself rich by working long hours at a profitable trade was something to be proud of ... was not even articulated, let alone familiar."[22] Although hard work would later become an essential part of the favored myth of bourgeois ascendancy,

---

[20] Mihoko Suzuki, *Subordinate Subjects: Gender, the Political Nation, and Literary Form in England, 1588–1688* (Aldershot: Ashgate, 2003) provides a thoughtful account of 1590s unrest in London and its various modes of representation (27–74).

[21] Richard Johnson includes a "Song of Sir Richard Whittington," with the usual elements—poverty, cat, etc.—in his *Crowne Garland of Goulden Roses* (London, 1612), but *Eastward Hoe* refers to "the famous fable of Whittington, and his puss" in 1605, suggesting it was already a commonplace by then, though there do not appear to be print references before the early seventeenth century.

[22] Stevenson, *Praise and Paradox: Merchants and Craftsmen in Elizabethan Popular Literature* (Cambridge: Cambridge University Press, 1984), 157.

in these early myths of upward mobility labor might be part of the life history of a rising urban elite, but it is not depicted as *causing* success. In the residual understanding of privilege on which these myths rely, labor simply could not serve as a mark of status.[23]

The major social theorists of the later sixteenth century all explicitly distinguish citizens (by which they mean wealthy merchants) from artisans, who share the attribute of laboring with noncitizens, even if they might jealously guard their own skilled status over the unskilled. In fact, Thomas Elyot emphatically asserts that it is the "multitude" alone (not high office holders) who constitute the "communaltye." The political role of the latter is restricted to submitting to their superiors, who "*by other mens labours, must also be meynteyned.*"[24] William Harrison likewise explains in his description of the "degrees of people" that "We in England divide our people commonlie into foure sorts, as gentlemen, citizens or burgesses, yeomen … [and] artificers, or laborers." Having identified gentlemen as those who "can live without labour" (if they are titled and landed) or at least "without manuall labor" (if they practice the professions, or are public servants), he distinguishes the "citizens" as second in rank following gentlemen, consisting of men who "are free within the cities, and are of some likely substance to beare office in the same." Because of the "substance" requirement, artificers are included *separately* from "citizens" among the "last sort of people" along with "day laborers and poor husbandmen" (even though artisans, legally, might too be citizens).[25] Thomas Smith makes the same division, and, of the last sort, emphasizes that "no account is made of them but onelie to be ruled," though they do, nonetheless, he notes, hold petty offices. Furthermore, like Harrison, he specifically lists "Shoomakers" among "Artificers" relegated to the lowest status category, and both, likewise, separate out city office holders "of some substance" as "Citizens" in their own category, just below "Gentlemen."[26] Thomas Wilson's "State of England, anno dom. 1600," composed very near the time in which the *Shoemaker's Holiday* appeared, also distinguishes "cives" [citizens] from "artisani" [artisans].[27]

While political theory does not tell the whole story of how things actually worked on the ground, we nonetheless need to recognize that it is not fully attentive to the politics of the time to collapse "artisan" and "citizen." At the very least, we

---

[23]   Michael Nerlich's *Ideology of Adventure: Studies in Modern Consciousness, 1100–1750*, trans. Ruth Crowley (Minneapolis: University of Minnesota Press, 1987) explores the pillaging (and transformation) of chivalric themes by merchants as capitalism emerges, but the contradictions that attend this practice could be further emphasized, especially with respect to "citizen history," as I attempt here.

[24]   Elyot, *Boke Named the Governour*, 4v, emphasis mine.

[25]   In Holdinshed's *Chronicles*, 156, 163.

[26]   Smith, *De Republica Anglorum* (London, 1583), 33.

[27]   Wilson, "State of England, anno com. 1600," in *Camden Miscellany*, vol. 16, (London: Camden Society, 1845), 17.

need to realize how contested status categories could be.[28] It simply was not the same thing to be "free" of the city as a wealthy draper or a goldsmith—that is, in the ruling group of one of the twelve elite guilds—and as a shoemaker, and this lends a heightened charge to Dekker's myth-making. Through its version of the Eyre story, *Shoemaker's Holiday*, like the period political theorists, is at pains to render the distinction between artisans and citizens manifest, despite the inability of many readers to see it now. A *citizen* history, in early modern understanding, then, is by no means an *artisan* history; the citizens who, in plays such as Dekker's, are being envisioned as historical actors on par with gentlemen, were also seen as divorced from what was still understood to be a lowering taint of manual labor in ways that artisans as such were not and could not be.[29] Wealth ("substance"), not labor, made a "citizen" in the *elite* sense of the word, as opposed to its technical, more expansive (guild-member, "free of the city") definition. Furthermore, wealth was not typically associated with hard work or even frugality at the time because wealth had its role to play in shoring up elite status in general—aristocratic as well as merchant. This is not to say, of course, that tensions did not emerge among these competing groups of elites along the way.

Indeed, *Shoemaker's Holiday* opens with the display of a seemingly unbridgeable rift between the "citizen" Mayor and the "courtier" Earl, which spurs them to attempt to prevent the marriage between their blood relations. Significantly, economic *ressentiment* gets expressed alongside stereotypical *hauteur*. The very first lines of the play draw attention to the discomfiting reality of merchant-citizens sometimes having more disposable wealth than Peers: "My Lord Mayor, you have sundry times / Feasted myself and many courtiers more. / Seldom or never can we be so kind / To make requital of your courtesy." The opening exchange between the self-identified "courtier" and the man who will shortly refer to himself as a "citizen" not only calls attention to uneasiness over disproportion in means and its relation to status, but immediately introduces labor as a contentious issue when the courtier sneers as his nephew's acquisition of shoemaking skills, while the citizen approves of it. Ultimately, however, the citizen's praise is contradictory because what it means to be elite is *not* recoded by the play as hard-working; high status is defined, as traditionally, by transcendence of labor. We never see Oatley engaged in labor of any kind, nor does he ever boast of having worked hard to achieve his status; indeed, we never see anyone who actually makes things described as a

---

[28] See Jonathan Barry and Christopher Brooks (eds.), *The Middling Sort of People: Culture, Society and Politics in England, 1550–1800* (New York: St Martins, 1994).

[29] Thus I agree with Stephen Maynard's claim in "Feasting on Eyre: Community, Consumption, and Communion in the Shoemaker's Holiday," *Comparative Drama* 32.3 (1998): 327–46, that the play displays an agonistic "claim to equality" of citizens with peers, but not that it therefore indicates that "people are fundamentally the same" or that "class" is not at issue. He occludes the play's participation in the making of the working class by proposing that the specific "tensions" attendant upon the emergence of capitalism are merely expressions of "essential" human "hostilities" better understood anthropologically than historically.

"citizen" in the play. That term, used only five times, is concentrated in the opening and closing scenes, when the all-important prospect of marital alliance between citizen and courtier is proposed. Furthermore, by rendering the upwardly mobile Simon Eyre responsible for the resolution of conflict between the representative of the traditional landed elites (the "courtier") and a new merchant-centered elite (the "citizen"), the play seems to demand a reading in terms of transition, though in intriguingly different terms than would become standard later on.

When Adam Delved and Eve Span, Who Was Then the Citizen?

Marx's concept of transition—"primitive accumulation"—reveals capital to have come into the world "dripping blood and gore," a product of violent dispossession.[30] Alternatively, mainstream views among political economists at the time explained the origins of poverty by the different dispositions of men—lazy and prodigal versus hard-working and frugal. Marx denounces this account as a "nursery tale" that obscures the quite different set of practices actually at work: legally-sanctioned theft, by which the world was sorted into owners and non-owners of capital. That is to say, he exposes dominant historical narrative as *counterfactual*. Intriguingly, Dekker, like the later bourgeois apologists critiqued by Marx, produces a "nursery tale"—a counterfactual account—concerning capital's origins, but it is a different tale than the one that would later become ascendant. Because capitalism did not yet exist in its fully-developed form and because the "Protestant work ethic" had not yet fully recoded labor's role in the highway to status, Dekker's play does not produce the myth that sorts ostensibly "diligent" owners from "lazy" workers. Instead, it negotiates the struggles for status between courtiers and citizens of the 1590s as if they had already been fully overcome long before in a politico-economic alliance of the two groups, while justifying the divorce of both from labor.

At the same time, the play mystifies the threat of discontent among the various social groups that are re-subordinated in this process by representing as amicable and desirable the division of the world into those who labor and those for whom they labor, with the latter alone assigned a historical role. This is so, paradoxically, not despite but because of the play's affirmative display of labor and the products of labor directly on stage. The shoes the young journeyman Ralph gives to his new wife, Jane, in the first scene, for example, are detailed as the product of a collective labor of love in Eyre's workshop: "Here, take this pair of shoes cut out by Hodge, / Stitched by my fellow, Firk, seamed by myself, / Made up and pinked, with letters for thy name" (1.239–41). Labor is here emphasized, just as the tools and practices of the shoemaking trade are referenced throughout the play.

Not only is work described, directed, commissioned, and sought, it is also performed before the audience's eyes. We see Hodge and the others in the workshop, at their "boards," in scene 13, and, in the previous scene, Jane "in a sempsters

---

[30]   *Capital: A Critique of Political Policy*, vol. 1, trans. Ben Fowkes (London: Penguin, 1976), 873–940.

shop" plying her needle to support herself while Ralph is in the army. Furthermore, commodities, such as Jane's shoes, are associated with care and craft; they effect and bind social relations through their circulation, from which labor is *not* effaced. For this reason, it is especially significant that Ralph locates his wife, when they become separated from each other during his military duty, by way of the shoes he had given to her, which are brought into the workshop by a servant as the model for a new pair: he recognizes his labor in them. Jane's labor, too, is underscored: in the very scene in which the shoes are transferred to her, Eyre takes Jane's hands and comments: "this fine hand, this white hand, these pretty fingers must spin, must card, must work, work … work *for your living*," labor which her amphibian suitor, the "citizen" *and* "gentleman" Hammon, who appears on the scene after Ralph is supposedly killed in action, will later find seductively charming: "how prettily she *works*" (1.217–20; 12.13). To put this in Marxist terms: London commodities in *Shoemaker's Holiday* are *unmystified*—they are clearly products of labor, even respected and community-affirming labor. Yet Hammon, like Oatley, never engages in any labor that we see, nor, ultimately, does Eyre, who has departed the workshop before the extended scene in which shoemaking is mimed. Eyre is also manifestly absent from the roster of laborers involved in the production of Jane's shoes. Labor, then, is displayed and appreciated as the purview of some characters, but just as emphatically divorced from others. Freedom from labor in this play invariably designates elite status: the very "freedom of the city" that, legally, was a freedom *to* labor, as John Archer properly points out in the essay that follows, was also, clearly, in the case of *elite* citizens, a freedom *from* it.

This state of affairs was not without contradictions and paradoxes. As we have seen, elite status and labor were at odds with each other in the period, but this meant neither that everyone approved of such a divide, nor that everyone who eluded labor was recognized as elite. A proverb already common in the fourteenth century and still current in the seventeenth captured a long tradition of recognized tension in the labor / non-labor distinction: "When Adam delved and Eve span, / Who was then the Gentleman?"[31] By the sixteenth century, elites also began developing novel institutions, such as workhouses, for the "idle."

Shoemaker's Holiday, too, concerns itself with idleness, but more discreetly. It does not denounce elite freedom from labor as would a leveling discourse, but neither does it disdain labor. It never associates rule or high status with labor, yet it forcefully imagines labor to be socially affirming and unifying. Intriguingly, hard work is also associated with aspirations to upward mobility, if not with its

---

[31]   See Albert Friedman, "'When Adam Delved … ': Contexts of an Historic Proverb," in *The Learned and the Lewed: Studies in Chaucer and Medieval Literature*, (ed.) Larry Benson (Cambridge: Harvard University Press, 1974), 213–30, who sets out the range of ways this phrase was used—conservative as well as radical. I would myself underscore, however, that these multiple codings indicate elite attempts to manage potentially revolutionary implications.

accomplishment.[32] Eyre rouses his sleepy household before seven in the morning to set them all to work. Hodge, Eyre's foreman, who has been given the workshop by the newly ascendant "Master Sheriff" Eyre, later urges the others: "To it, pell-mell, that we may live to be lord mayors or alderman at least" (13.3–4). It is not hard work, however, or even the workshop *per se*, that propels Eyre toward high office, but foreign trade bankrolled by Lacy the aristocrat, in the disguise of a Dutch shoemaker. Lacy mediates the shady deal for the cargo of a ship whose "merchant owner ... dares not show his head," a situation taken advantage of by Eyre (7.17–18). The play seemingly confirms the "Protestant work ethic" in its appreciative view of labor, but Dekker does not attribute either worldly success or the origin of the divide between rich and poor to labor any more than Marx does. It comes, rather, from merchant capital of obscure origins.

This obscurity has ideological significance. In Marx's account, primitive accumulation occurs as an effect of mass dispossession of the smallholder and the colonized, which establish the fundamental conditions of possibility for capitalism. A relation of mutual dependency arises between owners of capital (who do not work themselves because they are in a position to buy the labor of others) and the people who must sell their labor to them to survive, because they have been divorced from the means of production. Eyre's upward mobility, however, derives neither from hard work nor dispossession. So far is Eyre from profiting at anyone's expense (in London, in any case) that he "makes over" his workshop to his former foreman when he attains his first public office and proceeds to display luxuriant generosity in repaying debts and sharing his wealth, not only with Lacy and other elite stakeholders in his enterprise, but with the whole city in his endowment of Leaden Hall, and even with the vast population of London prentices, whom he treats to a feast at his inauguration, and for whom he declares an annual holiday (12.52–4). In Dekker's fantasy, then, when Eyre's boat comes in, all boats rise. Still, the play is less concerned, I would suggest, with establishing a "trickle down" theory of wealth than with contesting chronicle history's tendency to affirm traditional social hierarchy uncritically. Dekker's counter-thesis proposes that elite status should be expanded to include wealthy merchant citizens—indeed, the emphasis on Eyre's beneficence implies that he can fulfill this role as well or better than any aristocrat. *Shoemaker's Holiday* therefore deflects attention from the acquisition and unequal control of wealth to its dispersion.

In this respect, the citizen history play accomplishes for the city what Ben Jonson's "To Penshurst"—as read by Raymond Williams—will accomplish for the country.[33] This is not particularly surprising, since both urban and rural elites have an investment in asserting that their benefit to the larger population is greater than what they derive from it. Effacing labor by describing Penshurst as if Nature

---

[32]   Deloney, unlike Dekker, describes the early part of Eyre's career when he "labored hard daily." Neither Dekker nor Deloney attributes Eyre's success to labor, however.

[33]   Williams, *The Country and the City* (New York: Oxford University Press, 1973), 26–34.

alone provided for the Sidney family, and through it, for the whole countryside, Jonson not only effaces rural domination, but also the actual origin of the goods and services provided to those who depended upon the labor of others for their daily upkeep and comfort. While Dekker's play, with its elaborate displays of labor, seems to be doing something very different from Jonson's labor-erasing (and, therefore, mystifying) poem, we find ourselves on similar ground when we look to the origin of Eyre's wealth: the commodities in the Dutch ship are as unmediated by labor—as far as we see or hear—as are the flora and fauna on the country estate described by Jonson. They, too, are *mystified*. This is all the more so because Dekker changes the bill of lading of Deloney's ship, which is filled with fine cloth alone, to include foodstuffs. At a time of high inflation and poor harvests, such cargo would resonate in the stomachs as well as the minds of Dekker's audience. As Firk the clown-journeyman puts it: "O, sweet wares. Prunes, almonds, sugar candy, carrot-roots, turnips. O, brave fatting meat" (7.138–40). The delirious listing of these "fatting meat[s]," however, elicits no envy of Eyre by subordinates within the play, nor does it elicit curiosity as to their derivation: these commodities––unlike Jane's shoes—are never linked to any kind of labor. They are not only alien commodities, then, but alienated in the Marxist sense of mystified. That they are alien is underscored not only by the transactions in stage-Dutch necessary to acquire them, but also by their status either as luxury goods (imported fruit, nuts and sugar) or recently arrived cultivars to England in Dekker's sixteenth- not Eyre's fifteenth- century from agrarian experimentation and "improvement" in the Low Countries (carrots and turnips).[34] That these commodities are also alienated is underscored by their striking contrast with visibly labor-intensive Londoner-produced commodities.

This alienation appears to be contagious, however. Firk also codes the Shoemaker's feast at the play's end as an occasion of Cockaigne-like plenitude in which everyone is freed from labor and food seems to appear of its own accord: "venison pasties walk up and down piping hot like sergeants; beef and brewis comes marching in dry fats; fritters and pancakes comes trolling in wheelbarrows, hens and oranges hopping in porters' baskets, collops and eggs in scuttles, and tarts and custards comes quavering in malt shovels" (18.208–13). Jonson will later describe a similar fantasy feast in "To Penshurst." Through such mystifications, elite wealth sheds any infelicity in a spontaneous overflow of holiday abundance. In Dekker's play, though, this forgetting requires a moment of displacement: alienation is projected onto the alien, so that it can enter London, supposedly without any local cost, except to Eyre himself. Oatley comments sardonically when Eyre's great gains are described to him, "Well, he shall spend some of his thousands now,/ For I have sent for him to the Guildhall" (9.71–2). But above all

---

[34]   "Market gardening [of vegetables such as carrots and turnips] developed rapidly in the late sixteenth century—mainly in the 1590s—with the encouragement and active participation of alien immigrants from the Low Countries." Joan Thirsk, *Agrarian History of England and Wales*, vol. 4 (Cambridge: Cambridge University Press, 1967), 196–7.

the play carefully deflects potential uneasiness over the origins of Eyre's wealth onto the shady unnamed merchant, the foreign Other "who dares not show his head" (7.18).

Affect and Ascendancy

This attempted management of affect also drives the portrayal of subordinates as ultimately contented with their lot. The one moment in the play in which artisans appear to be potentially dangerous is pointedly not directed toward the city's ruling elites per se, but toward one citizen-turned-gentleman, Hammon, and his servants, when the shoemakers rescue Jane from them to return her to her husband Ralph. To be sure, Hammon is a "citizen by birth," as Oatley approvingly observes, and the appearance of a band of young men "all with cudgels, or such weapons" could correspond discomfiting closely to actual experiences of urban unrest by citizen viewers (6.61; 18, sd). However, by directing animosity toward Hammon alone, the play manages to critique its gentlemen—and citizens—but preserve them too. Hammon is rejected for being the wrong kind of citizen-gentleman: he merely apes gentlemanly speech, pastimes and manners, when the play's preferred norm is for citizen and aristocratic elites to collaborate in capital investment, as Eyre and Lacy do. The play crucially insists that the aristocracy needs to be more like the (elite) citizenry, not just the other way around. The threat of this status-offending suggestion (to traditional elites) is diffused by situating the crisis in a remote, mythical past, and depicting its resolution as involving no taint of labor. Lacy's shoemaking is not only temporary and strategic, but incidental to his earning the love of Rose, or providing the "earnest penny" to Eyre, who is, as we have seen, divided from labor altogether. Yet the threat of resentment from below to both groups of elites remains. To deal with it, the play transforms the Shrove Tuesday tradition of apprentice rioting into an orderly celebration of government benevolence.

There were other ideological means of negotiating this problem, so it is telling that Dekker does not use them. For example, Thomas Deloney's *Jack of Newberry* underscores that the claim to fame of this "worthy clothier of England" is that he "set continually five hundred poor people at work to the great benefit of the commonwealth." "Jack" himself explains the gap between rich and poor thus: "the poor hate the rich because they will not set them on work, and the rich hate the poor because they seem burdenous"—a view notable in its evasion of how there came to be rich and poor in the first place.[35] What it does propose, however, is that any unhappiness from below within the existing social hierarchy might be smoothed over by entrepreneurial solicitude. This is now a commonplace of capitalist ideology, but it was competing in the early modern period with a quite different account of how elites would earn "love": the suggestion that citizens

---

[35]   Deloney, *Jack of Newberry* (London, 1597), 363.

would fill in where aristocrats were failing in their traditional social obligations by providing hospitality and charity, a claim that Deloney also makes of Jack.

The tug of affect is thus particularly strong in *Shoemaker's Holiday*. As many critics have pointed out, the shadow side of London does creep into Dekker's cheerful play from time to time (Ralph's lingering war wound, for example, as well as his impressment in the first place). What is particularly striking about *Shoemaker's Holiday* just the same, however, is its attempt to insist on a certain leveling bonhomie among men of good will in all classes, while still maintaining a firm hierarchy of wealth and power. Eyre retains, from first to last, the blustery speech of a jestbook "merry" shoemaker—quite distinct a voice from that of Deloney's sober, God-fearing, cautious worry-wort. The aristocrat Lacy also assimilates himself easily into the workshop, earning the respect and camaraderie of men with whom he shares talk, song, drink and dance as well as labor, and to whom he refers in the end as "Sometimes [i.e., previously] my fellows" (20.144). Despite the seeming warmth of Lacy's comment, the (limiting) "sometimes" here is as significant as the (leveling) "fellows." Lacy sees labor as only a temporary condition ("I mean a while to work"). It is simply part of his disguise, an Ovidian metamorphosis from "high birth to bareness," which he rationalizes in a patronizing soliloquy (3.1–24). Disguise does not ultimately render his nobility or national solidarity irrelevant any more than divinity disappeared when classical gods transformed themselves into mortal or animal shapes to consummate sexual liaisons with earthly creatures in earlier myths. To the contrary, Lacy's transformation renders him a site for mediation of conflict between alien and native, aristocrat and citizen—as well as laboring and non-laboring populations.

This is so because, as we have seen, it is not principally through work but merchant's capital—provided by Lacy—that Eyre enters the ruling class. Like the magic beans of a fairy tale, or the Biblical talents, these few coins multiply, and secure Eyre's rapid rise. The marriage of Lacy and Rose merely confirms the alliance between citizen and courtier that has already been established by Lacy's portagues. In this way, the play proposes a collaboration of aristocrat and citizen in which they both become emergent merchant-capitalists who transcend the Biblical curse of labor by profiting at the cost of a foreign merchant—not local workers. One might almost imagine the playbill claiming, reassuringly: "no workers were harmed in the making of this play!" Eyre's rise appears to carry no threat to the local aristocracy either, fears of Lacy's uncle notwithstanding. Instead, it posits an alliance of elites in a new dispensation. For this reason, Lacy can be forgiven by both the king and the play for his dereliction of military duty. While pursuing his bride, he has been performing a new, but equally essential, elite social function: promoting national ascendancy by means of foreign trade rather than foreign wars through an alliance of citizen and court(ier), a project coded in the play as "love."

Eyre's role in this process is crucial, and suggests why a romance plot is combined with a citizen history plot: the historical role of the upwardly mobile citizen is to bring country and city together harmoniously in love—while managing any disgruntlement that might thereby emerge from below. Via Eyre, *Shoemaker's Holiday* effects in fantasy the union of key sectors of landed and mercantile wealth on which, in the long run, the emergence of capital was actually to depend in the analysis of historians such as Robert Brenner as it transforms the restiveness and resentments of subordinated groups into cheerful acceptance of their lot of laboring for others.[36] At the end of the play, an un-named "King"—his anonymity emphasizing his mythical authorizing function rather than his historicity—affirms Eyre's interventions. First he demands consent to the marriage of Lacy and Rose by challenging their recalcitrant relatives with a rhetorical question—"Dost thou not know that love respects no blood,/ Cares not for difference of birth or state?"—a speech implausible in the extreme outside a topsy-turvy fictional world (21.105–6). Then he attends the feast at the end of the play, legitimating the holiday that the—named—Simon Eyre declares, indicating that historical agency is being extended to citizens, whose money permits them to leave a historical mark on the *calendar* as well as the space of the city.[37] But not all citizens have such agency: only "princely" ones.

"Prince am I none, Yet am I Princely Born"

The ambivalent and anxious positioning of Eyre as a "prince" is perhaps the play's most explicit allusion to status crisis. Eyre repeatedly declares "Prince am I none, yet am I princely born"—or some variation on this paradoxical phrase (10.158). The very oddness of the formulation—which does not originate with Dekker, although he deploys it insistently—indicates an awkward attempt to negotiate vestigial "class" tensions as emergent capital competes with residual "feudalism" for ascendancy, giving some citizens new, prince-like powers, while noble families increasingly engaged in capitalized agriculture, or descended into debt and, perhaps, the necessity of "trade." Meanwhile, the vast majority of the population is still considered to be superfluous to history—nameless—as Dodger's relation of the battle "news" from France to Lincoln underscores:

> Twelve thousand of the Frenchmen that day died,
> Four thousand English, and no man of name
> But Captain Hyam and young Ardington. (8.8–10)

---

[36] Elite collaboration, as well as tension, is well established. In addition to Brenner's "Postscript," see, for example, Theodore K. Rabb, *Enterprise and Empire: Merchant and Gentry Investment in the Expansion of England, 1575–1630* (Cambridge: Harvard University Press, 1967).

[37] Eyre's fictional appeal to the "King" resonates "historically": direct commoner petitioning of Kings—bypassing aristocracy—was a long-standing strategy of resistance from below, here ideologically re-coded as an elite privilege. See Andy Wood, "'Poore men woll speke one daye': Plebian Languages of Deference and Defiance in England, c. 1520–1640," in *The Politics of the Excluded, c. 1500–1850*, (ed.) Tim Harris (New York: Palgrave, 2001). See also Alison Chapman, "Whose Saint Crispin's Day is it?," *Renaissance Quarterly* 54.4 (2001): 1467–94. Chapman argues that in *Henry V*, Shakespeare "fashions a shoemaker's holiday that celebrates monarchical instead of artisanal power," which resonates, in part, with my own argument (1482).

While a man like Ralph, maimed in war, pays the price of history in his person, he is still ultimately considered irrelevant to it. He is named in the play, to be sure, but not as a historical maker "of name." Eyre, meanwhile, is manifestly the featured agent of conflict (and plot) resolution.

Still, while depicting him as a historical agent, both Deloney and Dekker equivocate in their portrayal of Eyre, who, as Stow's account makes clear, was not a shoemaker—an extremely unlikely candidate for elite office. Firk comes close to rupturing the fantasy of upward mobility on which the Eyre myth is based in his observation, when informed by Ralph of the likelihood that several aldermen will not last long in their offices: "I care not, I'll be none" (8.41). In reply, Ralph encourages his fellow worker to root for Eyre's fantastical rise, diverting attention away from Firk's original, far more realistic, appraisal of a Cordwainer's prospects for attaining high office, by getting him to accept and acknowledge Eyre's exceptionality. Further mythifying the situation, Dekker fails to have Eyre "change his copy" to draper before he becomes Mayor, as Deloney does, thereby implying that a shoemaker could become mayor.

Any citizen, the play seems to imply, *might* become a man of name, but in the meantime should work diligently and appreciate the honor and wealth showered upon the fortunate few, as do Roger and Firk. Yet the play also recognizes that most people must work, and will not acquire name, and that, even if one does achieve name, it is not as a result of labor. When the citizen-turned-gentleman Hammon tries to lure the sempster Jane from her shop, she protests "I cannot live by keeping holiday," though he manifestly can (8.13). Perhaps most poignantly, Firk appreciatively explains that on every Shrove Tuesday he and his fellows will be "as free as my Lord Mayor," whose freedom (*from* labor, not *to* labor), however, persists (18.223). Like Marx, then, the play recognizes that some people manage to extricate themselves from the general curse of labor. The difference, of course, is that Dekker's play appears to approve of what Marx will later decry, though without resorting either to hard work or Providence as a rationale. In a moment of ideological flux between the dominance of "blood" status, with its contempt for labor, and an emergent affirmation of hard work, evident in respect for labor in the play, Dekker and other early apologists for elite citizens imagine a world of accidental success, which explains upward mobility without contaminating status with labor, or exposing the cost of elite status to the subordinated.

Although *Shoemaker's Holiday* contains several scenes in which the shoemakers assert what they take to be their rights (e.g., to hire a fellow journeyman, or to be protected from what they take to be insults from their mistress), then, the play always carefully limits both their claims and their threats—and depicts them as taken seriously—thereby suggesting that London's social structure addressed grievances successfully—just as a certain influential strand of historiography likes to suggest.[38] The counterfactual aspect of such claims, however, becomes starkly

---

[38] In addition to Rappaport, *Worlds Within Worlds*, see Ian Archer, *The Pursuit of Stability: Social Relations in Elizabethan London* (Cambridge: Cambridge University Press, 1991).

evident when we contrast them with the record of terroristic discipline of the commons via executions, workhouses, prisons and the like, as Francis Barker has argued.[39] Viewed, thus, it seems more correct to say that grievances were not so much addressed as repressed—obscured from view not only by elite assumptions in the period but also by the historiography that effectively (and affectively) affirms elite views even now.[40] The depiction of urban unrest in *Shoemaker's Holiday* stands in stark contrast with rebellious artisans and prentices featured in chronicle history plays, such as Jack Cade in Shakespeare's First Tetralogy. Real grievances make their way into the latter in the ventriloquized speech of rebels and rioters, when they explicitly raise the specter of radical leveling ("all the realm shall be in common"), views repressed in Dekker.[41]

This repression was necessary, and remains so, because despite broad agitation from below, the highest status category was expanding to include only a tiny portion of the citizenry, which disrupts traditional chronicle, but undermines traditional social order less than might at first appear, since it only slightly augments the cast of historical characters deemed worthy of name. To this end, *Shoemaker's Holiday* positions Eyre as a "Prince" without, apparently, rendering him any less a citizen. Eyre continues to play the merry man-of-the-people in affect after he is a Lord Mayor in substance, even suggesting that his demeanor—rather than Lacy's portagues—is the secret of his success: "Be as mad knaves as your master Sim Eyre hath, and you shall live to be sheriffs of London" (10.155–6). Being a populist and a prince at the same time, he has status and obscures it too. He seems to invent an urban version of the king's two bodies to inhabit his office; the citizen's two bodies permit him to assert princely privilege and common mirth at the same time ("be even as merry/ as if thou wert among thy shoemakers" the king urges him, when he is ushered, as Mayor, into the royal presence), pointedly bypassing the choice between courtier and citizen that Prince Hal supposedly has to make in Shakespeare's *Henry IV* plays (21.13–14). This distinction matters because of all the chronicle plays, the Second Tetralogy seems to have most immediately influenced Dekker in fashioning a plot which concerns Eyre's rise to great office from unlikely beginnings.[42] Shakespeare has Hal describe himself as a "madcap"—a word that Dekker, notably, uses to describe Eyre, who seems to be a

---

[39] Barker, *Culture of Violence: Shakespeare, Tragedy, History* (Manchester: Manchester University Press, 1993).

[40] Absence of overt, organized resistance—which was not negligible in early modern London in any case—does not prove satisfaction. See James Scott, *Weapons of the Weak: Everyday Forms of Peasant Resistance* (New Haven: Yale University Press, 1985).

[41] One need not agree with Annabel Patterson that Shakespeare is a man of the people to see that his chronicle histories at times voice such discontent. See *Shakespeare and the Popular Voice* (Cambridge: Blackwell, 1989). On *Henry VI* and *Shoemaker* in particular, see François Laroque, "'Blue-apron culture': La culture populaire dans *2 Henry VI* de Shakespeare et *The Shoemaker's Holiday* de Thomas Dekker," *RANAM* 39 (2006): 57–70.

[42] Thomas Worden traces out some of these echoes in "Idols in the Early Modern Material World (1599)," *Exemplaria* 11.2 (1999): 437–71.

composite of both the Prince and Falstaff, especially in his blustery mirth, which is sometimes pointedly Falstaffian, as at the end of the play, when Eyre quips with the king about his age, declaring himself "a very boy, a stripling, a younker" despite his fifty-six years.

When Dekker rewrites the process of Hal "becoming-Prince" in *Shoemaker's Holiday*, however, he produces a revisionist effect every bit as profound as Bale's recoding of King John for post-Reformation consumption. Eyre cannot be depicted as rejecting London, as Hal ultimately does, while being Lord Mayor of it. Hence, London is no longer a totalized foil against which the power and prestige of the court is consolidated; instead, the city is subjected to an internal social hierarchization that seeks to place a class-fraction of Londoners on par with their ostensible superiors at court, while altering the social function of the "high" to include capital investment. In the process, labor is segregated as the "low" part of the city so that London as a whole need not be (symbolically) separated from the court. At the same time, this gesture is mystified in a carnivalesque conviviality that, unlike Hal's cynical slumming, appears to render the former shoemaker just one Londoner among many, even as mayor. Yet Eyre's rise renders him, unlike his ostensible fellows, the equal of any "prince." His speech may remain peppered with the sort of slangy "gross terms" ("Corinthians," "Trojans," etc.) that Hal mocks. He may bond with his workers and keep the promise he made to the other prentices, when he was one himself, to repay them for a collective breakfast that he at the time could not afford. But the feast in the end is but a momentary relief from a life of labor to which the prentices, but not Eyre himself, will have to return. Like Hal, then, Eyre forms himself against laboring London, but positions himself as a prince *in* the city, forming something like a liberty of rule for himself within its bounds.

Dekker's displacement of the costs of this transition onto a foreign Other—the Dutch ship's mysterious captain—also has an instructive parallel in the Second Tetralogy. On his deathbed, Hal's father advises his son to "busy giddy minds/ with foreign quarrels, that action hence borne out/ May waste the memory of the former days."[43] In *Shoemaker's Holiday*, a merchant version of the Second Tetralogy emerges to complicate the narrowly dynastic history of chronicle drama. Like *Henry V*, Dekker's play raises the specter of France as an object of "aggressiveness," as the king declares in the final line that "Wars must right wrongs which Frenchmen have begun," but another front of battle—international trade— is foregrounded, and its role in uniting elites and securing national wealth, status and stability, prominently affirmed. This is a crucial significance of the origins of Eyre's wealth being explicitly attributed, as we have seen, to transactions with the alien. Overt aggression is not the only option for dealing with national "others," the play proposes. Without successful negotiation of and with the alien, neither Lacy nor Eyre would have accomplished their respective marital and mercantile

---

[43] William Shakespeare, *2 Henry VI*, in *The Riverside Shakespeare*, 2nd edition, (ed.) G. Blakemore Evans (Boston: Houghton Mifflin, 1997) 4.5.213–15.

triumphs. Just as important, they would not have accomplished them without each other. Most important, they would not have accomplished them without labor as the other of their elite status, a divide that appeared in the Henriad as "court" versus "city," and would later appear in bourgeois ideology as "hard working" versus "lazy," but in this early moment manifests as a fantasy of an elite who has laborless "rule"—and London too.

****

Citizen history holds the mirror up to labor in order to refuse the image as its own. A new labor-theory of value as a justification for economic inequality would emerge prominently only decades later after the revolutionary disruptions of mid-century and the incipient triumphs of a liberal-democratic agenda in figures such as John Locke, who wrote the script that capital would later put to use in the drafting of new tales of wealth's origin in labor. Dekker's play, despite its manifest respect for the artisanal, cannot imagine a self-made citizen elite as an effect of labor because this would be too dissonant with period understandings of status and rule, which were assumed to be by definition distinct from labor and those who performed it. Old myths or new, however, such tales expose actual historical struggles in their very eagerness to smooth them over. Pace Ferguson, then, there is nothing *accidental* about such struggles or their outcomes. Nevertheless, given the contradictions and historical variability of capitalism, its ideologies cannot spring coherently and fully-formed into the world: there are false starts, elaborate hybrids, odd detours, and—always—contestation that wrenches elite fantasies hither and yon. Exposing the changing face of such "mythic counterfactuals" is important for understanding not only distant historical processes, but also the versions that we inhabit now, since such tales, in their more recent forms, still do their share of work in a world in which some people, still, do not.

Chapter 2
Citizens and Aliens as Working Subjects in Dekker's *The Shoemaker's Holiday*

John Michael Archer

For Aristotle, the citizen was an adult male who did not work.[1] The Renaissance recurred, as is often claimed, to classical models, yet it reversed the Aristotelian canon of citizenship. Whether in the Italian city-states of the fourteenth century, or London during the sixteenth, citizens worked—or rather, they were supposed to work. In London, citizens were workers or masters of work, traders who worked at buying and selling, their sons, who were citizens by birth, and (less often) nobles who purchased citizenship outright, and with it, the right to work as a privilege of their citizen status. Great citizens were often merchants, rather than laborers, or even masters of workshops, but "trading" ideally remained bound to the trade that produced the goods they sold. Furthermore, London citizens of all sorts came to define themselves against illegitimate or non-citizen workers and, disproportionately, against alien workers in exile from the Low Countries. Aliens competed with citizens for labor, but symbolically, they vied for the illusive essence of citizenship as well, the prosperous citizen way-of-life, which took its legitimacy from the right to work and to trade that the freedom or citizenship proper bestowed on the subject. After reconsidering how the Tudor moral interlude stages the threatening figure of the Netherlandish urban immigrant, I will look closely at the device of alien disguise in Thomas Dekker's *The Shoemaker's Holiday*. Lacy's masquerade as "Hans" perpetuates the ethnic stereotype of the interludes, but it does so by converting that stereotype into a vehicle for contemporary anxieties about how different types of London citizen had assumed differing relationships to labor by the end of the sixteenth century.[2]

---

[1]   Aristotle, *Politics*, in *The Basic Works of Aristotle*, (ed.) Richard McKeon (New York: Random House, 1941), 1278a 6–10. This paper is a modified version of a lecture that was delivered at New York University in April 2003, and that also formed part of the seminar "Winter's Tales: Shakespeare and the North," Shakespeare Association of America, Philadelphia, April 2006. I'd like to thank the participants at those events.

[2]   I write "different types of London citizen," despite Crystal Bartolovich's useful emphasis on class differences between elite citizens and citizen artisans in the preceding paper. She is correct that work and the notion of citizenship were gradually diverging during the period. Nevertheless, livery companies or guilds typically contained members

Current theories of citizenship tacitly follow Aristotle in excluding work from the philosophical legacy of citizen subjectivity in modernity. Yet they often ground themselves in interpretations of the early modern European past as well. According to Etienne Balibar, it is the citizen who "comes after" the subject of political philosophy, in the aftermath of the European revolutions of the eighteenth century. Institutions such as medieval towns and corporations had provoked a return to classical Greek and Roman ideals of citizenship, yet it was not until the Enlightenment and its often violent consequences, he maintains, that the citizen emerged, albeit as a white, male, and thus incomplete figure.[3] Even though citizenship was originally restricted to the rights of certain men in law and custom, its philosophical character as the next placeholder of subjectivity made it potentially extendable. Through law and through force, women, colonial subjects, and others have successfully laid claim to citizen status. This is due to what Balibar calls the "indeterminacy" of citizenship, that is, "the possibility for any *given* realization of the citizen to be placed in question and destroyed by a struggle for equality."[4] A similar claim underlies Chantal Mouffe's radical-democratic reworking of the civic republican tradition of citizenship. Mouffe draws on Quentin Skinner, who, in tracing the figure of the citizen from Greek and Roman antiquity to the Italian Renaissance, argues that classical republicanism is not incompatible with modern

---

who labored in the craft and members who did not. Both were termed "freemen," and both attained the civic status of "citizen" by virtue of full company membership. While artisans in companies often opposed the masters and merchants who ran guilds, they also valued their citizen identity and sought to use it, in fact, to make claims upon elite citizens in what may be regarded as the class struggle over the division of labor. Whatever elite intellectuals in the Aristotelian political tradition like Sir Thomas Elyot may have written to exclude artisans from citizenship as a concept, then, skilled workers who were members of companies referred to themselves as freemen or citizens, and the authorities accepted and in fact insisted on that legal status for them. Citizen artisans regarded themselves as members of a kind of elite, too, over against semi-skilled workers, which included poor women like sempstresses such as Jane in our play, and those employed in more physical labor, who were hired by masters but who were not company members or citizens. Yet artisans struggled with company elites at various levels for control of their labor: journeymen complained that masters, say, employed too many apprentices to save paying wages, but journeymen also joined with masters in "yeomanry" associations within companies against the small number of wealthy "liverymen" who governed the guilds and set both working and trading conditions. Class antagonism in Marx's sense was present during the period: my point is that the highly-differentiated category of citizenship in fact reveals it, albeit in a prismatic and fractured way. I offer more detail on these terms and concepts in *Citizen Shakespeare: Freemen and Aliens in the Language of the Plays* (New York: Palgrave Macmillan, 2005), 13–15.

[3]	Balibar, "Citizen Subject," in *Who Comes After the Subject?*, (eds.) Eduardo Cadava, Peter Connor, and Jean-Luc Nancy (New York: Routledge, 1991), 38–9.

[4]	Balibar, "Citizen Subject," 53.

democracy precisely because its ideal of a common good rises above exclusion.[5] She argues that the manifest impossibility of attaining full democracy creates conditions that drive social change.[6] New identities, we might conclude, will always coalesce and lay claim to citizenship in the wake of recently enfranchised groups.

The idea that citizenship is in principle an expandable category suits the civic-republican model, with its emphasis on individual duty to a common good, but it is applied with difficulty to London and other northern European forms of citizenship, which were based on communal privilege. English citizenship in the late sixteenth century was a matter of economic rights for a large but still elite population of adult men: the right, above all, to work openly or freely in certain crafts and to sell the products of that work on the open market. Only people who lived in towns chartered by the crown could be called citizens or *freemen*, as in the Middle Ages. In London, it was necessary to become a member of a livery company, or craft guild, to become a citizen or attain *the freedom*: there were about 100 companies, but the twelve Great Companies dominated civic life. One first had to serve an apprenticeship to a master, then become a journeyman or wage laborer in the trade. The new journeyman often swore his oath of citizenship the same day he took his oath to the company; both oaths were sworn in London's Guildhall.[7] Companies often competed for work with one another, and so were doubly conscious of the real or perceived threats posed by non-citizens. Despite their hard work in and around the shop, which was often also the household, city women were rarely admitted to the freedom, even though girls were sometimes apprenticed and women were not formally denied company membership.[8] As a working form of subjectivity, and a form of subjectivity that proceeded from the selective accreditation of work itself, London citizenship was, for all intents and purposes, founded on exclusion.

Aliens or "strangers" were another group who were relegated to the non-citizen domain. Population estimates for aliens are difficult to settle upon, despite the successive census records the Elizabethan authorities tried to compile. There were around 8,000 aliens in London during the 1590s. Three-quarters of the London aliens were "Dutch," a term the English used for French-speaking Walloons as well as Dutch and Flemish speakers from the Netherlands. Germans (also sometimes called Dutch), some Italians, and especially French Huguenots

---

[5]   Mouffe, "Democratic Citizenship and the Political Community," in *Dimensions of Radical Democracy*, (ed.) Mouffe (London: Verso, 1992), 226–8.

[6]   Mouffe, "Preface: Democratic Politics Today," in *Dimensions of Radical Democracy*, (ed.) Mouffe, 13.

[7]   Steve Rappaport, *Worlds Within Worlds: Structures of Life in Sixteenth-Century London* (Cambridge: Cambridge University Press, 1989), 25–7; Ian W. Archer, *The Pursuit of Stability: Social Relations in Elizabethan London* (Cambridge: Cambridge University Press, 1991), 18–22, 100.

[8]   Rappaport, *Worlds Within Worlds*, 36–7.

formed the remaining 25 percent of the alien inhabitants. The Dutch revolt against Hapsburg Spain in the mid-1560s had greatly increased immigration, and more people arrived from the Low Countries with the fall of Antwerp in 1585. Still, with the total population of London approaching 200,000 during the last decade of the sixteenth century, aliens made up a very small percentage of the whole. The anxieties of livery company members were out of all proportion to whatever threat that competition from these workers posed. It is true that Dutch aliens were generally more skilled in trades like clothmaking than the English, and they certainly came to England with the intention of working. They often did so covertly in London and its suburbs, and openly in towns like Norwich, where the crown and Privy Council protected them in order to take advantage of their knowledge of the textile trade.[9] The city leaders of Norwich originated the proposal to settle Dutch aliens in their town in 1564, as Natasha Korda informs us in the following essay on the elaborate civic pageant staged there for Elizabeth I fourteen years later. In the latter part of the sixteenth century, well over a third of the inhabitants of Norwich came from the Netherlands. As Korda shows, their labor in the cloth trade was celebrated in a public display that featured young women from the community plying their skills at spinning and knitting before the queen. Such a spectacle would have been unheard of in London, with its numerically larger if proportionately smaller Dutch population, for complaints about alien families "setting women on work" were a staple of the livery companies.[10]

Many Netherlandish cities also defined their membership in an exclusionary guild-based fashion, and so Dutch immigrants of various sorts in London well understood the very mechanisms used to restrict, or rather to manage and exploit, their economic endeavors in the metropolis. As mentioned above, northern citizenship was not the potentially expandable category of the southern civic republican tradition or the late eighteenth-century revolutions in Europe. It was based upon economic exclusion and exploitation, a covert legacy the early modern north bequeathed to Enlightenment citizenship. This inheritance helps explain the persistence of slavery and lesser forms of bondage well into modernity, as Amanda Bailey's contribution to this volume attests. And as the mention of slavery suggests, ethnic and racial categories were partial products of economic distinctions. In the Spring of 1517, London apprentices and citizens had rioted against aliens from the Low Countries and elsewhere in what became known as "Ill May Day." Later in the century, food riots and other disturbances often had an anti-alien component, and companies complained to city and crown about alien

---

[9]   For population estimates, see *Immigrants in Tudor and Stuart England*, (eds.) Nigel Goose and Lien Luu (Brighton: Sussex Academic Press, 2005), 1–29. See also Laura Hunt Yungblut, *Strangers Settled Here Amongst Us: Policies, Perceptions and the Presence of Aliens in Elizabethan England* (London: Routledge, 1996), 13–14.

[10]   Archer, *Pursuit of Stability*, 131.

labor well into the seventeenth century.[11] The so-called "Dutch Church Libel" of 1593, a handbill in doggerel verse, capped decades of citizen resentment against the small but persistent alien presence by accusing Dutch Protestants of cowardice and treachery in allowing Spain to drive them from their homes. The authors of the Libel threatened the aliens with violence for undercutting English craftsmen and merchants, crowding the real-estate market, and engaging in usury.[12]

The populist charges of the Dutch Church Libel were anticipated by the drama earlier in the sixteenth century. The moral interlude, a mid-Tudor genre performed for both aristocrats in great houses and popular audiences in a variety of venues, seems an unlikely outlet for anxieties about strangers. Yet the interlude adapted allegorical personifications and the Vice figure from the morality play to stage debates on this and other topical issues. Court fashions, diplomacy, and the state of the realm were fair game; English military policy and the Reformation had placed Flanders on the agenda. Above all, the fusion of topicality and abstract virtue and vice in later interludes gave a moral tinge to political commentary. The combination of moralism and current events fostered what may be termed "national consciousness," at least among the elite audiences—that is, a sense of shared values and beliefs among English-speakers as subjects of the monarch and inhabitants of the realm and of its chief city, London. England and Englishness took on a specific ethical vocation in these mid-Tudor performances, implicitly supplanting the general "mankind" figure of the morality plays.

The anonymous *Enterlude of Welth and Helth*, from just before 1557, expresses a disdain for the Protestant aliens from the Netherlands that chimes with Mary I's Catholic policy.[13] Yet military matters and cultural differences, not religion, are the play's overt concerns, and account for its evident influence into Elizabethan times. The principal vices are Ill Wyll and Shrewd Wyt, who are made stewards of Helth and Welth and deplete their houses. They also bring in a "malaperte Fleming" called Hance, or Hans, Bere-Pot, whose name anticipates a series of future Hanses in the drama (l. 394). Another vice calls him a "scon rutter" (l. 386), mock-Dutch for a fine cavalry-officer, or bully. Hance enters singing, as Vices often do, but his song is entirely in what passes for Flemish (ll. 386–92). Clearly, we have a

---

[11]   See Rappaport, *Worlds Within Worlds*, 42–5; Archer, *Pursuit of Stability*, 1–7, 131–3; and Yungblut, *Strangers Settled Here*, 73–8.

[12]   The text of the Libel is provided by Arthur Freeman, "Marlowe, Kyd, and the Dutch Church Libel," *English Literary Renaissance* 3 (1973): 50–51.

[13]   *An Enterlude of Welth and Helth*, (ed.) F. Holthausen (Heidelberg: Carl Winters Universitätsbuchhandlung, 1922). References by line number will be included parenthetically. On this interlude's probable historical background, see T.W. Craik, "The Political Interpretation of Two Tudor Interludes: *Temperance and Humility* and *Wealth and Health*," *Review of English Studies*, n.s. 4 (1953): 98–108. For the pairing of this interlude and Ulpian Fulwell's *Like Will to Like* as contrasting vehicles for ethnic stereotype in an emerging national context, see the pioneering study by A.J. Hoenselaars, *Images of Englishmen and Foreigners in the Drama of Shakespeare and his Contemporaries* (Toronto: Associated University Presses, 1992), 41–3.

masculine, Netherlandish type here that was readily recognizable to the audience, though partly lost to us with other interludes from the period.

At the start of the interlude, Welth and Helth enter and debate their virtues. "I am Welth of this realme," that worthy declares, and vital to the nation, but Helth argues that Welth is nothing without him (ll. 14, 169–84). In the middle of the play, they reconcile under the leadership of a character called Remedi, or Remedy, who shows that only together can they bring fame to the kingdom, or "the comon welth and helth," not just the common-wealth (l. 584). Other nations will fear conflict with England—a great deal of stress is placed on a healthy army on the one hand and investment in artillery on the other (ll. 574–7). Hance Bere-Pot threatens this accord. His heavy dialect is comic, but is barely intelligible, and disrupts the flow of debate and instruction. He tells his audience that he is a "bumbardere," or gunner, and offers quantities of beer along with military expertise to his English hosts. He flatters them, but also endangers their wealth with war in the Netherlands and their health with drinking. Hance is also called "War," a personification of military expense, and he brags that he has transferred England's wealth to Flanders, where battle rages (ll. 395, 420). Remedy confronts Hance: where is he from? From the tavern in St Katherine's, he replies (l. 743). St Katherine's was a suburb where the Flemish community dwelt—in other words, Hance is from London itself.[14] Hance implies that he is here to stay, a part of the city's fabric. "There is too many aliaunts in this realm," Remedy protests (l. 750). According to the Oxford English Dictionary, the word "alien" had been used to designate "A resident foreign in origin and not naturalized, whose allegiance is thus due to a foreign state" since the 1330s; the *OED* gives a pertinent example from 1547 (*OED* B. 3.a). Hance is not only Dutch; he is an alien, both a non-subject of the crown and a non-citizen in the interlude's implicit urban milieu. In other words, Hance is a juridical as well as an ethnic "other." He is not treated as an outlaw in England, however, for he seems to enjoy some sort of protection from the authorities. "Fie on you aliants al, I say!" cries Remedy, "Ye can with craft and subtelti get Englishmens welth away" (ll. 754–5). Daunted, Hance reveals that he has been in England thirteen years, and also that he is a "scomaker," or shoemaker, as well as a gunner (l. 745). Just for a moment, he is allowed to reflect the situation of impoverished Flemish aliens in a hostile London. At the end of the interlude, the other vices laugh at Hance. Having fomented war, he is forced to return home to battle Spain himself: "This horson

---

[14]   See also the much fuller discussion of both interludes and George Wapull's *The Tide Tarrieth no Man* in Lloyd Edward Kermode, *Aliens and Englishness in Elizabethan Drama* (Cambridge: Cambridge University Press, 2009), 30–58. I attach more importance to the linguistic definition of the alien through both dialect and assimilation in these mid-Tudor plays than Kermode does, but I also find his emphasis on characters who embody the "alien within" England suggestive.

For St Katherine's, see John S. Burn, *The History of the French, Walloon, Dutch and Other Foreign Protestant Communities Settled in England* (London: Longman, Brown, 1846), 6.

Fleming was beshitten for fear, / Because he should voyde so soone" (ll. 815–16). The voiding of Hance's body matches his expulsion from the realm.

Ten years later, in Elizabeth's reign, a renewed Protestant England accepted another wave of Flemish immigration, but hardly welcomed it. *Like Will to Like*, a 1568 interlude by Ulpian Fulwell, takes its title from the proverbial idea that wicked people come in couples and reinforce each others' bad behavior.[15] Vice characters are accordingly paired off during the interlude, and a Flemish or Dutch twosome stand out from the abstract sins. The saying "Like will to like" is rendered topical: as in later libels, Netherlandish immigrants are implicitly accused of keeping to themselves. At the same time, one of the pair seems to affect assimilation to English society. Philip Fleming, as he is called, enters singing a drinking song, but speaks in unaccented English. He comes to rescue his drunken friend, once again called Hance, who does speak in a thick, if somewhat unidentifiable, dialect. We hear of a dream Hance has had: on board a ship sailing in a barrel of beer, he suddenly finds himself wafted from Flanders to France along with "a sort of knaves."[16] The audience presumably did not picture this as a touching "ship of the damned," but as a threatening confabulation of Flemish and Huguenot refugees whose next stop would probably be England. As for the well-spoken Philip Fleming, his first name, shared with the Spanish king, suggests the covert Catholic compromises and religious hypocrisy of which Protestant immigrants would continually be accused. Philip mixes well with the other vices while maintaining the natural bond with his "like": they both end up in the hospital with gout, scapegoated off-stage but also a permanent drain on English charity.[17]

Taken together, these moral interludes present a double image of the "Dutch," in the loose sense of this ethnic designation. In *Welth and Helth*, for instance, they are rich and successful economic competitors who absorb other nations' gold in exchange for arms and beer. In *Like Will to Like*, they are more clearly immigrants, bound together in refuge from an occupied homeland, although all the more devious for that. The earlier interlude recalls the late medieval image of the fabulously wealthy Flemings, while the later one reflects the reduced state of the Low Countries under Spanish rule between 1548 and the Dutch Revolt of 1566–1567. In the later Elizabethan and Jacobean periods this split deepened. By the 1580s, the Seven United Provinces of the North, chief among them Holland, had attained independence from Hapsburg Spain and were increasingly prosperous, the custodians of a rapidly growing overseas trading sphere. The ten southern provinces, including Flanders, remained under Spanish control, a source of apparently penniless religious exiles. Regional and other differences among Netherlandish strangers were not fully understood by the English. How could "the Dutch" be both poor and rich? Why should wealthy commercial competitors in the

---

[15]   Fulwell, *The Dramatic Works*, (ed.) John S. Farmer (London 1906; rpt. New York: Barnes & Noble, 1966).

[16]   Ibid., 25–6.

[17]   Ibid., 51.

emerging field of global trade be accepted as charity-cases by struggling London citizens? In the mid-sixteenth century, royal and civic authorities were already debating the effect that Netherlandish aliens, seemingly poor but with global contacts, might have on England, its well-being, and its religion.

By the end of the century, the crown had decided to protect Dutch aliens because they were generators of wealth and conduits for technological and financial innovations from the continent. Resentment of strangers from the Netherlands was left to London citizens and the public theater. Dekker's comedy *The Shoemaker's Holiday* provides a somewhat skewed perspective on contemporary anxieties about the Dutch. In tracing the rise of Simon Eyre, the madcap master-shoemaker of Tower Street and eventual Lord Mayor, it reveals how economic conflicts among native-born Londoners accompanied the new wave of anti-alien feeling. Rivalry with the Dutch evoked anxieties about identity and difference that transposed themselves to social distinctions within English society and its institutions. These distinctions were largely about differing relations to work.

In Dekker's play, as in its source, Thomas Deloney's prose work *The Gentle Craft*, Eyre is elected Sheriff of London by the aldermen before he becomes mayor.[18] "Welcome home, Master Shrieve," his wife greets him. "I pray God continue you in health and wealth" (10.147–8).[19] The recollection of the interlude title may be coincidental, proverbial as the phrase was, but reminds us that the morality tradition lives on in the public theater of the 1590s, albeit in a morally inconsistent form. Eyre's wife is also something of a Tower Street Lady Macbeth. It is unclear how Dekker regards the master shoemaker's political success: his riches both buy him power and place him under the expensive obligation of fulfilling office. Yet individual wealth is still linked to the health of the community, and in a competitive international context at that. Eyre is first noticed by the aldermen and made Sheriff because of the riches he suddenly acquired through dealing in commodities with a Dutch ship's captain and his off-stage merchant employer. The merchant has been forced into hiding for some reason (7.17–22). Probably an alien himself, he would be unable to trade in England unless he was a member of an English company, or was protected by the crown. Eyre offers the skipper "my countenance in the city" (7.145–6). He takes advantage of his status as London citizen to buy cheap from an economically excluded alien, and then sell dear, later taking Lord Mayor Oatley and an associate as partners in the venture (9.66–7).

Although the vessel comes from Candy, or Crete, its cargo is redolent of Holland's East Indian trade: sugar, civet, almonds, cambric, nutmeg, and a "tousand tousand ding," or things, in the play's bastardized Dutch dialect (7.3). Deloney's Eyre deals with a Greek captain whose ship comes from Candy and

---

[18]   Deloney, *The Gentle Craft*, in *The Works of Thomas Deloney*, (ed.) Francis Oscar Mann (Oxford: Clarendon, 1967), 121–5.

[19]   Dekker, *The Shoemaker's Holiday*, (eds.) R.L. Smallwood and Stanley Wells (Manchester: Manchester University Press, 1979). Further references to *The Shoemaker's Holiday* are to this edition, and will be cited parenthetically, by scene and line numbers.

is merely laden with fine cloth.[20] In a reversal of *The Enterlude of Welth and Helth*, merchandise in *The Shoemaker's Holiday* now flows into England from the Netherlands and its trading partners in the east. The English are now the indirect beneficiaries of a colonial form of primitive accumulation (see the preceding essay by Crystal Bartolovich). Furthermore, enterprising citizens like Eyre can make money from this transfer, transforming themselves from craftsmen to merchants, then to liverymen in their companies, and finally to aldermen, sheriffs, and mayors. The two aspects of "Dutch" aliens are in juxtaposition in Eyre's transaction: the Dutch proper are custodians of Old World wealth from a trading empire; when they enter London, however, they must go into hiding, like Flemish refugees, and cut their losses to the advantage of tolerant but clever freemen who are allowed to trade in the city. Furthermore, alien wealth calls attention to divisions between citizens who work in crafts and citizens who profit from such labor to become part of the city elite.

On top of all of this, Eyre makes his bargain with the Dutch skipper by means of Hans Meulter, the seemingly simple Flemish worker he has just employed. Hans introduces him to the captain and loans Eyre twenty Portuguese crusadoes to buy the exotic cargo (7.23–4, 130–37). Hans is, in fact, Rowland Lacy, an English nobleman supposedly sent to war who secretly remains in London to court Rose, the current Lord Mayor's daughter. Having run through his allowance while on the Grand Tour, Lacy had once holed up in Wittenberg and learned the craft of shoemaking there to win his passage home (1.19–31). As Hans, he penetrates the Mayor's shoemaker's household to throw himself at the Mayor's daughter's feet, literally, in one scene (15.28). Lacy adopts some sort of ethnic costume, probably huge breeches and a short doublet, and stage-Dutch speech to complete his disguise (3.1 note). "Yaw, yaw; ik bin den skomawker" (4.81), or "Yes, yes; I am the shoemaker," he announces to the shop, sounding like Hance Bere-Pot in the interlude. Dekker links Wittenberg to the Low Countries, as Marlowe does in *Doctor Faustus*, and preserves the old notion that the Dutch were expert shoemakers. The money that Hans lends Eyre is from the thirty crusadoes that Lacy's kinsman the earl of Lincoln gives him as a bribe to leave Rose (1.90). As Lord Mayor, Eyre returns the favor at the end of the play when he obtains the King's pardon for the draft-dodging Lacy.

Hans, as mentioned above, is the invariable name of Flemings or Dutchmen in the interludes. The link between Lacy's alter-ego and the morality tradition is also attested in formal terms. Dekker's Hans makes his first entry with a song in stage Dutch, just as the earlier Vice-figures did (4.41 SD). He enters to Eyre's shoemaking shop, and the journeymen immediately befriend this festive figure. The 1590s comedy, of course, is also radically unlike a mid-century interlude in lending the attributes of the Vice to its romantic hero, however disguised. The new London world of economic and ethnic competition partly justifies the Vice's tactics and renders moralistic condemnation of them simple-minded and belated.

---

[20]   Deloney, *The Gentle Craft*, 111–14.

Mocking—and self-mocking—ethnic disguise facilitates this transformation. London city comedy forcefully misreads the interlude tradition, maintaining a radically ironic relation with its immediate moral past. The fractured morality of wealth-generation is now civically, and nationally, healthy, and the difference between tolerating and tolling other Europeans is often hard to define.[21]

Toleration is the unlikely order of the day in Eyre's shop. Eyre keeps two journeymen, who threaten to quit unless their master hires Hans. Despite his stage-Dutch speech, they accept the Fleming because he bears "St Hugh's bones" (4.49), jargon for a shoemaker's tools, following a legend recorded in *The Gentle Craft*.[22] *The Shoemaker's Holiday* makes the thoroughly English St Hugh the patron of the trade. Dekker ignores the French legend of Saints Crispin and Crispinian, found in Deloney and familiar from Shakespeare's *Henry V*, even though the Cordwainers' Company themselves mounted a play on their Gallic patrons every October 25th.[23] A shared Protestantism was the reason many Flemish refugees had escaped to England rather than France upon the Spanish occupation of the Low Countries in the sixteenth century. Yet Londoners also resented their nominal coreligionists for deserting their native churches for the houses of worship grudgingly ceded to them in London. National and ethnic difference impinged upon Christian ideals in a complicated way, as the charges of hypocrisy in the Dutch Church Libel show.[24]

David Scott Kastan has influentially emphasized the "fantasy of social cohesion" in Hans's acceptance by the journeymen.[25] From the later 1560s onward, citizen tradesmen and their employees, including Cordwainers, had petitioned to regulate and even expel alien workers from London, and rioting by apprentices and journeymen in the mid-90s was partly against aliens as well as a host of other complaints.[26] Kastan sees *The Shoemaker's Holiday* as partly containing the anti-alien disruptions that threatened the city's order. But precisely how well did its fantasy of containment work, and how well was it supposed to work? One reason for the presence of Hans in the shop is that a real Dutch character of this name appears in Deloney's *The Gentle Craft* as a comic butt, along with his rival "John

---

[21]   For a contrasting view on the relation of Dekker's play to the moral interludes discussed earlier and their "Hans" figures, see Kermode, *Aliens and Englishness*, 137–8.

[22]   Deloney, *The Gentle Craft*, 87–9.

[23]   Ibid., 90–109. See also Charles C.H. Waterland Mander, *A Descriptive and Historical Account of the Guild of Cordwainers of the City of London* (London: Williams, Lea & Company, 1931), 196.

[24]   For the delicate balance between toleration of aliens and anti-alien sentiment in late sixteenth-century London and its comedy, see Jean E. Howard, *Theater of a City: The Places of London Comedy, 1598–1642* (Philadelphia: University of Pennsylvania Press, 2007), 8–11, and *passim*. Nigel Goose usefully questions the limits of a frequently-used term: "'Xenophobia' in Elizabethan and Early Stuart England: An Epithet too Far?" in *Immigrants*, (eds.) Goose and Luu, 110–35.

[25]   Kastan, "Workshop and/as Playhouse," in *Staging the Renaissance*, (eds.) Kastan and Peter Stallybrass (New York: Routledge, 1991), 152.

[26]   Rappaport, *Worlds Within Worlds*, 104, 35.

the Frenchman."[27] Dekker conflates these figures into a single Dutch disguise for Lacy. The young Lord soliloquizes about gods assuming humble shapes as he dons his outfit (3.1–24). His acceptance as Hans is made partly to depend on the pastoral device of lower-class disguise, in which true identity seems always to shine through the mask and secure good will. In a way, Dekker makes the acceptance of Deloney's Hans more rather than less plausible, at least according to literary convention, for he makes Hans a native Englishman after all. Furthermore, Dekker needed Hans for his disguise plot, and so avoided repeating common complaints about Flemish craftsmen hiding away in their own semi-legal shops, cornering markets, employing women, and the like. Nevertheless, I maintain that the obvious use of literary convention and the obvious absence of references to employment competition deliberately indicate a gap in the social text of the play. The contemporary popularity of *The Shoemaker's Holiday* was surely due to its relentlessly festive nature and frank celebration of tradesmen's values. The unlikely acceptance of Lacy-as-Hans amid the festivity, however, calls attention to itself, and thus becomes a sign of social disruption, of what cannot be safely depicted, and of what thus must be brazenly lied about to a knowing audience.

Besides, the audience gets to laugh at Hans, or Lacy's caricature of Hans, throughout his scenes, usually along with the tolerant but at best condescending journeymen Hodge and Firk. The song Hans sings as he enters is a drinking song thoroughly in the sub-tradition of the Netherlandish Vice, about a boor from Gelderland who was so drunk he could not stand (4.42–7).[28] Drunkenness was a key ethnic marker of the Dutch and Flemings in popular stereotype, as it was of the Germans, Danes and other northern Europeans. "O, he'll give a villainous pull at a can of double beer," Firk imagines. Hans's mock-language is also stereotypical, and Firk wants him as a colleague so he can learn some of his "gibble-gabble" (4.99–100, 51).

Margery, Eyre's hostile wife, calls Hans a "butter-box," (4.57) the first of many times this epithet is used in the play. Butter, even more than beer, was the principal attribute of the Fleming in England's disgusted but also fascinated eyes. In *Bartholomew Fair*, Ben Jonson imagines a man sinking into Ursula the Pig-Woman: "'Twere like falling into a whole shire of butter: they had need be a team of Dutchmen should draw him out" (2.5.87–8). Indulgence in butter represents the full life of the body. There are similar buttery moments in *Every Man in His Humor*, where the Flemish breed eat up butter (3.4.34–8), and *Volpone*, in which Dutchmen are imagined repeatedly swallowing whole pills of the stuff (1.1.41–

---

[27]   Deloney, *The Gentle Craft*, 118–21, 125–31.

[28]   On entrances of Dutch characters singing stage-Dutch songs as a probable convention adapted by Dekker from the interludes discussed above, see Peter M. McCluskey, "'Shall I Betray My Brother?' Anti-Alien Satire and its Subversion in *The Shoemaker's Holiday*," *Tennessee Philological Bulletin* 37 (2000): 44.

3).[29] When Rose runs off with Hans-Lacy, her father can't believe she would desert him for "A Fleming butter-box, a shoemaker" (16.42). Firk refuses to betray the couple, saying "Shall I prove Judas to Hans? No. Shall I cry treason to my corporation?" (16.98–100). More than craft loyalty spurs him. Firk has become invested in the pleasures of the Dutch stereotype he both mocks and identifies with, for it is both the necessary opposite and the fulfillment of his craft identity. Like Lincoln, he probably intuits Lacy's disguise at this point, admitting as much to the nobleman under questioning, yet he then says, "No, forsooth, I think Hans is nobody but Hans, no spirit" (16.125, 127–8). The stereotype has long since taken on a life of its own. "Hans" is, in fact, a spirit of a sort, although Firk insists on its self-identity, its bodily life.[30]

The momentary fear of intermarriage along ethnic as well as class lines in *The Shoemaker's Holiday* compliments Jonson's buttery image of erotic excess quoted above. Paradoxically, Flemings and other aliens were accused both of marrying within their closed communities and seeking to produce heirs with English wives.[31] There are hints in the play of the separateness, both self- and socially imposed, of London Flemings. While the English Cordwainers drink at the Boar's Head Inn in nearby Eastcheap, Hans and the Dutch captain are at the Swan (7.10). Several contemporary sources suggest this name connoted one or more inns owned and frequented by Dutch aliens.[32] In apportioning the day's work, Eyre stops Firk from making shoes for Rose's maid, Sybil: "fine ladies, my lads, commit their feet to *our* apparelling. Put gross work to Hans" (7.94, italics mine). It is work, "gross" as opposed to fine, that ultimately separates alien from citizen even in Eyre's tolerant shop. Sybil herself, let in on the secret of Hans's identity, promises Rose she will unite her with the supposed shoemaker: "I'll bind you prentice to the gentle trade" (11.91). Marriage is wittily meant, but women were sometimes apprenticed to trades. It is significant that aliens in particular were blamed for "setting women on work" secretly, and sometimes for marrying them off to newcomers who would then learn crafts like weaving from their wives, increasing competition.[33]

Marriage also figures in the chief subplot of *The Shoemaker's Holiday*. Eyre's former apprentice Ralph Damport has recently wed Jane, a servant in the master's household. He is soon conscripted for the French wars, a sad case for a man "but

---

        [29] References are from Jonson, *Five Plays*, (ed.) G.A. Wilkes (Oxford: Oxford University Press, 1988).

        [30] On the body in the play, particularly the masculine working body and its relation to female labor, see Ronda A. Arab, "Work, Bodies and Gender in *The Shoemaker's Holiday*," *Medieval and Renaissance Drama in England* 13 (2001): 182–212. I would add that as a figure of the "Dutch" alien, Hans, no less than Margery and her maid, serves as a screen upon which anxieties about bodily excess in labor and leisure are projected.

        [31] Archer, *Pursuit of Stability*, 131; Andrew Pettegree, *Foreign Protestant Communities in Sixteenth-Century London* (Oxford: Clarendon, 1986), 289.

        [32] See note to 7.10 in *The Shoemaker's Holiday*, 117.

        [33] Rappaport, *Worlds Within Worlds*, 57; Archer, *Pursuit of Stability*, 131.

newly entered," as Eyre's wife says, using the technical term for a journeyman's entry or passage from wage laborer to householder within a livery company (1.162).[34] Marriage usually accompanied a former journeyman's setting up his own shop. Ralph is not at the point of opening his own business yet. He does enlist the shop to make a special pair of shoes for Jane before he leaves, in lieu of a ring. The wealthier citizens, who sell rather than produce the specialties of their company, customarily buy their way out of military service. This is subtly hinted at, I believe, when the aldermen's money is promised to Lacy as the colonel in charge of mustering the London militias (1.66–8; Lincoln's explanation at lines 71–3 is clearly misleading). By the time Ralph returns from the war, he is wounded in the leg and Jane has run away from Margery, her silly but harsh mistress. Ralph searches for her, not suspecting that Hammon, a young "citizen by birth" who affects hunting and courtly language (6.61), has spotted Jane working as a seamstress in a shop. Hammon convinces her that Ralph is dead. Idle himself, he finds the spectacle of Jane's lowly labor erotic:

> How prettily she works! O pretty hand!
> O happy work! It doth me good to stand
> Unseen to see her. (12.13–15)

Jane's work is a species of alienated labor, if not precisely alien labor, to Hammon, and as such it is also a mark of his difference from her kind, as a woman and a worker. These differences excite him.[35] Hammon resides at the Sign of the Golden Ball in Watling Street, which is probably another shop, but one in a neighborhood where prosperous members of the Drapers' Company dwell (14.23–4 and note). To Jane and others he is also a "gentleman" (12.60). Dramas and satires of the period grant little subjectivity to women within the citizen sphere: they are passively virtuous, shop window displays to draw in customers, or desirable widows.[36] Jane is made into all three for a time. She gives in to the impressive Hammon and agrees to marry him; the wealthy citizen unwittingly commissions Ralph, working as a journeyman once more, to make his bride's wedding-shoes. Ralph recognizes

---

[34] The Merchant Taylor's court minutes address "young beginners and newly ENTERING into the world ... which word 'ENTERING' does strike a great impression into the heart." Cited in Rappaport, *Worlds Within Worlds*, 328. Margery's application to a recent bridegroom typically contains an unintended bawdy meaning as well.

[35] On alienated labor and the spectacle of women's work in the passage, see Wendy Wall, *Staging Domesticity: Household Work and English Identity in Early Modern Drama* (Cambridge: Cambridge University Press, 2002), 154–5. Arab also notes this moment ("Work, Bodies and Gender," 189). Kermode links the alien, alienated labor, and labor's re-appropriation through the related spectacle of the shoes that Ralph and his fellows have made for Jane (*Aliens and Englishness*, 144).

[36] See Leslie Thomson, "'As Proper a Woman as Any in Cheap': Women in Shops on the Early Modern Stage," *Medieval and Renaissance Drama in England* 16 (2003): 145–61.

the sample shoe, his parting gift, and resolves to break up the bigamist wedding at the church door with a gang of his fellow cobblers (14.58–61).

A riot scene follows that might well have caught the Master of the Revels' censoring eye—except that it depicts citizen against citizen, rather than citizens menacing aliens or aristocrats, and its politics are leavened by low comedy and resolved by a woman's decision. Ralph and his crew accost Hammon and his men at the Church with the traditional cry of London workers in revolt: "Down with them! Cry 'Clubs for prentices!'" (18.31–2). But even as the cry is repeated the focus switches from violence to Jane herself, who is asked to choose between the men. She chooses Ralph, and Ralph himself spurns Hammon's offer of twenty pounds for his wife: shoemakers do not turn their spouses into whores (18.88–95). Despite the shift to domestic comedy, it remains significant that a play with real and false Fleming characters in its main action also contains an episode of near-riot among tradesmen. The plots are kept separate, but the hot-button issues in each remain in telling juxtaposition, another deliberate gap in the text. Historically, the pancake feast of Shrove Tuesday, initiated by the fictional version of Eyre at the end of the play, was an occasion for apprentice riot in late sixteenth-century London.[37] Occluding revolt, or rather making it over into a personal struggle among romantic rivals, seems to be another instance of a dramatic fantasy that ultimately ensures social cohesion. The chastened Hammon, an elite citizen, is the stand-in for the aliens, at once prosperous and needy, who profit at craftsmen's expense and supposedly aspire to their women. In this, he deflects our doubts about the aristocratic Lacy, who pursues Rose while arranging the transaction with the Dutch skipper that profits her father as well as Eyre.

But the scene reveals deeper truths about contemporary disorder even as it attempts to smooth out the cracks and bumps in the social surface. So-called anti-alien disturbances in the 1590s were already about class and economic inequality, with aliens a convenient scapegoat, as Tom Rutter discusses in his essay in this collection. The Dutch Church Libel concludes by attacking the nobles:

> Nobles said I? nay men to be rejected,
> Upstarts that enjoy the noblest seats
> That wound their countries breast for lucres sake …
> By letting strangers make our hearts to ache.[38]

Furthermore, the Libel blames aristocrats partly to cover up divisions within craft guilds themselves. Many livery companies were preoccupied by conflict rather than cooperation between their artisanal and merchant members; compromise usually maintained order, but not without effort on the part of company leaders, and sometimes aldermen as well. It is significant that Hammon hires Ralph to make his bride's new shoes, and that Ralph recognizes the shoe he and his fellow-workers once made for Jane: differing relations to labor and its products set artisans

---

[37]   Rappaport, *Worlds Within Worlds*, 9; Archer, *Pursuit of Stability*, 1–3.

[38]   In Freeman, "Marlowe, Kyd, and the Dutch Church Libel," 51.

apart from elite citizens in *The Shoemaker's Holiday*, as Crystal Bartolovich argues above. Bartolovich points out that Eyre did not participate in the communal production of Jane's shoes. In an earlier exchange, she notes, Eyre takes Jane's hand but employs comic insults to distance himself from the imagined spectacle of its spinning and carding, just as Hammon later stands in gaze at its actual labor through the shop window (1.217–20). Class as well as gender differences in labor are at play in such scenes. In Dekker's sixteenth-century London, masters and artisans were often at odds. Craftsmen accused the merchants, who usually ruled the livery companies, of managing wholesale prices, restricting exports, and— tellingly—using alien labor against them. Elite citizens were also accused of usury by citizen artisans, a major but improbable charge against aliens alone in the Libel.[39] In avoiding a scene of anti-alien riot, Dekker actually exposes another layer of craftsmen's grievances beneath anti-alien feeling, but without drawing the censor's attention. It is comic action that partly diffuses the newly-revealed conflicts, but this is not really a case of containment or of social fantasy, at least if we take "fantasy" to mean mere wish-fulfillment. Overall, the scapegrace Lacy's disguise as Hans the Flemish shoemaker is a synecdoche for the play's festive use of stereotypical Dutchness to momentarily distract the popular audience from the elite abuses that Dekker wants ultimately to accentuate.[40]

It is finally unsurprising that Dutch alienage in *The Shoemaker's Holiday* should serve to cover conflicts within London citizenship as a form of working subjectivity. Anti-Dutch feeling among the English was an example of what Slavoj Zizek, citing a formulation of Jacques-Alain Miller, has called "hatred of the enjoyment of the other." As Zizek explains it, the other's enjoyment includes the work-habits of the alien community as well as its food, music, folkways, and leisure pursuits. Enjoyment in this sense does not mean pleasure, but rather the paradoxical satisfactions of everyday working life, the way-of-life that binds the community together. But the enjoyment of the other is always our *own* enjoyment in a misrecognized and excessive form.[41] The English had a lot in common with the "Dutch," particularly the English inhabitants of London, similarly urban and urbane, industrious and indulgent, Protestant and profane. Londoners retained a fondness for butter, and certainly for double beer, as the constant drinking in Eyre's shop attests. Although they were outsiders, Flemings and other northern

---

[39]   Archer, *Pursuit of Stability*, 24. Ian Archer's fourth chapter contains numerous references to the other grievances mentioned, although its point is to stress how constant internal negotiation over the enforcement of company ordinances allayed most artisanal grievances and secured a basic stability (140–8). See also Arab, "Work, Bodies and Gender," 193–4.

[40]   On this point, I disagree with Andrew Fleck's thorough and otherwise persuasive reading of the play, which parallels the containment of Hans as an alien figure with the supposed quelling of class and status conflict. See "Marking Difference and National Identity in Dekker's *The Shoemaker's Holiday*," *SEL* 46 (2006): 349–70.

[41]   Zizek, "Eastern Europe's Republics of Gilead," in *Dimensions of Radical Democracy*, (ed.) Mouffe, 196–9. Zizek cites an unpublished version of a lecture by Miller.

aliens were threatening to the English because they were so much like them. They competed for work, but the real competition was for what work meant to citizenship as a form of urban belonging. Dekker's play partly undoes the threat by comically gesturing toward it through Lacy's disguise as Hans Meulter, the hard-working butter-box. In doing so it unwittingly looks forward to the seventeenth century, when the sons and grandsons of immigrants were indeed accepted by livery companies and became citizens. In caricaturing the Dutch aliens among them, London citizens were satirizing themselves as well, then, working through their own social divisions over the changing relationship between citizenship and work.

Chapter 3
Staging Alien Women's Work in Civic Pageants

Natasha Korda

Massive numbers of Dutch- and French-speaking Protestant refugees, many of them skilled artisans, fled to England during the Dutch Revolt against Spanish Hapsburg rule (1568–1648) and the French Wars of Religion (1562–1598), as discussed in the previous essay.[1] Because many of the refugees, male and female, were skilled workers in the textile and clothing trades, their importation of new skills and technologies of manufacture had a huge impact on this sector of the economy.[2] Aliens from the Low Countries contributed vitally to the development of silk manufacture in England,[3] for example, introducing "new methods for throwing silk, new designs for damasks and other figured patterns, special knowledge of dyeing and finishing cloth, improvements in ribbon-weaving and knitting silk stockings."[4] They are also credited with improvements in linen-

---

[1]   As many as 100,000 refugees from the Low Countries are estimated to have settled in Western Europe, perhaps half of them in England. For a concise account of the impact of these religious conflicts on immigration to England, see Lien Bich Luu, *Immigrants and the Industries of London, 1500–1700* (Aldershot, England and Burlington, VT: Ashgate, 2005), 104–9. On the importation of skills, see Heinz Schilling, "Innovation Through Migration: The Settlements of Calvinistic Netherlands in Sixteenth- and Seventeenth-Century Central and Western Europe," *Histoire Sociale* 16 (1983): 7; Andrew Pettegree, *Foreign Protestant Communities in Sixteenth-Century London* (Oxford: Clarendon, 1986), 2; and Luu, *Immigrants and the Industries of London*, 90.

[2]   According to Luu, the "strangers were concentrated overwhelmingly in the clothing industry." *Immigrants and the Industries of London*, 106, 119–20. See also Linda Levy Peck, *Consuming Splendor: Society and Culture in Seventeenth-Century England* (Cambridge: Cambridge University Press, 2005), esp. Chapter 2, "'We May as Well be Silke-Masters as Sheepe-Masters': Transferring Technology in Seventeenth-Century England"; John J. Murray, *Flanders and England: A Cultural Bridge: The Influence of the Low Countries on Tudor-Stuart England* (Antwerp: Fonds Mercator, 1985), 149–75; and Nigel Goose, "Immigrants and English Economic Development in the Sixteenth and Early Seventeenth Centuries," in *Immigrants in Tudor and Early Stuart England*, (eds.) Nigel Goose and Lien Bich Luu (Brighton: Sussex Academic Press, 2005), 138–44.

[3]   Alfred Plummer, *The London Weavers' Company, 1600–1970* (London and Boston: Routledge and Kegan Paul, 1972), 16.

[4]   See also Luu, *Immigrants and the Industries of London*, esp. Chapter 6.

weaving and lace-making,[5] and with being largely responsible for the successful manufacture in England of the so-called "New Draperies"—smooth, light cloths such as bays, says, and mockados—which revitalized the English clothing market following years of commercial depression during the mid-sixteenth century.[6] Yet there has been no study of the ways in which this revolution in textile manufacture influenced different types of theatrical production or how it may have shaped contemporary dramatic depictions of aliens.

This essay focuses on the cloth and clothing manufactured by alien craftswomen from the Low Countries, and the ways in which they and their wares were staged in two civic pageants mounted during the Elizabethan and Jacobean periods. Previous discussions of alien women in dramatic criticism have tended to focus on prostitution or intermarriage with Englishmen, rather than on their productive work in various crafts and trades, and have thereby privileged the traffic *in* women over the traffic *of* women.[7] Elsewhere, I have examined the ways in which alien women's productive work in the starching trade influenced the material culture of plays staged by London's all-male professional playing companies in the commercial theaters.[8] The starched head- and neck-attires, such as ruffs and rebatos

---

[5]   Luu, *Immigrants and the Industries of London*, 115 and Murray, *Flanders and England*, 152.

[6]   B.A. Holderness, "The Reception and Distribution of the New Draperies in England," in *The New Draperies in the Low Countries and England, 1300–1800*, (ed.) N.B. Harte (Oxford: Oxford University Press, 1997), 217 and C.W. Chitty, "Aliens in England in the Sixteenth Century," *Race* 8 (1966–7): 131, 133.

[7]   Some important recent studies of the depiction of aliens in early modern English drama include: David Scott Kastan, "Workshop and/as Playhouse: *The Shoemaker's Holiday* (1599)," in *Staging the Renaissance: Reinterpretations of Elizabethan and Jacobean Drama*, (eds.) David Scott Kastan and Peter Stallybrass (New York and London: Routledge, 1991); A.J. Hoenselaars, *Images of Englishmen and Foreigners in the Drama of Shakespeare and His Contemporaries: A Study of Stage Characters and National Identity in English Renaissance Drama, 1558–1642* (Rutherford, N.J.: Fairleigh Dickenson University Press, 1992); Willem Schrickx, "Elizabethan Drama and Anglo-Dutch Relations," in *Reclamations of Shakespeare*, (ed.) A.J. Hoenselaars (Amsterdam: Rodopi, 1994); Ronda A. Arab, "Work, Bodies and Gender in *The Shoemaker's Holiday*," *Medieval and Renaissance Drama in England* 13 (2001); Emma Smith, "'So Much English by the Mother': Gender, Foreigners and the Mother Tongue in William Houghton's *Englishmen for My Money*," *Medieval and Renaissance Drama in England* 13 (2001): 165–81; John Michael Archer, *Citizen Shakespeare: Freemen and Aliens in the Language of the Plays* (New York and Houndmills, UK: Palgrave Macmillan, 2005); Ton Hoenselaars and Holger Klein (eds.), *Shakespeare and the Low Countries*, The Shakespeare Yearbook, vol. 15 (Lewiston: The Edwin Mellon Press, 2005); Jean E. Howard, *Theater of a City: The Places of London Comedy, 1598–1642* (Philadelphia: University of Pennsylvania Press, 2007); and Lloyd Edward Kermode, *Aliens and Englishness in Elizabethan Drama* (Cambridge: Cambridge University Press, 2009).

[8]   Natasha Korda, "Froes, Rebatos and Other 'Outlandish Comodityes': Weaving Alien Women's Work into the Fabric of Early Modern Material Culture," in *Everyday Objects: Medieval and Early Modern Material Culture and Its Meanings*, (ed.) Catherine Richardson (Burlington, VT: Ashgate, 2010), 95–106.

(flat, standing collars), that feature so prominently in Elizabethan and Jacobean drama, I argue, often point to off-stage dramas of economic production marked by gender, national identity, and the social dynamics of immigration. Dramatic depictions of Netherlandish women and their wares in plays were neither always nor simply xenophobic, but were marked by the native population's ambivalence towards the commercial supremacy of the Netherlands, which was at once admired and resented. This ambivalence was often projected onto Dutchwomen or "froes," whose skill at starching and bleaching fuelled the fashion in starched ruffs and rebatos. If the "stiffness" of starched linen came to "stand," as it were, for their assertive, "masculine" conduct in the world of work and commerce, its whiteness suggested their status as "paragons of domestic virtue" (e.g., their chastity, cleanliness and industry.)[9]

In what follows, I shift my attention from the representation of alien women in plays staged by native, professional playing companies, to consider how the cloth and clothing manufactured by alien craftswomen was staged in civic pageants mounted by the Netherlandish immigrant communities in Norwich and London—in which alien craftswomen and their daughters themselves participated. These pageants merit greater critical attention than they have thus far received, as they offer a fascinating example of pre-Restoration female performers in England.[10] Their featuring of the innovative products and skills introduced into England by alien artisans, including alien women, moreover, sheds new light on the gendered division of labor within and between the native and alien communities. And while such pageants present an intriguing example of the way in which cloth and clothing may function as what Peter Stallybrass and Ann Rosalind Jones call "material memories," what is memorialized here is not their present or past owners or consumers, as Jones and Stallybrass maintain, but rather their producers.[11] That is, the textile-wares fabricated by alien artisans were staged in such a way as to highlight and celebrate their status as "worked upon" (to borrow Marx's formulation,) thereby pointing to the domains of labor and praxis, and to social relations of production.[12] In this way, they foreground the semantic connection between "work" as both the act and the product of labor, as well as the more particular meaning of the term in early modern usage to signify both the "operation of making a textile fabric" and the fabric itself, often "as a distinctively feminine occupation" (see *OED*, "work, *n.*" 1 and 2, 16).

---

[9]   See Wayne E. Franits, *Paragons of Virtue: Women and Domesticity in Seventeenth-Century Dutch Art* (Cambridge: Cambridge University Press, 1993), 76–110; Simon Schama, "Wives and Wantons: Versions of Womanhood in Seventeenth-Century Dutch Art," *Oxford Art Journal* 3 (1980): 5–13.

[10]   For other examples of Pre-Restoration female performers in England, see *Women Players in England, 1500–1660*, (eds.) Pamela Allen Brown and Peter Parolin (Aldershot, England and Burlington, VT: Ashgate, 2008).

[11]   Jones and Stallybrass, *Renaissance Clothing and the Materials of Memory* (Cambridge: Cambridge University Press, 2000).

[12]   Lloyd D. Easton and Kurt H. Guddat, trans., *Writings of the Young Karl Marx on Philosophy and Society* (New York: Doubleday, 1967), 400.

****

The Returns of Aliens living in early modern London contain a wealth of information regarding Netherlandish immigrant craftswomen's work in the textile and clothing trades. Some worked in occupations that would have competed with low-status, native women's work, such as spinning, twisting, carding, and combing wool, or working as a sempstress, needlewoman, botcher, whitster, or laundress. Other alien women, however, worked in occupations that drew on more sophisticated, imported skills, such as starching, dyeing, tapestry-, fine lace- and button-making, millinery, as well as many occupations connected to the manufacture of silk. Still other alien women worked in trades that in England were male-dominated (e.g., "linen draper," "taylour," or "merchaunt").[13] A significant number of alien women worked as silk-weavers, an occupation considered to be the province of men by the London Weavers' Company.[14] Others ran businesses in linen-weaving, silk-weaving, thread-dyeing, and -selling (as well as such non-textile-related businesses as shoemaking and brewing), some of which were quite successful judging by the numbers of alien and English workers they employed. Thus, for example, one widow who worked as a silk-throwster employed a total of seventeen people, while two others ran successful starching businesses, one employing eight English women and the other nine.[15]

In such workshops the skill of starching and other imported skills connected to the manufacture of silk and luxury-attire circulated among alien women and were gradually transmitted to native women as well. One might think that the transmission of skills between alien and native women would have placated native resentment of alien artisans for refusing to share trade secrets, yet the gendered

---

[13]   See R.E.G Kirk and Ernest F. Kirk (eds.), *Returns of Aliens Dwelling in the City and Suburbs of London from the Reign of Henry VIII to that of James I, 1523–1571*, vol. 10, part 1, *Publications of the Huguenot Society of London* (Aberdeen: University Press, 1900), 424, 426–7, 429. R.E.G Kirk and Ernest F. Kirk (eds.), *Returns of Aliens Dwelling in the City and Suburbs of London from the Reign of Henry VIII to that of James I, 1571–1597*, vol. 10, part 2, *Publications of the Huguenot Society of London* (Aberdeen: University Press, 1902), 13, 15, 18, 25, 30, 33, 50, 53, 60, 66, 119–20, 129, 261–65, 269, 175, 285, 315, 326, 355; R.E.G Kirk and Ernest F. Kirk (eds.), *Returns of Aliens Dwelling in the City and Suburbs of London from the Reign of Henry VIII to that of James I, 1598–1625*, vol. 10, part 3, *Publications of the Huguenot Society of London* (Aberdeen: University Press, 1907), 224, 229, 339, 345–6, 350, 381, 385; and Irene Scouloudi, *Returns of Strangers in the Metropolis, 1593, 1627, 1635, 1639: A Study of an Active Minority* (London: Huguenot Society of London, 1985), 139, 147, 155, 157, 158, 161–3, 165–8, 170, 172, 174, 176, 179, 180–81, 184–5, 187–91, 200–202, 204, 206, 208–9, 211, 213–14, 217.

[14]   See Kirk and Kirk (eds.), *Returns of Aliens, 1523–1571*, 431–2, 43, 451, 455; Kirk and Kirk (eds.), *Returns of Aliens, 1571–1597*, 263; and Scouloudi, *Returns of Strangers*, 195, 199–200.

[15]   See Scouloudi, *Returns of Strangers*, 82, 170, 178, 181–2, 184, 197, 199–200, 208, 213, 219.

division of labor in early modern England precluded such a favorable reception. London guildsmen, who wished to maintain their prerogative over all skilled textile-work frowned upon the exchange of imported skills between women in an unsupervised setting. In 1595, the yeomen of the Weavers' Company thus lodged a complaint against the aliens that included the accusation that alien craftswomen were disseminating their skills to others who were not entitled to them, and were thereby "open[ing] and discover[ing] the secrete of our Occupacion" to "those that never deserved for it."[16] The perceived (and often sexualized) threat posed by alien women's work and unregulated dissemination of skills was perhaps exacerbated by the fact that alien single-women and widows often lived together in small or large groups sometimes all working in the same trade. These all-female households and widow-run boarding houses in the environs of the theaters may in turn have reinforced the association of "Dutch widows" with prostitutes, an association that appears frequently in contemporary plays.[17]

That Dutch working women were often represented as prostitutes in dramatic literature is perhaps not surprising given the general tendency to sexualize female labor during the period. Mistress Quickly famously comments on (while inadvertently suggesting the justification for) this tendency in *Henry V*, when she claims she "cannot lodge and board a dozen or fourteen gentlewomen that live honestly by the prick of their needles, but it will be thought [she] keep[s] a bawdy-house straight" (2.1.32–5).[18] It is precisely because of this tendency, however, that the veracity of the Dutch courtesan stereotype should not be taken for granted.[19]

---

[16]   Frances Consitt, *The London Weavers' Company*, vol. 1 (Oxford: Clarendon, 1933), 313–14.

[17]   In Thomas Middleton's, *A Trick to Catch the Old One* (1608), the phrase "Dutch widow" appears no fewer than six times, including three times in rapid succession when one of several "old ones" in the play, Walkadine Hoard, discovers he has been tricked into marrying a courtesan posing as a wealthy widow, and shouts "A Dutch widow, a Dutch widow, a Dutch widow!" (5.2.107). The pay-off of this joke is set up earlier in the play, when Hoard is told that "Dutch widow" is a cant term for prostitute, and is so tickled by the term that he vows "I shall remember a Dutch widow the longest day of my life" (3.3.20–21)—as he indeed does when he discovers that he is married to one. See Thomas Middleton, *A Trick to Catch the Old One*, (ed.) Valerie Wayne, in *Thomas Middleton: The Collected Works*, (eds.) Gary Taylor and John Lavagnino (Oxford: Oxford University Press, 2007). The sexualization of Dutch women appears perhaps most famously at the center of John Marston's *The Dutch Courtesan* (1603). See John Marston, *The Dutch Courtesan*, (ed.) M.L. Wine (Lincoln: University of Nebraska Press, 1965).

[18]   William Shakespeare, *Henry V*, (ed.) J.H. Walter (London and New York: Routledge, 1990).

[19]   It is surprising that critics have accepted the veracity of the Dutch courtesan stereotype, given the skepticism with which male immigrant stereotypes, such as that of the Flemish drunkard, have been scrutinized. Hoenselaars speaks of an "age-old tradition of Dutch prostitutes in London." Hoenselaars, *Images of Englishmen and Foreigners*, 117. Jean Howard likewise refers to the "long-standing centrality of Dutch frows to London's illicit sexual economy." Howard, *Theater of a City*, 152.

This is not to suggest that there were no Dutch prostitutes in London. Given the economic challenges that immigrant women faced, some undoubtedly did turn to sex-work to earn a living. However, it is also clear, based on the evidence of the Alien Returns, that many made a living in a variety of other ways, and some of them a very good one given the numbers of workers they employed. Indeed, the visibility of Dutch women textile workers in London gave rise, as we have seen, to resentment on the part of London guildsmen for the perceived discrepancy between the gendered division of labor within the native and alien communities.

The elision and/or sexualization of alien craftswomen and their wares in plays staged by the all-male professional playing companies in London's commercial theaters stands in stark contrast to their depiction in civic pageants staged by England's immigrant communities, which sought to defend the benefits brought to the native economy by skilled immigrant laborers. The alien artisans of London and Norwich produced these pageants—quite literally with their own hands—for royal progresses and coronations during the reigns of Elizabeth I, James I, Charles I, and Charles II.[20] Through their hands–on participation in every aspect of the pageants' staging (including writing texts and inscriptions, fabricating textiles, building stages and triumphal arches, painting tableaus, designing costumes and properties, etc.), alien artisans brought imported skills, technologies, materials, and iconography to bear on native dramatic forms.

Civic pageants staged by immigrant communities in England had the important function of petitioning current or new monarchs for the continuance or renewal of their Royal Charters and privileges.[21] Ole Peter Grell demonstrates that such pageants often included gifts to the monarch of luxury textiles or other wares that "served as a reminder of the value of the refugee craftsmen to the economic life" of England.[22] This value was also exemplified—and materially recollected—in the costumes, properties, and scenic aspects of the pageants, which may have figured into the motivation of native civic authorities in allowing immigrant communities to stage them, for such pageants were extraordinarily expensive to produce. By drawing on the financial resources of immigrant merchants and artisans, city guilds, and corporations were able to reduce their own expenditure in the entertaining of monarchs. Yet scholarship on these entertainments has hitherto said little about their staging of alien women's skilled textile work, which occupied a prominent place in their iconography and performance.

The earliest civic pageant staged by aliens in England was performed for the queen in Norwich in 1578, during one of her summer progresses. Norwich had the largest population of immigrant textile workers outside of London,

---

[20]   See Chapter 7 of Ole Peter Grell, *Calvinist Exiles in Tudor and Stuart England* (Aldershot, UK: Scolar Press, 1996).

[21]   Ibid., 163.

[22]   Ibid.

which specialized in the production of the New Draperies.[23] The community was established after 1564, when the city authorities approached the Duke of Norfolk with a scheme to revive the local economy (which was "in much distress by the decay of the Worsted Manufacture") by inviting thirty Dutch and Walloon master artisans and three hundred of their servants skilled in the "making of Flanders Commodities of wool" including "Bayes, Sayes, Arras, Mockadoes, and such like" to settle in the city.[24] The project was extremely successful, resulting in a population far beyond the original quota: at the time of the pageant there are estimated to have been some 6,000 strangers living in Norwich (more than 50 percent of whom were women,) out of a total population of 14,000–15,000.[25] Norwich "stuffs" were renowned for their extraordinary variety (they included both expensive and more affordable fabrics in a diverse array of colors and designs,) and for their innovative mixing of wool with other threads, such as linen and silk. Between 1567 and 1586, the volume of New Draperies produced in Norwich increased from 1,200 to 38,700.[26]

The native population initially "raised many Clamours" against the stranger community, particularly when the alien artisans refused to hand over their "Book of the Drapereye," which was "written in Dutch" and contained trade secrets, including "excellent Orders and Rules, about the making of Bays, Fustians … Lace and Fringe, Tufted Mockadoes, Currelles, and all other Works mingled with Silk, Saietrie, or Linnen Yarn."[27] By the time of the pageant, however, they appear to have "found Favour," at least among certain city authorities, who recognized that "the Generality of the Strangers were of good & honest Conversation," and were "convenient and profitable for its Common Weal, by their keeping not only their own People, but many others at work, to the great Advantage of the City and adjacent Country."[28] The alien artisans also found favor with the queen, who interceded on their behalf when disputes arose, "reminding" the complainants

---

[23]   In 1571 the population of strangers in Norwich is estimated to have been 4,000, out of a total population of 16,000. Murray, *Flanders and England*, 36.

[24]   Francis Blomefield, *The History of the City and County of Norwich* (Norwich, 1745), 200–201; R.H. Tawney and Eileen Power (eds.), *Tudor Economic Documents: Being Select Documents Illustrating the Economic and Social History of Tudor England*, vol. 1 (London: Longmans, Green and Co., 1924), 298–9. See also Nigel Goose, "Introduction: Immigrants in Tudor and Early Stuart England," in *Immigrants in Tudor and Early Stuart England*, (eds.) Goose and Luu, 18.

[25]   Blomefield, *History of Norwich*, 206–7; Goose, "Immigrants and English Economic Development," 141–2.

[26]   Goose, "Immigrants and English Economic Development," 140–42.

[27]   Blomefield, *History of Norwich*, 205. On the initial tensions between the native and alien artisans in Norwich, and the aliens ultimate integration in the 1570s, see Laura Yungblut, *Strangers Settled Here Amongst Us: Policies, Perceptions, and the Presence of Aliens in Elizabethan England* (London: Routledge, 1996), 52–6.

[28]   Blomefield, *History of Norwich*, 207.

of "the Advantage accruing to the City from ... the Number of People being employed, which before had nothing to support them."[29]

The first Norwich pageant, performed by the "Artizans Strangers" in Saint Stephen's Street, thus aimed to remind the local community of the commercial success of the New Draperies, and to demonstrate the fruits of that success to the queen.[30] It took place on a forty-foot long scaffold or stage, above which was written: "The Causes of this Common Wealth are ... " and among these causes, "Idlenesse expelled" and "Labour cherished."[31] The front of the stage was "beautified with Painters Work, Artificially expressing to Sight, the Pourtraiture of ... several Looms, and the Weavers in them (as it were working)." Over each of the seven looms was written the name of the woven-work it produced, which included New Draperies (such as "Russels," "Darnix," and "Tuft Mockado,") broad silks ("Caffa," a rich silk cloth similar to damask,) and narrow silk wares ("lace" and "Fringe."). It is significant that the immigrant community chose to give the New Draperies toponymic names, which pointed to their countries of origin: "Russels," also spelled "Ryssillis," for example, was named after Rijssel (the Flemish name for Lille) and "Darnix," was named after the Flemish town Dornick (or Tourney.)[32] In naming the New Draperies, the alien artisans were therefore claiming their own cultural heritage. They may also have been asserting their proprietary interest in the skills associated with their manufacture, as on several occasions the alien weavers insisted upon their exclusive right to "search and seal" such fabrics, including "a new Work called Bombasins [or bombazines]," claiming that "the Dutch first invent[ed]" it.[33] Yet the politics of naming the New Draperies did not go uncontested: native craftsmen claimed that many of these fabrics with "outlandish" names were new in name only, accusing the strangers of inventing newfangled nomenclature for already existing fabrics in order to claim exclusive rights over their manufacture, and as a marketing ploy. "In demonstration therof," they argued, "a buffyn, a catalowne, and the pearl of beauty are all one cloth ... the same cloths bearing other names in times past."[34] In advertising the toponymic

---

[29]   Ibid., 202–203.

[30]   Ibid., 231.

[31]   Ibid. See also B.G., *The Joyfull Receyving of the Queenes Most Excellent Majestie into Hir Highnesse Citie of Norwich* (London, 1578), B4r–B4v.

[32]   Holderness, "New Draperies in England," 221–2. "Tuft Mockado," also originally produced in Flanders, is probably named after the French "moucade" (a deep pile fabric resembling velvet, made of wool and/or silk), and perhaps the Italian "mocaiardo" (a kind of mohair), but is also associated, once it is Englished, with the term "mock," as in "mock-velvet" (*OED*). The term itself thus nicely mocks or mimics the aping of foreign terms, skills and fashions that spurred the economic success of the New Draperies in England.

[33]   Blomefield, *History of Norwich*, 207. On the "mobile confusion of invention, innovation, and imitation" that characterized relations between the native and alien weavers of Norwich, see Holderness, "New Draperies in England," 225ff.

[34]   Cited in Robin D. Gwynn, *Huguenot Heritage: The History and Contribution of the Huguenots in Britain* (London and Boston: Routledge and Kegan Paul, 1985), 63.

names of the stuffs produced at Norwich in the pageant, the alien weavers were thus insisting upon their contribution to and proprietary interest in the revitalization of the city.

Above the painted and labeled looms on the stage stood the alien weavers who had "made the said several Works, and before every Man the Work in Deed" (i.e., in front of each weaver lay a bolt of the fabric his own hands had produced). By metonymically pointing to the labor of the workers who stood proudly behind them, the materially presented bolts of fabric bore eloquent testimony to the skills of the immigrant artisans who had produced them. The materiality of these "Norwich stuffs" was further heightened in the staging of the pageant, insofar as the fabrics were displayed directly above the two-dimensional, painted tableau of the looms. In choosing to put the actual products of their labor (the "Work in Deed") on display, the alien weavers were reminding the queen both of the work necessary to produce them, and of the material fruits of that work. As stage-properties, the "Norwich stuffs" were presented as something "worked upon" by the hands of aliens.

The work of alien craftswomen also occupied a prominent place in the pageant. At one end of the stage sat "eight small Women Children spinning Worsted Yarne; and at the other End as many knitting of Worsted-Yarn Hose." The peculiar phrase "small Women Children" suggests that the "Women" knitters were "slender," "graceful," "inferior in rank" and/or "young," if not actually children (*OED*, "small, *a.* and *n.*²," 1.a., 3.a., 3.c., 16). Most likely, all 16 were young women or girls, but even if some of the knitters were boys, the phrase makes clear that their labor was coded as female. The term "small" also evokes the fineness of the work they produce, as "small yarne" or apparel was "fine in texture or structure" (*OED*, "small, *a.* and *n.*²," 11). It is the fineness of the "Worsted Yarne" that necessitates its being spun and knit by the slender fingers of young women or children.

The gendered division of labor in the pageant visually subordinates women's work (spinning and knitting) to men's (weaving) by deeming only the latter worthy of pictorial representation (probably by skilled Dutch painters), while placing the former at the margins of the stage. It does so, perhaps, to diffuse native artisans' complaints that alien women were usurping the male prerogative of skilled labor. Yet in doing so, the pageant ironically renders the actual labor of the female spinners and knitters *more* visible than that of the male weavers. Although the ostensible aim of this staging may have been to suggest the higher level of skill associated with weaving (whose trade secrets had to be protected and kept hidden, unlike the purportedly less skilled work of the spinners and knitters,) it nonetheless accorded the dexterity of the girls greater prominence in the pageant's staging, as the queen was able to watch the nimble fingers of the girls as they skillfully spun and knit stockings onstage.

The worsted stocking industry was considered to be an offshoot of the New Draperies, and along with the latter was one of the great success stories of Elizabethan "projects" involving imported immigrant skills and labor. Centered in Norwich, although it soon "spread like wildfire," according to Joan Thirsk, the industry "ranked second only to the New Draperies as a user of long wool [such as worsted] and employer of handicraft labor."[35] The demand for stockings throughout England was enormous: Thirsk estimates that around ten million pairs were needed to dress the whole population per annum.[36] The Norwich jersey and worsted stockings, produced of fine wools with improved knitting techniques, were also in high demand on the Continent and were exported abroad.[37] By presenting young rather than adult women engaged in the labor of spinning and knitting (rather than weaving,) the alien community advertised their contribution to the native economy in an unthreatening way.

Between the spinners and knitters stood a "pritty Boy richly apparelled, which represented the Common-Wealth of the City." Upon Elizabeth's arrival he praised the industry of Norwich to her as follows:

> Most Gracious Prince, undoubted Soveraigne Queene,
> Our only Joy next God, & chiefe Defence,
> In this small Shew, our whole Estate is seen,
> The Wealth we have, we find proceede[s] from thence[:]
> The idle Hand hath here no Place to feed,
> The painfull Wight hath still to serve his need. ...
>
> *Pointing to the Spinners*
> From combed Wool we draw this slender Thread,
> *Pointing to the Looms*
> From thence the Looms have dealing with the same,
> *Pointing to the Works*
> And thence again in Order do proceed,
> These several Works, which skilful Art doth frame:
> And all to drive Dame Need into her Cave,
> Our Heads and Hands together labour'd have.
>
> We bought before, the Things that now we sell,
> These slender Imps, their works do pass the waves, ...
> Thus thro' thy Help, & Aid of Power Divine,
> Doth Norwich live, whose Hearts & Goods are thine.[38]

The text of the pageant works in tandem with its textiles to highlight the imported skills that have allowed Norwich to produce and export goods it had formerly purchased from abroad ("We bought before, the Things that now we sell,") thereby enriching the "Common wealth" of both the city and nation. The speaker particularly emphasizes the export of worsted stockings, made by the "slender

---

[35]   Joan Thirsk, *Economic Policy and Projects: The Development of a Consumer Society in Early Modern England* (Oxford: Clarendon Press, 1978), 44–7, 60.

[36]   Ibid., 5.

[37]   Ibid., 45.

[38]   Blomefield, *History of Norwich*, 231 and G., *Joyfull Receyving*, B4v.

Imps" onstage, whose "works do pass the waves." By highlighting their gendered labor, the pageant presents a chaste image of Dutch femininity, one that taps into contemporary depictions of Dutch women as paragons of Protestant domestic virtue and industry, and attempts to dispel the countervailing image of Dutch women as promiscuous commercial agents, if not as prostitutes.[39]

Certainly, the "small Women" spinners and knitters present a fascinating example of female performers in the provinces, at a time when London's professional playing companies were all-male. Yet to call them "female players" would be misleading, as it is crucial to their performance and to the meaning of the pageant as a whole, that they are workers "in deede," who are not merely performing work, but are actually working, producing a product ("Goods") for the queen, who is able to observe their skills in action. The girls are included in the performance, it would seem, precisely because of the dexterous techniques practiced by their "slender Imp[ish]" fingers. The "skilful Art" of the "Artizans Strangers" presented in the pageant is not the art of players, but of workers. That is, the pageant's significance depends upon its performance by artisans, whose closely guarded skills are not easily imitable. If the skills performed and depicted are to be imitated by the native population, it will be because they are trained by alien artisans.

If, on the other hand, some or all of the child-knitters who performed in the pageant staged by the alien community were native girls, the pageant would have the further significance of staging for Elizabeth the positive impact of the immigrant artisans on the local economy through their transmission of skills to and employment of the local population. In contemporary documents, Norwich officials express their gratitude for the large numbers of poor people "set on worke" by alien craftspeople.[40] We know from contemporary censuses taken of the poor in Norwich and elsewhere that anywhere from 60 to 90 percent of people receiving parish poor relief during the period were female, many of them widows with children.[41] A clue as to how we are meant to interpret the status and significance of the "small Women Children" who performed in the pageant appears in the second painted tableau on the front of the stage, described as "the Pourtraiture of a Matron, and two or three Children, and over her Head was written these Words: Good Nurture Changeth Qualities."[42] If the motto and the children depicted were intended as a gloss on the children in the pageant, it may refer to

---

[39]   See Franits, *Paragons of Virtue*, 76–110 and Schama, "Wives and Wantons," 5–13.

[40]   Through the alien artisans' manufacture of "commodities as have not been wrought here before," they maintained, "many ruinous houses are redified, the city profited, [and] the poor maintained by working from begging." Cited in Yungblut, *Strangers Settled Here*, 111.

[41]   Tim Wales, "Poverty, Poor Relief and the Life Cycle: Some Evidence from Seventeenth-Century Norfolk," in *Land, Kinship, and Life Cycle*, (ed.) R.M. Smith (Cambridge: Cambridge University Press, 1984).

[42]   Blomefield, *History of Norwich*, 231.

the alien artisans' positive influence on the local community, implying that before their arrival Norwich's poor were idle, but now they are set to work ("The idle Hand hath here no Place to feed.") Under the positive influence or "Nurture" of Dutch industry and industriousness—an exemplary Protestant virtue that brings together religious devotion, cleaver marketing, hard work and manual skill ("Our Heads and Hands together labour'd have") and that is figured as female—"Dame Need" has been driven "into her Cave."

The figure of the "Matron" may refer to the alien women who have taught the girls (whether native or alien) the skills of spinning and knitting. It may also be intended to flatter the queen for having the foresight to establish the alien settlement at Norwich, thereby "nurturing" and protecting her own subjects. This identification was reinforced several days later by the Minister of the Norwich Dutch Church, who delivered an oration to Elizabeth, praising her as the "Nurse" of true religion and protector of the immigrant community.[43] The pageant and oration both work to dispel native complaints that Netherlandish artisans had emigrated for economic rather than religious reasons by representing their skilled industry as an expression of their religious devotion, and as a benefit to the commonwealth. The pageant's presentation of the chaste girls' virtuous industry seems to have been especially effective in this regard: the exhibition, we are told, "pleased hir Majesty so greatly, as she particularly viewed the knitting & spinning of the Children."[44] Three days later, the minister of the Norwich Dutch Church delivered a speech to Elizabeth thanking her for her hospitality and generosity and presenting her with a silver cup, "very curiously and artificially wrought" by a Dutch artisan.[45] Elizabeth expressed her appreciation for the pageant by donating thirty pounds to the refugee churches.[46]

The iconography of Dutch industry in general, and of Dutch women's skilled textile work in particular, appears even more prominently in the coronation pageant held for King James in 1604, entitled *The Magnificent Entertainment:*

---

[43]   Ibid., 238.

[44]   A description of this pageant may also be found in Raphael Holinshed, *The Third Volume of Chronicles ... Augmented, and Continued ... to the Yeare 1586* (London, 1587), 1290–91. See also David Bergeron, *English Civic Pageantry, 1558–1642* (Columbia: University of South Carolina Press, 1971), 39. Bergeron also describes several civic pageants staged in the Low Countries during Elizabeth's reign, which may have influenced the pageants staged by the immigrants in Norwich and London: a pageant staged in Antwerp for the Duke of Anjou, accompanied by the Earl of Leicester in 1582, and five pageants staged for the Earl of Leicester himself in 1586 (in Antwerp, the Hague, Haarlem, Amsterdam and Utrecht), when he was sent to the Low Countries by Elizabeth. These pageants contain many similar features, such as the female personification of the various cities by "damsels," and the celebration of their respective industries. Bergeron, *English Civic Pageantry*, 46–55.

[45]   Blomefield, *History of Norwich*, 237.

[46]   Raingard Esser, "Immigrant Cultures in Tudor and Stuart England," in *Immigrants in Tudor and Stuart England*, (eds.) Goose and Luu, 167.

Given to King James ... As Well by the English as by the Strangers, staged at seven triumphal arches throughout the city.[47] The third triumphal arch was financed, designed, built, and its associated pageant staged, by the Dutch merchants of London at the Royal Exchange.[48] According to its primary designer, architect Conraet Jansen, the Dutch community's decision to erect their own triumphal arch was intended to "honour the King and show their gratitude to God and the City."[49] At the center of the front side of the arch, as Thomas Dekker describes it, was a "spacious square roome" with "Silke Curtaines drawne before it, which (upon the approch of his Majestie)" were drawn to reveal a stage on which sat "17. yong *Damsels*, (all of them sumptuously adorned, after their countrey fashion,) ... in so many Chaires of State, and figuring in their persons, the 17. *Provinces of Belgia*" (ll. 481–4).[50] The sumptuous adornment of the "Dutch" damsels—the term "Dutch being used loosely during the period to refer to anyone from the Low Countries or regions directly adjacent—was not only meant to symbolize the immigrant community's nostalgic investment in the seventeen provinces of a

---

[47]   The pageant was postponed for a year due to plague. The seven opulent triumphal arches, which contained niches that functioned as stages for live actors, were designed by the architect Stephen Harrison, and engravings by William Kip were later published in *The Arches of Triumph*, described in John Nichols (ed.), *The Progresses, Processions, and Magnificent Festivities of King James the First*, vol. 1 (London: J.B. Nichols, 1828), 329–401.

[48]   The Dutch community invested over £1,000 in the arch, as against the £4,100 the City and livery companies invested in the five other arches (the sixth being financed by the Italian merchants). Grell, *Calvinist Exiles*, 168.

[49]   Ibid, 166. Jansen published a pamphlet on the event for the London Dutch community entitled *Beschryvinghe vande Herlycke Arcvs Trivmphal ofte Eere Poorte vande Nederlandtsche Natie Opgherecht in London* (Middleburgh, 1604). Grell draws on Jansen's pamphlet extensively in his account of the Dutch community's role in producing the pageant. See also Gervase Hood, "A Netherlandic Triumphal Arch for James I," in *Across the Narrow Seas: Studies in the History and Bibliography of Britain and the Low Countries: Presented to Anna E.C. Simoni*, (ed.) Susan Roach (London: British Library, 1991).

[50]   The text of the Dutch merchants' pageant may be found in Thomas Dekker, "The Magnificent Entertainment Given to King James," in *The Dramatic Works of Thomas Dekker*, (ed.) Fredson Bowers, vol. 2 (Cambridge: Cambridge University Press, 1953–1961), 229–31. See also Bergeron, *English Civic Pageantry*, 78–80. "Belgia, which we commonly call Netherland ... is divided into 17. provinces, viz. The Dukedomes of Brabant, Limburg, Lutzemburg and Guelders: the Earledomes of Flanders, Artois, Henault, Holland, Zeland, Namure and Zutphen, the Marquisat of the sacred Empire, the Seignories of Friesland, Mechlin, Utrecht, Overissel and Groningen, all territories rich, plentifull and exceeding populous." G. Botero, *The Worlde, or An Historicall Description of the Most Famous Kingdomes and Common-Weales Therein* (London, 1601), 30–31. Cited in Cyrus Hoy, *Introductions, Notes, and Commentaries to Texts in "The Dramatic Works of Thomas Dekker,"* (ed.) Fredson Bowers, vol. 2 (Cambridge: Cambridge University Press, 1979), 144.

united "Belgia," but also functioned as a material testament to the fruits of their industries and industriousness.

The rear of the arch was devoted entirely to praising Netherlandish industry, and the economic benefits brought to England by the immigrant community. At the top of the arch was a statue of *Prudentia*, who "served to promote crafts and trade," and underneath her a painting of *Diligentia*, *Industria*, and *Labor* with the inscription "*Artes perfecit, Sedulitate Labor.*"[51] Below them were the arch's three passageways: the central one was designated as the "passage of State" for King James, on either side of which were two "lesser" passageways for the thoroughfare of commoners. Over one of the latter passageways, according to Dekker, was a painted tableau of "Dutch Countrey people, toyling at their Husbandrie; women carding of their Hemp, the men beating it, such excellent Art being exprest in their faces, their stoopings, bendings, sweatings, &c. that nothing is wanting in them but life (which no colors can give)" (ll. 564–74). Over the other lesser passageway was a painting of "men, women and children (in Dutch habits) ... busie at other workes: the men Weaving, the women Spinning, the children at their Hand-loomes, &c. Above whose heads, you may with little labour, walke into the *Mart*, where as well the *Froe*, as the *Burger*, are buying and selling, the praise of whose industrie (being worthy of it) stands publisht in gold" (ll. 584–90).[52] Jansen's account of these two paintings suggests that alien women's skilled textile work was featured even more prominently. As Grell translates, the first painting depicted "all sorts of needlework, sewing, stitching, crocheting, and so on," while the second depicted "spinning, weaving 'in the Dutch manner' and other crafts associated with the cloth trade."[53] In this pageant, the industry of Dutch craftswomen is deemed worthy of pictorial representation at great expense.[54]

---

[51] Grell, *Calvinist Exiles*, 170.

[52] The Latin inscription that follows praises the commerce and the energy of craftspeople, whose industry banishes idleness and preserves the commonwealth.

[53] Grell, *Calvinist Exiles*, 172.

[54] Indeed, among the four Dutch artists employed to paint these tableau was the painter Marten Droeshout, uncle to the engraver of the same name who produced the famed portrait of Shakespeare (wearing a starched rebato) for the First Folio. One of these Droeshouts (possibly the younger engraver, or his brother Martin Droeshout) later did the engravings of the arch for a pamphlet describing the event published by Jansen. Hood, "Netherlandic Triumphal Arch," 75. E.A.J. Honigmann has argued that the elder Droeshout provided the limning on which the engraving of Shakespeare was based, pointing out that he lived near Shakespeare, who was at this time lodging with the Huguenot Mountjoys. "Shakespeare and London's Immigrant Community," in *Elizabethan and Modern Studies: Presented to Professor Willem Schrickx on the Occasion of His Retirement*, (ed.) J.P. Vander Motten (Gent: Seminarie voor Engelse en Amerikaanse Literatuur, R.U.G., 1985), 144–8. The other three artists were Daniel de Vos and Pauwels van Overbeke (who were brought over from Antwerp at considerable cost), and the immigrant Adriaen van Sond from Breda, described as "painter to the King." Grell, *Calvinist Exiles*, 166–7.

As in the Norwich pageant, a "Boy, attyred all in white Silke" delivered a speech written by members of the immigrant community[55] to the monarch explaining the meaning of the pageant in Latin. In Dekker's translation, he says to James:

> *Plentie* (daughter to *Industrie*) layes the blessings both of Countrey and Cittie, in heapes at thy feete. ... Wee (the *Belgians*) likewise come, to that intent: a Nation banisht from our owne Cradles; yet nourcde and brought up in the tender boosome of Princely Mother, *ELIZA*. The *Love*, which wee once dedicated to her (as a Mother) doubly doe wee vow it to you, our Sovereigne, and Father; intreating wee may be sheltred under your winges now, as then under hers. (ll. 689–97)

As in the Norwich pageant, "plentie" is here figured as the natural daughter of Dutch "industrie": yet industry will continue to beget plenty only if "nourcde" by James's love, as it had been at the "boosome of Princely Mother, *ELIZA*." Contemporary accounts suggest that the arch was very well received by James, who "admired it greatly; it was so goodly, top and top many stories, and so high as it seemed to fall forward ... pictures of great art, cost, and glory ... a speech of wonder ... thus the Dutch and French spared for no cost to gratify our King."[56] At night, the arch was illuminated both from without and from within (through colored glass in its obelisks) creating a spectacular light show that "caused crowds of people to gather around" it for several nights running.[57]

The emphasis on Dutch "Industrie" and labor evidenced by the verisimilar "toyling," "carding," "beating," "stoopings, bendings, sweatings," "Weaving," "Spinning," "buying and selling," and, according to Janssen, needlework, sewing, stitching, and crocheting, depicted on the arch contributes to the pageant's clear intent to secure James's economic, as well as religious, support or "shelter" by representing the Dutch community, notably featuring female artisans and retailers, as contributing to, rather than depleting, England's "common wealth." As a result of the alien weavers' industry, "Plentie" will lie "in heapes at [James's] feete." The prominence of the seventeen "damsells" at the center of the arch, who emblematize

---

[55] The speech was written by Jacob Cool, a wealthy silk merchant and self-taught classicist, who was the nephew of Abraham Ortelius, the famous Antwerp cartographer, and by Raphael Thorius, a refugee physician and poet from Flanders. Grell, *Calvinist Exiles*, 165.

[56] Dugdale, the chronicler, confesses himself to have been transfixed by "the glory of this Show," which "was in my eye as a dream, pleasing to the affection, gorgeous and full of joy: and so full of joy and variety, that when I held down my head, as wearied with looking so high, methought it was grief to me to awaken so soon." Gilbert Dugdale, *The Time Triumphant Declaring in Briefe, the Arival of our Soverainge Liedge Lord, King James into England, his Coronation at Westminster: Together with his Late Royal Progresse ... Shewing also, the Varieties and Rarities of Al the Sundry Trophies or Pageants, Erected ...* (London: 1604), A5v. Cited in Grell, *Calvinist Exiles*, 173. See also Esser, "Immigrant Cultures," 168.

[57] Grell, *Calvinist Exiles*, 174.

the seventeen provinces of the Low Countries, draws on a longstanding iconographic tradition of allegorized female figures in civic pageantry. Yet the sumptuous material adornment of the damsels, when coupled with the visual depiction of the industry of Dutch women in producing and marketing such wares, moves beyond the purely allegorical by drawing attention to the "stuff" of their costumes (all of them are "sumptuously adorned, after their countrey fashion") and even of the "Silke Curtaines" drawn before them, as "worked upon" by their own hands. The youth of the damsels, like that of the "small Women Children," renders this work unthreatening by reinforcing the image of the Dutch as "a Nation banisht from [their] owne Cradles" and in need of shelter and nurturance.

The presentation of Netherlandish women and their wares in civic pageants stands in striking contrast to their representation in plays performed by the all-male, native, playing companies on London's professional stage, where their labor was typically sexualized or effaced.[58] The fashion-driven stage, like the culture at large, was transformed by the new textiles, starched ruffs, head-attires, and other items manufactured by alien artisans, and relied on the power of these eye-catching costumes and properties to attract audiences. It was left to the alien communities themselves to recollect through their civic performances the labor that was congealed in these most fetishized of commodities.

---

[58]   For exceptional depictions of Dutch froes' productive labor on the professional stage, see Korda, "Froes, Rebatoes and Other 'Outlandish Comodityes."

Chapter 4
Osmologies of Luxury and Labor: Entertaining Perfumers in Early English Drama[1]

Holly Dugan

At a key moment in *Much Ado About Nothing*, the drunkard, Borachio, reports a court rumor to the bastard, Don John: Don Pedro intends to woo Hero for Claudio. Borachio comes by this information surreptitiously:

> Being entertained for a perfumer, as I was smoking a musty room, comes me the Prince and Claudio, hand in hand in sad conference. I whipped me behind the arras, and there heard it agreed upon that the Prince should woo Hero for himself and, having obtained her, give her to Count Claudio.[2]

In a play whose plot relies on eavesdropping, innuendo, rumor, and confused identities, such an exchange seems hardly noteworthy. Surely Borachio could be "entertained for," or engaged as, a perfumer; in the social world of Messina, he is a jack-of-all-trades, a henchman for hire, and by his own admission, "a goodly commodity, being taken up on [other] men's bills" (3.3.171). Borachio's mutability contrasts with other characters in the play. Balthasar's song reinforces his role as courtly singer, just as Friar Francis's name identifies his vocation, and Dogberry is defined by his role as constable of the watch. Most notably, Don John's anti-social melancholy marks him as "a plain-dealing villain" (1.3.30). He admits: "I cannot hide what I am" (1.3.12–13). Borachio can, however, and such mutability is critical to the play's plot: over the course of the play, he "entertains" as a perfumer, a court musician, and as Hero's lover.[3] His entertainments demonstrate a

---

[1]   I would like to thank Thomas Dungan for generously sharing his research on London's earliest perfumers with me. I would also like to thank Michelle Dowd, Natasha Korda, an anonymous reviewer, and the participants of the 2008 SAA seminar on working subjects for their thoughtful critiques of earlier drafts of this essay.

[2]   All citations are from William Shakespeare, *Much Ado About Nothing*, (ed.) A.R. Humphreys (London: Methuen, 1981), 1.3.54–60.

[3]   The English verb "entertain" derives from the French "entretenir," meaning to maintain or to hold between. Associated with the rituals of courtship, such entertainments reinforced social conditions and status. By the late sixteenth century, however, the term also connoted pleasurable activities between two or more people, including amusements and merriments. For more, see William Beatty Warner, *Licensing Entertainment:*

new kind of occupational mutability, one that hinged upon increased consumption of luxury goods while downplaying the labor required to produce them. Unseen and unnoticed, Borachio's perfumed entertainments cloak the laborer-for-hire in the scents of hospitality, providing Don John with both means and opportunity to strike at the heart of Messina's social networks.

It is significant that Borachio "entertains" as a perfumer. His labor of dispensing scented smoke is linked to other meaningful "nothings" in the play, namely, his plot to ruin Hero's reputation. The term connoted both traditional forms of hospitality and newer forms of wage labor during the period, including amusements and leisure activities like the theater.[4] Both meanings coalesced in the professional identity of perfumer, whose invisible labor was increasingly vital to elite domestic life, yet whose olfactory presence sparked fears about other unseen influences within England's markets and interior spaces. Entertained as a perfumer, Borachio's labor affords him a metaphoric and material stealth: hidden behind the arras, and behind scented smoke, he learns valuable information about the domestic world of Messina.

Though occupations associated with new kinds of luxury consumption were perceived by some to be "much ado about nothing," insofar as they required a great deal of labor to produce inconsequential fripperies, Borachio's performance as a perfumer nonetheless demonstrates how the invisible labor of perfuming came to define the working subjectivities of those performing it. First cloaked by their perfumes and later defined by them, early modern England's perfumers document important phenomenological approaches to luxury goods other than consumption. As perfume emerged as a popular commodity in London's luxury markets, and the labor of perfumery involved selling perfumes rather than fumigating rooms with them, strong scents were increasingly associated with the bodies of perfumers, demonstrating that sensory associations between the smells of labor and of luxury were anything but intrinsic. Though one might assume that the labor of fumigating a room with smoky perfumes would infuse such scents into the clothing, hair, and pores of the laborer more than merely selling *prêt-à-porter* commodities, claims about the stench of perfumers only appeared after the labor of perfumers shifted from service to merchandizing. This shift greatly expanded economic opportunities to those shut out of London's traditional guild systems, namely, alien men and English women. These later perfumers were negatively defined by the smell of their wares, their bodies represented as reeking on early English stages and their occupational mutability strongly checked by the olfactory presence of luxury perfumes.

The Elevation of Novel Reading in Britain, 1684–1750 (Berkeley: University of California Press, 1998), 231.

 [4]   See, for example, the *OED* definitions for the verb "entertain," especially nos. 5 (referring to wage labor and service), 10 (referring to leisure activities / amusement) and 13 (referring to hospitality).

This essay examines how paradoxical claims about the smell of luxury and labor accrued around the occupational identity of the perfumer, and how scented entertainment shaped the labor of perfuming and the working subjectivities of those associated with it. Reading the economic histories of England's early perfuming industries alongside representations of perfumers on the early modern stage, I argue that the economic and theatrical histories of English perfumers were intertwined. Although the theater was one example of the new kinds of "idle occupations" or entertainments associated with luxury goods, it staged broader cultural anxieties about changing labor structures, linking xenophobic and misogynistic fears about the role of aliens and women in the marketplace to an emerging discourse about the scent of labor.

Though links between certain kinds of labor and specific smells were not new on early English stages—late medieval mystery plays, for example, routinely utilized the noxious smell associated with butchers and chandlers to stage the harrowing of hell—the embodied effects of perfumery were. Unlike butchers or chandlers, whose industrial scents were noxious and thus increasingly associated with certain spaces, perfumers were believed to embody the exotic scents of their cosmetic wares, a cultural belief strengthened by the relative rarity of perfumers in early modern London. Despite their prevalence on stages in the late sixteenth and early seventeenth centuries, perfumers were not a common presence in English markets until the 1620s, when the first commercial perfume shops opened in London's luxury markets. These shops were owned mostly by those ineligible for guild membership, particularly alien men and English women. Perfumers were a common presence on London's stages well before perfume was a merchandisable commodity. Borachio's smoky entertainments thus document both a growing cultural demand for perfumes but also a burgeoning cultural fascination with perfumers in English culture. Defined by their expertise and control over invisible, ephemeral, and influential scent ingredients, early modern perfumers challenged existing social networks of trade and exchange. As such, they became a focal point for new anxieties about London's shifting economies, and were increasingly associated with the smell of the oddly transient, mutable, beguiling and illusory commodities they offered for sale.

In what follows, I examine this complicated history from two distinct vantage points, arguing that the stage history of early English perfumers provides one way of approaching the phenomenological relationship between the occupational identity of perfumer and the concoctions he or she sold. The economic history of early modern London's nascent perfume industry provides another. Read together, these two histories document a chiastic relationship between the scent of luxury perfumes and the labor associated with producing and merchandizing them. London's perfume industry, like other industries associated with luxury goods, provided those excluded from the traditional guild-system lucrative economic opportunities. As these entrepreneurs prospered, the strong scent of perfume was increasingly used to stigmatize them in theatrical representations. London's perfumers thus "entertain" in a variety of ways on stage: they are deceptive, vulgar, grotesque, and, ironically, malodorous. Perfumes, such representations seem to suggest, are deceptive tools of social advancement, evinced by those outsiders who manufactured or sold them, yet not by those who consumed them. The stage and economic histories of London perfumers thus demonstrate how certain luxury goods challenged and redefined the concept of malodorous labor and the working subjectivities of those associated with it.

Economic Histories: Selling Perfumes

Perfume's ephemeral materiality and the labor of perfuming shaped the occupational identity of London's perfumers. Between 1580 and 1630, however, the labor of perfuming changed greatly, raising important questions about how and why phenomenological associations of malodorous smell came to be associated with the bodies of perfumers. Like Borachio, London's early perfumers were employed in aristocratic households. As their names suggested, perfumers scented objects *per fume*, or through smoke. Though a variety of guilds sold imported perfume ingredients, like ambergris, civet, storax, benjamin, and musk, perfumers did not. Rather, one hired a perfumer to air a room. The labor of fumigating or perfuming defined the occupational identity of a perfumer, rather than the scent of the perfumes themselves. And, because only the most elite Londoners could afford such luxury, perfumers were associated with the labor of hospitality. Perfumes, as store-bought commodities, were not available before the last quarter of the sixteenth century and were not readily available in London's markets until the end of the first quarter of the seventeenth century.[5] Thus, within London's economic system, perfume was more commonly understood as a verb, not a noun. Borachio, for example, is cloaked behind the smoke of his perfumes; they do not betray his presence in the room.

Part of this stemmed from residual belief in perfumery as a medicinal application. Scented fumigations were a relatively easy way to protect oneself from a variety of airborne illnesses, including the plague, the pox, and other endogamous diseases, linking practices of domestic hospitality to those of health. The earliest perfumers in London worked for royal apothecarists, distilling perfumes and scenting and fumigating royal chambers. Apothecarists at this time were under the purview of the Grocers' Guild, who had a monopoly on importing and selling

---

[5]   Some fashion historians point to the "Earl of Oxford's" perfume as England's first recognizable perfume commodity; however, this is most likely an anachronistic term. It is named after a gift of Italian perfumed gloves, which Edward de Vere, the Earl of Oxford, gave to Queen Elizabeth as a gift in 1573. The queen adored the gloves, igniting a trend. Though one can purchase the Earl of Oxford's perfume in modern-day gift shops in Oxford, Elizabethans would have recognized the scent under a different name: ambergris, or gloves dressed in the "Spanish manner." For more on early modern perfume, see Holly Dugan, "Ephemeral History of Perfume: Scent and Sense in Early Modern England," PhD diss., University of Michigan, 2005.

aromatic ingredients.[6] Perfume ingredients like ambergris, storax, civet, musk, and benjamin were coded as either spices or drugs and sold by Grocers or Grocer-Apothercarists.

Though such ingredients could be consumed, they also could be burnt (at great expense) and used to fumigate royal and aristocratic homes. For example, John Hemingway, royal apothecarist to Henry VIII, Edward VI, and Elizabeth I, and a Warden of the Company of Grocers, recorded large quantities of perfumes in his six-month "midsummer" inventory of 1564.[7] These perfumes included rosewater scented with cloves, used to perfume the Banquetting House, Counsel Chamber, Great Chamber, and Chapel. Such perfuming was not unique. The Queen's elaborately embroidered robes were also scented with rosewater, benjamin and storax. And, in the summer of 1564, Elizabeth I's mistresses of the bedchamber used two pounds of orris powder (made from the root of iris flowers) to scent the room with a perfuming pan. Perfumes were also used to air the great chambers at Hampton Court, Richmond, Sheen and Westminster, along with litter or rushes.[8]

Royal perfuming practices sparked consumer desire for these luxury goods. Consumption of perfumed items, particularly scented gloves, dramatically increased in the last quarter of the sixteenth century, particularly among the English elite. As perfume became associated with luxury, demand increased for ready-made perfumes and imported aromatic ingredients. Between 1600 and 1620, the value of imports increased by forty percent.[9] By the early seventeenth century, perfume described a host of scents, applied in numerous ways, to a multitude of objects. Perfume was part of London's growing luxury markets, sold by a diverse array of tradespeople.

Given such varied ingredients and applications, confusion and contestation emerged over who should control (and regulate) the production, sale, and consumption of perfume. Early Stuart policies responded to the increases in consumption and importation, encouraging domestic production of luxury items when available and reorganizing London's guilds to reflect new import patterns.[10] Terminology was important to defining which company had purview over these profitable aromatics. As foreign aromatic ingredients entered London markets,

---

[6]   Leslie Gerard Matthews, *The Royal Apothecaries* (London: Wellcome Historical Institute, 1967), 68.

[7]   Ibid.

[8]   Hemmingway sent two pounds of orris powder each month to one of the Queen's mistresses of the bedchamber. See Matthews, *The Royal Apothecaries*, 71.

[9]   Linda Levy Peck, *Consuming Splendor: Society and Culture in Seventeenth Century England* (New York: Cambridge University Press, 2005), 13.

[10]   Early Stuart policy sought to develop luxury manufacturing at home, thereby reducing the number of imports. As Linda Levy Peck has argued, new patents for luxury manufacturing increased substantially between 1617 and 1640. See Peck, *Consuming Splendor*, 19 and chapter 2.

they were coded as spices or drugs. During the last quarter of the sixteenth and first quarter of the seventeenth centuries, categorical differences intensified. Disputes emerged between the Royal College of Physicians, the Worshipful Society of Grocers, and a small subset of apothecaries who struggled to control the lucrative trade of spiced aromatics like ambergris, civet, benjamin, storax, and labdanum.

The Apothecaries emphasized perfume's medicinal applications, arguing that perfume ingredients were drugs and should be regulated accordingly. James I agreed: in 1617 the Worshipful Society of Apothecaries was formed. Apothecaries successfully captured the lucrative market for aromatics in the seventeenth century by emphasizing their use as drugs rather than spices (which were already under the purview of the Grocers' Company). Others wishing to profit from these same imports needed a new way to market aromatics. Perfumes, as ready-made luxury commodities, were one way to do this. By the time the title of "perfumer," as an occupational identity, emerged in London, it tended to describe precisely those who were barred from inclusion within early modern guilds: aliens and women.

Phenomenological associations between the labor of perfuming and the bodies of perfumers thus focused upon these two groups of workers, linking the malodorous smell of perfumery with the foreign, feminine bodies of perfumers. A cursory study of the data on perfumers captured from London's Alien Returns suggests that, although the number of alien perfumers did not dramatically change between 1571 and 1638, their relationship to London's economic markets did. The Returns suggest that the labor of perfuming shifted from distillation to merchandizing. As a result, ready-made perfumes, as commodities, defined the occupational identity of perfumer, rather than the work of distillation or fumigation. The later Returns also reveal new kinds of labor associated with the work of perfumery: the 1593 Return, for example, lists six "dressers of Spanish leather" and three "aquae vitae" distillers and the Returns of 1627, 1635, and 1639 list six perfumers, 11 leather dressers, three distillers of strong waters, and one seller of sweet powders.

There were a few resident alien perfumers in London in the late sixteenth century. These Italian and French perfumers worked in a manner similar to Borachio, working at court, scenting objects with smoke. Because of such associations, perfumers were often represented as elite, effeminate, and foreign. When Hotspur decries the effeminacy of the King's messenger in Shakespeare's *Henry IV, Part I*, he maintains that he is "perfumed like a milliner."[11] The term "milliner" meant either a person from Milan or a seller of luxury goods and women's wares made in Milan. Hotspur objects to the presence of the unnamed Lord on the battlefield, focusing on his Italian perfumes. Not surprisingly, these early perfumers

---

[11] All citations are from William Shakespeare, *Henry IV, Part I*, (ed.) A.R. Humphreys (London: Methuen, 1960), 1.3.35.

worked hard to establish deep roots in the community. By the 1590s, many of them had English wives or apprentices and anglicized surnames.[12]

Perhaps due to such efforts, or due to the fact that perfume was a lucrative commodity, more and more ready-to-wear perfumes were manufactured domestically and "perfumer" emerged as an English occupational identity. Though these English purveyors were undoubtedly influential within London's markets, their prominent presence only served to underscore the difficulty in determining whether perfumes were domestically produced. For example, an inventory "of the Apparaile & bedding that the Adventurers have bestowed upon each of the younger woemen now sente" to Virginia in August of 1621 included a pair of perfumed "white Lambe gloves," supplied by William Piddock, perfumer.[13] That perfume was included among supplies used by early colonists suggests its prevalence in English markets and the complicated role of smell within the contact zone. Although it is impossible to know for certain if Piddock was English, it is probable, for there is no mention of Piddock in any of London's Alien Returns. English perfumers clustered in the East End in the early 1620s, but by the 1630s, most perfumers were located in the West End, where Italian, French, Irish, Dutch, Welsh and Scottish shop owners sold ready-made perfumes.[14] Such data suggests that it would have been possible to create associations between perfumery and the spatial zones where it was procured (much like medieval associations between butchery, the noxious smell of slaughtering, and the margins of cities). Yet this did not occur; rather, the economic success of the foreign perfumers in the West End galvanized xenophobic associations between the strong scent of perfume and the labor of perfumery.

As the term "perfume" expanded to include new kinds of luxury products largely manufactured outside the formal economy regulated by the guilds, more and more of London's most successful perfumers were alien men and English women, who clustered in London's emerging luxury markets in the West End. Alien perfumers moved from the city's central and eastern parishes (near the Royal Exchange and established French and Italian communities along Threadneedle Street) towards the wealthier, western parishes along the Strand, near the New Exchange and Westminster, whereas English perfumers remained in the East End.

---

[12] For example, Frauncis Lucatella from earlier returns became "Francis Lucatell" just as Gilliam Bysco became "William Bisco." See Irene Scouloudi, *Returns of Strangers in the Metropolis, 1593, 1627, 1635, 1639* (London: Hueguenot Society of London, 1985), chapter 4.

[13] "William Piddock, perfumer, submitted a bill for twelve pairs of them at four shillings the dozen pairs." David R. Ransome, "Wives for Virginia, 1621," *The William and Mary Quarterly* 48.1 (1991): 16.

[14] Bartholomew Benson was a perfumer of Artillery Lane, Richard Hooke was a perfumer in St. Magnus parish near Bridefoot Street, along with Henry Shawcroft and Henry Coleman of the parish of St. Botolph, near Aldersgate. I am grateful to Thomas Dungan, who shared his research on these perfumers. See Calendar of the Middlesex Session Records, Vol. 3, 32, 155, 389.

Such shifts allowed perfume to emerge as a profitable—and popular—luxury commodity valued for its exotic status. Perfumer, as an occupational identity, was associated with the act of merchandizing, rather than manufacturing, perfumes and the smell of strong scents with those employed in London's luxury markets rather than those fumigating aristocratic homes. Such shifting olfactory associations fueled xenophobic and misogynistic theatrical representations on London's stages, which often equated the deceptive, cosmetic allure of perfumes with those marketing them.

In the late sixteenth century, luxury goods were concentrated in the Royal Exchange. Though we know very little about the inventories of the shops in this Exchange, the sole piece of archival evidence, Thomas Deane's inventory for his haberdashery shop, includes pomanders, i.e., small, metal globes that functioned as plague preventatives when filled with aromatic gums and resins.[15] Deane's inventory suggests that most of the small shops were crowded with ready-made goods. Most shops were five feet by seven and a half feet, which made it almost impossible to manufacture crafts in them.[16] Strong aromatics would have overwhelmed these cramped, dark stalls, and many shoppers would have experienced the smell of perfume even if they chose not to purchase it. Such first-hand, phenomenological experience of passive olfaction by London's elite consumers undoubtedly reinforced xenophobic and misogynistic stereotypes about the smell of perfumers encountered elsewhere.

Cultural representations of perfumers conflated the smell of the laborer with the scents sold in his or her shop. A preacher in Oxford, for example, utilized strong, second-hand smells to emphasize how the power of sermons could even reach those who only passively listened: "If any man, sayth Chrysostome upon John, do sit neare to a perfumer, or a perfumers shop, even against his will he shall recevie some savour from it: much more shall he who frequenteth the Church, recevie some goodness from it."[17] Linking the strong scents of the perfumer's shop with the scent of the perfumer, this preacher draws upon what must have been a common experience (even for churchgoers in Oxford) of smelling both, imagining that each produces a "savour" that was impossible to ignore. Though perfume was an ephemeral, luxury commodity, it powerfully defined the perfumer's identity through what was perceived to be the smell of luxury markets.

The association of such scents with the occupational identity of perfumers strengthened with the building of the New Exchange. Completed in 1609, the New Exchange, known as "Britain's Burse," focused almost exclusively on exotic, and

---

[15]   Kay Staniland, "Thomas Deane's Shop in the Royal Exchange," in *The Royal Exchange*, (ed.) Ann Saunders (London: London Topographical Society, 1997), 59–67.

[16]   Linda Woodbridge, "The Peddler and the Pawn: Why Did Tudor England Consider Peddlers to Be Rogues?" in *Rogues and Early Modern English Culture*, (eds.) Craig Dionne and Steve Mentz (Ann Arbor: University of Michigan Press, 2004), 157.

[17]   George Abbot, *An Exposition upon the Prophet Jonah Contained in Certaine Sermons, Preached in S. Maries Church in Oxford* (London, 1600), 239.

imported, luxury items. Its location on the Strand, the main thoroughfare between Westminster and the City, was designed to entice luxury trades to drift west and out of the City.[18] It succeeded; by the 1630s, the New Exchange defined all that was fashionable about the emerging West End district of London.[19] Its covered arcades hosted a number of shops that specifically focused on imported luxury goods, particularly exotica like porcelain, feathers and perfumes. The shops in the New Exchange were cheaper and larger than at the Royal Exchange, yet the Earl of Salisbury's leases required merchants to focus on a particular trade, encouraging the development of specialized luxury trades, including perfume shops.[20] The highest rents were on the second level. Perfumers, along with other luxury purveyors, were prevalent on the second floor of the exchange.

Foreign men and English women were the most prominent perfumers in the New Exchange. According to the renewal of leases in 1633, there were at least three perfume shops on the second floor, including Queen Henrietta Maria's perfumer, Jean-Baptiste Ferreine, whose shop was one of the largest in the Bourse. William Dungen, listed as a perfumer in the 1635 Alien Returns, leased two shops next door to one another, one next to a Mary Jelley, "a sempstress" and "seller of French wares," and the other to a Mrs. Hassett, "perfumer," one of the first English women explicitly labeled as such. Mrs. Hassett was most likely an abbreviation of Blennerhassett; George Blennerhassett was a neighbor of Dungen's and a fellow shopkeeper, with two haberdashery shops—the George and the Black Bear—on the lower level of the Exchange. Blennerhassett was a prominent merchant, selling many items to the Earl of Salisbury, his landlord. Mrs. Hassett, "perfumer," was probably George's wife; her association with Blennerhassett and with Dungen would have made her a prominent retailer of perfumes to the landed gentry.[21]

Other sources suggest that there were additional perfume shops, including Anne Clarges's shop, the Spanish Gypsies. Clarges, later known as the "Monkey Duchess" after she married the Duke of Abermarle, sold perfumed washballs and powders in the New Exchange.[22] Clarges's unusual marriage and satirical title demonstrates how female perfumers, as purveyors of luxury goods, were believed to be upwardly mobile, dangerously exploiting aristocratic connections in ways others could not.[23]

---

[18]   J.F. Merrit, *The Social World of Early Modern Westminster: Abbey, Court, and Community* (Manchester: University of Manchester Press, 2005), 159.

[19]   See Jean Howard, *Theater of a City: The Places of London Comedy* (Philadelphia: University of Pennsylvania Press, 2007), 156.

[20]   See Peck, *Consuming Splendor*, 52.

[21]   Dungen had two other partners in his perfuming business: Thomas Richards, a Welshman, and Thomas Mazzine, a second-generation Italian.

[22]   See Jacob Larwood and John Camden Hotten, *The History of Signboards* (London: John Camden Hotten, 1866), 424.

[23]   For an example of contemporary satires of Clarges, see Andrew Marvell's "Third Advice to a Painter," in *Poems on Affairs of State, 1660–1714*, (ed.) George deForest Lord (New Haven: Yale University Press, 1963), 75.

If Clarges exploited perfume's elite associations, she certainly was not alone. Ferreine, like other perfumers and merchants in the Bourse, emphasized the New Exchange's royal connections. Perfumers in the last quarter of the seventeenth century expanded such affiliation beyond spatial terms: Edmund Bolsworth's advertisement for his perfume shop, the King's Arm and Civit-Cat, located near Temple Bar, contained the royal stamp, as did most of the shops of the New Exchange.[24] Others were opportunistic, rather than elitist, expanding the term to include other lucrative commodities like tobacco. Perfumers increasingly sold snuff and tobacco-related products. Dungen's two shops, the Phoenix and the Orange Tree, in the New Exchange demonstrate that perfume encompassed both ready-made scents as well as tobacco, or "Indian" perfume. The Phoenix's fiery classical allusions and the Orange Tree's fruity theme demonstrate the growing fashion for fumes and for Continental scents, particularly floral essences. By the end of the seventeenth century, perfumers were also tobacconists: William Trunket, "London perfumer," a late-seventeenth century perfumer located near Temple-Bar, sold "all sorts of snuff, perfumes, essences, French and Hungary Waters Retail."[25] The connection between perfume and tobacco would increase across the seventeenth century, as both commodities were routinely satirized by Puritan commentators for their vaporous, insubstantial qualities.

The popularity of ready-made perfumes inspired others to take up the labor of perfuming in order to participate in such fashionable consumption. Recipe books of early English housewives contain numerous recipes for perfumes, emulating the distilled waters, scented powders for linens, or perfumed sundries, like gloves or ribbons sold in London's luxury markets. The labor of perfuming, when performed in English homes, produced very different results, depending on the quality and quantity of the ingredients used. Housewives' perfume-recipes from the period reflect the same ingredients most likely used in the composition of ready-made commodity perfumes, but they also reveal both individual preferences and market availability, documenting the widespread appeal of "luxury" in the seventeenth-century.[26]

For example, Margaret Yvelerton's 1621 "Booke of Phisicke Surgery Preserves and Cookery with Sundrie Other Excellent Receites" contains recipes for medicines and other receipts useful for maintaining both health and domestic life. It also contains a number of receipts for producing scents if commercial ones were unavailable or too expensive. To perfume apparel, for example, she advises to keep it clean and "perfume it often either with some red powder burned or with

---

[24]   See Folger MS X.d. 525. Bolsworth also was listed as a haberdasher in a later defeasance of mortgage. See also East Sussex Records Office MS AMS6270/68.

[25]   See Halliwell Phillips MS 1239. Trunkett's perfume inventory from 1732 emphasizes perfumed powders and pomatum.

[26]   Women's recipes for perfumes are numerous in their manuscript cookbooks. See, for example, British Library MSS ADD 28320, ADD 27466, ADD 28320, Eggerton 2214, Eggerton 2197, Yale MS Osborn Shelves B226, and Wellcome MS 363.

Juniper."[27] To make sweet water, she emphasizes using whatever sweet herbs are available: "take all maner of sweete hearbes and pottle or gallon of faire water, fill yt till you have out all the water, fill yt againe and fill the styll with rose and beaten cloves, put to yt and fill it till you have out all the water." Similarly, she provides a receipt "to make sweete bags with little cost."[28] These recipes are varied in their applications: Mary Dogget's receipt book, for example, includes recipes for pomander-bracelets, a perfume for a sweet bag, another for "sweet bags and sweet water," and instructions on how to perfume gloves. Yvelerton's and Dogget's perfumes undoubtedly involved a good bit of labor. The prevalence of such recipes in women's manuscripts suggests that many housewives thought such labor worthwhile, if it produced a luxury good like perfumed gloves.

Published cookbooks explicitly addressed these new markets for luxury goods, allowing women who lived further from the capital's shopping districts to create their own fashionable perfumed items.[29] Simon Barbe's *French Perfumer*, for example, targets "Persons of Quality and Condition," who can "afford themselves leisure enough to gather Flowers at their Country Seats, and make use of them for Perfumes," not only for "diversions" but also saving "the Expence of buying them at Extravagant Rates in Shops."[30] By the end of the seventeenth century, the labor of perfuming had itself become a diverting form of entertainment for the elite and the would-be elite. Barbe's perfumed "diversions," like Borachio's scented "entertainments," define the pleasure of perfume as ephemeral and intoxicating, so much so that it diverts the mind from labor even as it is being performed.[31]

Although the labor of perfuming was defined as a tool of pleasurable diversion, the occupational identity of perfumer was increasingly associated with fraudulent diversions. Such fears concentrated on cosmetic and economic deception, rather than sensory transformation. Richard Braithwaite's "Advice to a Gallant" warns that a perfumer can only make one a "neat *Outward Man*," who might nevertheless be "inwardly" unsuitable to "intelligible company." Because their "*Bark* is better than the *Body*," such consumers should have a cinnamon tree as their emblem, subtly mocking the signboards of perfumery shops.[32] Thomas Brown even doubts the association of perfumery with foreigners, warning potential consumers that

---

[27] See Wellcome MS 182.

[28] It directs one "Take the buttons of Roses dryed and watered with Rosewater three or foure times put to them Muske powder of cloves Sinamon and a little mace mingle the roses and them together and putt them in little baggs of Linnen with Powder." See Ibid, 186.

[29] See Wendy Wall, *Staging Domesticity: Household Work and English Identity in Early Modern Drama* (New York: Cambridge University Press, 2002).

[30] Barbe, *The French Perfumer* (London, 1697), A2v.

[31] Diversion, from the French *divertissement*, translates as "entertainment".

[32] Brathwaite, *The Captive Captain, or, The Restrain'd Cavalier* (London, 1665), E2r– E2v.

"a Perfumer will pretend that his Essences came from *Montpellier*, or *Florence*, tho he made them at home."[33]

As this brief survey demonstrates, the labor of perfuming changed dramatically in the seventeenth century. The influx of aliens in London, along with the building of the New Exchange, redefined the occupational identity of "perfumer," aligning it with ready-made luxury commodities rather than the work of fumigating or perfuming a room. Whereas in the sixteenth century, the labor of perfuming was a crucial, if invisible, part of elite entertaining and rituals of hospitality, by the end of the seventeenth century, such labor became more visible, and at times entertaining in its own right, demonstrating the widespread impact of luxury consumption. By the end of the seventeenth century, even the labor of perfuming had been absorbed by consumer desires for perfume, yet this did little to challenge negative cultural associations with those merchandizing such commodities.

Such shifts provided those previously excluded from London's guilds with an economic opportunity to thrive, yet left them vulnerable to a host of cultural stigmas about the role of such labor in London. Perfume was believed to be an exotic, effeminate, luxury commodity rather than an act of labor, which allowed alien men and English women to merchandize it successfully. Once solely the purview of the elite, produced by laborers employed in royal households, perfume now infiltrated England's luxury markets and domestic realms, as more and more aliens and women sold it and as English housewives took up the labor of perfuming. As such, it was increasingly thought of as a deceptive tool of social advancement: strong scents could mask old identities and create new ones. As the next section demonstrates, London's stage histories document that "entertaining" perfumers are malodorous buffoons and social climbers, rather than successful entrepreneurs.

Stage Histories: Selling Perfumers

Prior to the 1630s, perfumer was not a widely recognized profession in London. Despite this fact, there are a striking number of perfumers in late Elizabethan and early Stuart plays: besides Shakespeare's *Much Ado About Nothing* (1598), perfumers appear in Marston's *What You Will* (1601), Jonson's *Cynthia's Revels* (1601), Chapman's *Sir Giles Goosecap* (1601), Heywood's *If You Know Not Me, You Know No Bodie, Part II* (1605–1606), Middleton's *A Trick To Catch the Old One* (1608), Jonson's *Bartholomew Fair* (1614), and *A New Way to Pay Old Debts* (1625), Massinger's *The Fatal Dowry* (1632), and Mabbe's closet drama, *The Spanish Bawd* (1631), an English translation of Rojas's *Celestina*.[34] Some of

---

[33]   Brown, *A Collection of Miscellany Poems, Letters, &c. by Mr Brown, &c.* (London, 1699), 204.

[34]   Though Mabbe's play is a closet drama and was not performed on English stages in this period, I include it in this analysis for its exploration of female perfumers, particularly its coinage of the term "perfumeress."

these perfumers are fumigators; most are purveyors of perfume. Almost all are associated with deception. Whereas the economic history of perfumers outlined above reveals how the term perfume changed from an act of labor into a luxury good, the theatrical history of perfumers documents not only a profound cultural fascination with the purveyors of such popular goods but also a widespread (and paradoxical) belief that the purveyors of such elite, expensive, and sweet-smelling perfumes stank. As these representations demonstrate, the smell of perfume continually defines the occupational identity of the perfumer as a malodorous and deceptive social outsider.

Early representations of perfumers emphasized their outsider status. Like Borachio in *Much Ado About Nothing*, these early perfumers were associated with masquerades, deceptions, bed tricks, class transgressions and other theatrical plots hinged to social climbing. Their perfumes or fumes are often dangerous tools within such plots. In *Much Ado About Nothing*, scented fumes conceal Borachio, allowing him to spy on elite intimacies. In other plays, perfumes have almost diabolical power. For example, perfumes are dangerous aphrodisiacs in Shakespeare's *A Midsummer Night's Dream*, Middleton's *Women Beware Women*, and Massinger's *The Renegado*. Such representations hinted at unseen dangers of foreigners and foreign commodities infiltrating England's domestic realms.[35]

On English stages, xenophobic fears about London's changing economic demography coalesced around representations of malodorous, foreign perfumers. Though Italian and French perfumes symbolized the power of the theater to transform and transport audience members, representations of Italian and French perfumers dwelled upon a connection between bodily smell and occupational expertise. These plays explore the effects of perfuming. In them, the smell of their labor defines the perfumer's occupational identity. As the production and consumption of luxury perfumes increased in London and "perfumer" emerged as a recognizable—and profitable—profession practiced predominantly by foreigners and women in English markets, early fascination with the labor of perfuming waned and was replaced by outright satire in plays. Perfumers became effeminate, ridiculous fops, stinking of their own commodities. Their role in these theatrical markets and shops creates the allure of luxury, only to dispel it. Whereas once their labor was, to borrow Borachio's apt description, perfumed entertainment, in these later plays, perfumers stink onstage.

The shift of perfumery from a service industry or craft to a merchandising industry is one way to understand this stage history. In Marston's *What You Will*, perfumers' wares are part of the play's engagement with identity, social structures of marriage, commerce, and theatrical fantasy. In this play, Francisco Soranzo,

---

[35]   For more on how Catholic incense was reconfigured as perfume on English stages, see Jonathan Gil Harris, "The Smell of Macbeth," *Shakespeare Quarterly* 58.4 (2008): 483–4. On early modern English Protestant fears about Catholics, see Frances Dolan, *Whores of Babylon: Catholicism, Gender and Seventeenth-Century Print Culture* (Ithaca: Cornell University Press, 1999).

a perfumer, impersonates the play's hero, Albano, a merchant presumed to have drowned at sea, in order to delay the marriage of Albano's wife, Celia, to Laverdure, a Frenchman. As George Geckle summarizes, "the point [of the play] is that three men will by *wit* attempt to thwart the *will* of both Laverdure and Celia."[36] When Albano returns, he assumes the identity of Soranzo, associating the loss of his identity with the elusive, ephemeral aspect of the perfumer's wares, both the ones he purports to sell and those Soranzo wears to impersonate him:

> And now my soul is skipp'd into a perfumer, a gutter master ... the world's turned juggler, castes mistes before our eyes ... if Albanos name were liable to scence, that I could taste or touch or see, or feele it, it might tice beleefe, but since tis voice, and ayre, come to the Muscat boy. Franscisco, that's my name tis right, I, I, What do you lack? What do you lack right that's my cry (E3v-E4r).

Echoing the perfumer's commercial cries, "What do you lack?" Albano describes his loss of self in terms of perfume's lack of substance, mutability, and capacity to transform or deceive. Misty airs confuse the eye and Albano's identity is reduced to airy nothings. The play does not ascribe any lingering scent to Soranzo through which his identity as the real perfumer might be discerned; rather, it deploys the art of perfumery metaphorically to capture the elusiveness of identity.

By contrast, Ben Jonson's nameless perfumer in *Cynthia's Revels* proudly asserts a professional identity grounded in technological knowledge that counters the social privilege of "protean" courtiers who use his wares to "perfume their hair." Amorphous, perhaps the most degenerate of courtiers, purchases perfumes and declares that he "shall be simple, to discouer [his] simples." The perfumer retorts,

> Simple? ... I have in it muske, civet, amber, phoenicobalanus, the decoctions of tumericke, sesame, nard, spikenard, clamus, odoratus, stacte, opobalsamum, amomum, storax, ladanum, aspalathum, opoponax, oenanthe. And what of all these now? What are you the better?[37]

Answering Albano's aristocratic, ventriloquized cry of "What do you lack?" in Marston's play with a stunning array of complex, perfume ingredients, Jonson's perfumer ridicules the courtier's desire for "simple" simples. Distilling his disdain, the perfumer's "simples" are anything but; his professional mastery of perfuming challenges Amorphous' assertion of social privilege. Despite such mastery, he finally asserts his expertise through the consumer's direct experience of the commodity. When Amorphous queries if the perfume is "rich," the perfumer commands him to "taste it, smell it," and concludes: "I assure you it is pure Benjamin" (X3v). The play thus associates perfume with hedonistic pleasure and ultimate luxury. Earlier

---

[36] See Geckle, *John Marston's Drama: Themes, Images, Sources* (Madison, N.J.: Fairleigh Dickinson University Press, 1980), 93. All citations of the play are from Marston, *What You Will* (London, 1607).

[37] See Jonson, *Cynthia Revells*, in *The Workes of Benjamin Jonson* (London, 1616), 4.3, T3r.

in the play, Mercury satirizes Hedon's penchant for luxuries by locating it within London's economic map: "He is thought a very necessary perfume for the presence, and for that only cause welcome thither: six milliners shops afford you not the like scent" (R3v). Hedon's seeks a perfume that can out scent those produced by six milliners, producing a unique luxury "presence" that defines his identity.

Heywood's representation of perfumers echoes this point, demonstrating how the commodity came to define perfumers on stage and off. The second part of *If You Know Not Me, You Know No Bodie* (1605) dramatizes the building of Gresham's Royal Exchange in the 1570s. In its depiction of London's early luxury markets, tradesmen stink. Quick, servant to the yeoman, Honesty, brags that he has "served Sent the Perfumer, Tallow the Currier, Quarrell the Glasier, and some three or foure more of our poore smelts so this morning" (C3r). Perfuming, tanning, and glazing are all professions known by their olfactory stench, as Quick jokes. Smelts, small fish known for their distinctive odor, mark this class of malodorous professionals. Such jokes define the identity of the perfumer solely in terms of his/her distinctive stench. Here, scent is an indelible marker of working subjectivity, rather than a tool of protean, social mobility or mutability. In Middleton's *A Trick to Catch the Old One* (1608), a play whose plot revolves around a courtesan's ability to impersonate a rich, country widow, the identity of perfumers is described by Hoard as refreshingly obvious: "perfumers, of all men, had need carry themselves uprightly; for if they were once knaves, they would be smelt out quickly" (4.4.40–41).[38] The perfumer, who "desires to be entertained" by the newly wealthy Hoard, is already "under his nose" (4.4.65, 70). Yet if the scent of the perfumer's own working subjectivity is cast as indelible, his wares nonetheless have the power to transform the scent, and hence the identity, of others: Hoard himself asks the perfumer to "cast a better savour upon the knaves, to take away the sent of my Taylores feet, and my Barbers Lotioum-water" (4.4. 70–73).

As perfume became more readily apparent in London's luxury markets, consumption of perfumes required its own form of olfactory expertise. George Chapman's eponymous Gyles Goosecappe is described as having "an excelent skil in al maner of perfumes, & if you bring him gloves fro[m] fortie pence, to forty Shillings a paire he will tell you the price of them to two pence."[39] Goosecappe's ability to purchase perfumes morphs into an extended joke about perfumery and seduction: according to his servant, Tales, Goosecappe will perfume Lady Penelope's gloves "most dilicately, and give them the right Spanish Titillation," a "pretty kinde of terme newe come up in perfuming, which they call a Titillation."[40]

---

[38] All citations are from Heywood, *The Second Part of If You Know Not Me, You Know No Bodie* (London, 1606) and Thomas Middleton, "A Trick To Catch the Old One," (ed.) Valerie Wayne, in *The Complete Works of Thomas Middleton*, (eds.) Gary Taylor and John Lavagnino (Oxford: Oxford University Press, 2007), 373–414.

[39] See Chapman, *Sir Gyles Goosecappe Knight A Comedie Presented by the Children of the Chappell* (London, 1606), Actus Secundi, Sæna Prima, D3r–v.

[40] Ibid.

Goosecappe's foppishness flirts with labor, as his titillations become distillations. Like the perfumed diversions in Barbe's *French Perfumer*, Goosecappe's "titillations" demonstrate how consuming perfumes could be construed as entertainment.

As *Gyles Goosecappe* makes clear, representations of perfumers in early modern drama change in the first quarter of the seventeenth century as perfumes become recognizable commodities. The perfumer, now a retailer of perfumes, emerges as a stereotype, a theatrical, effeminate fop whose aim is profit. For example, in the 1620 Salisbury "show or play of 12 parts," courtiers of King James's Scottish bedchamber lampooned a wide range of identities, professional or otherwise. Linking performances of class and ethnicity to theatricality, Lord Buckingham and his men entertained themselves as an Irish footman, a western pirate, a Welsh advocate, a cobbler and "teacher of Birds to whistle," a "neat" barber, a tailer, a merryman, a cook, a bearward, a perfumer, and finally, a Puritan "that marred the play." Here, the perfumer seems anything but a legitimate occupation; rather, he is part and parcel of the theatrical world of the "play" that the Puritan seeks to mar. Likewise, the page in Massinger's *The Fatal Dowry* (1620), describes his "lord, tailor, a perfumer, a barber, and a pair of monsieurs," concluding miserably: "three to three; as little wit in the one as honesty in the other" (Hr). Perfumers, Massinger's play suggests, are witless and dishonest.[41]

Finally, in Mabbe's 1631 translation of Rojas's *Celestina,* the eponymous "perfumeresse" manufactures deception. She is an "honest whore" and "a grave matrone," dwelling near the Tanners on the outskirts of the city, rather than in its fashionable center. Her economic power is geographically and economically circumscribed. Working "six severall Trades" to make a living, Celestina was a

> Laundresse, a Perfumeresse, a Former of faces, a Mender of crackt maiden-heads, a Bawd, and had some smatch of a Witch … at home in her owne house shee made perfumes, false and counterfeit Storax, Benjamin, Gumme, Anime, Amber, Civit, Powders, Muske and Mosqueta: Shee had a chamber full of Limbecks, little vials, pots, some of earth, some of glasse, some brasse, and some tinne, formed in a thousand fashions. Shee distilled sweet-waters, of Roses, of Flowers, of Oranges, of Jesmine, of three-leafed Grasse, of Woodbine, of Gilly-flowers, incorporated with Muske and Civit, and sprinkled with wine.[42]

Latent in this representation of a "perfumeresse" is a deep cultural ambivalence about women's creation of perfumes. Rather than asserting professional expertise through "rich" and "pure" Benjamin, Mabbe's perfumeresse "counterfeits" perfumes, using them to repair maidenheads and faces. Like Borachio, Mabbe's

---

[41]   *Calendar of State Papers and Manuscripts Relating to English Affairs Existing in the Archives and Collections of Venice and in Other Libraries of Northern Italy: 1619–1621*, vol. 16, (ed.) Allen B. Hinds (London: H.M. Stationery Office, 1947), 290. See also Massinger, *The Fatall Dowry* (London, 1632).

[42]   All citations are from Mabbe, *The Spanish Bawd* (London, 1631), 15.

perfumeresse is a jill-of-all-trades, wrecking just as much havoc on the social world of this play. However, her "entertainments" are diabolical rather than professional. Reversing the gendered implications of perfuming practices that sought to "impregnate" objects with burning fumes, Mabbe's perfumeresse seems to have more in common with the weird sisters in Macbeth than she does with Mrs. Hasset of the Royal Exchange.[43]

Conclusion

As this brief survey of theatrical and economic histories of perfumers suggests, the sweet smell of perfume defined both the labor of perfuming and the working subjectivities of perfumers. The scent of perfume was thus part of a complicated, shifting smellscape, one in which the sweet scent of luxury was conflated with the labor producing it. Both, I argue, were defined as "entertainment." Although these stage representations often mocked perfumers as malodorous, deceptive social climbers, they document the emergence of perfumer as a recognizable occupation in early modern London. Borachio's performance, like those of other entertaining perfumers on early modern stages, shaped emerging cultural associations about the art of perfumery.

Defined by their expertise and control over an invisible, ephemeral, and influential commodity, early modern perfumers produced and challenged established social networks of trade and exchange. As such, they offer a unique way to understand the development of occupational identities, the relationship between the smells of luxury and labor, and other meaningful "nothings" staged in Shakespeare's *Much Ado*, such as the link between social status and theatrical deception. "Entertained" as a perfumer, Borachio's occupational identity of "perfumer" afforded him a metaphoric and material stealth: hidden behind the arras, and behind scented smoke, Borachio learns valuable information about the social world of Messina. And, as I have tried to demonstrate here, the ephemeral labor of such scented entertainments also provides valuable information about how early modern London's social and economic realms shaped phenomenological responses to perfumers' bodies. Perfume's unique ephemerality was not just consumed by London's elites, but it also shaped the occupational identities and working subjectivities of those making and selling it, fueling both economic opportunity and xenophobic fears about outsiders and their unseen influence in London's markets.

---

[43] Ian Donaldson, "Looking Sideways: Jonson, Shakespeare, and the Myths of Envy," *Ben Jonson Journal* 8 (2001): 1–22. On the connections between Mabbe's bearded perfumeresse and the weird sisters, see Mark Albert Johnson, "Bearded Women in Early Modern England," *SEL* 47.1 (2007): 1–28.

Chapter 5
Englishmen for My Money: Work and Social Conflict?

Tom Rutter

A recurrent and obvious dynamic in early modern citizen comedy is the opposition between those who do and those who do not have to work for a living.[1] If, as Theodore B. Leinwand suggests, this form of drama is characterized by "social conflict" in which "Merchant-citizens, gentleman-gallants, and wives, whores, widows, and maids represent gender or status groups," then what this often amounts to is conflict between men whose income derives from commercial labor and men whose income derives from land.[2] The role of female characters in such conflicts is not, of course, a necessarily passive one: in *Theater of a City: The Places of London Comedy, 1598–1642*, Jean E. Howard emphasizes the scope these comedies offer for female agency in the form of entrepreneurialism, self-reinvention, and the pursuit of pleasure, and indeed the alternative title of the play discussed in this chapter, *A Woman Will Have Her Will*, indicates that an interest in the desiring female subject is present from the beginnings of the genre.[3] However, as well as comprising a range of gendered status groups in their own right, female characters frequently offer a means by which social conflicts can be played out in sexual terms: as Douglas Bruster puts it, for example, the cuckoldries of urban comedy tap into a myth whereby the "patiently productive husband … is robbed and mocked by a picaresque opportunist." "Methods of labor constitute the crux of the struggle," with the craftiness of the seducer pitted against the patient craft of the husband: in the words of Quomodo, the villainous merchant-usurer in Middleton's *Michaelmas Term* (1604–1606), "They're busy 'bout our wives, we 'bout their lands" (1.2.112).[4]

---

[1]   I use the term "citizen comedy" on the grounds that its terms of reference are potentially broader and more inclusive than those of "city comedy," which Brian Gibbons describes as "distinct in its satiric mode from chronicle plays like *The Shoemaker's Holiday*" in *Jacobean City Comedy*, 2nd edition. (London: Methuen, 1980), 1.

[2]   Leinwand, *The City Staged: Jacobean Comedy, 1603–1613* (Madison: University of Wisconsin Press, 1986), 8–9.

[3]   Howard, *Theater of a City: The Places of London Comedy, 1598–1642* (Philadelphia: University of Pennsylvania Press, 2007), 114–61.

[4]   Bruster, *Drama and the Market in the Age of Shakespeare* (Cambridge: Cambridge University Press, 1992), 50–51; Thomas Middleton, *Michaelmas Term*, (ed.) Theodore B. Leinwand, in *Thomas Middleton: The Collected Works*, (eds.) Gary Taylor and John Lavagnino (Oxford: Oxford University Press, 2007).

It is only in the pursuit of pleasure that the young gallant tends to busy himself, however. The figure of the prodigal, who so often appears in this type of comedy, is by definition an idle one, and it is invariably by "the morality of thrift and industry" that such characters "are judged and found wanting"—even when, as in *Eastward Ho!* (1605), this bourgeois morality is itself parodically subverted.[5] Jonson, Chapman, and Marston's play rests on the comically overstated contrast between the idle Quicksilver and the dutiful Golding, "two prentices, the one of a boundless prodigality, the other of a most hopeful industry" (1.1.77–9). While Golding's labor in his vocation is rewarded (with comically absurd speed) with the rank of alderman, penurious downfall awaits Quicksilver, whose social attitudes are encapsulated in his exhortation, "be like a gentleman, be idle; the curse of man is labour" (1.1.114–15).[6]

If "class warfare" between citizens and gentry, or workers and non-workers, is indeed central to early modern citizen comedy, then it is curious that arguably the earliest comedy in this tradition is one where such conflict is made firmly subordinate to other rivalries.[7] William Haughton's 1598 play *Englishmen for My Money* has been called "the first London comedy," "the earliest city comedy," "the first English stage comedy set specifically in London."[8] Its plot seems to offer an archetypal citizen-comic structure, having at its center the widowed merchant Pisaro, who wishes to marry his three daughters, Laurentia, Marina, and Mathea, to three merchants, Vandal, Alvaro, and Delion. The daughters, however, prefer three gentlemen, Heigham, Harvey, and Walgrave, in whom admiration for Pisaro's daughters is joined by the desire to regain through marriage the lands they have mortgaged to him. Walgrave's vow, "We'll work our lands out of Pisaro's daughters, / And cancel all our bonds in their great bellies" (4.1.114–15) seems to offer a classic instance of the way in which the sexual intrigue of citizen comedy can serve as a metaphor for class-based economic conflict.[9] However, the thing that makes *Englishmen for My Money* atypical is, of course, the sentiment referred to in its title. Though Laurentia, Marina, and Mathea seem to have inherited the English nationality of their mother, Pisaro is Portuguese, while Vandal is Dutch,

---

[5]   Alexander Leggatt, *Citizen Comedy in the Age of Shakespeare* (Toronto: University of Toronto Press, 1973), 33–53, 49.

[6]   Ben Jonson, George Chapman and John Marston, *Eastward Ho!*, (ed.) C.G. Petter (London: Benn, 1973, repr. A & C Black, 1994).

[7]   Leggatt, *Citizen Comedy*, 9.

[8]   Leggatt, *Citizen Comedy*, 7; Leinwand, *The City Staged*, 7; Howard, *Theater of a City*, 38.

[9]   William Haughton, *Englishmen for My Money*, in *Three Renaissance Usury Plays*, (ed.) Lloyd Edward Kermode (Manchester: Manchester University Press, 2009). The current essay was drafted before Kermode's edition appeared, and in its original form cited the first quarto of the play, *English-men for My Money; or, A Pleasant Comedy, Called, A Woman Will Have Her Will* (London, 1616).

Alvaro Italian, and Delion French.[10] Socio-economic rivalry between gentlemen and merchants is thus joined with national rivalry between Englishmen and foreigners.

If critical reactions to the play are anything to go by, the former struggle seems to take a firm second place to the latter. Leinwand disqualifies the play from consideration in *The City Staged* on the grounds of "the jingoism that motivates the tedious plot":

> Haughton's uncritical endorsement of the careers of three thriftless English gallants, and his wearisome mockery of their rivals—three wealthy, foreign merchants—suggests that he is uninterested in either the conflict, or the sources of the conflict, that pitted one status group against another.[11]

However, even critics more generously disposed towards the play have tended to privilege the national competition above the socio-economic one, concurring with A.J. Hoenselaars's view that "the issue of nationalities is central" and "underlies nearly all relationships and incidents in the play."[12] "Anti-alien feeling was at a pitch during the early 1590s," as Emma Smith notes, and this provides an important element of the play's non-dramatic context. Smith goes on to emphasize the problematization of national identity inherent in the sisters' mixed family background, reading *Englishmen for My Money* in the light of both the "legal complexities of maternal inheritance" and "the symbolic complexities of the trope of the mother tongue."[13] Howard sees the play as an attempt to deal with anxieties concerning the presence and influence of foreign merchants within the City of London and to give a socially mixed audience a stronger sense of their own identity as Londoners, although she does note how, in "what was to become a stock convention of city plays, a merchant is ... outsmarted by members of the impoverished landed gentry who compensate for shallow pockets with their witty charm."[14]

One reading of the play that does devote significant space to socio-economic as well as national rivalries is that of Lloyd Edward Kermode, who sees Pisaro as the embodiment of contemporary fears regarding the increasing pervasiveness of usury in English economic life. Kermode identifies *Englishmen for My Money* and *Jack Drum's Entertainment*, written by John Marston in 1600, as successive stages in the "metamorphosis of the usurer ... from foreign Jew to English non-Jew," for while Mamon, the usurer in Marston's play, shares Pisaro's stereotypically Jewish

---

[10] Emma Smith, "'So much English by the Mother': Gender, Foreigners, and the Mother Tongue in William Haughton's *Englishmen for My Money*," *Medieval and Renaissance Drama in England* 13 (2000): 173.

[11] Leinwand, *The City Staged*, 7.

[12] Hoenselaars, *Images of Englishmen and Foreigners in the Drama of Shakespeare and His Contemporaries* (Rutherford: Fairleigh Dickinson University Press; London: Associated University Presses, 1992), 53–4.

[13] Smith, "'So much English by the Mother,'" 166, 177.

[14] Howard, *Theater of a City*, 29–49, 44.

large nose, he does not share his foreign nationality (it should be pointed out that neither character is either unambiguously Jewish or unambiguously non-Jewish). The resident foreigner Pisaro serves as a warning that the supposedly alien vice of usury is increasingly gaining a foothold in London (a warning that will be borne out by the English Mamon), and the gallants' successful courting of his daughters enables them to overcome at once "the father's usury ... and the daughters' mixed birth."[15] National pride and economic anxiety are thus inextricably intertwined in the play. However, Kermode, like the other critics I have briefly surveyed above, treats Pisaro essentially as an outsider, or at best as an interloper; the conflict he isolates in the play is between the English and a practice (usury) perceived to be non-English.[16] In the analysis that follows, by contrast, I shall be focusing on tensions central to the play that relate only incidentally to nationality: in particular, the tensions between working and non-working subjects that, as I have suggested above, are integral to citizen comedy. I shall argue that Haughton's play uses xenophobia as a distraction from these tensions, and that its reasons for doing so relate to the circumstances of the London theatre prior to 1599.

The fact that critics of *Englishmen for My Money* have interested themselves primarily in questions of national identity may simply reflect modern interpretational priorities, but I would suggest that it also reveals something about how the play works. While commentators have tended to regard the play's nationalism as its defining feature, another way of seeing it is as a distraction from the other social conflicts at work in *Englishmen for My Money*—conflicts which would become much more evident in later plays like *Michaelmas Term* and *Eastward Ho!*, but which can nevertheless be observed in Haughton's play. Pisaro's opening soliloquy, for example, identifies him not only as an international merchant and a usurer, but as the class enemy of gentlemen:

> I wax rich, though many gentlemen
> By my extortion comes to misery:
> Amongst the rest, three English gentlemen
> Have pawned to me their livings and their lands,
> Each several hoping—though their hopes are vain—
> By marriage of my daughters to possess
> Their patrimonies and their lands again. (1.1.19–25)

Pisaro's subsequent remarks suggest that he does not merely see gentlemen like Heigham, Harvey and Walgrave as victims to be exploited, but as representatives

---

[15]   Lloyd Edward Kermode, "After Shylock: The 'Judaiser' in England," *Renaissance and Reformation* 20.4 (1996): 6, 11. Material from this article is incorporated in Kermode's introduction to *Three Renaissance Usury Plays*, which offers a detailed account of early modern debates concerning usury and of the way questions of nationality and religion figured in those debates. Kermode also provides a survey of literary and dramatic treatments of the usurer, and of the critical literature relating to the three plays included in his edition.

[16]   Hoenselaars similarly notes in passing that Haughton can be seen as interrogating the mercantilist ethic "in a contemporary and recognizable domestic setting," "introducing a Jewish foreigner to represent the reprehensible element" (*Images of Englishmen*, 55).

of a way of life that he despises. Berating the scholar Anthony for acting as a go-between for the gentlemen and his daughters, he complains that Anthony has been "Urging the love of those I most abhorred": "Unthrifts, beggars—what is worse" (1.1.144–5). He manifests this disapproval directly to the gentlemen later in the play, admonishing them, "Will you be wived? First learn to keep a wife. / Learn to be thrifty; learn to keep your lands; / And learn to pay your debts" (4.1.129–31). His lack of sympathy for them seems to be grounded in a bourgeois ethic of thrift and good husbandry, without the complacent irony that allows Touchstone in *Eastward Ho!* to ask, "How would merchants thrive, if gentlemen would not be unthrifts?" (1.1.32–3).

It is not only Pisaro who expresses class-based sentiments in terms of work and idleness, or thriftiness and unthriftiness. The gentlemen's indebtedness to him seems to derive less from a need for ready cash to make specific purchases than from a sense that being a gentleman requires a careless prodigality with money. As they approach Pisaro in the Exchange with a view to borrowing more, Heigham explains to him that gentlemen "must want no coin, / Nor are they slaves unto it, when they have" (1.3.62–3)—the unspoken implication, perhaps, being "nor are they slaves unto it *as you merchants are*." Their sense of a class identity is unappealingly manifested later on in the scene in their treatment of a sunburnt Post, or courier, newly arrived from Spain:

Heigham. Came you, sir, from Spain lately?

Post. Ay, sir. Why ask you that?

Harvey. Marry, sir, thou seems to have been in the hot countries, thy face looks so like a piece of rusty bacon. Had thy host at Plymouth meat enough in the house when thou wert there?

Post. What though he had not, sir? But he had, how then?

Harvey. Marry, thank God for it, for otherwise he would doubtless have cut thee out in rashers to have eaten thee. Thou lookst as thou wert through broiled already.

Post. You have said, sir, but I am no meat for his mowing, nor yours neither. If I had you in place where, you should find me tough enough in disgestion, I warrant you.

Walgrave. [*Makes to draw a weapon.*] What, will you swagger, sirrah? Will ye swagger?

Browne. [*To Walgrave.*] I beseech you, sir, hold your hand! [*To Post.*] Get home, ye patch! Cannot you suffer gentlemen jest with you?

Post. I'd teach him a gentle trick, an I had him of the burse; but I'll watch him a good turn, I warrant him. (1.3.179–96)

The gentlemen's belief that the Post's complexion gives them license to ridicule him derives from the way in which (as Kim F. Hall observes when discussing Mary Wroth's *Urania*) white skin in the Renaissance served to articulate class difference as well as racial difference. Whiteness is "the sign of membership of (or aspiration to) a leisured, aristocratic class in which bodies are purest white because they can escape signs of labor such as exposure to the sun."[17] Conversely, the Post's tanned skin is the sign of his status as a worker. It is not clear whether the merchant Browne's dismissal of him, "Cannot you suffer gentlemen jest with you?," indicates acceptance of this ideology or merely the sense that for those involved in merchandise and its related activities, being mocked by gentlemen goes with the territory. At any rate, the gentlemen themselves are ready to invoke their class status as a rationale for their treatment of Pisaro, Harvey describing as "a gallant jest" the idea of taking him up on the invitation to dinner he inadvertently extended to them (1.3.313).

Social tensions like these are identifiable in the play, and while they might be called class-based or status-based, class allegiance inescapably involves a particular relationship with work. Pisaro's servant Frisco complains in his opening speech that "A man were better to live a lord's life and do nothing, than a serving creature and never be idle" (1.1.153–4), and his association of high social status with idleness echoes Sir Thomas Smith's definition of a gentleman as someone able to "live idly and without manuall labour."[18] However, such lines of conflict, visible though they are, are much less noticeable than the national conflicts to which critics of the play have tended to devote more space. To an audience, much more striking than the fact that Pisaro's preferred suitors are merchants is the fact that they are foreign, since we are reminded of it whenever they open their mouths:

> *Alvaro.* Me dincke such a piculo man as you be sal have no de such grande lucke madere.

> *Delion.* Non; da Monsieur, an he be so grande amorous op de damoisella, he sal have Mawdlyn de witt wenshe in de Kichine by maiter Pisaro's leave. (2.1.135–9)

It is their status as foreigners, more than their status as merchants, that Pisaro's daughters find objectionable, and their satirical descriptions of their suitors partake of the play's general atmosphere of crass xenophobia:

> *Mathea.* My Frenchman comes upon me with the 'sa, sa, sa.
> Sweet madam pardone moy I pra.'
> And then out goes his hand, down goes his head,
> Swallows his spittle, frizzles his beard ... (2.3.19–22)

[17] Hall, *Things of Darkness: Economies of Race and Gender in Early Modern England* (Ithaca: Cornell University Press, 1995), 209.

[18] Smith, *De Republica Anglorum*, (ed.) Mary Dewar (Cambridge: Cambridge University Press, 1982), 72.

Not only is national rivalry central to the play's dramatic effect: it cuts across class boundaries to unite the English characters against the foreign threat to English maidenhood. At the beginning of the play, Anthony, the tutor to the three sisters, passes on letters and gifts from their English lovers, as well as urging their suits; Pisaro's accusation that Anthony has favored them "all because they are your countrymen" (1.1.146) is confirmed by Anthony's later explanation, "To help my countrymen I cast about, / For strangers' loves blaze fresh, but soon burn out" (4.2.58–9). This solidarity between the needy scholar and the idle gallants persists throughout the play and contrasts noticeably with the social disengagement and class envy evident in scholars like Asper/Macilente in Jonson's *Every Man Out of His Humour* (1599) and Laureo in Dekker, Chettle and Haughton's *Patient Grissil* (1599–1600). For his part Frisco, Pisaro's serving-man, expresses hostility towards his master's intentions and encourages Heigham, Harvey and Walgrave to take advantage of his master's absence: "My master is abroad and my young mistresses at home. If you can do any good on them before the Frenchman come, why so! Ah, gentlemen, do not suffer a litter of languages to spring up amongst us" (1.2.102–5). As Emma Smith notes, in Frisco's invocation of "a litter of languages" "the unspeakable possibility of international marriage and its mongrel offspring is transferred to the resultant linguistic progeny."[19] Charged with leading Vandal by night from Bucklersbury to his master's house, Frisco asks, "what wise man in a kingdom would send me for the Dutchman? Does he think I'll not cozen him?" (2.3.276–7). Tricking foreigners seems to be something any right-thinking English serving-man would do on principle—although Frisco does subsequently express his intention to "have a fling at the wenches" in Vandal's place (3.1.12–13). The English gentlemen similarly misdirect the foreign suitors to prevent them from keeping the nocturnal meeting with his daughters that Pisaro has arranged:

Alvaro. I pray de grazia, wat be dis plashe? Wat do ye call dit street?

Heigham. What, sir; why, Leadenhall: could you not see the four spouts as you came along?

Alvaro. Certenemento Leadenhall. I hit my hed by de way—dare may be de voer spouts. I pray de grazia, wish be de wey to Crutche Friars?

Heigham. How, to Crutched Friars? Marry, you must go along till you come to the pump, and then turn on your right hand. (3.2.56–64)

Leggatt justifies his claim that *Englishmen for My Money* is the first citizen comedy with the observation that Haughton seems "to use his local colour with the self-consciousness of an innovator," and here the fetishizing of London's streets and street furniture (the spouts, the pump) is much in evidence.[20] Like their broken

---

[19]   Smith, "'So much English by the Mother,'" 173.
[20]   Leggatt, *Citizen Comedy*, 7.

English, the inability of the foreigners to decipher this topography symbolically excludes them from the community the play celebrates, as well as presenting a practical obstacle to success with Pisaro's daughters.[21]

While rivalries between workers and non-workers are certainly discernible in *Englishmen for My Money*, then, they are both less obvious than national rivalries and to some extent mitigated within the play by those rivalries, as potentially antagonistic groups (gentlemen, scholars, serving-men) collaborate in vanquishing the alien threat. The critics to whom I have already referred offer a variety of explanations for the play's treatment of foreigners: the need to "lay the blame for England's economic problems at the door of some hated Other" (Kermode); to "construct legible and recognizable fictions of both Englishness and non-Englishness in order to produce an idea of national identity" (Smith); to "negotiate ... the alien presence at the heart of London's merchant world" (Howard).[22] I do not wish to dispute any of those suggestions, but as to the more specific question of why class antagonisms should be subordinated to national ones, I would offer a further explanation that relates to the circumstances of the London theatre in 1598.

Between the years 1594 and 1599, the London theatrical marketplace was dominated by the Lord Chamberlain's Men, who performed mainly at the Theatre prior to the opening of the Globe, and the Lord Admiral's Men at the Rose. The Children of Paul's had ceased playing in 1590, apparently following the Marprelate affair, and for most of the 1590s London's theatergoing culture does not seem to have been particularly stratified on social grounds, the Chamberlain's and the Admiral's running "a similar repertoire of plays" that tried to appeal to "a homogeneous, all-inclusive social range."[23] Performing as they did in large, open-air theatres that could seat thousands at a time, it did not make sense for either company to seek to restrict its audience appeal to one particular group, and indeed Roslyn Lander Knutson has argued that a significant element of each company's commercial strategy was to copy the successes of the other.[24] However, when the Children of Paul's recommenced playing in 1599, to be followed by the Children of the Chapel in 1600, both companies seem to have attempted to capitalize on the small size of their playhouses and the relatively high cost of entrance by presenting

---

[21]   Howard points out, however, that "The joke seems to depend on what in truth was an unstable distinction between aliens and native Londoners that obscures not only how long many stranger merchants resided within the city and how extensive their knowledge of it could be, but also how many English-speaking Londoners were foreigners, that is, people born elsewhere in England and not officially made free of the city and at least initially having little familiarity with it" (*Theater of a City*, 40–41).

[22]   Kermode, "After Shylock," 5; Smith, "'So much English by the Mother,'" 165; Howard, *Theater of a City*, 38.

[23]   Andrew Gurr, *Playgoing in Shakespeare's London*, 2nd edition. (Cambridge: Cambridge University Press, 1996), 153, 158.

[24]   Roslyn Lander Knutson, *The Repertory of Shakespeare's Company 1594–1613* (Fayetteville: University of Arkansas Press, 1991), 40.

their drama as socially exclusive, as in the following extract from *Jack Drum's Entertainment* (1600):

> *Sir Edward.* … I sawe the Children of *Powles* last night,
> And troth they pleasde mee prettie, prettie well,
> The Apes in time will do it hansomely.
>
> *Planet.* Ifaith I like the Audience that frequenteth there
> With much applause: A man shall not be choakte
> With the stench of Garlicke, nor be pasted
> To the barmy Jacket of a Beer-brewer.
>
> *Brabant Junior.* Tis a good gentle Audience …[25]

While it is far from certain that such passages reflected a genuine absence of workers from the playhouses of the children's companies, it can more safely be said that plays written for both companies sought to depict their performance spaces as socially elevated and to distance their form of theatre from the idea of work, with its connotations of social inferiority.[26] Work took on a significance in distinguishing between different theatrical cultures that it had not had before. Furthermore, it has been argued that one effect of this attempt by the children's companies to align themselves with the social elite was to encourage a divergence between the repertories of the adult companies, the Admiral's and the Earl of Worcester's Men "catering for an increasingly narrow and conservative citizen taste," the Chamberlain's "competing with the boys and their new fashions" while trying to maintain a broad audience base.[27]

The subordinating of social rivalries to national ones that I have tried to identify in *Englishmen for My Money* can be seen as reflecting an earlier period, when both main adult companies attempted to appeal to a wide range of theatergoers and when a straightforward alignment either with a non-laboring elite or with laboring commoners would have been undesirable. A comparable dynamic can be observed in Thomas Dekker's play *The Shoemaker's Holiday* (Admiral's Men, 1599), where (in David Scott Kastan's words) "the social and economic tensions that are revealed"—in particular, friction between classes, and between English and foreign artisans—are obscured by a festive conclusion in which "Rafe and Jane are reunited, Lacy and Rose are wed, and class conflicts dissolve in the harmonies celebrated and confirmed in the Shrove Tuesday banquet in Leadenhall."[28]

---

[25] Gurr, *Playgoing in Shakespeare's London*, 26–7; John Marston, *Jacke Drums Entertainment* (London, 1601), H3v.

[26] Tom Rutter, *Work and Play on the Shakespearean Stage* (Cambridge: Cambridge University Press, 2008), 99–106.

[27] Gurr, *Playgoing in Shakespeare's London*, 157.

[28] Kastan, "Workshop and/as Playhouse: Comedy and Commerce in *The Shoemaker's Holiday*," *Studies in Philology* 84 (1987): 324.

(A somewhat different view of *The Shoemaker's Holiday*, not dissimilar to my own reading of *Englishmen for My Money*, is put forward in the current collection by John Archer, who sees the play's cartoon xenophobia as contributing to its festive atmosphere.) In *Englishmen for My Money*, national oppositions help to paper over class conflicts, rather than being resolved with them at the end of the play; but here, as in Dekker, the plot leads to a romantic ending in which Pisaro allows himself to be brought into the festive community:

> Is it even so? Why, then, I see that still,
> Do what we can, women will have their will.
> [.   .   .   .   .   .]
> And, gentlemen, I do entreat tomorrow
> That you will feast with me, for all this sorrow. (5.1.295–6, 304–5)

As Kermode points out, "Pisaro is finally the accepting father of comedy, not the 'Judas-like' villain his own words proclaim him at the beginning."[29] While the English gentlemen's contest with the foreign suitors ends with the latter's defeat, their struggle with the semi-Anglicized merchant-usurer gives rise to feasting and reconciliation.

In keeping with her view of *Englishmen for My Money* as in part a response to the presence of foreign merchants in London, Howard sees the festive conclusion of the play as a defusing of the threat Pisaro poses: "it is the work of the play's narrative structure to make this powerful alien presence pass—through his daughters' marriages—harmlessly into the national fabric, trailing his wealth behind him."[30] While the play's national conflict may be resolved with Pisaro being subsumed into Englishness, however, the same cannot be said about the socio-economic conflicts evident in *Englishmen for My Money*. There is substantially more in Pisaro's final speech than a mere capitulation to the inevitable:

> *Moore.* Master Pisaro, 'tis in vain to fret
> And fume and storm: it little now avails.
> These gentlemen have, with your daughters' help,
> Outstripped you in your subtle enterprises.
> And, therefore, seeing they are well descended,
> Turn hate to love, and let them have their loves.
>
> *Pisaro.* Is it even so? Why, then, I see that still,
> Do what we can, women will have their will.
> Gentlemen, you have outreached me now,
> Which ne'er, before you, any yet could do.
> You that I thought should be my sons indeed
> Must be content, since there's no hope to speed.
> Others have got what you did think to gain,

---

29   Kermode, "After Shylock," 12. The reference is to 1.1.28.
30   Howard, *Theater of a City*, 46.

And yet, believe me, they have took some pain.
Well, take them, there; and with them, God give joy.
And, gentlemen, I do entreat tomorrow
That you will feast with me, for all this sorrow.
Though you are wedded, yet the feast's not made:
Come, let us in, for all the storms are passed,
And heaps of joy will follow on as fast. (5.1.289–308)

The speeches of Pisaro and Moore interpret the events of the play in terms of commercial competitiveness: Pisaro has been "outstripped" and "outreached" by the English gentlemen, exceeded or surpassed in "subtle enterprises."[31] He uses the striking phrase "heaps of joy" to describe the prize they have gained, conflating marital bliss with the heaps of coin they may expect, and in a reversal of his earlier scorn for the idle gentlemen alludes to the labor or "pain" they have undergone in achieving their end. Furthermore, the language of outstripping and outreaching, and the reference to storms in the penultimate line, creates an implicit link between Pisaro's three daughters (one of whom, of course, is called Marina) and the three English ships, "the *Fortune*, your ship, the *Adventure*, and *Good Luck* of London," he earlier believed had been more literally outstripped by Spanish galleys (1.3.106–7), but which were saved by the weather.[32] In Alvaro's description, "after un piculo battalion, for un half hour de come a wind fra de north, and de sea go tumble here, and tumble dare, dat make de galleys run away for fear be almost drowned" (1.3.246–9). While one might expect the pirates to stand for the Englishmen stealing Pisaro's daughters from him, their foreignness and their ultimate lack of success mean that they are more closely paralleled by Vandal, Alvaro, and Delion. Pisaro assimilates the industriousness and ingenuity of the English gentlemen to his own mercantile ethic, rather than seeing the two as fundamentally opposed.

The sense that there is something in the gentlemen's amorous intrigues that mirrors Pisaro himself has been quietly anticipated in the play. His comment on the gentlemen in his opening speech, "For though I gild my temples with a smile, / It is but Judas-like, to work their ends" (1.1.27–8) is recalled in Walgrave's vow to "work our lands out of Pisaro's daughters" (4.1.114). Pisaro's pride at having "overreached the Englishmen" (4.1.5) parallels the promise Anthony makes to them, "I'll overreach the churl, and help my friend" (1.2.54), and for their part when the gentlemen attempt to extricate Anthony from the predicament his disguise as a Frenchman has placed him in, Harvey's expression of fear that "all our market will be spoiled and marred" (2.3.77) suggests that he has internalized the vocabulary of merchandise. The suggestion that the ostensibly idle gentleman may have something of the merchant in him is something we find elsewhere in citizen comedy: in the second part of Thomas Heywood's *If You Know Not Me You Know Nobody* (1605), for example, Sir Thomas Gresham, celebrated by the play as

---

[31]   *OED*, "outreach, *v*.," 4a and "outstrip, *v*. 1," 2.
[32]   *OED*, "outstrip, *v*. 1," 1; "To run or move faster than."

the founder of the Royal Exchange, comes to reflect on the roguery of his prodigal nephew with the words "When I was yong I doe remember well, / I was as very a knave as he is now," as if to imply that his escapades are an excellent preparation for a career as a merchant.[33] In *Englishmen for My Money* the rival work of Pisaro and the gentlemen, and the attempts at mutual overreaching that we see, lead up to a climax that involves Pisaro's defeat in the struggle for control over his daughters, but the victory of a mercantile ethic of industriousness and competition.

Ultimately, it is the working world of Pisaro and his fellow merchants, rather than the leisured world of Harvey, Heigham and Walgrave, that is central to *Englishmen for My Money*. As Howard points out, the Royal Exchange is a "principal setting" for its action, with a substantial scene that comprises almost an eighth of the play being set there.[34] To a striking extent, the play dramatizes the activities of which a merchant's work consists. We see Pisaro discussing the arrival of English ships with his fellow merchants, arguing over the payment of a bill of exchange, bargaining over the price of some cloths, receiving a letter from his factor, and trying to defer payment of several moneys until the Exchange Bell rings to announce the end of the day's business. The style of the letter, which Pisaro reads out, makes an effective contribution to the scene's verisimilitude:

> Our duty premised, and we have sent unto your worship sack, Seville oils, pepper, Barbary sugar, and such other commodities as we thought most requisite. We wanted money; therefore we are fain to take up £200 of Master Towerson's man, which by a bill of exchange sent to him, we would request your worship pay accordingly. ... The news here is that the English ships, the *Fortune*, your ship, the *Adventure*, and *Good Luck* of London, coasting along by Italy towards Turkey, were set upon by two Spanish galleys. What became of them we know not, but doubt much by reason of the weather's calmness. (1.3.100–5, 106–10)

Haughton seems to have based the wording of the letter on the practice of contemporary merchants and their employees, as its style resembles that of the sample letters included in John Browne's *The Marchants Avizo* (1589):

> After my duetie remembred unto your Worship ... you shall againe understand that on the 24. day of October, within 16. daies after our departure from Kingrode, we arrived here at Lisbon (God be thanked) in good safetie, and the Minion and the Gabriel also. ... I have according unto your remembrance laden for you in the Gabriell, 6. Kintals and 2. Roves of pepper, which cost the first pennie 50. Duckets the Kintal.[35]

By means of its lengthy and detailed depiction of the Royal Exchange, *Englishmen for My Money* dramatically realizes the daily lives of merchants—something that

---

[33]   Heywood, *If You Know Not Me You Know Nobody Part II*, (ed.) Madeleine Doran (Oxford: Malone Soc., 1935), lines 961–2.

[34]   Howard, *Theater of a City*, 32.

[35]   Browne, *The Marchants Avizo* (London, 1589), 10–11.

cannot be said of its portrayal of gentlemen, for whom no spatial equivalent of the Exchange is dramatized in the play. The nearest thing we get is Frisco's description of St Paul's, where he has been trying to find Pisaro a replacement for Anthony and where he remembers seeing a "great store of company that do nothing but go up and down and go up and down, and make a grumbling together" (2.2.12–14). The Exchange scene's focus upon buying and selling and upon the fates of the various ships also reminds us that unlike Shylock (with whom Pisaro has obvious affinities, as a widowed, possibly Jewish money-lender whose daughters marry against his wishes), Pisaro makes money through merchandise as well as usury— an important distinction as far as his status as a worker is concerned. Usurers were accused of earning their bread through others' labor, breaking "the First Law, that was made for Mankinde, after the Fall; which was, *In sudore Vultus tui comedes Panem tuum*; Not, *In sudore Vultus alieni*." The usurer's guaranteed profits distinguish him from the merchant, "the *Usurer* being at Certainties, and others at Uncertainties," as Francis Bacon put it.[36] That Pisaro is at uncertainties is clearly conveyed by his discomfiture at the news of his "late excessive loss" (1.3.137) to the Spanish galleys (it is this, indeed, that leads him distractedly to invite the English suitors to dinner instead of the foreigners). This vulnerability both makes him potentially more sympathetic as a character and adds legitimacy to his work.

The relatively positive treatment of Pisaro, whom we see going about his daily business, who is included in the play's festive ending, and whose citizen values can be said to dominate it, is one of the things that makes *Englishmen for My Money* somewhat atypical of the citizen comedy genre. Another is the way it distracts our attention from the class tensions that structure it by emphasizing national rivalries. In this essay, I have argued firstly, that these class tensions are inextricably connected to different relationships with work, and secondly, that the play's minimizing of them locates it in a historical moment when the principal London playing companies were both attempting to maintain a broad social appeal. Less than two years later, however, these same divisions would be re-emphasized by dramatists attempting to distance the children's companies from the socially degrading notion of work; and in the years that followed, they would be played upon in a variety of citizen comedies from *The Honest Whore* to *The Knight of the Burning Pestle*. Their presence in *Englishmen for My Money* is an important factor in the play's claim to priority in this particular tradition.

---

[36]   Bacon, *The Essayes or Counsels, Civill and Morall* (London, 1625), 239, 241.

Chapter 6

Will Kempe's Work:
Performing the Player's Masculinity in
Kempe's Nine Daies Wonder

Ronda Arab

Gender cannot be understood outside of its intersection with social hierarchy or estate, or in a postindustrial world, class. Early modern masculinities and femininities came into existence as effects of the various material conditions that constituted social groupings, such as occupation, wealth, friends and connections, lineage and kinship. From wherever they originated, the discourses constructing what it meant to be a working man varied from those constructing what it meant to be an aristocratic man. There was no single "masculinity" in early modern England, and the working man performed his masculinity in iterations that were distinct to his place in society.[1] This is not to say that his iterations of manliness did not or could not challenge patriarchal hierarchies that attempted to keep the working man in his place, but rather to observe that more critical attention might be paid to the conditions—discursive and material—that produced the various gendered subjectivities of the working man. Some of those discursive and material conditions were controlled by the dominant elite and some came from the world of work itself, with its various hierarchies, but their overall effect were subjectivities that can be called iterations of working "class" manliness.[2]

---

[1]   Studies of early modern masculinities include Bruce R. Smith, *Shakespeare and Masculinity* (Oxford: Oxford University Press, 2000); Will Fisher, *Materializing Gender in Early Modern Literature and Culture* (Cambridge: Cambridge University Press, 2006); Coppélia Kahn, *Man's Estate: Masculine Identity in Shakespeare* (Berkeley: University of California Press, 1981); and her more recent *Roman Shakespeare: Warriors, Wounds, and Women* (New York: Routledge, 1997); Mark Breitenberg, *Anxious Masculinity in Early Modern England* (Cambridge: Cambridge University Press, 1996); Thomas King, *The Gendering of Men, 1600–1750: The English Phallus* (Madison: The University of Wisconsin Press, 2004); Elizabeth A. Foyster, *Manhood in Early Modern England: Honor, Sex and Marriage* (New York: Longman, 1999); Alexandra Shepard, *Meanings of Manhood in Early Modern England* (Oxford: Oxford University Press, 2003); and Ronda Arab, *Manly Mechanicals on the Early Modern English Stage* (Selinsgrove, PA: Susquehanna University Press, forthcoming).

[2]   Following on David Kastan, I use the term class here in its "abstract social sense" as a hierarchizing category dividing privileged from less and non-privileged social groups rather than as a "properly historical" category. I do not mean to invoke Marxist theories of

In the following essay, I will examine one such construction of a working man's masculine subjectivity, that narrated by Will Kempe in his *Kempe's Nine Daies Wonder*. In 1600, Kempe, the son of a printer or a gentleman's servant[3] and one-time actor and clown for the Lord Chamberlain's Company, danced a morris dance from London to Norwich over a period of nine days, in order to raise money for himself from sponsors of his activity; shortly afterwards, he published his account of that dance. His tract relays to us two intersecting performances: within the narration of the theatrical performance of the morris dance is revealed a performance of masculinity by a self-identified working man. I will argue that, with his theatrical performance as the foundation for his textual self-creation, Kempe's narrative functions as a performative speech act that mediates discourses of masculinity, work, and the professional player by writing the player as a skilled working man whose dancing is his labor. In constructing the professional player as a working subject, Kempe's text not only rehearses for us celebratory discourses of the working male body as admirably strong, powerful, and skilled, he also locates the player within these discourses in order to confute the many accusations of idleness and effeminacy levelled at workers of the theater in early modern England. But dominant discourses of the working man as often—or more often—demonized him as a potentially violent and riotous threat than valorized his industry and vitality. Kempe's self-narration also reveals an acute awareness of these denigrating discourses in his defensive denials of all immoderate behavior; it is as though his iteration of the respectable working man must take them into account. In order for Kempe successfully to perform a valorized version of masculinity, which appears to be the aim of his pamphlet, he must intervene in and challenge dominant constructions of the working man's masculinity that kept the working man in his place.

Kempe consistently identifies his dancing as labor. When his activity leads to injury, he reports "finding remedy by [the] labor that had hurt mee, for it came in a turne, and so in my daunce I turned it out of my service againe";[4] his final dance into Norwich, he tells readers, involves "great labor" and "toyling": "with great labor I got thorow that narrow preaze into the open market place. Where on the crosse, ready prepared, stood the Citty Waytes, which not a little refreshed my weariness with toyling thorow so narrow a lane, as the people left me" (C3r). Significantly, he reports with pride that the buskins he wore from London dancing into Norwich were nailed to the Guildhall wall (Dr); his labor thus becomes honored by and associated with the established institution of respectable, skilled labor. He also consistently describes himself in physical terms, in that way taking part in available discourses

---

economic divisions that are not fully applicable to early modern England. Kastan, "Is There a Class in this (Shakespearean) Text?" *Renaissance Drama* 24 (1993): 150.

[3]   S.P. Cerasano, "The Chamberlain's-King's Men" in *A Companion to Shakespeare,* (ed.) David Scott Kastan (Malden, MA: Blackwell Publishers, 1999), 331.

[4]   Will Kempe, *Nine Daies Wonder* (London, 1600), B. Further references are given parenthetically in the text.

of the working man. What shows up most explicitly in *Kempe's Nine Daies Wonder* are celebratory discourses of the male working body. As with many working men, Kempe's physical vitality is a source of celebration—we see in his account how the strength and power of the working body is a crucial component of masculine pride. Morris dancing was physically demanding and highly skilled, and Kempe emphasises his own athleticism in his account: under good conditions he dances ten miles in three hours and is "so light … on [his] heeles, that [he] count[s] the ten mile no better than a leape" (C1r). The distance between London and Norwich is more than one hundred miles, and road conditions in the sixteenth century were not good: his endeavor was an impressive one. His fans try to keep up, but with limited success: two young men who dance in the mud with him on day four get stuck there (B2r); a butcher gives up after a half mile ("ere ever we had measur'd halfe a mile of our way, he gave me over in the plain field, protesting, that if he might get a 100. pound, he would not hold out with me") (B3r); the Host of Rockland manages to follow him for only two fields, although he set out to be his guide from Rockland to Hingham (C2r); and when he leaves Hingham for Norwich, the five young men determined to stay by his side are "running all the way" (C3r). Interestingly, two who do relatively well dancing with Kempe are young women: a fourteen year-old maid and a "Lusty Country lasse." But even the fourteen year-old is "ready to lye downe" (B2r) after an hour, and the country lass is in a "pittious heate" after a mile. Kempe's body, he tells us, is one with "well labor'd limbes"; his "pace in dauncing is not ordinary" (B3r) and "not for footemen" (C3r–C3v). Thus while positioning himself within a discourse that celebrates the capacity for physical exertion of the laboring man, he also asserts his professional status: he is a professional at this particular form of manly, physical work, as evidenced by his out-performance of these ordinary working folk. He shows the pride of the tradesman at his skill, in this case dancing, in his good-natured boasting.

Kempe's prowess excites cheer and pleasure; from the very beginning, there are crowds of admiring well-wishers following "through thicke and thin" (B1r), giving money, "harty prayers and God-speedes" (A3r). By day three the "fiftie in the companie"(B1r) of the previous day has swelled to two hundred; on day six his spectacle hijacks that of the Chief Justice of Bury, who was entering the town at another gate at the same time as Kempe, only to have the "wondring and regardless multitude … [leave] the streetes where he past to gape at" Kempe instead (C1r). Kempe's physically-active body is a visually exciting one, a site of aesthetic value. This is not surprising; the early modern theater operated on the assumption that there was pleasure in viewing the male body, and many plays make clear that a particular mode of that pleasure was in watching the strong male body at work. Plays such as Thomas Dekker's *The Shoemaker's Holiday*, William Rowley's *A Shoemaker, A Gentleman*, John Lyly's *Sappho and Phao*, and Robert Greene's *George a Greene, the Pinner of Wakefield*, to name a few, offer up the laboring man's body as an interesting and exciting spectacle, visually foregrounding his manly strength and skill and in many instances staging work, foregrounding the tools of skilled labor, or narrating its processes. In *The Shoemaker's Holiday*, for instance, which enacts the production of shoes onstage, skilled labor, productivity, and vigorous, work-hardened bodies define English masculinity, and claims to political power and social status for artisans are forged on the basis of this masculinity.[5] Despite their trade company associations, the status of professional players as gainfully employed workers was contested, as many scholars of the early modern commercial theater have discussed, most recently Tom Rutter.[6] Players' performances of manly strength and skilled labor in plays such as the above worked to associate them with the manly working men of the skilled trades where many of them, in fact, had personal connections;[7] this alignment might have been in response to anti-theatrical critiques of their idle effeminacy. Kempe's dance participates in this dramatic aesthetic of the physically powerful working body on display and in the ideological work of constructing the player's body as at one with the vital, skilled, industrious laboring body.

Sixteenth- and seventeenth-century masculinities were defined at once through and in opposition to the body. Ideal masculinity, most often associated with elite men, was according to dominant discourses achieved through outward signs of bodily strength and refinement as well as through controlling passions and desires that were understood to originate from the body—any excess of sorrow, anger, vengefulness, appetite, lust, etc., could be considered unmanly behavior. Displaying the characteristics of what Mikhail Bakhtin has termed the closed or classical body, ideal masculinity distanced itself from the body's messy passions

---

[5]   See Ronda Arab, "Work, Bodies, and Gender in *The Shoemaker's Holiday*," *Medieval and Renaissance Drama in England* 13 (2001): 182–212.

[6]   Rutter, *Work and Play on the Shakespearean Stage* (Cambridge: Cambridge University Press, 2008). Rutter argues that "in representations of actors on the public stage of the 1590s, theater professionals made a conscious effort to respond to [the charge that acting was an illegitimate occupation,] portraying actors as skilled and industrious craftsmen" (27). This aspect of his argument is similar to my argument about Will Kempe, although Rutter does not explore the aesthetics and politics of the body of the laboring man (whether theatrical or craft), nor his masculinity.

[7]   Trade company membership was widespread among actors, owners, managers, and playhouse builders. See David Kathman, "Grocers, Goldsmiths, and Drapers: Freemen and Apprentices in the Elizabethan Theater," *Shakespeare Quarterly* 55.1 (2004): 1–49, for a thorough account of the imbrication of the world of the trade companies and the world of the commercial theater. See also Roslyn Knutson for evidence of long-held personal and professional guild practices that were common among theater workers, who, she argues, probably accepted them as the norm because of their craft guild backgrounds: *Playing Companies and Commerce in Shakespeare's Time* (Cambridge: Cambridge University Press, 2001). Paul Yachnin offers a similar argument about "theatrical artisans" (311); the theater, he argues, maintained the marks of craft labor, and the creators of the theater were more like artificers than merchants buying and selling goods, despite the many contemporary references to the theater as a market. See Yachnin, "'The Perfection of Ten': Populuxe Art and Artisanal Value in *Troilus and Cressida*," *Shakespeare Quarterly* 56.3 (2005): 306–27.

and functions and was in this sense more mind than body.[8] Somewhat paradoxically, the assertion of mind over body involved in this construction of manliness was underwritten through displays of *bodily*, physical strength, which was seen as a reflection of mental and spiritual control. Canons of masculinity could be used to reinforce social hierarchies through denigrating representations of working bodies as open and out of control; however, the emphasis on bodily strength in early modern idealizations of masculinity also offered a means by which celebratory discourses of working men might be constructed. While the elite man who did not labor was understood to develop strength from physically skilled activities such as jousting, fencing, riding, and hunting, working men were perceived to develop great physical strength through their daily labor and in this way could also achieve this valued masculine trait.

Celebration of the physically vital, low-born body, such as that seen in *Kempe's Nine Daies Wonder*, appears in a great deal of popular literature of the early modern period, including the plays mentioned above, and numerous ballads and prose works. In part two of Thomas Deloney's *The Gentle Craft*, a rich shoemaker, "lusty Peachey," and his men are repeatedly victorious in a series of swordfights with two sea captains.[9] Deloney's *Thomas of Reading* and his *Jack of Newbury* also narrate artisan prowess; the clothiers of the former provide King Henry I with an army[10] and Jack of Newbury, a weaver, supplies 250 of his workmen to fight against the Scottish invasion: "there is not, for the number, better souldiers in the field,"[11] a nobleman tells the queen. Numerous ballads were written with similar themes: one such ballad, "The Honor of a London Prentice," features an apprentice of common stock who performs superhuman feats at arms for the honor of Queen Elizabeth.[12] Yet representations that champion the power of the working male body have been neglected in literary studies, despite the dialogue that exists between these literary representations and other, non-literary discourses of the culture. The health manuals of the period, which equate labor and exercise,[13] emphasize the importance of physical activity—"vehement moving" (1)—and draw attention to

---

[8]   Bakhtin, *Rabelais and His World*, trans. Helene Iswolsky (Bloomington: Indiana University Press, 1984).

[9]   Deloney, *The Gentle Craft, The Novels of Thomas Deloney*, (ed.) Merritt E. Lawlis (Bloomington: Indiana University Press, 1961), 213–18.

[10]   Deloney, *Thomas of Reading*, in *Shorter Novels*, vol. 1 (London & Toronto: J.M Dent & E.P. Dutton, 1929).

[11]   Deloney, *Jack of Newbury*, in *Shorter Novels*, vol. 1 (London & Toronto: J.M Dent & E.P. Dutton, 1929), 31.

[12]   Charles W. Camp, *The Artisan in Elizabethan Literature* (New York: Columbia University Press, 1923), 18–19.

[13]   Thomas Cogan notes that labor can signify exercise—"Hippo. is wont to take this worde labor for exercise"—and uses the words interchangeably: "Labor then, or exercise, is a vehement moving, the end whereof is alteration of the breath or winde of man." Cogan, *The Haven of Health* (London, 1596), 1. Further references are given parenthetically in the text.

the advantages working men have over learned and idle men, that is, the social elite. As Thomas Elyot writes in *The Castel of Health*, "sluggyshness dulleth the body, labor doth strength it, the first bringeth the incommodities of age shortely, the last maketh a man long tyme lusty."[14] Thomas Cogan, in the many-times published *The Haven of Health*, notes that "it be proved by experience" that laborers "for the most part be stronger than learned men" (1), and asserts that husbandmen and craftsmen "live longer and in better health, than Gentlemen and learned men" (3) because labor "increases heat"—the most manly of complexional qualities—which allows for better digestion and "nourishing" (2).[15] Having been toughened by labor, men of the "base occupations" could be seen to embody the masculine qualities necessary for that most masculine of activities, war. Both Mathew Sutcliffe and Gerat Barry note that "many men of lowe degree and base linadge have attained unto great dignitie, credit, and fame" as soldiers,[16] pointing out the importance of being "rebuste or stronge of boddy" (10) and not overly "curious [fussy]" (3)[17] about food and drink. Thomas Proctor, in *Of the Knowledge and Conduct of Warres*, concurs, railing that "delicate custome, and licentious living spoyled of all valure"[18] and arguing that working men make the best men of war:

> for their exercyse or trade of lyfe, first it is cleare, that the stronger, better breathed, and harder man of bodie by nature or custome, is the more avaylable for warres: and therefore it is to conclude, that men of such occupations, as are accustomed most to labor with the strength of their armes, are to bee preferred for this purpose, as smythes, butchers, masons, dyggers in mynes, Carpenters, & most principallye the husbandman, both for his wonted enduringe of hardnes in fare, and of all weathers and toyle in the fielde, beeinge also for the more parte, of honest inclination, & thriftie, which be good partes in a souldier. And the daintier sorte of serving men & riotous fellows, are least profitable herein. (21–2)

Admiring, respecting, celebrating, or simply acknowledging enhanced strength and vigor built up from physical labor, military and health manuals provide an account of the male worker's body that underwrites literary representations found in plays, ballads, and Will Kempe's autobiographical account. In their intersection with new religious discourses promoting activity over monastic learning and

---

[14] Elyot, *Castel of Health* (London, 1539), 48v.

[15] The texts of both Cogan and Elyot were published multiple times in the early modern period. Elyot's *Castel of Health* was published at least ten times between 1539 and 1610; Cogan's *Haven of Health* was published at least seven times between 1584 and 1636.

[16] Barry, *A Discourse of Military Discipline Devided into Three Boockes, Declaring the Partes and Sufficiencie Ordained in a Private Souldier, and in Each Officer* (Brussels, 1634), 2. Further references are given parenthetically in the text.

[17] Sutcliffe, *The Practice, Proceeding, and Lawes of Armes* (London, 1593), 13.

[18] Proctor, *Of the Knowledge and Conduct of Warres* (London, 1578), 19. Further references are given parenthetically in the text.

work over idleness, accounts such as these directly and indirectly write the active, lowborn body as a particularly English Protestant one.

Kempe's masculine strength, like that of the shoemaker's in Dekker's play, Jack of Newbury's weavers, and the fierce apprentice-soldiers of so many ballads, embodies some of the manly traits most valued by cultural authorities, but is of a rougher hue than those associated with elite men in early modern literary representations. Yet high canons of bodily behavior were not uniformly valued: the suave, cool, controlled courtier with his perfectly refined bodily countenance, for example, was sometimes seen as in danger of effeminization through *overrefinement*. The denial of vulgar corporeality involved cultivating a perfectly groomed exterior that could be seen as dangerously similar to the feminine realm of artifice, fashion, and superficiality, undermining the strength of the self-contained "classical" body.

The rougher corporeality of the strong-bodied working man, on the other hand, evidenced the manly humor of blood, which in turn produced the heat that was responsible for fierce, fearless action. Passionate action was antithetical to reason, the highest achievement of manliness, attained through a perfect balance of the bodily humors; yet if a perfect, reasonable temperament could not be achieved— and anatomists conceded that it rarely could—"the second best [was] for blood to dominate the other humors"[19] because an aggressive, forceful manliness could be a "reviving force." Thus, in Shakespeare's *Henry IV, Part 1* Hotspur's heated ferocity elicits admiration from the king and is not only compared favorably to the dissolute Prince Hal (until Hal reforms) but also to the "neat, and trimly dress'd"[20] lord who brings messages to the battlefield and is presented as a parody of courtly refinement, with "his chin new reap'd" (1.3.34), his body "perfumed like a milliner" (1.3.36), and his speech peppered with "holiday and lady terms" (1.3.46). Hotspur exemplifies uncontrolled masculine heat—admirable yet too excessive to be a perfect exemplar of ideal manliness. Kempe embodies the same admirable, quintessentially English vigor as Hotspur, but without his uncontrolled excess; in this way he offers a greater challenge to elite canons of masculinity than Hotspur, in that he is neither too hot, like the aristocratic warrior, nor too refined, like the perfumed courtier.

Kempe's Nine Daies Wonder likewise demonstrates how celebrations of the working man might eschew elite dictates of "classical" perfection and instead be grounded in characteristics of the Bakhtinian "open body." Kempe makes a great deal of the injury he sustains early on in his journey; on the second day of dancing he strains his hip and "indure[s] exceeding paine," but decides not to "trouble a Surgeon" (B1r) and dances on. Here, the bodily integrity and wholeness of the idealized, elite, manly body are challenged as qualities

---

[19] Smith, *Shakespeare and Masculinity*, 20.

[20] William Shakespeare, *1 Henry IV*, in *The Norton Shakespeare: Based on the Oxford Edition*, (eds.) Stephen Greenblatt et al. (New York: W.W. Norton, 1997), 1.3.33. Further references are given parenthetically in the text.

necessary to masculinity. Manhood here calls attention to its own vulnerability: Kempe boasts of his lameness, rather than concealing it. Wounds, and especially blood, as Gail Paster convincingly demonstrates, often "assume[d] the shameful attributes of the incontinent female body as both cause of and justification for its evident vulnerability and defeat."[21] Kempe's text offers a quite different model. Unlike aristocratic displays of manliness, which celebrate the body's perfection,[22] Kempe's advertisement of his injury exhibits no shame in his pain, only pride that he endures it without calling a surgeon. Nor is his dance-induced injury an indication of vulnerability or failure; rather, his extreme physical exertion is represented as having its own curative properties. To quote again: "I held on, finding remedy by labor that had hurt mee, for it came in a turne, and so in my daunce I turned it out of my service againe" (B). As Kempe names his dance as labor, we are reminded that working men like Kempe relied on bodily exertion to bring in their bread. In Kempe's text labor is pain and injury, but it is also the means to strength and vitality. Pain and injury thereby become signifiers of the powerfully vital force that is the working male body.

Although Kempe is ambivalent towards the crowds that follow him (discussed further below), his autonomy is not compromised by his dependency on the crowd; to the contrary, he relies on the power of publicity both in his original endeavor (the public dance is an enterprise to gain money) and in his written account (which aims in part to shame non-payers into rendering their payments). This dependency on public discourse is aggressively self-generated; Kempe is unabashed in his public bid for payment and in his complaint against sponsors who "will … [not] willingly be found," claiming that he "wil have patience, some few daies longer," but then "wil draw a cattalogue of al their names," marking an "H" next to the honest men and a "K" in front of the "ketlers & keistrels" that haven't respected their promise (D2r).

Kempe's proximity to the multitude is not represented as a taint to his manhood; on the contrary, he expresses pride in their cheering presence, adoration and exhortations, as he catalogues their increasing size and exuberance. The crowds, in fact, turn Kempe's dance into a collective activity; throughout the nine days, sundry merry-making well-wishers join in and dance with him, disrupting

---

[21]   Paster, *The Body Embarrassed: Drama and the Disciplines of Shame in Early Modern England* (Ithaca: Cornell University Press, 1993), 92. Paster also shows how anxiety about involuntary male wounds is evident in reconfigurations of male bloodshed as "voluntary and therapeutic" (96), but makes clear "the psychic precariousness of this kind of assertion" (97), using Coriolanus's refusal to show the plebeians his wounds "and beg their voices in his election" (97) as her example. As Paster writes, "Janet Adelman is surely right to see this horror as rooted in his fear of dependency" (97). Coriolanus is urged to display his wounds as marks of pride, indications of his bravery on the battlefield, but the "psychic precariousness" of the process of displaying such ambiguously gendered attributes as bodily wounds prevents him from doing so, particularly since its purpose involves seceding his individual political autonomy to the multitudes.

[22]   I am thinking of such courtly activities as jousts and tournaments.

the boundary between spectator and spectacle. Kempe's manhood is not defined through the self-sufficient individuality of his body, but in relation to the bodies that surround him. Moreover, the bodies that join with his in dance are described in terms that emphasize their Bahktinian corporeality: the butcher who dances for a half mile is a "lusty tall fellow" (B3r); the Host of Rockland who manages to follow Kempe for only two fields is a "good true-fat-belly" (C2r) who likes his "Nut-browne Ale" (C2v); Kempe's most determined partner, a "Lusty Country lasse," has "thicke short legs," "fat sides," and "browne hips" that go "swig a swag," and she ends a successful mile in a "piteous heate" (B3r; B4r). These bodies (and others that are mentioned) are the source of merriment and laughter as well as commendation, as is Kempe's own; his treatise celebrates bodies that run counter to dominant constructions of power and worth, which emphasized the qualities of spirit and reason over corporeality. But while Kempe celebrates the men and women who join him in the dance, he always outdoes them, thus elevating his body as a professional one, even as its professional activity involves including non-professional bodies in its sphere.

Furthermore, Kempe always remains in control. While Kempe celebrates the lusty appetite for ale of his hearty Host of Rockland (who "will drinke, and stille be dry, / And quaffe with every company") (C2v), he himself maintains a moderate appetite throughout, refusing the urgings of those who would encourage him to drink:

> [I] had small rest with those that would have urg'd me to drinking. But, I warrant you, Will Kemp was wise enough: to their full cups, kinde thanks was my returne, with Gentleman like protestations, as 'truly, sir, I dare not,' 'It stands not with the congruity of my health.' (A3r)

Here, Kempe demonstrates his ability to perform the forms of elite, masculine civility in both his moderation and in his "gentleman like" speech; moderation was the bulwark of gentility, according to Richard Braithwaite, because it was "*a subduer of our desires to the obedience of Reason, and a temperate conformer of all our affections; freeing them from the too much subjection either of desires or feare,*" and it was "a note of distinction betwixt man and beast."[23] It was moderate physical appetite that led to balanced bodily humors, and in turn, the desired reasonable temperament. The theme of moderation is again reinforced in Kempe's recording of a conversation between himself and a gentleman, Master Foskew, "that had before trauailed a foote from London to Barwick." Foskew, veteran of the roads, gives Kempe "good consaile to obserue temperate dyet for [his] health, and other aduise to bee carefull of [his] company" (B3r). The juxtaposition of discourses at this moment is telling; temperate diet, that insurer of masculine reason and health, is discussed alongside a warning about the dangers of Kempe's mingling in bad company. One begins to see something more in Kempe's insistence

---

23   Braithwaite, *The English Gentleman* (London, 1630; Amsterdam & Norwood, N.J.: Walter J. Johnson, Inc, 1975), 306.

on his moderation: a concern with his own reputation that might be characterized as an internalization of regulatory discourses of the dominant, hierarchical culture that constructed the player as dissolute and the working man as indulgent of his bodily appetites. Kempe does not, his account lets us know, pass the time between dances raising a glass in the tavern with bad *or* good company. This concern with reputation is evident throughout Kempe's account, and suggests his simultaneous participation in and modification of contemporary discourses that denigrated working men's masculinity.

Kempe's assertion of his moderate habits performs textually a congruence between the experiences of working men and elite discourses of masculinity; he creates a refined working man. His assertion of his moderation, with all it suggests about careful self-regulation, can be understood as an element of a defensive anxiety that runs through the text. It is clear that Kempe is well aware of certain negative constructions of the working man, and in particular, of the "professional player" that abounded in his society. The respectability of any sort of theatrical activity was dubious to some segments of the population; Kempe's dance from London to Norwich occurs at a time when conservative preachers and other social authorities railed against dancing, the theater, and wandering the countryside. Dancing the countryside might easily be construed as akin to wandering it, an activity associated with vagrants and "masterless" men, an association that would have seemed especially threatening when the man dancing was himself a masterless commoner and gathering large crowds—potential breeding grounds of riot, sedition, and all manner of crime—in his wake. In celebrating his own dance as a form of labor, rather than mere roguish idleness, Kempe simultaneously defends himself against these imagined accusations.

In the unstable socio-economic period of sixteenth- and seventeenth-century England, enclosures were denying many their traditional access to land, and an impoverished rural proletariat was created; as a result, unemployed or underemployed craftsmen, farm workers, and other laborers often participated in food riots and other protests. The 1590s in particular were a period of social instability and unrest;[24] Roger B. Manning cites thirty-five outbreaks of disorder in London between 1581 and 1602.[25] Some of the least privileged of the working classes, along with discharged soldiers, wandered the countryside seeking work, begging or thieving. Such people were frequently stigmatized as vagrants and subject to the strictures of Elizabethan poor laws. Able bodies untethered from

---

[24] E.P. Cheyney characterizes the 1590s as a period of crisis, plague, harvest failure, massive price inflation, heavy taxation, depression in overseas trade and in the volume of domestic demand, large-scale unemployment, and escalating crime and vagrancy. See Ian Archer, *The Pursuit of Stability: Social Relations in Elizabethan London* (Cambridge: Cambridge University Press, 1991), 9. Even Steven Rappaport, who argues for the essential stability of London in the sixteenth century, agrees that the final decade was a tumultuous one: see Rappaport, *Worlds Within Worlds: The Structure of Life in Sixteenth-Century London* (Cambridge: Cambridge University Press, 1989), 11–17.

[25] Manning, *Village Revolts*: *Social Protest and Popular Disturbances in England, 1509–1640* (Oxford: Clarendon Press, 1988), 187.

the patriarchal authority of a household-workshop, or uncontrolled by the masters of the household to which they belonged, were viewed as a potential threat to the social and political order.[26] A description by John Stow makes clear what a formidable force of destruction a crowd of London rioters might unleash:

> The Apprentices of London are so considerable a Body, that they have sometimes made themselves formidable by Insurrection and Mutinies in the City, getting some Thousands of them together, and pulling down Houses, breaking open the Gates of Newgate, and other Prisons, and setting the Prisoners free. ... But they have been commonly assisted, and often egged on and headed by Apprentices of the Dregs of the Vulgar, Fellows void of worthy Blood, and worthy Breeding; yea, perhaps not apprentices at all, but forlorn Companions, masterless Men, and Tradeless, and the like.[27]

In this vision of the crowd, protesting tradesmen are joined with and become not fully distinguishable from vagrants, rogues, and thieves.

Kempe is a masterless man and a more-than-able body at a time when social tensions meant that the celebrated, strong, low-born body could also be a scary body. Leveraging his claim to respectability through insisting on his professional status, he construes his working masculinity in terms of temperance, moderation, and skill, as well as strength and vigor, and thereby diffuses its threat. Although he gathers crowds, he is clearly not a Jack Cade, the artisan rebel-leader in Shakespeare's *2 Henry VI*—a role he likely played in the 1590s—as Cade and his fellow artisan rebels, with their work-hardened bodies and the tools of their trades, use their power, skills, and weapons to generate bloody disorder and challenge social hierarchy.[28] For all his obvious exultation in the crowds' adoration, Kempe insists that he tries to get away from them, and is not, like the charismatic Cade, intentionally creating them: "in the evening I tript to Ingerstone, stealing away from those numbers of people that followed mee: yet do what I could, I had about fiftie in the company, some from London, the other of the Country thereabout, that would needs when they heard my Taber, trudge after me through thicke and thin" (Br). Although Kempe's venture would have been a failure had no one taken note of it, he nevertheless wants to claim that the crowds gather against his will. Moreover, he reacts vehemently to the arrest of two cutpurses and their companions taken in the crowd that followed him from London, fervently dissociating himself from them and all their lot when officers query the possibility of an association:

---

[26]   See Manning, *Village Revolts*; A.L. Beier, *Masterless Men: The Vagrancy Problem in England 1560–1640* (London: Metheun, 1985); Buchanan Sharp, *In Contempt of All Authority: Rural Artisans and Riot in the West of England, 1586–1660* (Berkeley: University of California Press, 1980); and Patricia Fumerton, *Unsettled: The Culture of Mobility and the Working Poor in Early Modern England* (Chicago: University of Chicago Press, 2006).

[27]   John Stow, *Stow's Survey of London* (London: Dent, 1965), 332–3.

[28]   See Ronda Arab, "Ruthless Power and Ambivalent Glory: The Rebel Laborer in *2 Henry VI*," *Journal for Early Modern Cultural Studies* 5.2 (2005): 5–36.

> Whereupon the officers bringing them to the inn, I justly denied their acquaintance,
> saving I remembred one of them to be a noted Cut-purse, such a one as we tye
> to a poast on our stage, for all people to wonder at, when at a play they are taken
> pilfering. … To be short, I thought myselfe well rid of foure such followers, and
> I wish hartily that the whole world were clear of such companions. (B1r)

That the officers brought the thieves to the inn where Kempe was staying suggests
that they may have suspected a criminal alliance between them, indicating that
Kempe may well have had reason to be defensive about his activity. Kempe is
almost accused of being an accomplice; the potential for the morris-dancing
journeyer to be taken for a vagrant thief is clear here. Perhaps this is the sort of
thing the "lying Ballad-makers" (A3r) wrote about, whom Kempe rails against
over and over. Near the beginning, in passages within, and in a "*humble request*"
(D3r) at the end of his account, Kempe maintains as one of his objectives setting
the record straight against these "pittifull papers, pasted on every poast, of that
which was neither so nor so" (D2r). The *Nine Daies Wonder* is Kempe's self-
"spin"; he is wresting control of his image from others, who have taken his person
and "neer hand rent [it] in sunder with [their] unreasonable rimes" (D3r).

Kempe's other explicit purpose in publishing his account is his "duety to expresse
with thankefulness the kind entertainment [he] found" (D2r). This motive seems
integrally bound up with his desire to present himself as an honest, sober citizen. It
is difficult not to read the dedication of so much space to the reputable gentlemen
and gentlewomen who offer him hospitality as a name-dropping reminder to his
detractors that he has worthy supporters. He begins with a dedicatory epistle to
Mistress Anne Fitton, maid of honor to Queen Elizabeth, seeking her "protection."
Kempe behaves here like the actor he in fact was, seeking aristocratic endorsement
to legitimate his theatrical activity, and to keep it outside of the discursive realm
of the vagrant wanderer.[29] He then begins his account by noting that the expedition
started on the first Monday of Lent—thus managing an allusion to asceticism—and
describes it as a journey "from the right Honorable the Lord Mayors of London,
towards the right worshipfull (and truly bountifull) Master Mayors of Norwich"
(A3r), thus framing it between two pillars of respectability and authority. During
the weeks that follow he is given hospitality by many:

> At Melford, divers gentlemen met mee, who brought me to one master Colts,
> a very kinde and worshipful Gentleman, where I had unexpected entertainment
> till the Satterday. (B4r)

After dancing on the Saturday mentioned above, he has dinner at a rich widow's,
with about thirty gentlemen—a "woman of good presence: and if a foole may
judge, of no small discretion" (B4r). A week later a Sir Edwin Rich gives him

---

[29]   Acting troupes required the official patronage of a noble in order to avoid possible
prosecution as vagrants under the "Act for the Punishment of Vagabonds" of 1572. See
Andrew Gurr, *The Shakespearean Stage, 1574–1642* (Cambridge: Cambridge University
Press, 1992), 27.

"entertainment in such bountifull liberal sort, during [his] continuance there Satterday and Sunday" that Kempe feels he is at a loss for words: "I want fit words to expresse the least part of his worthy usage of my unworthiness" (C1r–C1v). Kempe becomes even more effusive when he reaches Norwich and receives "plenty of good chere at the Mayors," declaring,

> his bounty, and kinde usage together with the general welcomes of his worshipful
> brethren, and many other knightes, Ladies, Gentlemen and Gentlewomen, so
> much exceeded my expectation, as I adjudg'd my selfe most bound to them
> all. (D1r)

In its self-narration and self-performance, *Kempe's Nine Daies Wonder* presents the complex, often contested constructions of masculinity mapped onto the male working body in general, and that of the player in particular. Kempe presents himself as a physically powerful man who embodies many of the positive traits that discourses of the early modern working man constructed. Kempe's self-alignment with discourses of the manly, vigorous working man seems intended to confute contemporary attacks on playing. At the same time, while associating himself with working bodies in general, he must distance himself from the other working bodies he comes into contact with in order to assert playing as a trade. There must be a distinction between his dancing abilities and those of the well-wishers who join him along his route; for his activity to be that of a professional, his skill at it must surpass the skills of his amateur fans. But while Kempe's text is full of mirth and merriment, it is clear that he is well aware of negative constructions of the working man when he tells his readers of his refusal of all drink, when he laments the difficulty of dispelling the crowds that follow him, when he vehemently disassociates himself from the cutpurses found in that crowd, and associates himself with as many respectable names as possible. These aspects of Kempe's pamphlet show his vulnerability to the cultural construction of the powerful working man as a threat to social order, a potential force of destruction.[30] In order to reclaim the player as a respectable working man, he must contend with these discourses.

Discursive constructions of the working man have been understudied in scholarship on early modern literary masculinity, and most studies that do exist give little attention to seeking out the means by which working men of the early modern period represented themselves. *Kempe's Nine Daies Wonder*, written by a self-identified working man, offers a rare glimpse of a working man relaying his own version of his experience of masculine subjectivity; as a cultural construction of a working man's subjectivity written by a self-identified working man, it stands as a particularly valuable historical artifact.

---

[30]   They show as well how the literary "no bad intentions" topos can emerge out of actual material conditions.

Chapter 7
The Rogues' Paradox:
Redefining Work in *The Alchemist*

Elizabeth Rivlin

Ben Jonson's *The Alchemist* opens with a cultural cliché about the dangers of leaving a servant idle. With the plague having descended upon London, a master, Lovewit, leaves his house in the City to the care of his servant, Face. But his trust proves to be misplaced:

> Ease him corrupted, and gave means to know
> A cheater, and his punk; who, now brought low,
> Leaving their narrow practice, were become
> Cozeners at large: and only wanting some
> House to set up, with him they here contract,
> Each for a share, and all begin to act.[1]

The transition from definable "practice" to wide-ranging criminal enterprise is disposed of quickly: Face merges seamlessly with the "cozeners," Subtle and Dol. Together, the three move beyond petty crime to pursue a more expansive scheme. The Argument thus presages an apparent evolution: *The Alchemist*'s anti-heroes cheat narrow definitions of work and re-create themselves as gleeful agents in a burgeoning market economy of investment and profit. Idleness and criminality are transformed into a mode of work that paradoxically promises freedom from labor.[2] On a first reading, *The Alchemist* might thus seem to be about redefining work in terms of an emerging capitalist ethos, one that provides greater opportunity for subjects on the periphery of the economy to gain productive entry.

Yet the possibility of construing the rogues' aversion to labor as compatible with this ethos is complicated in *The Alchemist* by the continued presence of hierarchical structures of service, which prove indispensable to the livelihoods, and perhaps even the survival, of these marginal figures. The play implies a division between older forms of labor, associated with subservience, physicality, and toil, and newer

---

[1]   Ben Jonson, *The Alchemist*, (ed.) Elizabeth Cook (London and New York: A & C Black and W.W. Norton, 1991), "The Argument," 3–8. Hereafter, line references are in the main text.

[2]   On criminality and its negotiations with "legitimate" society in *The Alchemist*, see Jonathan Haynes, "Representing the Underworld: *The Alchemist*," *Studies in Philology* 86 (1989): 18–41.

forms of work, which produce profit seemingly without labor, even as it shows these categories collapsing back into each other. This essay argues that *The Alchemist* balances an emergent capitalist fantasy with an entrenched narrative in which the conventions and strictures of hierarchically organized labor renew their claims on the rogue characters. I use "capitalist" to designate an economy in which labor was becoming more portable and exchangeable, and in which the accumulation of profit increasingly depended on owning the labor of others. In theory, the transition to capitalism enhanced the possibilities for individual advancement and weakened hierarchical structures; in a capitalist economy, anyone could seek profit, as the rogues do, for example, by taking shares in a venture. However, Jonson suggests that in a milieu of seemingly limitless opportunism, some restrictions still obtain, for as the play illustrates, those who lack the capital to control labor are ultimately excluded from investment and ownership and resigned to labor for others. *The Alchemist* offers a window onto the changing forms of early modern work, while intimating that this shift may result in a retrenchment, at least for some groups of people.

One group negotiating significant change, the play proposes, was workers in the contemporary theater. *The Alchemist* delights openly in its meta-theatrical dimensions; the conditions of labor it portrays are inseparable from those that produced it. Since the Blackfriars house in which Jonson sets the action refers transparently to the Blackfriars playhouse in which the play was performed, the rogues' "works" comment not only on work generally, but also more specifically on work in the early modern theater. Shareholders in licensed London theatrical companies such as the King's Men (who commissioned *The Alchemist*) were no rogues.[3] Like Jonson's characters, however, theater people were increasingly guided in their concept of work by principles of investment and risk, fueled by the expectation of profit. Also like their fictional counterparts, they continued to depend upon more traditional forms of labor. If Lovewit's masterless house conjures newly available economic subject positions only to show the limits of that imagining, Jonson is quick to remind his audiences of the analogies to the theatrical workplace they are visiting. The history of the early modern theater suggests a complexity in perceptions of work that the drama, particularly in its final acts, both embodies and evades. Examining that history in relation to *The Alchemist* illuminates how individuals in a changing economy conceived of their work, and in turn defined their subjectivities, according to competing models that

---

[3]   The Elizabethan statute of 1572 famously grouped unlicensed "Comon Players in Enterludes" under the rubric of "Roges Vacaboundes and Sturdy Beggers." Quoted in Andrew Gurr, *The Shakespeare Company, 1594–1642* (Cambridge: Cambridge University Press, 2004), 85. Gurr argues that the most important effect of the statute was to launch the licensing system for playing companies. By the early seventeenth century, shareholders in the King's Men were in the position of largely controlling their own investments, risks, and profits.

invited upward mobility and deferred it, that detached from the materiality of labor and reconfirmed it.

Alchemy is the governing conceit of the play, and its theatrical power derives from its mutability. It functions as a prime business motive for the rogues, and often demands extenuating labor. Face, Subtle and Dol establish an alchemical enterprise that lures people with the promise of great wealth and social prestige. No chemical alchemy takes place, the rogues' gamble being that their customers will pay in advance for their services. As their scheme requires, the rogues are under immense pressure to juggle the multiplying demands made by an ever-increasing number of aspirants, with the result that they are forced to work harder and harder to maintain their fraudulent enterprise. The distance, illusory to begin with, between simulated and actual labor collapses altogether as they struggle to satisfy their clients' expectations. As Jonson foretells in the Argument's last line, their goal of getting rich at the expense of others finally evaporates altogether, the flurry of roguish labor—"casting figures, telling fortunes, news, / Selling of flies, flat bawdry" (10–11)—along with the rogues themselves, disappearing in "fume[s]" (12). Master Lovewit's return at the end of Act 4 precipitates the rogues' reversion to low status. While Face, back in the role of servant, gets to share the material benefits of the cons with his master, Subtle and Dol are left with nothing.

Alchemy is also Jonson's metaphor for the desire to inflate oneself, subjectively, economically, and socially, that drives rogues and gulls alike, and a joke about the extremity of self-delusion they endorse in this pursuit.[4] Throughout, Jonson plays on the applicability of alchemical terms and concepts to the private and cultural imaginings of his characters. "Projection," for example, which refers to a technical stage in the transmutation of metal into gold, also describes the cognitive process by which longings express themselves as a tangible, if ultimately unrealized, outcome. Moreover, a "project" referred, in Joan Thirsk's words, to "a practical scheme for exploiting material things," precisely the sort of capitalist enterprise upon which the rogues embark.[5] For transformation to "project" itself long enough for the gulls to keep investing their money in the rogues' venture, alchemy's lack of substance—its essential non-being—must be balanced with its continually deferred promise. The gull Mammon asks Subtle, "When do you make projection?" and is met with a characteristic response: "Son, be not hasty" (2.3.101–2). Although they manipulate the meanings of alchemy, Face, Subtle, and Dol Common, no less than their gulls, fall victim to its allure. The rogues wish to convert their human acts of labor into work performed by their capital,

---

[4]   It has been commonplace for critics to discuss the inflationary (and deflationary) implications of alchemy in the play. See, for example, John Mebane, "Renaissance Magic and the Return of the Golden Age: Utopianism and Religious Enthusiasm in *The Alchemist*," *Renaissance Drama* 10 (1977): 128.

[5]   Thirsk, *Economic Policy and Projects: The Development of a Consumer Society in Early Modern England* (Oxford: Clarendon Press, 1978), 1.

not by themselves. But their projection, like their project, ends up only reasserting the materiality of their labor. Subtle may put off Mammon by professing the need to "iterate the work" (106), but his words later take on an unwanted resonance as Subtle and his partners unceasingly repeat their machinations with alchemical props and their encounters with increasingly dissatisfied clients. Jonson exposes a persistent gap between the dream of "a work" that creates profit without human labor and the reality of difficult and toilsome labor that cannot be relied upon to produce any profit at all.[6] Trapped by the incommensurability of alchemical desire and the difficult labors that desire entails, the rogues in fact have more to lose than anyone else.[7]

Most labor in early modern England took place under the rubric of service.[8] Subtle, Face, and Dol were instantly recognizable to contemporary audiences and readers as "rogues," who avoided legitimate forms of labor largely by avoiding service. A more economically sensitive interpretation is that such figures had a fluctuating relation to service during a period when long-term service offered increasingly uncertain prospects.[9] When Subtle accuses Face of having been

---

[6] In discussing the growth of industrial capitalism, Marx describes the English East India Company as dispensing contracts to investors "under conditions whereby they, cleverer than the alchemists, made gold out of nothing." *Capital: A Critique of Political Economy*, vol. 1, trans. Ben Fowkes (New York: Vintage, 1977), 917. Eric Wilson extends a Marxist analysis to highlight the fetishistic value attached to wished-for products of alchemy in Jonson's play, resulting in "a symptomatic confusion of persons and things." "Abel Drugger's Sign and the Fetishes of Material Culture," in *Historicism, Psychoanalysis, and Early Modern Culture*, (eds.) Carla Mazzio and Douglas Trevor (New York: Routledge, 2000), 119. A similar reification exists in the transformation of the activities of work into "a work," a process that Theodore Leinwand discusses in *Theatre, Finance and Society in Early Modern England* (Cambridge: Cambridge University Press, 1999), 134. Leinwand is interested, as I am, in the ways that Jonson depicts the capitalist venture, contrary to its fantasy presentation, as demanding extraordinary amounts of labor.

[7] My claim runs counter to Andrew Gurr's assertion that the gulls, "who all lose their wealth," actually suffer more than the rogues in *The Alchemist*'s ending. While Gurr is right to say that Face, Subtle and Dol "simply revert to the status they all occupied before the play began," he downplays the precariousness of their status when compared to the security enjoyed by most of the gulls, who in many cases have invested surplus capital and have more reliable resources for generating new income. Gurr, "Prologue: Who is Lovewit? What is he?" in *Ben Jonson and Theatre: Performance, Practice and Theory*, (eds.) Richard Cave, Elizabeth Schafer, and Brian Woolland (London and New York: Routledge, 1999), 14.

[8] Ann Kussmaul describes the wide-ranging reach of service in the early modern period: "servant," she writes, refers both to one who worked for and was supported by a master, and to "all those who worked for others." Kussmaul, *Servants in Husbandry in Early Modern England* (Cambridge: Cambridge University Press, 1981), 6.

[9] Several essays in this volume examine the often dramatic impact of the destabilization of service. Amanda Bailey's "Custom, Debt, and the Valuation of Service Within and Without Early Modern England" explores how indentured servants were represented as traversing bondage and liberation, the latter achieved by entering into debt in

merely "the good, / Honest, plain, livery-three-pound-thrum" (1.1.15–16), he is gesturing towards the familiar type of the domestic servant. This is hardly the only prototype of service encountered in the play, however; Dol and Subtle have also engaged in service, albeit in less permanent positions where compensation was correspondingly unpredictable.[10] Dol's main employment is as a prostitute, while Subtle has apparently flitted from one "course" (5.4.146) or subsistence scheme to another. What Face calls "your conjuring, cozening, and your dozens of trades" (1.1.40) might have been inscribed in popular rogue literature as a willful rebellion against gainful, steady employment, but recent scholarship has confirmed that the pull of necessity is a more realistic explanation.[11] Face's recollection of Subtle standing on a street corner, sniffing pies he cannot afford to buy, "like the father of hunger" (27), tells that story clearly. Shifts in the labor market, together with the rise of monetary exchange, spawned what Patricia Fumerton has usefully defined as an "economy of 'unsettledness,'" a de facto community that included "not only the legally vagrant, but also the 'respectable' yet unstable servant and apprentice classes," continually on the move, sometimes geographically and other times simply occupationally, piecing together survival through ad hoc combinations of licit and illicit work.[12] Understanding the play's scenario in an unstable economic context allows us to read the rogues' setting up house as just another move in an ongoing dialectic between constraint and opportunity for those engaged in or at the margins of service. If for Face his master's departure gives him a chance to improve his economic status, for Subtle and Dol it surely also augurs a comparatively stable interlude in their itinerant existences.

---

a credit economy. In Bailey's analysis, the servant's obligation becomes the condition of his or her freedom. The impulse to manage the disordered situations of servants is evident as well in Michelle Dowd's "Desiring Subjects: Staging the Female Servant in Early Modern Tragedy," which shows that Jacobean tragedies coped with "unruly" female servants by disposing of them in narratives of marriage and simultaneously displacing their agency, thus stripping them of their dangerous and uncomfortable significations. Both Bailey and Dowd locate in the literary treatment of servants a social recursiveness similar to that which I see in *The Alchemist*.

[10]   On the expansion of marginal service activities, see Peter Clark and Paul Slack, *English Towns in Transition 1500–1700* (London: Oxford University Press, 1976), 78. Natasha Korda discusses women's subsistence labor in "Labors Lost: Women's Work and Early Modern Theatrical Commerce," in *From Script to Stage in Early Modern England*, (eds.) Peter Holland and Stephen Orgel (Houndmills, UK and New York: Palgrave, 2004), 195–230.

[11]   See, for example, William Carroll, *Fat King, Lean Beggar: Representations of Poverty in the Age of Shakespeare* (Ithaca: Cornell University Press, 1996) and Linda Woodbridge, *Vagrancy, Homelessness, and English Renaissance Literature* (Urbana: University of Illinois Press, 2001).

[12]   Fumerton, *Unsettled: The Culture of Mobility and the Working Poor in Early Modern England* (Chicago and London: The University of Chicago Press, 2006), 11.

Jonson's audiences would have been familiar with the type of the lazy and avaricious rogue popular in "cony-catching" literature, whose objective is to avoid honest labor at all costs and accrue wealth through dishonest means. In *A Caveat for Common Cursitors*, for example, Thomas Harman sketches a typical portrait of a rogue, dubbed an "upright man," as a former soldier or "serving-man, and weary of well-doing, shaking off all pain, doth choose him this idle life."[13] In a bit of circular logic, another sixteenth-century commentator hypothesizes that rogues do not work "by reason their sinews are so benumbed and stiff through idleness as their limbs, being put to any hard labour, will grieve them beyond measure. So as they will rather hazard their lives than work."[14] The rhetoric of avoidance that runs through rogue literature serves as an important background for contemporary assumptions about rogues in *The Alchemist*. Their plot, audiences know without having to be told, is premised on an evasion of rigid hierarchical structures of authority and of moral conventions of industry and diligence.

One of Jonson's characteristic ironies is that the rogues' desire to be both idle and rich, when taken on its merits, is almost identical to the hopes expressed by their victims. What is suspect in such a sentiment when expressed by Face, Subtle, and Dol or their antecedents in rogue literature, of course, is their egregiously forthright attempt to violate their rightful occupational and social stations as servants, apprentices and laborers.[15] As Jonson intimates, however, this sin is committed equally by the gulls, among them a lawyer's clerk, a druggist, a country yeoman, and a pair of Anabaptists. All of these figures fantasize about achieving powerful positions, and all attempt to realize their fantasies by procuring "magical" enhancements to their material goods, their personal abilities, or their professional status. The agents of the gulls' illicit advancement are, however, the rogues, and it is they who conveniently shoulder the burden of responsibility for the social and commercial aspirations of more "legitimate" members of society. In this way, as Craig Dionne argues about the cony-catching texts, "the otherness of underworld villainy gives voice to the anxieties of a social disruption brought about by the very practices that empowered London's new corporate class: self-advancement through histrionic manipulation of the social and linguistic registers of court and

---

    [13]   Harman, *A Caveat for Common Cursitors, Vulgarly Called Vagabonds* (1566) in *Rogues, Vagabonds, & Sturdy Beggars*, (ed.) Arthur F. Kinney (Amherst: The University of Massachusetts Press, 1990), 115.

    [14]   From a 1596 letter by Edward Hext, Somerset J.P., to Lord Burghley, quoted in Christopher Hill, *Liberty Against the Law: Some Seventeenth-Century Controversies* (London: Allen Lane; The Penguin Press, 1996), 52.

    [15]   Catherine Gimelli Martin makes a similar point about the "commercial speculation" which is practiced by most of the play's characters, but which is rewarded or punished in discrepant fashion. Martin locates the distinction as being between forms of capitalism performed, respectively, by Subtle and Face. "Angels, Alchemists and Exchange: Commercial Ideology in Court and City Comedy, 1596–1610," in *The Witness of Times: Manifestations of Ideology in Seventeenth Century England*, (eds.) Katherine Z. Keller and Gerald J. Schiffhorst (Pittsburgh: Duquesne University Press, 1993), 128.

state."[16] In this vein, Face and his partners serve as representations of the culture's ambivalence about the changing criteria for elite status.

These socio-economic anxieties center in *The Alchemist* on how work in an urban, commercial space is being re-calibrated to emphasize mobility and ambition over preservation and sustenance. Self-advancement is the driving motive for Jonson's characters, irrespective of their initial access to economic and social capital, and it is precisely the cross-class availability of capitalist modes of work that Jonson highlights, and undermines, so effectively. The discourse of "venture," used by both gulls and rogues, indicates the nature of the work that these characters imagine themselves performing. The vision is already present in The Argument, with the mention of each rogue "contract[ing]" for a "share" of the investment. Early on, Dol refers to their partnership as the "venture tripartite" (1.1.135) between her and her two co-conspirators. Her rhetorical questions, "All things in common? / Without priority?" (135–6), imply a contractual agreement that has established equal shares of investment and profit. Work is transformed from labor conducted at the orders and on behalf of a master to a collaborative project undertaken on the initiative and for the benefit of shareholders. Mammon plays up the distinction between the "venture" and other kinds of work when he articulates his relationship to the coveted philosopher's stone. After his friend Surly opines that the man who acquires the stone must be "one free from mortal sin," Mammon counters: "But I buy it. / My venture brings it me" (2.2.99, 100–101). The humor lies in Mammon's unabashed substitution of money for morality, but equally telling is his substitution of venture for traditional forms of labor. There is no suggestion that Mammon expects to *do* anything in particular; his commitment to the work of the venture is secured, rather, by his monetary investment and the personal risk it signifies. Once initiated, the venture becomes the actor, that which "brings" and labors on the investor's behalf.

The absence of industry and diligence in Mammon's vision taps into the fear that commerce, trade, and other kinds of capitalist enterprise might subvert the economic and social virtues that were commonly associated with work. The detachment of capitalist work from labor in *The Alchemist* is evident not only in the implications of the "venture," but in its sometime synonym, the word "work," which appears thirty times in the play, most often in reference to grand alchemical projects. Representative is Subtle's pronouncement: "This is the day, I am to perfect for him / The *magisterium*, our great work, the stone" (1.4.13–14).[17] Defined less by occupational labor than by creative and contractual outcome, the work described by both rogues and gulls centers on a projection of hopes and gains, a perfect

---

[16] Dionne, "Fashioning Outlaws: The Early Modern Rogue and Urban Culture," in *Rogues and Early Modern English Culture*, (eds.) Craig Dionne and Steve Mentz (Ann Arbor: The University of Michigan Press, 2004), 55.

[17] As a noun in the play, "work" functions more often as "an act, deed, proceeding, business" (*OED*, "work, *n.*," I.1) than as an "action involving effort or exertion directed to a definite end, esp. as a means of gaining one's livelihood; labour, toil; (one's) regular occupation or employment" (*OED*, "work, *n.*," I.4).

analogue for, or even a realization of, commercial enterprise. Seven mentions of "work" come as verbs. These uses enhance the capitalist redefinition of work and tend to occur at moments when Jonson's characters are advising one another or themselves about how to produce transformative or manipulative effects in other people or things. Mammon imagines making Dol into his consort and showing her off at court: "Set all the eyes / Of court afire, like a burning glass, / And work 'em into cinders" (4.1.139–41), while Dol teases Mammon, "You are pleased, sir, / To work on the ambition of our sex" (4.1.129–30). To "work" or "work on" something or someone is an essentially self-serving act designed to advance the overall project. Far from connoting laborsome activity, it entails subverting societal expectations and circumventing moral requirements in order to accrue capital.

As it turns out, Face, Subtle, and Dol have not exactly liberated themselves from labor; on the contrary, they are entangled in precisely the subservience and toil from which they seek to escape. Face exposes this irony in one of his rants against Subtle: "You must have stuff, brought home to you, to work on? / And, yet, you think, I am at no expense, / In searching out these veins, then following 'em, / Then trying 'em out" (1.3.104–7). Although the stress on capital investment—here, "expense"—remains, Face gives an early reminder that the grandiose illusion that they are projecting entails good old-fashioned labor. The raw material or "stuff" of their schemes, namely, the gulls, must be identified, pursued, and lured to the house. Face wants to show Subtle that such efforts require not only money but also the fulfillment of a series of delimited, disciplined tasks. Indeed, the rogues are forced to labor ever more intensively as the conflicting demands of the gulls multiply, ratcheting up the effort needed to keep the facade of the great work intact. By Act 3, Face is evincing frustration at labors that have failed to "yield us grains," using an extended metaphor in which he is the "mill-jade," or horse whose laborious, circular march powers a grain mill (3.3.6, 5). We are always behind the scenes with the rogues, and the result is that we may be struck more by the sheer drudgery involved in keeping such complex schemes afloat than by the thrill of getting a glimpse into London's underworld.[18]

Although the emergent capitalist discourses of *The Alchemist* initially seem to herald a departure from the constrictions of service, the rogues' plans are predicated upon "serving" gulls. As the plot grows increasingly dense, the demands of service grow more intense. In the intent of the rogues, "to serve" means to trick or to dupe, but in carrying out this intent, the rogues end up serving the gulls in a more conventional fashion. The relationships that the rogues establish with their proposed victims both mimics and merges with the bond of servant and master. The venture depends upon appearing to cater to the gulls' desires, and the appearance must be sustained, the rogues soon find, through the actual labor, as well as the appearance, of service. As the pace quickens to a frenzy in Acts 3 and 4, the rogues are at the beck and call of their gulls, improvising "some device" (3.5.57) to keep each one placated. From the rogues' perspective, they are juggling

---

[18]	As Leinwand puts it, "A Blackfriars house is transmuted not only into an alchemical workshop and a dream machine but into a sweatshop." *Theatre, Finance and Society*, 131.

a set of false hopes along with the exits and entrances of the gulls. Yet Jonson also displays the perspective of the gulls, who surprisingly often act like satisfied masters. In his dealings with Sir Epicure Mammon, Face insists, "I have blown, sir, / Hard, for your worship" (2.2.21–2). Mammon, in response, is so pleased with Face's services that he promises him exalted positions as "master / Of my seraglio" (2.2.32–3) and a "lord's vermin" (2.3.330) once the philosopher's stone comes to fruition. To serve their own pleasurable delusions, the gulls require the rogues' labor.

The Alchemist has a story to tell about work at a transitional moment in early modern England. The quandary that Face, Subtle, and Dol face—the more strenuously they try to avoid the commitments of labor and service, the more inextricably they are bound to them—reveals the limits of socio-economic change for those at the lower levels of the social hierarchy. Jonson's rogues are at once emboldened and restricted by the fluidity in definitions of work. By embracing commercial enterprise, these marginal characters—in common with characters all along the social spectrum—see the possibility of advancement and profit without the traditional burdens of labor. Yet their only access to the capitalist sphere is by performing the skills that they already have. In other words, the end of labor cannot be envisioned outside of the paradigm that the servant or laborer attempts to escape; thus the conditions of their labor repeatedly and recursively continue.

Though Face and Subtle each play several roles, they do not stray far from service positions. Face alternates between turns as "suburb-captain" (1.1.19; a general purveyor of vice in the extramural Liberties) and as the alchemist's servant, Lungs. In impersonating a doctor of alchemy, Subtle appropriates a somewhat higher rank; but the "cunning-man" (1.2.8), though accorded an obsequious reverence by the gulls, is soon revealed to be more akin to a pander or pimp, managing an illicit but highly sought-after service, than the scholarly master to whom he bears a passing resemblance. He also is briefly disguised in 3.5 as "a Priest of Fairy," a minister of the "Aunt of Fairy" from whom Dapper hopes to inherit a fortune. Even their disguises, then, remain elevated versions of service.

The case of Dol invites inquiry into how working roles for marginal women might have compared to those of their male counterparts. In Acts 2–4, Dol appears mostly as a lord's sister wooed by Mammon, while in Act 5, she takes the part of the Fairy Queen to the hapless Dapper. The fact that among the co-conspirators, only Dol projects herself into aristocratic or royal identities that seem to transcend, however parodically, the urban marketplace, reveals how work economies map onto sexual economies in ways that eroticize and seemingly elevate the labor of women. Dol is identified first and foremost in *The Alchemist* with prostitution, an occupation that, as Jean Howard has suggested, "figures a market economy that can feel like it knows no boundaries."[19] Dol's fluidity gestures towards the lack of

---

[19]   Howard, "Sex and the Early Modern City: Staging the Bawdy Houses of London," in *The Impact of Feminism in English Renaissance Studies*, (ed.) Dympna Callaghan (Basingstoke, UK: Palgrave Macmillan, 2007), 123.

a firm divide between prostitution and other forms of labor and service available to women in the lower ranks of society.[20] Her labors encompass, but are not limited to, the sale of her body. She is clearly an equal sharer in the "venture tripartite," and takes as active a role as her male partners in managing the business; indeed, she is listed in the *dramatis personae* as "their colleague." She halts the feud in 1.1 that threatens to dissolve the venture; she provides crucial communication between the enterprise and its clientele ("I have told 'em, in a voice, / Thorough the trunk, like one of your familiars" [1.4.4–5]); and she plots to relieve Dame Pliant of her jewels (5.4.74). Moreover, Dol's prostitution, as the play portrays it, involves meticulous planning and work that go far beyond the labors of sex itself. In readying herself for a sexual encounter, Face notes that "she must prepare perfumes, delicate linen, / The bath in chief, a banquet, and her wit" (3.3.20–21). It is evident from such examples that prostitution is part of broader commercial prospects.

The prostitute's lack of circumspection applies as well, Howard maintains, to her ability to work her trade virtually anywhere and in virtually any guise, truisms borne out by Dol as she plies her sexual wares in Lovewit's "respectable" Blackfriars house and in disguise as a noblewoman. There is an implied fungibility between Dol's props and skills and those possessed by women of high rank who similarly rely on personal and luxurious enticements to woo suitors on the marriage market. Prostitution proves particularly malleable for Dol, allowing her both to engage in multiple facets of the commercial economy and to translate herself believably from a woman of sexual and other petty commerce to a virginal lord's sister involved in an elite marital commerce.[21] The interchange between gender and economics allows Dol to impersonate classed identities that are beyond the pale for Face and Subtle. In some ways, Dol is reminiscent of the increasingly commercialized female servant, whose threat of disorderly independence, as Michelle Dowd has shown, is managed through upwardly mobile marriage.[22]

---

[20]   Korda addresses how the "networks of commerce" through which many women sustained themselves with a combination of regulated and unregulated work were intertwined with the early modern stage. See "Women's Theatrical Properties," in *Staged Properties in Early Modern English Drama*, (eds.) Jonathan Gil Harris and Natasha Korda (Cambridge: Cambridge University Press, 2002), 202–29, and "Labors Lost."

[21]   Howard makes the point that "whore" city comedies depict fluid conversions between prostitutes and respectable wives ("Sex and the Early Modern City," 131). Jonson teases at, but does not carry through with, a conversion narrative of this sort in *The Alchemist*, not only by stressing the similarities between Dol and elite women, but also through Face and Subtle's plot to prostitute the widow Dame Pliant when they find themselves with one too many clients on their hands.

[22]   Dowd argues that female servants in the period increasingly cultivated "marketable skills and proficiencies in a commercial labor economy," practices that were at once associated with the prospect of advancement and the threat of women's "disorderly independence." "Labours of Love: Women, Marriage and Service in *Twelfth Night* and *The Compleat Servant-Maid*," *The Shakespearean International Yearbook* 5 (2005): 118, 112.

Yet Dol's narrative trajectory ultimately resists marriage. Her meetings with Mammon mimic those of a woman of elite status, without actually securing her such status through marriage. Despite her flexibility, Dol is limited, as are her male counterparts, by her marginality: She *is* the prostitute whom it was feared other female servants might become. It is the nominally respectable widow, Dame Pliant, rather than she, who marries at the end of the play. Dame Pliant is, after all, "a rich one" (5.3.86), while Dol evidently possesses little beyond the "velvet gown" (5.4.134) with which she is ultimately sent packing. Impersonation never yields to transformation for the rogues in *The Alchemist*, and ultimately Dol is no exception. Her work in the play points to continuities between urban women of disparate economic status, while restoring the boundaries between them.[23]

Work in *The Alchemist*, I have argued, does not offer the rogues a true portal from their peripheral and precarious status to the respectability that might allow them to flourish in the new economy. Although critics have associated performance, disguise, and role-playing with social mobility, the efficacy of such methods proves limited in Jonson's play. The rogues are not the only disappointed aspirants in the play; most of the gulls are also sent away empty-handed. With the possible exception of Surly, however, the gulls already have a foothold in society: they have capital to invest in their ventures, whereas those who possess little to begin with remain dispossessed.[24]

It is no accident that Face makes a literal return to servitude when Lovewit arrives at the end of Act 4 to reclaim his house. The recursive logic that Jonson traces practically demands that Face must ultimately scrape together an appeal to his master's largesse to save his place. By leveraging his influence with Lovewit, Face manages to defraud his co-conspirators and hold onto the "pelf" that the three had stolen from the gulls. Yet he does so at the cost of a far more valuable prize: the young, wealthy widow, Dame Pliant, whom he had intended to marry himself. Because Lovewit's social authority and power obviously trump that of his servant, the latter must surrender his best hope for advancement to his master. The disguise of the Spanish don that he had planned to wear to fool the widow into marriage is worn by Lovewit instead, affirming that elite disguises are more efficacious for those whose status is already assured. Lovewit confirms hierarchical privilege when in his final speech he promises to show his gratitude to Face "and help his fortune" (5.5.151). In the last lines of the play, Face tells the audience that "this pelf, / Which I have got, if you do quit me, rests / To feast you often, and invite new guests" (163–5). The audience is left to wonder whether Face's newly-acquired capital will finally allow him to leave his master's service and establish

---

[23]   It may be true, as Karen Newman claims, that in Jonson, "the relations of all the women to commodification are represented as the same, which tends to level class differences," but in *The Alchemist*, the (dis)possession of capital becomes the crucial marker of class difference between women. "City Talk: Women and Commodification in Jonson's *Epicoene*," *ELH* 56 (1989): 512.

[24]   Hill, *Liberty Against the Law*, 60.

his own household and hospitality, or, as seems more likely, he will remain bound to the master at whose pleasure he keeps his hard-fought treasure.

If Face, Subtle, and Dol try with mixed results to perform capitalism by "acting" on their shares, thus hoping to transform their relationship to labor and profit, capitalism was itself being performed in London theaters daily, in ways that *were* transforming the relationship between labor and profit. Just two years before the first performance of *The Alchemist*, the King's Men had assumed occupancy of the indoor Blackfriars playhouse. The collaborative nature of the rogues' shareholding, as well as the fact that in *The Alchemist* rogues and gulls are ultimately engaged (even if sometimes unwittingly) in a shared venture, offers a striking parallel to the innovative business arrangement that the King's Men had cultivated since 1594, when a group of players and theater entrepreneurs took shares to form a company then called the Lord Chamberlain's Men. Based on the shareholding principle, in 1599 the Burbage brothers formed a core group of "housekeepers" who together bore the risks and rewards of building the Globe theater and eventually of taking over the Blackfriars playhouse. For those who owned shares, and especially for housekeepers, to work for the King's Men was to participate in a capitalist venture akin to that imagined by Jonson's characters. Indeed, the highest levels of the company were occupied increasingly by the housekeepers, who could expect significantly greater profits than standard company shareholders.[25]

For other members of a playing company, enjoying the fruits of a capitalist economy could not be taken for granted. The ranks were filled by hired hands, who worked steadily or occasionally, as players or behind the scenes, in exchange for "wages ... paid by the year or the week or even the day."[26] Near the bottom of this continuum, comparisons to Fumerton's "unsettled" subjects become more apt. The possibility that an outlay of money might replace labor must have seemed like a chimera, or perhaps even an irrelevance, to many of the working subjects who made playhouses function day in and day out. In this sense, *The Alchemist* helps us to glimpse the unglamorous working conditions of those who made the playing companies and theaters run.

Hierarchies of work underwrote theatrical productions in the Blackfriars as surely as they inscribe plot action in Lovewit's house. This does not mean that divisions in theatrical labor and work always fell neatly along socio-economic lines, although some critics have been quick to draw parallels between occupational identities in the companies and in the play. Reading theater history back into the play, Gurr argues that Lovewit, the owner of the house who returns to collect on the labor of others, stands in for the housekeepers of the King's Men, and

---

[25] As Gurr explains, housekeeping shares were not even necessarily controlled by active participants in the company; they could be sold or passed on by inheritance, and many shares in the first decades of the seventeenth century became dissociated from the King's Men in that fashion. *Shakespeare Company*, 118.

[26] Gurr, *Shakespeare Company*, 89. Out of a company of fifteen at the turn of the century, almost half of the members were hired labor rather than shareholders.

that "Jonson saw the housekeepers as the affluent idlers who profiteered from the tricks the players entertained their customers with."[27] Based on his investigation of lawsuits involving the Blackfriars, Leinwand understands Lovewit as a prototype for Richard Burbage, the "absentee landlord who conveniently returned to the scene at just the moment the Blackfriars company was in shambles."[28] In these metatheatrical allegories, Jonson recognizes property ownership as marking the crucial division between "haves" and "have-nots" in the theatrical economy.[29]

Yet to draw such exact parallels between characters and their historical counterparts misses a fundamental point about work and working identities in the theater: while socio-economic divisions certainly did reproduce themselves within the playing companies, those divisions were neither stable nor predictable. For one thing, the emphasis on monetary investment and reward hides from view the material labors that most sharers in the early seventeenth century continued to perform, whether acting in plays or managing the company's affairs.[30] As *The Alchemist* shows, the onstage and offstage components of theatrical production required labor-intensive exertions, intellectual and physical, and not only on the part of hired hands. Moreover, in the King's Men, the seven housekeepers who collaborated on the Globe doubled the roles of "impresario-playhouse-landlord and player-tenant."[31] For a housekeeper at once to occupy the position of employer and employee, manager and worker, property-owner and renter, master and servant, was to break down boundaries between social and economic categories of work. The documentary evidence on the King's Men supports the mixed nature of early modern work in and for the theater, which was grounded in labor that made good on an investment, transforming it from inert to active status.

The economic subject positions of theater workers were heterogeneous, shaped in part by the growing imperatives of a market economy, but also by older traditions of service work associated with craft guilds and noble patronage.[32] David Kathman

---

[27]   Gurr, *Shakespeare Company*, 116–17.

[28]   Leinwand, *Theatre, Finance and Society*, 137–8. See also Melissa D. Aaron, "'Beware At What Hands Thou Receiv'st Thy Commodity': *The Alchemist* and the King's Men Fleece the Customers, 1610," in *Inside Shakespeare: Essays on the Blackfriars Stage*, (ed.) Paul Menzer (Selinsgrove, PA: Susquehanna University Press, 2006), 72–9.

[29]   In "*The Alchemist* and the Emerging Adult Private Playhouse," *SEL* 45 (2005): 375–99, Anthony J. Ouellette gives an interesting twist to such readings: he views Face as the play's winner because he is not only a charismatic player but also an aspiring playwright, and one who, like the shareholders in the King's Men, has a stake in the permanent property.

[30]   Gurr, *Shakespeare Company*, 89.

[31]   Ibid., 112.

[32]   See William Ingram's hypothesis in *The Business of Playing: The Beginnings of the Adult Professional Theater in Elizabethan London* (Ithaca and London: Cornell University Press, 1992) that "Everyone involved in the enterprise in this period, including the vast majority of writers for the stage, would have seen his activity (I believe) indifferently as an art, a craft, and a means of producing wealth" (16).

has demonstrated that the livery companies and their apprenticeship system served as an important mechanism and model for socio-economic relations within the playing companies.[33] Adult players, who were also freemen of various guilds, took on boys as apprentices and trained them in the theater, using them in female roles and producing both future sharers and hired men. The latter often went on both to become free of livery companies and to have long careers as players.[34] We might speculate further that the fraternal, cooperative ethos of the guilds was formative for the sense of communal purpose, even teamwork, that Gurr and others have argued characterized the companies, a purpose that did not obviate hierarchy but operated within its requirements. Meanwhile, the London companies continued to function with the license of their noble and royal patrons; formally, players were servants of the aristocracy, with certain accompanying privileges.[35] If structures of work in the theater were indebted both to the venture and the craft, the theater also remained a scion of aristocratic service.

Even as the London theater was becoming "professionalized" and finding new ways to authorize and legitimate the work of its practitioners, spectators of different ranks within the theater saw no contradiction in, and in some cases relied materially on, inhabiting more than one occupational position, just as the players themselves did.[36] The early modern theater was a transitional workplace, entangled like many other urban institutions in multiple economies and paradigms of work.

Company records indicate that Face was played consecutively by two housekeepers / sharers in the King's Men: Nathan Field (also at various times a boy player and playwright) from 1615–1619, and Joseph Taylor after 1619; while Lovewit was likely played by Robert Benfield, who began as a hired man and evolved first into a sharer and by the 1630s into a housekeeper.[37] Unlike Face and Lovewit, the players behind these roles did not revert to a strict occupational stratification; rather, they were men who ascended the ranks of company hierarchy, who likely did or had done manual and physical labor, who learned parts and donned costumes, and who did or would make investments that rendered them

---

[33]   David Kathman, "Grocers, Goldsmiths, and Drapers: Freemen and Apprentices in the Elizabethan Theater," *Shakespeare Quarterly* 55 (2004): 1–49. See also Stephen Orgel, *Impersonations* (Cambridge: Cambridge University Press, 1996), 64–74, on implications of the guild structure for the playing companies and their modes of representation.

[34]   Kathman, "Grocers, Goldsmiths, and Drapers," 4.

[35]   Ingram, *Business of Playing*, 89. On the relation of players to different paradigms of service, see David Schalkwyk, *Shakespeare, Love and Service* (Cambridge: Cambridge University Press, 2008).

[36]   Ingram, *Business of Playing*, 49. Kathman's research shows that even prominent people in the theater were often aligned with non-theatrical trades and crafts: for example, one of the King's Men's most celebrated players, Robert Armin, was apprenticed as a goldsmith and later made free of the company. "Grocers, Goldsmiths, and Drapers," 18, 38–9.

[37]   Gurr, *Shakespeare Company*, 220, 227, 243. More details on early casts of *The Alchemist* are provided by James A. Riddell, "Some Actors in Ben Jonson's Plays," *Shakespeare Studies* 5 (1969): 285–98.

property-owners and stakeholders. Their fluid histories, like Jonson's own, are a counterpoint to the regressive leanings of the play's ending, a reminder that the play invites us to look for signification both within and beyond its fictionality.[38]

The Alchemist uses the theater as metaphor and microcosm for the retrenchment of hierarchies of work and identity in a developing capitalist economy. The play also reflects on the early modern theater as an institution in which traditional and emerging taxonomies of work collided and merged, and in which the same subject might in the course of a working life be both a Face and a Lovewit, sometimes both at once. In the drama, the rogues struggle in vain to transcend the labor that their status confers. In the theater, labor was irreducible and omnipresent, requiring tremendous work at moments of supreme illusion that seemed the most effortless. It was in the theater that work mapped onto identity more flexibly, and was less affixed to concepts of permanent character than in Jonson's imagining. When Face, in his final speech, tells the audience, "My part a little fell in this last scene, / Yet 'twas *decorum*" (5.5.158–9), he evokes the resilience of categories of work and subjectivity as well as their self-conscious artificiality.

---

[38] As numerous commentators have observed, Ben Jonson was free of the tylers and bricklayers, and he thought enough of his membership to pay his dues to the company for quite some time after he had become an established playwright. Kathman, "Goldsmiths, Grocers and Drapers," 31–2.

Chapter 8
Desiring Subjects:
Staging the Female Servant in
Early Modern Tragedy

Michelle M. Dowd

The third act of Shakespeare's *The Winter's Tale* (first performed in 1611) stages a scene of loss and redemption, death and transformation that is intimately connected to matters of genre. The death of Antigonus paired with the finding of the infant Perdita by the Bohemian shepherd occasion a striking shift in the play's tone and formal momentum. As the shepherd tells his son: "thou met'st with things dying, I with things new-born" (3.3.113–14).[1] But this oft-discussed transition in the play's mood and structure is also, perhaps surprisingly, associated with women's service. When the shepherd first comes across Perdita alone on the seacoast, he exclaims: "Though I am not bookish, yet I can read waiting-gentlewoman in the scape. This has been some stair-work, some trunk-work, some behind-door-work. They were warmer that got this than the poor thing is here" (3.3.72–6). The shepherd interprets the abandoned infant as the product of a "scape," or sexual escapade, involving a waiting-gentlewoman and probably conducted furtively (i.e., under the stairs, in a trunk, or behind a door). Historically speaking, the shepherd's analysis of the scene corresponds to what we know about illegitimate births among women in service. Despite the fact women in service in early modern England were generally expected to remain chaste and were not permitted to marry, "the typical unmarried mother who was brought before the secular courts was the maidservant who had been impregnated by her master or fellow servant."[2] Given these circumstances, Shakespeare's shepherd might be forgiven for jumping so quickly to his conclusions.

What interests me most about this passage, however, is not the "accuracy" of the shepherd's assumptions per se, but the fact that the *narrative* of the sexually deviant female servant proves to be especially useful at this key juncture in the play. This particular story, after all, is not just an analytical assessment of the probability of the child's origins, but rather an embellished, even fanciful account

---

[1]   All citations of Shakespeare's plays refer to *The Riverside Shakespeare*, 2nd ed., (ed.) G. Blakemore Evans (Boston: Houghton Mifflin, 1997) and will be given parenthetically in the text. For all primary texts, dates in parentheses indicate the year the work was first published, unless otherwise indicated.

[2]   See Sara Mendelson and Patricia Crawford, *Women in Early Modern England* (Oxford: Oxford University Press, 1998), 97–8.

that conjures up lurid images of a female servant engaged in "behind-door-work." Deployed at the very moment in which the play switches gears from tragedy to comedy (or at least to tragicomedy), the shepherd's tale offers a sort of generic bridge, providing a temporary explanation of Perdita's origins that allows the plot to move forward toward eventual resolution. Moreover, the story itself is a generic mixture: although the furtive sexual rendezvous and the presumably illegitimate child presage tragedy, the tone and diction of the shepherd's relation imply comedy, even farce. Visible only as an abstract, sexualized figure in the shepherd's narrative, the waiting-gentlewoman remains shadowy and indeterminate, yet also oddly central to the generically hybrid plot of Shakespeare's romance. Indeed, I would suggest that her narrative importance is directly related to the deferral and eventual effacement of the potentially tragic consequences of her story.

In what follows, I turn my attention to early modern tragedy—the genre that the shepherd's narrative seems both to invite and resist—in order to explore in greater detail the ways in which women's service work gets ideologically deployed in dramatic narratives. Tragedy may initially seem an unlikely genre to examine for traces of women's work (in comparison, for instance, to domestic comedies that focus on the daily workings of the household), but I am particularly interested in the ways in which tragic form, especially in plays that give sustained attention to female servant characters, both occludes and enables specific narratives of women's service. These narratives actively re-imagine and discursively delimit the cultural meaning of female service during a transitional period in English economic history. Looking primarily at Thomas Dekker, John Ford, and William Rowley's *The Witch of Edmonton* (first performed in 1621) and Rowley and Thomas Middleton's *The Changeling* (first performed in 1622), I argue that these Jacobean tragedies stage the sexual vulnerability of the female servant in part as a cautionary narrative about domestic order and the shifting parameters of the institution of service. At the same time, the formal trajectories that shape the plots of female servants derive much of their force from the cultural fantasies of marriage and domestic harmony that tragedy seems generically designed to resist. As such, these formal features and oddly romanticized narratives of female service substitute fictions of desire for the real sexual coercion and economic imperatives that attended England's increasingly commercialized labor market.

The early seventeenth century was a particularly uncertain time for the institution of domestic service in England. About sixty percent of those aged fifteen to twenty-four were servants living in the households of families other than their birth families, and young women were more often employed in service than in any other occupation.[3] Women from nearly all ranks of society worked as servants

---

[3]   See Mendelson and Crawford, *Women in Early Modern England*, 92–4 and Keith Wrightson, *Earthly Necessities: Economic Lives in Early Modern Britain* (New Haven: Yale University Press, 2000), 32–3. For the increase in female household servants during the early modern period, see Anne Laurence, *Women in England 1500–1760: A Social History* (London: Phoenix Giant, 1994), 134–5 and Ilana Krausman Ben-Amos, *Adolescence and Youth in Early Modern England* (New Haven: Yale University Press, 1994), 151.

in domestic settings, ranging from scullery maids to ladies-in-waiting (including, we may presume, the shepherd's "waiting-gentlewoman"). Yet, despite their ubiquity, female servants were not always easily absorbed into social hierarchies, largely because the nature of those hierarchies was changing as England moved toward a more widespread wage-based system of labor. By the beginning of the seventeenth century, due in part to the sharp reduction in the size of aristocratic households, increasing numbers of servants were negotiating yearly contracts with their masters rather than assuming long-term positions.[4] Because female domestic servants had been removed from their birth homes and their parents' supervision, their social status was especially ambiguous. Often, these women were viewed as sexually vulnerable and potentially disorderly singlewomen; indeed, the 1563 Statute of Artificers, which stated that local officials could order unmarried women aged twelve to forty into service, was based on the principle that unmarried and masterless women were inherently disorderly.[5] While in service, women were often subject to the sexual advances of their masters or fellow servants, and the public penalties for these liaisons would usually fall most heavily on the female domestic. In his analysis of seventeenth-century female servants' accounts of sexual relations with their masters, Tim Meldrum notes three recurring themes: "the tensions that were created within households, the breaking of bonds that resulted, and the almost inevitable loss of place for the servant who conceived."[6] These

---

[4]   See A.L. Beier, *Masterless Men: The Vagrancy Problem in England 1560–1640* (London, Methuen, 1985). For the gradual replacement of the feudal ideology of service with a wage-labor system in the period, see Michael Neill, *Putting History to the Question: Power, Politics, and Society in English Renaissance Drama* (New York: Columbia University Press, 2000), 28–39; Wendy Wall, *Staging Domesticity: Household Work and English Identity in Early Modern Drama* (Cambridge: Cambridge University Press, 2002), 201–3; Mark Thornton Burnett, *Masters and Servants in English Renaissance Drama and Culture: Authority and Obedience* (New York: St Martin's, 1997), 4–5 and 8–9; and Mary Ellen Lamb, "Tracing a Heterosexual Erotics of Service in *Twelfth Night* and the Autobiographical Writings of Thomas Whythorne and Anne Clifford," *Criticism* 40.1 (1998): 1–7. For contemporary concerns about the increasingly mercenary nature of service, see Walter Darell, *A Short Discourse of the Life of Servingmen* (London, 1578) and I.M., *A Health to the Gentlemanly Profession of Servingmen* (London, 1598).

[5]   See Mendelson and Crawford, *Women in Early Modern England*, 96. For the potential challenge to social order posed by singlewomen, see also Paul Griffiths, *Youth and Authority: Formative Experiences in England 1560–1640* (Oxford: Clarendon Press, 1996), 358–9 and Amy M. Froide, *Never Married: Singlewomen in Early Modern England* (Oxford: Oxford University Press, 2005). For the connection between service and vagrancy in the period, see also Patricia Fumerton, *Unsettled: The Culture of Mobility and the Working Poor in Early Modern England* (Chicago: University of Chicago Press, 2006), 12–32.

[6]   Meldrum, "London Domestic Servants from Depositional Evidence, 1660–1750: Servant-Employer Sexuality in the Patriarchal Household," in *Chronicling Poverty: The Voices and Strategies of the English Poor, 1640–1840*, (eds.) Tim Hitchcock, Peter King, and Pamela Sharpe (New York: St Martin's Press, 1997), 48.

tensions, together with the often disastrous emotional and economic consequences of rape or pregnancy, meant that women in service, despite their familiar presence in early modern homes, were often regarded as transient, potentially disruptive and sexually available.

Dekker, Ford and Rowley's domestic tragedy *The Witch of Edmonton* dramatizes many of these social uncertainties. As befits its genre, the play begins where more comedic narratives involving female service usually leave off—with a marriage.[7] In the play's main plot, Winifred, a maidservant of Sir Arthur Clarington, has married Frank Thorney, a gentleman's son who is also in Sir Arthur's service. The marriage legitimizes Frank and Winifred's unborn child; Winifred admits that Frank has had "conquest of my maiden-love" and Frank reassures her that, "Thy child shall know / Who to call Dad now" (1.1.33, 4–5).[8] Young working women in city comedies are frequently subject to the sexual advances of their male suitors, but Winifred is vulnerable to both a fellow servant and, we learn a few scenes later, her master. Learning of Winifred's marriage to Frank, Sir Arthur interprets the event as a clever ploy of hers to allow them to continue their sexual liaison without suspicion; as he tells her, "now we share / Free scope enough, without control or fear, / To interchange our pleasures" (1.1.170–72). Sir Arthur's diction emphasizes mutuality at the expense of coercion, representing their liaison as a collaborative act of interchange and sharing rather than as manipulation. When she acts confused about his meaning, he reminds her of their "secret game" (1.1.176), another euphemism that associates her with furtive, but mutual, sexual exploits (much like the "behind-door-work" in the shepherd's narrative) instead of with sexual and social powerlessness. Although the rhetoric of this exchange posits Winifred's sexual relations with Sir Arthur as mutual rather than enforced, the scene challenges that conclusion through Winifred's reference to Frank's "conquest," an appropriate metaphor for Winifred's defenselessness.

Winifred's situation makes legible the fact that for early modern women, service was frequently a form of sexual as well as social subordination. Although female servants had been associated with disruptive sexuality in popular literature dating back to the thirteenth and fourteenth centuries, these earlier tales tended to focus on lecherous maidservants who used their occupations as covers for sexual escapades rather than on servants' sexuality vulnerability.[9] By the seventeenth

---

[7]   For a fuller discussion of the teleological marriage plot as it relates to early modern comedy, see my essay, "Labors of Love: Women, Marriage, and Service in *Twelfth Night* and *The Compleat Servant-Maid*," *Shakespearean International Yearbook 5* (2005): 103–26 and its expanded version in *Women's Work in Early Modern English Literature and Culture* (New York: Palgrave Macmillan, 2009).

[8]   Thomas Dekker, John Ford, and William Rowley, *The Witch of Edmonton*, (ed.) Arthur F. Kinney (London: A & C Black, 1998). All citations will refer to this edition of the play and will be given parenthetically in the text.

[9]   See Michael Goodich, "*Ancilla Dei*: The Servant as Saint in the Late Middle Ages," in *Women of the Medieval World: Essays in Honor of John H. Mundy*, (eds.) Julius Kirshner and Suzanne F. Wemple (Oxford: Basil Blackwell, 1985), 121–5.

century, as Susan Amussen has demonstrated, servants faced a contradiction in the household in which they worked because they were simultaneously protected and threatened by their masters. A master was in theory "supposed to ensure the moral behavior of his servants, but he could also force them to have sex with him."[10] Female servants were understood as sexually available within the households in which they were employed and were often not protected by "normal community controls on extramarital sex."[11] Characters such as Winifred expose these domestic contradictions as they become caught up in their potentially tragic consequences. Although muted by Sir Arthur's euphemistic rhetoric and Frank's bland reassurances, Winifred's sexual vulnerability is nevertheless a necessary precondition of the play's tragicomic plot. As an emblem of the crisis of domestic authority and social order, the pregnant, single maidservant sets the stage for the violence and disorder that will presumably follow.

As in *The Winter's Tale*, however, the potential tragedy of Winifred's situation is staged only to be systematically deferred over the course of the plot. Violence and disorder *do* certainly follow in the course of the play, but Winifred is oddly immune from much of it, and her own story is discursively reworked so as to separate her from the tragedy that befalls many of the play's other characters. Sir Arthur's rhetoric of sexual partnership begins to distance Winifred from the taint of sexual scandal in the very first scene of the play, as we have seen. Furthermore, by opening the play with Frank's assurances of marriage, Dekker, Ford, and Rowley simultaneously elicit and disarm "[t]he threatening figure of the single, pregnant, potentially masterless woman."[12] Indeed, despite Sir Arthur's prodding, Winifred is firmly resolved not only to marry Frank but also to end her affair with her master, proclaiming: "I will change my life, / From a loose whore to a repentant wife" (1.1.192–3). Because she refuses to comply with his desires, Winifred is forced to leave Sir Arthur's service, another event that would mark her as masterless and socially displaced if she hadn't so fortuitously married Frank. As if to highlight the neat coincidence of her termination as a servant and her fortunate entrée into married life, Winifred marks the occasion by announcing her own parallel moral transformation. In plotting the course from

---

[10]   Amussen, "Punishment, Discipline, and Power: The Social Meanings of Violence in Early Modern England," *Journal of British Studies* 34.1 (1995): 14.

[11]   Amussen, "Punishment, Discipline, and Power," 15–16. For the sexual vulnerability of female servants, see also Garthine Walker, "Rereading Rape and Sexual Violence in Early Modern England," *Gender and History* 10.1 (1998): 1–25; Marjorie Keniston McIntosh, "Servants and the Household Unit in an Elizabethan English Community," *Journal of Family History* 9.1 (1984): 20–21; Griffiths, *Youth and Authority*, 273–6; Laura Gowing, *Common Bodies: Women, Touch and Power in Seventeenth-Century England* (New Haven: Yale University Press, 2003), 59–65; Meldrum, "London Domestic Servants," 52–7; and Martin Ingram, *Church Courts, Sex and Marriage in England, 1570–1640* (Cambridge: Cambridge University Press, 1987), 259–81.

[12]   See Helen Vella Bonavita, "Maids, Wives and Widows: Multiple Meaning and Marriage in *The Witch of Edmonton*," *Parergon* 23.2 (2006): 88.

"loose whore" to "repentant wife," Winifred transforms Sir Arthur's rhetoric of jocular sexuality into a new story, a tidy conversion plot that promises a coherent narrative trajectory just at the moment when her occupational and social position seem most precarious. The tragic consequences of Winifred's tenure in service are thus staged only to be hastily displaced by more comforting plotlines involving repentance and marriage.

The reassuring idea that women would get married immediately after leaving positions in service was a popular one in early modern England, one bolstered by the increasingly transitory nature of service by the early seventeenth century and by the expectation that women could work as servants in order to gain the practical skills they would need as wives and to delay their marriages until they became more economically feasible. Yet this social ideal frequently jarred with reality. Many former servants were never able to marry for financial reasons, and poverty caused a great many others to delay their marriages long after they left their positions as domestics.[13] The fact that contemporary comedies romanticize women's movement from service to marriage is unsurprising; that a tragedy like *The Witch of Edmonton* should do so warrants further scrutiny. Winifred's hasty marriage does not transform her story into the stuff of romantic comedy, but it does, at least initially, substitute the formal *structure* of comic resolution for the fallen-from-grace narrative of tragic loss that her initial situation seems to presage.

Yet if the play offers a marriage plot to assuage concerns about Winifred's social displacement, that move is only partially successful at best. Although Winifred is spared the most disastrous outcomes of being a single, pregnant, out-of-work maidservant—such as poverty, abandonment, criminal prosecution, or death—her marriage to Frank is hardly the end of her troubles. When Frank marries Susan Carter later in the play, the union that was supposed to legitimize Winifred and her child quickly becomes a bigamous one. The neat trajectory that propelled Winifred out of service and into a life of marriage and moral certainty is quickly thrown into disarray by Frank's second marriage, which not only taints the legitimacy of the first but also forces Winifred to return to service in the guise of a male page in order to mask her husband's illicit relationships. In staging this return to service, the play, as Mark Thornton Burnett has argued, "explores the options available to the abandoned woman servant forced to find a legitimate social niche."[14] Although married and thus ostensibly assigned a clear social place, Winifred remains at least symbolically abandoned by both husband and master. Unlike the function of cross-

---

[13]   For service as a transitional position, see Ann Kussmaul, *Servants in Husbandry in Early Modern England* (Cambridge: Cambridge University Press, 1981), 4; Wrightson, *Earthly Necessities*, 32; Mendelson and Crawford, *Women in Early Modern England*, 92–6; and Judith Weil, *Service and Dependency in Shakespeare's Plays* (Cambridge: Cambridge University Press, 2005), 18–23. On service as preparation for marriage, see Judith M. Bennett and Amy M. Froide, "A Singular Past," in *Singlewomen in the European Past, 1250–1800*, (eds.) Bennett and Froide (Philadelphia: University of Pennsylvania Press, 1999), 9–10 and Ben-Amos, *Adolescence and Youth*, 227–32.

[14]   See Burnett, *Masters and Servants*, 135.

dressing in a comedy such as *Twelfth Night*, in which Viola dons male disguise as a means of self-preservation and, as Jean Howard has argued, as a "holding place" until she returns to the heterosexual marriage economy,[15] Winifred's act of cross-dressing effectively disallows her any closure that she might otherwise have gained by marrying Frank. Susan, Frank's second wife, has been told that Winifred (as a male page) was "commended" to her husband by Sir Arthur. Telling the disguised Winifred that Frank was also one of Sir Arthur's servants, Susan remarks: "That title methinks should make you almost fellows, / Or at the least much more than a servant; / And I am sure he will respect you so" (3.2.59–61). Susan's syntactically hesitant lines locate Winifred in the murky space that exists between being "almost fellows" and being "much more than a servant," denying her the social stability promised by marriage in lieu of service. Both her disguise and Frank's bigamy effectively preclude her from publicly claiming her status as a wife, a series of events that destabilizes the institution of marriage itself as a force of social order in the play.[16] Marriage in *The Witch of Edmonton* is hardly a celebratory end to service or even to sexual improprieties, but an expedient arrangement that initiates a new scenario of sexual and social disorder.

Even so, the conclusion of Winifred's story is far more positive than this series of potentially tragic events might suggest. Despite her mistreatment throughout the play—including the fact that she is saddled with a bigamous husband-turned-murderer-turned-executed-criminal—Winifred ultimately escapes the fate of many female servants who appear in historical narratives as vagrants or destitute single mothers. Indeed, even though it appears that she will be left, in Frank's words, "unprovided" and "unfriended" after his death, the Justice rules that Sir Arthur must pay her "a thousand marks" for "his abuse" of her, a sum to which Sir Arthur willingly agrees (5.3.65, 66, 158, 156). Winifred thus receives a generous monetary payment that saves her from poverty, while also acquiring the spiritual authority that accompanies the role of grieving widow. As he is being taken to execution, Frank specifically plots out this role for his "much wronged" bride (5.3.63). He tells her:

> there is payment
> Belongs to goodness from the great exchequer
> Above; it will not fail thee, Winifred;
> Be that thy comfort. (5.3.69–72)

Winifred assents to this designation as a pseudo-martyr figure, telling the gathered company that she will survive as the "monument" of Frank's "loved memory," a memory that she will preserve "[w]ith a religious care" (5.3.100–102). Her

[15] See Howard, *The Stage and Social Struggle in Early Modern England* (London: Routledge, 1994), 93–128.

[16] On the destabilization of marriage in the play, see Bonavita, "Maids, Wives and Widows," and Lisa Hopkins, "Ladies' Trials: Women and the Law in Three Plays of John Ford," *Cahiers Elisabéthains* 56 (1999): 53.

transition from "loose whore" to "repentant wife" is superseded by her final status as a widow with "modest hopes" (Epil. 5), who is literally granted the final word in the play when she addresses the audience in the epilogue. Winifred's story is thus both a cautionary one—a potent reminder of the sexual and social disruptions that can stem from women's work as domestic servants—and a fanciful one, in which real concerns about poverty, vagrancy, and sexual scandal are displaced by more reassuring narratives that emphasize women's seemingly effortless transitions from servant to wife to widow. It would be a mistake, however, to conclude unequivocally that this surprisingly happy ending constructs the subjectivity of female servants in positive terms. All of the more "favorable" subject-positions that Winifred inhabits in the play—such as the role of grieving widow or her designation as Sir Arthur's sexual "partner" rather than his abused servant—are carefully delimited and scripted by others. Sir Arthur deflects any suggestion of overt sexual coercion in the first scene, and the Justice, Frank, and Sir Arthur provide a frame for understanding her story of service and its end, an end that coincides with widowhood rather than with marriage. In staging Winifred's oddly romanticized narrative, *The Witch of Edmonton* announces and then averts tragic catastrophe. Yet it suggests that tragedy is prevented not through the agency of the servant herself, but rather by virtue of her fortuitous circumstances and the intervention of her male superiors.

In deflecting her potential tragedy, Dekker, Ford, and Rowley allow others to plot and define Winifred's experiences both during and following her tenure in service. This is a discursive strategy common to many tragedies of the period, even those with relatively minor female servant characters. In *Arden of Faversham* (1592), for instance, a domestic tragedy intensely interested in the relationships between masters and servants, Susan, the servingmaid of Alice Arden and sister to Alice's lover, Mosby, serves primarily as a pawn in Alice and Mosby's plot against Arden.[17] Susan has only a handful of lines in the entire play, yet she figures prominently as the subject of Alice and Mosby's marriage negotiations on her behalf. In order to enlist their assistance in murdering Arden, Alice and Mosby promise Susan in marriage to both Michael, Arden's servant, and Clarke, the painter who devises the (unsuccessful) poisoned painting. Susan is thus entered into two competing marriage plots of which she is entirely unaware. Even a letter that Michael prepares for Susan, in which these competing narratives are solidified and explained, is intercepted by Arden, who rails against Michael for wanting to

---

[17]   Noteworthy studies of this play and its master-servant dynamics include: Frances E. Dolan, *Dangerous Familiars: Representations of Domestic Crime in England 1550–1700* (Ithaca: Cornell University Press, 1993), 20–58; Lena Cowen Orlin, *Private Matters and Public Culture in Post-Reformation England* (Ithaca: Cornell University Press, 1994), 15–78; and Garrett A. Sullivan, Jr., *The Drama of Landscape: Land, Property, and Social Relations on the Early Modern Stage* (Stanford: Stanford University Press, 1998), 31–56.

marry "so base a trull" (3.28).[18] Although neither of Susan's marriage prospects is ever realized in the play, her hypothetical marriage is nonetheless a necessary fiction that fuels Mosby's and Alice's murderous plans. Ultimately, Susan is herself sentenced to death, even though she has minimal complicity in the murder of Arden (she tells Mosby innocently that she "knew not of it till the deed was done" [18.20]). As a subordinate member of a household in which subordinates have rebelled against their master, Susan is positioned in the play as guilty by association. Her own narrative of service and the marriage trajectories in which she is unwittingly inserted are so rigorously controlled that they take shape in the drama almost exclusively through the words of others. However, the silencing of Susan in this tragedy also hints at what is imagined to be the dangerously unpredictable nature of female servants—those "base trulls" who must be carefully managed, scripted, and scrutinized lest they (in Arden's words) become part of a "crew of harlots, all in love" (3.25).

Rowley and Middleton's tragedy *The Changeling* is similarly interested in the potential sexual disorder caused by female servants, but it shares with *The Witch of Edmonton* a pattern of deferral and redeployment whereby the story of the female domestic is manipulated and redefined for strategic purposes. However, in the overtly tragic ending of Rowley and Middleton's play (compared with the tragicomic redemption of Winifred) chaos and violence command the stage more viscerally and at greater length.[19] Diaphanta, Beatrice's waiting-woman in *The Changeling*, figures as both a pawn in a larger plot and as a character who, like Susan in *Arden of Faversham*, must be scripted by others in the face of her own silence. Diaphanta's primary role in the play is to substitute for Beatrice on her wedding night with Alsemero; Beatrice pays the virgin Diaphanta one thousand ducats to take over her "first night's pleasure" in order to hide the fact that she herself is no longer a virgin (4.1.88).[20] Eager to accept Beatrice's offer, Diaphanta giddily exclaims: "The bride's place, / And with a thousand ducats! I'm for a justice now: / I bring a portion with me; I scorn small fools" (4.1.128–30). The

---

[18]   *Arden of Faversham*, (ed.) Martin White (London: A & C Black, 1982). All citations will refer to this edition of the play and will be given parenthetically in the text.

[19]   For the link between disloyal servants and sexual ambition in the play, see Michael Neill, "'A woman's service': Gender, Subordination, and the Erotics of Rank in the Drama of Shakespeare and his Contemporaries," *The Shakespearean International Yearbook* 5 (2005): 127–44. Neill's discussion, however, focuses on De Flores rather than Diaphanta. Burnett argues that the play is "preoccupied with larger crises in service" and that it "uncovers pervasive concerns about dependency ... and the fixity of hierarchical schemes." See "*The Changeling* and Masters and Servants," in *Early Modern English Drama: A Critical Companion*, (eds.) Garrett A. Sullivan, Jr., Patrick Cheney, and Andrew Hadfield (New York: Oxford University Press, 2006), 307.

[20]   William Rowley and Thomas Middleton, *The Changeling*, (ed.) Douglas Bruster, in *Thomas Middleton: The Collected Works*, (eds.) Gary Taylor and John Lavagnino (Oxford: Oxford University Press, 2007). All citations will refer to this edition of the play and will be given parenthetically in the text.

bed trick to which she so willingly accedes positions Diaphanta's lusty sexuality quite strikingly within a marriage plot in which she both literally and figuratively takes over the "bride's place"—dowry and all. Like Winifred's bigamous marriage to Frank, however, Diaphanta's tryst is tainted by illicit sexuality. Not only is her wedding night an adulterous one, but Diaphanta almost ruins Beatrice's scheme when she overindulges in her sexual rendezvous, "devour[ing] the pleasure with a greedy appetite" (5.1.3). As formal stage device run amok, the bed trick in this play contorts and parodies the culturally assumed passage of women from service to marriage and characterizes Diaphanta as unreliable and sexually voracious. It also casts doubt on her subservience within the domestic hierarchy, compelling De Flores, Beatrice's lover and partner in crime, to exclaim in exasperation: "Who'd trust a waiting-woman?" (5.1.15). As the clock strikes one and then two with no sign of Diaphanta, Beatrice joins De Flores in berating her servant, saying that "this whore forgets herself" (5.1.23). While the play successfully paints Diaphanta as a lusty and disobedient servant, a cautionary emblem of the disorder that women's service can engender in domestic settings, it also offers a fantasy version of that disorder by displacing all blame onto the servant herself and by rerouting her actions to align with marriage—however contrived and unsatisfactory. In Diaphanta's narrative, as in Sir Arthur's euphemistic description of his relationship with Winifred, the sexual relationship between a female servant and her master is defined in terms of lascivious and disorderly female desire rather than coercive male prerogative. Furthermore, the play discursively manages even this potentially disruptive sexuality by siphoning it off into a contorted marriage trajectory through the dramatic device of the bed trick.

As a substitute and, ultimately, a scapegoat for her mistress, Diaphanta bears a resemblance to Margaret in Shakespeare's *Much Ado About Nothing* (1600). At the crucial turning point in that play, Borachio's wooing of Margaret, Hero's attending gentlewoman, "by the name of Hero" (3.3.146), leads Claudio and Don Pedro to denounce Hero publicly as a "rotten orange" who is "but the sign and semblance of her honor" (4.1.32, 34). Of course, *Much Ado* is a comedy and this error is rectified in the end, but the substitution of waiting-woman for mistress nevertheless initiates generic tensions, precipitating the play's temporary transition into tragedy, epitomized by Hero's presumed death. Though it is not recognized as such until the play's conclusion, the presumed sexual laxity of a female servant once again heralds domestic chaos and tragedy. Like Diaphanta, Margaret's indecorous behavior at "her mistress's chamber-window" (3.3.146–7) threatens to taint her mistress's honor. Yet the resolution of this misunderstanding at the conclusion of Shakespeare's comedy works doubly to sanitize Hero's own reputation, both by clearing her name outright and by rhetorically shifting suspicion onto the schemers Don John and Borachio, as well as onto Margaret herself. As Leonato tells the gathered company, although Claudio and Don Pedro are innocent, "Margaret was in some fault for this, / Although against her will, as it appears / In the true course of all the question" (5.4.4–6). Tragedy is averted, but only by displacing Hero's blame onto Margaret, who is both granted agency as a kind of conspirator (she was "in some fault") and simultaneously denied it (the act was "against her will"). Like Winifred and the shepherd's waiting-gentlewoman, Margaret is granted a central role in *Much Ado*'s narrative arc that is directly related to her assumed lasciviousness, but the potentially tragic consequences of her indiscretions are subsumed by the play's romantic resolution. This resolution, however, still requires a specific version of Margaret's story in order to be successful. Conveniently at fault "against her will," Margaret escapes the more extreme penalties imposed on characters such as Don John, yet remains vaguely guilty of sexual improprieties—enough so, at least, to reassure the audience of Hero's innocence by comparison.

As is the case with Margaret in *Much Ado*, Diaphanta's sexual escapades have a significant afterlife of their own. Ultimately Diaphanta must be killed because of her complicity in Beatrice and De Flores's scheming; De Flores sets fire to Diaphanta's chambers to lure her out of Alsemero's bed, then meets her in her chambers and shoots her. Yet Diaphanta's death is not the end of her narrative, as it is for Susan in *Arden*. When questioned by her father, Vermandero, about Diaphanta's "accident," Beatrice concocts an entirely new narrative about her service:

Vermandero: How should the fire come there [to Diaphanta's chamber]?

Beatrice: As good a soul as ever lady countenanced,
                     But in her chamber negligent and heavy:
                     She 'scaped a ruin twice.

Vermandero: Twice?

Beatrice: Strangely, twice, sir.

Vermandero: Those sleepy sluts are dangerous in a house,
                     And they be ne'er so good. (5.1.102–7)

Beatrice and Vermandero rewrite Diaphanta's death as deserving, or at least as inevitable, by inserting her into the position of the bad, "negligent" servant. By calling her a "sleepy slut"—a phrase that, for contemporary audiences, conjured a range of problematic meanings, including a dirty, slovenly or untidy woman, a troublesome or awkward creature, a drudge, a foul slattern, or a woman of low or loose character—Vermandero implies that not only her sexual behavior but also her lack of diligence in her household tasks is to blame for her death.[21] Vermandero's insult thus simultaneously emphasizes Diaphanta's lower class status, her failure in her household duties, and her sexual improprieties. Beatrice goes even further than insulting Diaphanta after her death; by inventing two prior incidents in which Diaphanta narrowly "'scaped a ruin," Beatrice establishes a narrative pattern of slothful service after the fact.

---

[21] *OED*, "slut, *n.*," 1 and 2. Judith Haber argues that Diaphanta's lack of sexual fears "underscores her lower status" in "'I(t) could not choose but follow': Erotic Logic in *The Changeling*," *Representations* 81 (2003): 81.

The narrative that Beatrice and Vermandero conveniently provide for Diaphanta defines her in terms of laziness, sexual indecorum, and domestic disorder, creating a picture of service that, not surprisingly, runs directly counter to advice given to female servants by seventeenth-century conduct book writers. Hannah Woolley, for example, who wrote several books on domesticity later in the century, includes a great deal of specific advice for female servants in her manual, *The Compleat Servant-Maid* (1677). Woolley warns her readers to "encline not to sloth or laze in bed" and to "be neat, cleanly, and huswifely in your clothes," and later in the treatise she forbids "wantoning in the society of men," advice that Diaphanta, the "sleepy slut," clearly ignores—at least, according to Beatrice.[22] In terms of dramatic effect, Woolley's practical advice pales in comparison to Beatrice's racy story and that, of course, is precisely the point. Displacing both the mundane economic details common to treatises like Woolley's and the historical risk of sexual coercion and abuse, Rowley and Middleton offer up the female servant as both delicious entertainment and crucial mechanism of the tragic plot. Both in the bed trick and after her death, Diaphanta's narrative is provided to the audience through the mediated language of those characters who *need* her to function as the "sleepy slut" or negligent servant in order for their own dramatic plots to succeed. *The Changeling* represents Diaphanta's story of service as a malleable commodity that can be manipulated to provide closure and an appropriately cautionary message about sexual disorder. The artificial nature of Diaphanta's posthumous narrative, however, signals the degree to which this sense of closure is contrived, tentative, and ultimately illusory. The fanciful and nearly excessive scripting of Diaphanta's service—similar to what we saw with Winifred in *The Witch of Edmonton* and Susan in *Arden of Faversham*—attempts to provide a feeling of certainty and finality, but cannot completely erase the threat to household order posed by Diaphanta, the "sleepy" and "dangerous" slut.

The dangers implicit in the work of domestic service are writ large in tragedies such as *The Changeling* and *The Witch of Edmonton*, as these plays, befitting their genre, place sustained attention on the potentially disastrous consequences of female service in the patriarchal household. At a time when the institution of service was gradually being redefined in terms of temporary, wage-based contracts rather than sustained social relationships, these narratives serve a cautionary function, warning audiences about the uncertainties and instabilities that these female workers potentially bring into English homes. What is more surprising and ultimately more interesting about these plays, however, is the way in which romanticized plot structures manage at times to permeate the tragic mode. Winifred as sexual partner and later grieving widow and Diaphanta as "sleepy slut" are dramatic fantasies that depend on the deflection of the far more common historical narratives of economic hardship and, most notably, sexual subordination and abuse. There is, therefore a cultural use-value to these fictions that goes beyond their

---

[22] Woolley, *The Compleat Servant-Maid; Or, The Young Maidens Tutor* (London, 1677), B1v and D7v.

cautionary function. The tragic genre creates a space in which concerns about the sexual vulnerability of women in service can be vividly, even tantalizingly, aired. Yet in these plays that tragic drive is superseded and narratologically transformed into far more palatable stories. Crucially, those stories are told by others. The subjectivity of the female servant thus emerges only at a distant remove, and is defined largely in terms of social powerlessness, criminality, or excessive sexual desire. The fanciful narratives that structure these plays—particularly those that rewrite sexual coercion as female lasciviousness—in no way benefit the servant herself, though they do ameliorate the potentially more devastating aspects of her story, presumably for the benefit of the audience, which can enjoy the salacious entertainment on offer without considering too deeply the more troubling stories of women's service and its aftermath.

These plays thus perform a culturally useful balancing act, creating a space—albeit a largely negative one—in which female servants emerge as dramatic subjects, while also displacing those subjects when dramatically necessary. Like the shepherd's waiting-gentlewoman or Margaret in *Much Ado*, the stories of female servants are poised between tragedy and comedy. As narratives, they are generic hybrids, and the complications they invoke are likewise resolved through generic means. Plays as divergent as *The Winter's Tale* and *The Witch of Edmonton* turn to romanticized plotlines to leave the problems of "behind-door-work" and "secret game[s]" behind. In doing so, however, these plays turn sexual vulnerability itself into a fictional narrative, replacing the real danger of coercion that obtained in master-servant relationships with a discursive fantasy of female desire. In this scenario, fictional narrative does the work of distancing messy social realities by rendering them salacious entertainment and therefore of limited social threat. As a result, it becomes far too easy to align ourselves with the shepherd in *The Winter's Tale* and "read waiting-gentlewoman in the scape."

Chapter 9
Domestic Work in Progress Entertainments[1]

Sara Mueller

In a genre noted for its allegorical, mythological, and even typological presentation of the English aristocracy and its country estates, it comes as something of a surprise that two progress entertainments performed for Queen Elizabeth staged the mundane domestic work of the queen's aristocratic female hosts. Yet Lady Elizabeth Russell's 1592 entertainment at Bisham featured her own daughters doing needlework, and the entertainment staged at Harefield in 1602 by Sir Thomas Egerton and Lady Alice Egerton, Dowager Countess of Derby, explicitly represented Lady Egerton as a demanding, hardworking, and exemplary housewife. Although parts of both entertainments are deeply conventional examples of the progress genre, their focus on the proper, orderly, daily execution of women's unpaid work is a decidedly novel method of communicating the wealth and noble status of the hosting family, the central aim of any progress entertainment.[2] Admittedly, progress entertainments do routinely boast of the hard work involved in hosting the queen, such as the lengthy list of the Earl of Hertford's renovations to his estate in the printed account of Elizabeth's visit to Elvetham published in 1591 (A2v–A3v).[3] Progress entertainments also regularly include spectacles which required a tremendous amount of labor to execute. Sir Francis Carew, for instance, unveiled a cherry tree at least a month out of season for Elizabeth at Beddington

[1]   I would like to thank The Huntington Library, Wilfrid Laurier University, Queen's University, and the Social Science and Humanities Council of Canada for supporting my work on this project.

[2]   Studies of the role of progress entertainments in performing court power and noble status include Jayne Elisabeth Archer, Elizabeth Goldring, and Sarah Knight (eds.), *The Progresses, Pageants, and Entertainments of Queen Elizabeth I* (Oxford: Oxford University Press, 2007); Mary Hill Cole, *The Portable Queen: Elizabeth I and the Politics of Ceremony* (Amherst: University of Massachusetts Press, 1999); William Leahy, *Elizabethan Triumphal Processions* (Aldershot: Ashgate, 2005); David Scott Kastan, "'Shewes of Honour and Gladnes': Dissonance and Display in Mary and Philip's Entry into London," *Research Opportunities in Renaissance Drama* 33 (1994): 1–15; and James Sutton, *Materializing Space at an Early Modern Prodigy House: The Cecils at Theobalds, 1564–1607* (Aldershot: Ashgate, 2004).

[3]   Hertford's renovations included enlarging the house, erecting new buildings, constructing a new hall, and digging a large crescent-shaped pond in which many ships and boats were placed (A3–A3v).

in 1599.[4] While the conceit suggests that the queen's mere presence was enough to trump nature and bring back spring, it surely would have been obvious that this feat was much more likely to have been achieved by Carew's labor as well as that of his workers.[5] The Bisham and Harefield entertainments are exceptional in their dramatization of the process—and not just the result—of women's labor. It is my contention that just as the transition from a feudal to a mercantilist, proto-capitalist economy and the opportunities for new kinds of work outside of traditional guilds prompted some commercial playwrights to examine this new economy and its workers, so too were these changes influential—albeit in a very different way—to Bisham and Harefield's performances of nobility and class legitimacy.

Both the Russell and Egerton entertainments depict their estates as fertile, rustic, well-managed farms that are models of domestic virtue. Central to these representations of idealized noble husbandry are the performances of domestic work by aristocratic women whose dedicated labor demonstrates synecdochically the commitment of the host to the proper governance and care over the estate as a whole. This idealized representation of the aristocratic country house is, in large part, a conservative reaction to the changes in aristocratic life brought about by new economic and social conditions at the end of the sixteenth century and the beginning of the seventeenth century. New urban and commercial opportunities meant that aristocratic men made less of their incomes from rents from their tenant farmers and spent more of their time away from their country houses pursuing potentially more lucrative sources of income.[6] Aristocratic women assumed the managerial roles abandoned by their husbands and took on the complicated day-to-

---

[4]   Jean Wilson, *Entertainments for Elizabeth I* (Woodbridge and Totawa: D.S. Brewer, 1980), 24.

[5]   Hugh Plat's account of how Carew accomplished this feat dwells on Carew's labor: "This secret he [Carew] performed by straining a Tent or cover of canvas over the whole tree, and wetting the same now and then with scoope, or horne, as the heat of the weather required; and so, by withholding the sun-beames from reflecting upon the berries, they grew both great, and were very long before they had gotten their perfect cherry colour: and when he was assured of her Majesties coming, he removed the Tent, and a few sunny days brought them to their full maturity." *The Garden of Eden* (London, 1659), 165–6.

[6]   Kari Boyd McBride, *Country House Discourse in Early Modern England: A Cultural Study of Landscape and Legitimacy* (Aldershot: Ashgate, 2001), 91–2. Moreover, Felicity Heal and Clive Holmes argue that many members of the gentry who needed to work to supplement traditional agricultural incomes "became involved directly or indirectly in trade or finance." They did so, Heal and Holmes argue, "not … as an exogenous activity, but in an endeavour to exploit the nonagricultural potential of their estates—sinking mines, investing in facilities to process or transport their product, encouraging urban growth in the vicinity of their lands. There are few examples of gentlemen whose involvement in industry or trade was not related intimately to the development of the potential of their estates." *The Gentry in England and Wales, 1500–1700* (Stanford: Stanford University Press, 1994), 127. Even if the motivation for participating in commercial ventures was to enrich one's country estate, such ventures still compromised the ideal of the gentleman as patriarch whose wealth came from the management of his tenant farmers.

day administration of country estates. These changes in aristocratic life fostered a widespread representational crisis, since noble self-presentation dating back to the Tudors was founded upon patriarchal possession, presence, and governance of their estates.[7] Tudor ideology held that on a noble country estate "every individual [had] an immutable social and geographic place and [was] fixe[d] ... within a network of duties and responsibilities."[8] Since the physical presence and governorship of the patriarch had become less of a condition of country life, and since his ties to the land were no longer self-evident, it became necessary to perform these ideals of nobility even though the social conditions behind the ideals were no longer a reality. Indeed, according to Kari Boyd McBride in *Country House Discourse*, "early modern England invented ... the late-medieval country estate as the symbol of good housekeeping."[9]

With the diminished presence of noblemen on the country estate, women began to play a greater role in performing noble ideology, just as they assumed a greater role in estate management. Bisham and Harefield's novel representational strategy of focusing on women's work is, then, a canny response to changing social and economic conditions. In terms of the performance of noble ideology, aristocratic women were increasingly associated with their country estates to the extent that "the fiction of timeless values of a chivalric culture that defined noble status" was accomplished by the enclosure of women in the country house.[10] The idealized aristocratic household depended on the performance of conservative gender politics because, as McBride writes,

> nobility and legitimacy were understood to be fundamentally and ontologically male. That is, the exercise of power depended on a distinction between masculinity and femininity or, more accurately perhaps, on the control of everything associated with the feminine by those who claimed the fullness of masculine privilege. ... [A]s country house poems, conduct literature, and private writings demonstrate again and again, the virtuous wife is central to the ideal estate, her virtue both dependent on and significant of her husband's particularly noble virility.[11]

---

[7]   Felicity Heal writes that there was so much anxiety about the departure of elites from the country that proclamations were issued "from the 1590s to the later 1630s ... [which] forbade the gentry to live in or about the city outside the law terms, and specifically required them to return to their country houses for the Christmas period." *Hospitality in Early Modern England* (Oxford: Clarendon, 1990), 18.

[8]   Andrew McRae, "Husbandry Manuals and the Language of Agrarian Improvement," in *Culture and Cultivation in Early Modern England: Writing the Land*, (eds.) Michael Leslie and Timothy Raylor (Leicester and London: Leicester University Press, 1992), 35.

[9]   McBride, *Country House Discourse*, 1. McBride's book focuses on country house poems, miniatures, and portraits, all of which she describes as "pocketbook icons of the signifying landscape that served to legitimate authority apart from the land itself, which was nonetheless effectively present in its representations" (12). The progress entertainment does not figure into McBride's analysis.

[10]   Ibid., 91–2.

[11]   Ibid., 5.

Although McBride focuses on how women exemplified the values of the country house by their passive enclosure in it, Bisham and Harefield employ a different strategy—dramatizing women's labor—to demonstrate the household's embodiment of idealized nobility. Moreover, although both entertainments define the country estate as a place of unchanging noble values and patriarchal presence and control, the entertainments by their very focus on women's domestic labor— and not men's—resist an uncomplicated endorsement of nostalgic noble ideals. Instead, the entertainments acknowledge in their focus on women's active labor the new realities of country life in the changing economy. Alongside Bisham and Harefield's necessary assertion of traditional, patriarchal, and noble legitimacy, both entertainments foreground a very timely recognition of women's importance and changing roles on country estates, a recognition that acknowledges the material and symbolic contributions of women to their estates. While Bisham and Harefield are largely reactionary aristocratic cultural productions that shrewdly strove to perform familial status by imagining an idealized noble reality that no longer existed, both entertainments also invoke the very social and economic changes they appear to deny. They assert the presence of nostalgic ideals on their land, but the entertainments articulate with their focus on female labor that these ideals are nothing but fiction and instead intimate that the new realities of life on country estates presented powerful and even potentially radical possibilities for early modern women.

The performance of domestic work in progress entertainments had the potential then to promote both familial status and personal power. It was essential, though, that Bisham and Harefield's depiction of female labor successfully negotiate aristocratic prejudices against labor, since part of what defined nobility in the early modern period was living a life of leisure free from work. Certain kinds of unpaid labor—including household management, husbandry, and chaste pursuits like needlework—were forms of work appropriate for those of high rank, and these were just the kinds of aristocratic work depicted at Bisham and Harefield. According to Andrew McRae, however, even these kinds of work had to overcome base associations. In husbandry manuals, the subject of McRae's study, the work of husbandry was transmuted into an occupation suitable for the gentle classes "by commuting physical labor into the daily rounds of supervision. In this sense the landlord can claim himself a 'husbandman' in a slightly pastoralized transformation of Virgil's figure from the *Georgics*."[12] Bisham and Harefield employ representational strategies similar to those of the husbandry manuals. Both entertainments use elements of the georgic, emphasizing the land as a cultivated farm, focusing on its proper management, and celebrating dutiful labor on the estate.[13] The entertainments also incorporate pastoral elements more familiar in

---

[12]   McRae, "Husbandry Manuals," 41.

[13]   The garden was a far more common way of describing the cultivated, controlled environment in progress entertainments. See Jayne Elisabeth Archer and Sarah Knight, *Elizabetha Triumphans*, in *The Progresses, Pageants, and Entertainments of Queen Elizabeth I*, (eds.) Archer, Goldring, and Knight, 9.

progress entertainments, including Russell's daughters' roles as shepherdesses and the investment of both entertainments in rusticity and elevated language. The performances of women's labor at Harefield and Bisham admit no base associations, instead encoding the Russell and Egerton households as on the one hand virtuous, well-governed, and noble, while on the other hand making clear just how valuable and authoritative women's work was in their country houses.

In addition to the necessity for nobles in general to perform a nostalgic conception of their identity, the Russell and Egerton households both had particular reasons for asserting their noble legitimacy. Neither the Russell nor the Egerton household came close to embodying the feudal ideals that were valorized in the period, and the conservative identities performed by the women of the Russell and Egerton households were not accurate representations of their lives. Both Russell and Egerton led remarkable, privileged lives that were far from ordinary. Russell was a patron, translator, and one of the famously well-educated daughters of Sir Antony Cooke.[14] Egerton was a noted patron of Spenser, Milton, and others; she would later perform in at least two Jacobean court masques; and she was a central part of the Northern court of the Stanley family before her second marriage to Egerton.[15] Accordingly, performances of conservative noble ideology like Bisham and Harefield's were especially important given the incongruity of these families to the noble ideal and of these women to conservative domestic ideals. Moreover, the genre of the progress entertainment was a particularly potent medium for articulating familial meaning. In addition to staging one's wealth and status for the queen, for other aristocrats, for local onlookers, and for readers of accounts of the entertainment, progress entertainments featured a conceptual transformation of house and household into a stage upon which the ideals, values, status, and aspirations of the host were performed.[16] For Alison Findlay, women's performances in the household always manifest this kind of "spatial practice" where lived reality and imagined reality collide, and where the performance is at once a representational space and a representation of space, in Henri Lefebvre's terms.[17]

---

[14] For more on Russell, see Mary Ellen Lamb, "The Cooke Sisters: Attitudes Toward Learned Women in the Renaissance," in *Silent But for the Word: Tudor Women as Patrons, Translators, and Writers of Religious Works*, (ed.) Margaret Patterson Hannay (Kent: Kent State University Press, 1985), 107–125.

[15] For details about Egerton, see French R. Fogle, "'Such a Rural Queen': The Countess Dowager of Derby as Patron," in *Patronage in Late Renaissance England: Papers Read at Clark Library Seminar 14 May 1977* (Los Angeles: William Clark Memorial Library, 1983), 3–28.

[16] See Helen Cooper, "Location and Meaning in Masque, Morality, and Royal Entertainment," in *The Court Masque*, (ed.) David Lindley (Manchester: Manchester University Press, 1984), 137 and Michael Leslie, "'Something nasty in the wilderness': Entertaining Queen Elizabeth on her Progresses," *Medieval and Renaissance Drama in England* 10 (1998): 54.

[17] Alison Findlay, *Playing Spaces in Early Women's Drama* (Cambridge: Cambridge University Press, 2006), 3–4, 11. Henri Lefebvre defines representations of space as the "dominant space in any society" (39), whereas representational spaces are instead spaces that are "directly *lived* through [their] associated images and symbols" (39). Representations of

At the same time, however, the performances of domesticity by these women move beyond a simple re-imagining or re-conceptualization of domestic space. The women's performances of feminine domesticity in the explicitly theatrical context of the progress entertainment obscure the line between performance and reality to assert a particular understanding of their familial—and even personal—meaning. In such an important state context, and in a genre with incredible potential to shape familial reputation and social status, women's performances of labor at Bisham and Harefield did nothing less than accomplish the most important cultural work required of the aristocracy in this time of economic and social change. While the progress entertainment was a powerful venue to assert familial propaganda, it is essential that both entertainments prevent their audiences from easily accepting the fiction of that familial propaganda. Instead, the performance context of the Bisham and Harefield entertainments works to suggest that not only are the families legitimately noble, but so too is the authority of Elizabeth's aristocratic female hosts. This aspect of the performances at Bisham and Harefield suggests that alongside the conservative aim of these performances lies a radical acknowledgement of social change as well as a validation of the different social configurations made possible by economic change. Women's performances of domestic work thus signify doubly in progress entertainments. While the performances' manifest object was to declare the legitimacy of the host family, the subtext strove to legitimate, value, and give credit to the power of women's labor on the country estate.

Bisham, 1592

Remaining records of Queen Elizabeth's visit to Bisham indicate that she was greeted with an entertainment written by Lady Elizabeth Russell herself and performed, in part, by Russell's own daughters, Anne and Elizabeth.[18] Most of

---

space are linked to order, power, and the relations of production, but representational spaces are "linked to the clandestine of underground side of social life, as also to art." *The Production of Space*, trans. Donald Nicholson-Smith (Oxford: Blackwell, 2007), 33. Lefebvre explains how a single space can hold radical and conservative connotations at once.

[18]   Alexandra Johnston first established Russell's likely authorship. "The 'Lady of the farme': The Context of Lady Russell's Entertainment of Elizabeth at Bisham," *Early Theatre* 5.2 (2002): 71-85. The entertainment was published anonymously with two other entertainments given for the queen's progress that summer. Johnston's argument about Russell's authorship has been accepted by Alison Findlay, *Playing Spaces*, 80–81; Claire McManus, *Women on the Renaissance Stage: Anna of Denmark and Female Masquing in the Stuart Court, 1590-1619* (Manchester: Manchester University Press, 2002), 85; and Peter Donaldson and Jane Stevenson, "Elizabeth I's Reception at Bisham (1592): Elite Women as Writers and Devisers," in *The Progresses, Pageants, and Entertainments of Queen Elizabeth I*, (eds.) Archer, Goldring, and Knight, 207–226. The case for Russell's daughters being the performers who play "the Virgins keeping Sheepe, and sowing their samplers" (Aii) is supported by Pan's description of them as daughters of the owners of the farm: "you are but the Farmers daughters of the Dale, I the god of the flocks that feede upon the hills" (Aii).

Bisham's critics understand the objective of Russell's daughters' performance to be an attempt to promote the girls as potential ladies-in-waiting to the queen (positions they eventually attained.)[19] Russell's daughters' performance also presented Bisham as a model of Protestantism, feminine virtue, proper governance, and nobility. Such a performance was especially important for Russell because aristocratic anxieties about noble status hit particularly close to home in her case. Russell was twice widowed; her second husband, John, Lord Russell, did not live long enough to inherit the earldom of Bedfordshire; she did not possess a very large estate in Bisham; and her aims for her daughters "demanded great revenues" and even greater social status.[20] For a woman of limited means, but with limitless ambition for her daughters, performing the ideals of nobility was very important for Russell. At the same time, the pride Russell takes in her dominion over her estate is evident throughout the entertainment, not in the least when at the end of the entertainment the goddess Ceres speaks for Russell and welcomes Elizabeth to her home (Aiiijv). Although she must perform conventional conservative notions of nobility, Russell's entertainment also registers just how different her realm is from that ideal.

As an aristocratic widow living in her own home, Russell enjoyed an unusual position in her household and had far more freedom than would have been afforded most married or never married women.[21] Despite, and perhaps because of her widowhood and exceptional status, Russell's entertainment is in many ways very conventional in its promotion of the nobility and legitimacy of her family through feminine virtue. The entertainment staged at Bisham consisted of three scenes that took place on the queen's approach to the house: a "Wilde" man greeted the queen the furthest distance from the house; Russell's daughters performed their dialogue at the half-way point on the queen's approach; and at the entry to the house, Ceres delivered the personal message from Russell, presented a crown of wheat to the queen, and ceded to Queen Elizabeth her authority over the estate. The form of entertainment coincides with the conventions of the genre and the entertainment promotes, as it must, traditional ideals of nobility, but Bisham does not let its

---

[19] See especially Johnston, "The 'Lady of the Farme,'" 77 and Findlay, *Playing Spaces*, 81.

[20] Felicity Heal, "Reputation and Honour in Court and Society," in *Transactions of the Royal Historical Society* 6 (1996): 166. Russell's anxiety over land possession would come to a head in her fight with Charles Howard over Donnington Castle. The Castle had been willed to Russell but was given by Queen Elizabeth to Howard in 1600 to reward him for his naval service. See Heal, "Reputation and Honour," 163.

[21] Alice Friedman writes that wealthy aristocratic widows "exercised considerable independent authority over their families and households" since they were "no longer subject to either parental authority or their husbands' control and too old to serve as intergenerational or interfamilial conduits through their offspring." "Architecture, Authority, and the Female Gaze: Planning and Representation in the Early Modern Country House," *Assemblage* 18 (1992): 50.

audience forget Russell's own power and the extent to which her reign over her estate undermines the very noble ideology it performs.

The scene performed by Russell's daughters is the most pertinent to my discussion of the performance of aristocratic women's work in progress entertainments. In the scene, Russell's daughters perform needlework, and they fend off Pan's advances by describing their work. The images they sew are so virtuous and complimentary to Elizabeth that once they decipher their work for Pan, he breaks his phallic pipe and declares his allegiance to the queen (Aiiij). Claire McManus finds that the Bisham entertainment presents needleworking as "a quasi-linguistic medium, predicated through gender," since the content of the women's dialogue is so closely related to the images they sew on their samplers.[22] Indeed, on coming upon the girls at work on their samplers in the field, Pan asks them to explain the meaning of their work to him. The girls respond by deciphering the allegorical significance of each figure they have made:

> PAN. … what is wrought in this sampler?
>
> SYB. The follies of the Gods, who became beastes, for their affections.
>
> PAN. What in this?
>
> ISA. The honour of Virgins who became Goddesses, for their chastity.
>
> PAN. But what be these?
>
> SYB. Mens tongues, wrought all with double stitch but not one true.
>
> PAN. What these?
>
> ISA. Roses, Egletine, harts-ease, wrought with Queenes stitch, and all-right. (Aiii)

Despite the pastoral nature of this scene, its interest in the girls' proper execution of their work is more georgic. The girls demonstrate their mastery not only of different kinds of stitches, hence displaying their sound education and hard work at mastering their craft, but they also reveal their mastery of the precepts of feminine virtue, since their work glorifies chaste virgins and castigates double-speaking men and foolish gods. The content of the girls' speeches would have appealed particularly to Elizabeth, both because the kind of virtue evidenced by the speeches was just what she looked for in her ladies-in-waiting, but also because the powerful model of virginity articulated by the girls so closely echoes Elizabeth's representation of her own virginity.[23]

---

[22] McManus, *Women on the Renaissance Stage*, 185.

[23] The girls also reveal in this passage their education in the classics and the ways in which that education shaped their virtue positively. Elizabeth Russell was famously well-educated, and the value of humanist education to shape the virtue of women is an important and polemical subtext to this exchange between Pan and Russell's daughters.

Embroidery was a high-status occupation, but this is not to say that it was not work, and necessary work, for elite women. According to Marla Miller, it was "skilled work—requiring skills that not every woman possessed—but also ... was difficult, mind-numbing, eye-straining, back-breaking labor."[24] Early modern usage of the word "work," in fact, often referred specifically to women's needlework.[25] Bisham itself is emphatic that needlework constitutes proper aristocratic work. Pan asks the women, "How doe you burne time, & drowne beauty in pricking of clouts, when you should be penning of Sonnets? You are more simple then the sheepe you keepe, but not so gentle" (Aiiv). The implication of Pan's question is that the girls work too hard on their needlework and that their labor marks them not as gentlewomen who, he thinks, should labor only over sonnets, but as a less "gentle" sort who are devoted to their work above all else. Furthermore, Pan's use of the word "clout" to describe the fabric the women sew indicates its worthlessness, since a clout is "A piece of cloth (*esp.* a small or worthless piece, a 'rag'); a cloth (*esp.* one put to mean uses, e.g. a dish-clout.)"[26] The question Pan asks highlights the girls' virtue and Pan's own depravity, since it shows the women spending their time on the kind of work that will enhance their virtue instead of on pursuits that would compromise it, like writing sonnets.[27] Sybilla and Isabella demonstrate that real nobility comes from hard work, discipline, and feminine virtue. Moreover, it is centrally important that the girls' "clouts" are their samplers. In the sixteenth and seventeenth centuries, unlike today, "samplers were not for display, but were evidence of a girl's progress and could be kept rolled up in a workbox as a record of patterns and techniques."[28] The sampler provides evidence of one's education in the craft and documents the work done over a period of time by its maker. The content of Isabella and Sybilla's samplers demonstrates the alignment of their learning about sewing techniques and their education in proper feminine virtue.

Findlay has argued that Russell's entertainment created a feminine space in which "the naturalness of the masculine heroic is undermined, and women dominate nature."[29] For Findlay, the needleworking scene is a "metaphor for constructing the world according to one's own agenda," where, when the women embroider flowers like "roses, eglantine and heart's ease (all flowers associated

---

[24]   Miller, *The Needle's Eye: Women and Work in the Age of Revolution* (Amherst: University of Massachusetts Press, 2006), 4.

[25]   *OED*, "work, *n.*," II.,16.

[26]   *OED*, "clout, *n.*¹," II., 4.

[27]   See Linda Dove, "Mary Wroth and the Politics of the Household in 'Pamphilia to Amphilanthus.'" in *Women, Writing, and the Reproduction of Culture in Tudor and Stuart Britain*, (eds.) Mary E. Burke, Jane Donawerth, Linda L. Dove, and Karen Nelson (New York: Syracuse University Press, 2000), 141-56 on the negative implications of women's sonnet writing.

[28]   Liz Arthur, *Embroidery 1600–1700 at the Burrell Collection* (Great Britain: Glasgow Museums, 1985), 59–60.

[29]   Findlay, *Playing Spaces*, 81.

with Elizabeth I,) [they] … erase any distinction between culture and nature."[30] Bisham certainly performs a vision of nature controlled and mastered by the proper governance and work done on the estate, but to understand Bisham as an anomalously feminine realm that rewrites the patriarchalism of the country house misses the ways in which the entertainment's is at once invested in conventional noble ideology at the same time as it strives to challenge that ideology. Although Russell herself is represented in the entertainment as "the Lady of the farme," Pan describes Isabella and Sybilla as "the Farmer's daughters of the Dale" (Aiiv). The entertainment does not imagine away patriarchy but instead invokes the memory of a dead patriarch who was, in the fiction of the entertainment at least, involved in the care of the land. While this might be convincing to readers of the printed entertainment who were not present at the event or for audience members ignorant of Russell's widowhood, in performance the mention of the absent patriarch works less to invoke his memory than it does to draw attention to Russell's sole control over her estate. Moreover, that needleworking is the work the women perform further demonstrates the simultaneous conservative and radical gender politics of the entertainment. Recent scholarship on women's needlework has attempted to reclaim it as a creative endeavour instead of one associated with women's subjection, even though needleworking was so frequently used as a signifier of feminine virtue in conduct literature.[31] The submissive posture of the needleworker, the downward glance of her eyes, and the consuming nature of the work made it an activity that was endorsed by even the most rigid of conduct book writers.[32] While needleworking in the entertainment does signify a kind of radical agency (where the women defy Pan's dismissal and understanding of their work), the entertainment also presents their work as indicating their embodiment of the conservative cultural ideal.

Given Bisham's emphasis on proper labor on the estate, it is appropriate that this entertainment includes some very georgic descriptions of the fruits of that labor. Sybilla delivers a speech which lauds not just Queen Elizabeth's stewardship of England, but of the proper husbandry of Bisham:

---

[30]   Ibid, 81.

[31]   Following Rozsika Parker's foundational *The Subversive Stitch: Embroidering and the Making of the Feminine* (London and New York: Routledge, 1989), scholars have seen needleworking as not just a sign of feminine subjection, but as a creative and expressionistic medium. Indeed, needleworking is frequently understood as a creative outlet where women could express their concerns and where, as Dympna Callaghan's reading of John Taylor's pattern book, *A Needle's Excellency* (1634) reveals, there is even the possibility of bawdy play. "Looking Well into Linens: Women and Cultural Production in *Othello* and Shakespeare's England," in *Marxist Shakespeares*, (eds.) Jean E. Howard and Scott Cutler Shershow (London and New York: Routledge, 2001), 53–82.

[32]   See Lena Cowen Orlin, "Three Ways to be Invisible in the Renaissance: Sex, Reputation, and Stitchery," in *Renaissance Culture and the Everyday*, (eds.) Patricia Fumerton and Simon Hunt (Philadelphia: University of Pennsylvania Press, 1999), 189–90.

SYB. By her it is (*Pan*) that all our Carttes that thou seest, are laden with Corne, when in other countries they are filled with Harneys, that our horses are ledde with a whipp: theirs with a Launce, that our Rivers flow with fish, theirs with bloode: our cattel feede on pastures, they feede on pastures like cattel. (Aiiiv)

It is significant that Sybilla delivers this speech because more than anything else, the performance of Russell's daughters demonstrates Bisham's exemplification of the ideals of the English nobility. The sisters' performance of domestic work at Bisham transforms Russell's household into a model of late medieval nobility, where women's devoted, proper, everyday work proves the virtue, nobility, and legitimacy of the entire estate. At the same time the entertainment does not let its audience—and especially Elizabeth, who would understand best of all the negotiation that Russell's entertainment accomplished between conservative and radical gender ideologies—forget just how contemporary the situation at Bisham is and how its success and nobility really stems from a woman's work, will, and authority.

Harefield, 1602

Sir Thomas and Lady Alice Egerton hosted Queen Elizabeth at Harefield on what would be her final summer progress in late July 1602 with an entertainment that, like Bisham, was interested in simultaneously performing noble status and legitimacy as well as intimating the fictional nature of that performance of status and legitimacy. The authorship of the entertainment is undetermined, although it has been suggested that the verse speeches were written by Sir John Davies and the prose speeches were by John Lyly.[33] The entertainment was never printed in full, but it did circulate widely in manuscript.[34] As at Bisham, the entertainment at Harefield presents its owners, and especially Lady Alice Egerton, as dedicated household managers who preside over a fertile, emphatically noble estate. There were many reasons, in addition to aristocratic anxiety about noble status, why it was important for the Egertons to perform antiquated notions of nobility in their entertainment at Harefield. Lady Egerton's trustees bought Harefield for her in 1601, just after she and Egerton were married in 1600. Alice Egerton thus acquired the Harefield estate only a year before she hosted Elizabeth.[35] As a new

---

[33] Mary Erler, "'Chaste Sports, Juste Prayses, & All Softe Delight': Harefield 1602 and Ashby 1607, Two Female Entertainments," *The Elizabethan Theatre* 14 (1996): 4.

[34] For more on the circulation of the text in manuscript, see Gabriel Heaton, "Elizabethan Entertainments in Manuscript: The Harefield Festivities (1602) and the Dynamics of Exchange," in *The Progresses, Pageants, and Entertainments of Queen Elizabeth I*, (eds.) Archer, Goldring, and Knight, 227–44.

[35] Lady Alice Egerton had money of her own, inherited from her first husband. Although much of the estate had been willed to her, Egerton engaged in a dispute with the new earl of Derby over the inheritance that was not resolved until 1609. For more details, see Cedric Brown, *John Milton's Aristocratic Entertainments* (Cambridge: Cambridge University Press, 1985), 16.

couple in a home which had been purchased with the money of its mistress, it was important for Sir Thomas and Lady Alice Egerton to establish the nobility of their marriage and their stewardship of the land.[36] Although Egerton's first husband, Ferdinando Strange, the fifth earl of Derby, was of a very old and wealthy family, Alice Egerton's own family, the Spencers, were not of the same stature.[37] Sir Thomas Egerton himself "was a very important self-made man at court," but not nearly as well born as Strange and certainly not as wealthy.[38] Under this weight of circumstance, performing the ancient values of the aristocracy was vital to the success not only of the entertainment, but to the social success of their marriage as well. The representation of the estate as a bastion of ancient, noble, patriarchal ideals does not, however, overshadow the very well-known ways in which this notorious family did not live up to those ideals. The entertainment, in its focus on Alice Egerton instead of Thomas Egerton, positions her as a proper domestic manager at the same time as it reminds its audience that the estate is really hers, protected from coverture. As at Bisham, although nostalgic noble ideology is invoked at Harefield, it is not invoked in a way that allowed its audience to forget contemporary realities.

The opening and closing scenes of the entertainment are those most relevant to Harefield's representation of Lady Alice Egerton's domestic labor.[39] The scene with which Elizabeth was greeted took place at Harefield's dairy house. Joane, a dairy maid, mistakes the queen and her retinue for "idle hearvest folkes" (3.588) and tries to put them to work, following the precise instructions of her mistress on what to do when potential laborers arrive on the property. In the scene, Joane and Richard, a Bayliff, debate where the visitors should stay, what their status is,

---

[36]   It is arguable that the entertainment alludes directly to the new purchase of the estate. Joane tries to dissuade the queen's party from going to the main house, arguing that the main house cannot accommodate lowly strangers as well as she can in her dairy house:
> I pray you hartley forsooth, come neare the house, and take a simple lodging with us to-night; for I can asuere you that yonder house that he talks of [Harefield] is but a Pigeon-house, which is very little if it were finisht, and yet very little of it is finisht. And if you belive me, upon my life Lady, I saw Carpenters and Bricklayers and ther Workmen about it within less than those two howers. Besides, I doubt my Mr. and Mrs. are not at home; or, if they be, you must make your own provision, for they have noe provision for such Strangers. (587)

The litotes deployed in Joan's speech communicates to Elizabeth just how fit Harefield is, and how much work has been done just for her stay. The declining standards of hospitality that were so frequently lamented in the period are the subject of the joke here.

[37]   Brown, *John Milton's Aristocratic Entertainments*, 16.

[38]   Ibid, 16. Egerton also had the aim to return fully to grace after his role in the Essex affair. See Felicity Heal, "Giving and Receiving on Royal Progress," in *The Progresses, Pageants, and Entertainments of Queen Elizabeth I*, (eds.) Archer, Goldring, and Knight, 60.

[39]   The other parts of the entertainment—including "*The humble Petition of a guiltless Lady, delivered in writing upon Munday Morninge, when the rainbow was presented to the Q. by the La. WALSINGHAM*" are more conventional celebrations of the queen and do not deal as much with the themes of women's labor.

and how they can best meet the high expectations of their mistress. The Bayliff disagrees with Joane's assessment of the social status of the group and wishes to lead them on to the manor house:

> B. Goe to, gossip; your tongue must be running. If my Mrs. should heare of this, I faith shee would give you little thankes I can tell you, for offeringe to draw so faire a flight from her Pigeon-house (as you call it) to your Dayrie-house.

> JO. Wisely, wisely, brother Richard; I faith as I would use the matter, I dare say shee would give me great thankes: for you know my Mrs. charged me earnestly to retaine all idele hearvest-folkes that past this way: and my meaning was, that, if I would hold them all this night and to-morrow; on Monday morening to carry them into the fields; and to make them earne their entertaynment well and thriftily; and to that end I have heere a *Rake* and *Forke*, to deliver to the best Huswife of the company. (587–8)

Joane and Richard's debate puts Egerton's own housewifery at the forefront of the entertainment. Egerton's "earnest charge" to Joane about how to deal with laborers mirrors Thomas Tusser's advice in his immensely popular *Five Hundred Points of Good Husbandry* (1580) about how to inform servants of their duties. Tusser emphasizes the careful instruction of servants in the proper management of an estate:

> 5   Where husband and huswife, be both out of place,
> there servants to loiter, and reason their cace. (124)

and

> 14   The laborers gentle, keppe this as a lawe,
> make child to be civill, keep servant in awe. (125)

Joane's certainty regarding what to do to please her mistress, especially in keeping everyone on the estate working and not idle, demonstrates her mistress's fine job in training her, even if Joane is too dim to recognize the difference between royalty and day laborers. Moreover, the reverence with which both servants speak of Egerton and her wishes indicates that she does keep them in "awe" and that Egerton's household, despite the comic mishaps of Joane, is run the way an ideal domestic establishment should be run.

The entertainment depicts Egerton's domestic role as tending to the needs of her household, managing it, and keeping it in a way that is congruent with the ideals of prescriptive literature and, accordingly, with the ideals of the country estate. The Harefield entertainment asserts Egerton's domestic virtue and her embodiment of the ideals of virtuous femininity as a manager and a conscientious housewife. It is Elizabeth, of course, whom Joane proclaims to be "the best Huswife of the company" (3.588) and to whom is presented jewels in the shape of a rake and a fork, which she is to use the next day when she is put to work. The entertainment makes clear, however, that Egerton is a superb housewife, since Egerton's work, and not Elizabeth's, exemplifies the noble functioning of the Harefield estate as a whole. At the same time, since Alice Egerton actually owned the estate, and since her marriage did not correlate easily with the noble ideologies the entertainment performed, the implications of Egerton's management carried different and less conservative significations such as the possibility for female autonomy and successful female estate management outside of patriarchal control.

Like Bisham, Harefield trumpets the fruits of the proper labor of the land in the style of the georgic when Joane boasts of the fine country foods she will serve the queen and her retinue in reward for their hard labor on the land (3.587). The description of Harefield's wealth of plain, fresh food produced on the estate promotes the fecundity of the farm and is evidence of the Egertons' proper, noble management of their estate. Yet it is Harefield's closing scene that consolidates the entertainment's representation of the estate as a model realm of noble life replete with an able housewife managing affairs, a plentiful farm, and a household organization where everyone knows his or her place in the hierarchy. In this scene, a monologue is delivered by "Place," a personification of Harefield itself performed by an actor dressed in *"a partie coloured roabe, like the brick house"* (3.588). Although Jane Archer and Sarah Knight intimate that Place could be female, they presume the character is gendered male.[40] However, Place's characterization as a "widow" and the congruity between her situation and that of noble women enclosed in country houses strongly suggests that Place ought to be understood as female. If we accept that Place is gendered female in the context of the entertainment, her speech can be read as dramatizing the enclosure of women in the country house, although the speech registers ironically since Alice Egerton, who was very active in court and city life, did not live the kind of life that Place laments:

> Sweet Majestie, be pleased to looke upon a poor Wydow, mourning before your Grace. I am this *Place*, which at your comming was full of joy: but now at your departure am as full of sorrow. I was then, for my comfort, accompanied with the present cheerful *Time*; but now he is to depart with you; and, blessed as he is, must ever fly before you: But alas! I have noe wings, as *Time* hath. My heaviness is such, that I must stand still, amazed to see so greate hapines so sone bereft mee. Oh, that I could remove with you; as other circumstances can! *Time* can go with you; *Persons* can goe with you; they can move like Heaven; but I, like dull Earth (as I am indeed), must stand unmovable. I could wish myself like the inchaunted Castle of Love, to hould you heere for ever, but that your vertues would dissolve my inchauntment. Then what remedy? As it is against the nature of an Angell to be circumscribed in *Place*, so it is against the nature of *Place* to have the motion of an Angell. I must stay forsaken and desolate. You may goe with majestie, joy, and glory. (3.593–4)

Place laments that while others may leave the estate to continue to be in the queen's presence, she, like "dull earth," must stay in one location. While Place's

---

40   Archer and Knight, *Elizabetha Triumphans*, 10.

monologue evokes the helplessness of women and their necessary absence from public life, Egerton's representation as an accomplished housewife lends her a kind of "working subjectivity," since her performance of labor had such important consequences for Egerton and her family's future success. The representation of Place as a woman who knows she must perform the duties required of someone of her station articulates very directly the entertainment's use of women to legitimate the country house, although the ironic contrast made between Place and the mobility of women like Alice Egerton and Queen Elizabeth herself suggests that alternatives to the enclosure Place experiences not only exist, but were already the lived reality of aristocratic women. Place evokes the conservative ideal at the same time as she demonstrates just how different and more empowered Egerton was from that ideal.

As much as Bisham and Harefield imagine away the economic and social conditions that saw the emergence of new workers in London, both entertainments create—and even validate—new working subjects in their representations of women's work. Just as the Dutch female artisans and retailers that Natasha Korda discusses in her contribution to this volume assert the value of their labor in their performances for James I, so too did aristocratic women's performances in progress entertainments demonstrate publicly both the reality and importance of the work women did in country estates. In this light, the performances of domesticity at Harefield and Bisham are necessary and powerful tools for asserting familial and class legitimacy at the same time as they provided the opportunity for women like Egerton and Russell, who found themselves in positions of authority that did not coincide with traditional roles for women, to assert their competency, power, and legitimacy. As the entertainments examined in this article reveal, the women of Bisham and Harefield were instrumental in promoting the appearance of unchanging, feudal values required by their class not necessarily in their passive enclosure in country homes but through the active and agential embodiment of the signifiers of feminine virtue in their performances of domestic work. The agency these women demonstrate would be significant even if they were unable, unwilling, or even uninterested in recasting the place of women in the stratified and rigidified world of the country house. That the entertainments at Harefield and Bisham became venues of personal as well as familial legitimization is the greatest testament of all to the newfound authority assumed by Russell and Egerton. It does not stretch plausibility too much to think that perhaps this aspect of the entertainment might have been what appealed most of all to their primary audience—a woman who herself continually had to negotiate between traditional values and her own power.

Chapter 10
"You take no labour": Women Workers of Magic in Early Modern England[1]

Molly Hand

In studies of magic in early modern culture, discussions of sorcery and witchcraft predominate. Workers of magic—those for whom magic was a professional trade—are obscured by powerful images of male magicians as overreaching tragic heroes and women witches as victims. How can we recuperate magic as a professional practice chosen by women? How can we overcome the powerful associations of women with witchcraft and victimhood?

This essay takes up the task of locating women workers of magic as active agents for whom magic is an enabling practice and a trade by which they earn a living. I examine representations of such women in John Fletcher and Philip Massinger's *The Prophetess* (1622), as well as Edmond Bower's pamphlet *Doctor Lamb Revived, or Witchcraft Condemn'd in Anne Bodenham* (1653) and Ben Jonson's *The Alchemist* (1610). While each of these texts invokes negative cultural assumptions about women, each also questions such assumptions, implicitly or explicitly. In the character of Delphia, Fletcher and Massinger create a working woman magus who is meant to out-Prospero Prospero. Doll Common, a whore and confidence trickster, is also a worker of magic; in early modern terms, she is a juggler, a performer of illusions and staged magic tricks. Anne Bodenham is tried and condemned as a witch, but Bower's pamphlet actually shows her to be a cunning person, someone who offered magical services such as finding lost or stolen items, providing love tokens or protective charms, prognosticating, healing the sick, and "unwitching" or counteracting *maleficia*. In contrast to witches, who were ascribed their identities by others, cunning folk and jugglers chose and fashioned theirs. These expressions of agency and professionalism suggest new ways of thinking about women's magical practices and about performed magic as labor both on and off stage. In the face of the many contemporary texts in which women's positions as "working subjects" were demonized or obscured, the representations I discuss invite us to reconsider our notions about magical practice, women's status as agents or as victims, and women's occupations in early modern culture.

[1] I am grateful to Michelle Dowd and Natasha Korda for inviting me to contribute to this volume and for helpful feedback as I honed this essay. Thank you to the Renaissance group at FSU for commenting on an early draft, and to Bruce Boehrer for feedback on a later one.

"Workers of wonders"

Early modern representations of magic as work are rare. In that these three characters, Delphia, Anne Bodenham, and Doll Common, are composite figures whose magical identities include elements borrowed from other more narrowly defined magical types—the witch, the magician, the cunning person, and the juggler[2]—they are less easily distinguished and relegated to a pre-identified category that would exclude the possibility of perceiving them as workers. For, while the former two magical types listed above, the witch and the magician, were decidedly not workers, the latter two might be. Cunning folk exchanged their services for payment in cash or kind. Their profession was a valued one, and apparently sometimes a profitable one, as cunning folk were numerous. Some estimates suggest that at least one cunning person resided within walking distance of most English households.[3] They might be itinerant workers, paying housecalls to clients, or operate their business within their own homes. Cunning folk had clients ranging from the very poor to members of the elite. Yet, these magical practitioners were also viewed with mistrust, as the example of Bodenham attests—as "good witches" who worked counter-magic, had they too entered into a tacit compact with the devil? Protestant divines and demonologists thought so.[4]

Jugglers were similarly ambiguous and perceived with ambivalence. They might be legitimate, giving licit performances at court, in fairs, or as a part of traveling shows; licit jugglers staged acts before an audience who knew they were seeing a magic show. Jugglers might also be illicit performers, akin to "cony-catchers," whose magic acts were aimed at cozening poor gulls. Doll and the "venture tripartite" in *The Alchemist* are of the latter group. Licit or illicit, on stage or off, the staged magic of jugglers required real work, including practice, manipulation of various props, and hiring and training of confederates who would then share in the profits. Whether or not those profits were ill-gotten, they were the juggler's income, which audiences willingly exchanged for entertainment, or which "private" audiences unwittingly gave in return for the deception.[5]

---

[2]   I employ these terms when distinguishing among magical figures according to their specific practices and characteristics as indicated in early modern demonological discourse; I employ the term "practitioner of magic" when referring to magical figures more generally, or to figures in whom elements of discrete magical identities are combined.

[3]   Owen Davies, *Popular Magic: Cunning-Folk in English History* (London: Hambledon and London, 2003), 67–8.

[4]   William Perkins, for example, believes that cunning people are even more dangerous than maleficent witches, as they drew people towards idolatry and superstition—the "bad witch" might harm the body, but the "good witch," or cunning person, endangered the soul. *A Discourse of the Damned Art of Witchcraft* (Cambridge, 1610), 174–6. Cited hereafter in text.

[5]   Philip Butterworth's recent study of early modern jugglery, *Magic on the Early English Stage* (Cambridge: Cambridge University Press, 2005), is rich with detail and examples.

More frequently represented in early modern culture and more frequently studied by scholars are the witch and the magician, both of whom were usually viewed in opposition to work. As David Hawkes indicates in his essay in this volume, the question of who actually performed the supernatural phenomena— the magical practitioner or the devil—was fundamental to demonological debate. Demonologists and divines, like James I and William Perkins, argued that neither witches nor magicians actually performed the feats attributed to them; instead, the devil or his minions performed the desired tasks, but only after the magical practitioner had entered into a demonic compact. William Perkins explains: "It is a point of policie, not to be readie at every mans command to doe for him what he would, except [the devil] be sure of his rewards, and no other meanes will serve his turne for taking assurance hereof, but this covenant" (45). The depiction of the devil as the "real" worker of magic is present in many early modern representations, from Marlowe's *Doctor Faustus* to Rowley, Dekker, and Ford's *The Witch of Edmonton.*[6]

The influential skeptic Reginald Scot did not accept that corporeal beings could enter into contracts with spiritual ones, yet he also perceived witches and magicians as nonworkers. In general, the Neoplatonic magus was portrayed as male, educated, cosmopolitan, and of the "better sort."[7] Not needing to work for a living, he was at leisure to study humanist philosophy and learn the occult arts. By contrast, the witch was typically depicted as female, impoverished, old, disfigured, uneducated, and marginalized by the community. These figures' incentives for practicing magic varied as well. James I describes their motives as

> Curiositie in great ingines: thirst of revenge, for some tortes deeply apprehended: or greedie appetite of geare, caused through great poverty. As to the first of these, Curiosity, it is onelie the inticement of Magiciens, or Necromanciers: and the other two are the allureres of the … Witches.[8]

Revenge and poverty appear as motives in Scot's treatise as well; however, Scot places blame with the community that refuses to help the ostensible witch. For

---

[6] For a slightly different take, see David Hawkes's essay in this volume, which argues that the devil, like money or fetishized commodities, is a performative sign, an efficacious image that seems to "work" because human practitioners of magic mistakenly believe it has the power to do so.

[7] Reginald Scot, *A Discoverie of Witchcraft* (1584; repr., Carbondale: Southern Illinois University Press, 1964), 58. On the Neoplatonic magus, see Barbara Howard Traister, *Heavenly Necromancers: The Magician in English Renaissance Drama* (Columbia: University of Missouri Press, 1984); D.P. Walker, *Spiritual and Demonic Magic from Ficino to Campanella*, Studies of the Warburg Institute, 22 (London: Warburg Institute, 1958); and Frances Yates, *Giordano Bruno and the Hermetic Tradition* (Chicago: University of Chicago Press, 1991).

[8] James I, *Daemonologie*, (ed.) G.B. Harrison (1597; repr., Oxford: Bodley Head, 1924), 8.

him, the accused witch is an unemployed woman depending on the community for assistance. Her constant demands begin to annoy her neighbors, who deny her charity the next time she comes begging. When those neighbors' children grow ill or their livestock become lame, they conclude that the witch has placed a curse on them.[9]

This model, sometimes called "charity denied," has been influential in modern studies of witchcraft, not only because it appears in the work of the most thoroughgoing early modern skeptic, but also because it has been espoused by Keith Thomas in his magisterial *Religion and the Decline of Magic*. Thomas's study usefully maintains a focus on the socio-economic context in which witchcraft accusations emerge. Yet, "charity denied," like most paradigms, effaces some important nuances. A recent body of scholarship complicates the model.[10] Studies by Clive Holmes and Deborah Willis demonstrate that women accused of witchcraft were not always pitiful victims; they were often bad neighbors who demanded goods, slandered community members, or took property without asking first.[11] Witchcraft accusations may also have been expressions of larger political conflicts within communities, rather than of differences in socio-economic status and disdain for the poor, as Annabel Gregory has shown.[12]

Furthermore, Thomas's acceptance of the notion that charitable giving was in decline in early modern England means that, while he correctly sees the discourse of witchcraft in relation to the vilification of the poor as displayed in the early modern discourse on poverty, he quickly blames the secularization of poor relief for increased socio-economic anxiety at the village level.[13] Even if the laws led to a gradual decrease in charitable giving at the individual level, there is no conclusive evidence that they were responsible for a subsequent increase in witchcraft accusations. The Poor Laws of 1598 and 1601 created funds for the relief of the poor through taxation.[14] "Witches," if lame or widowed, might have been considered "deserving poor," though if they were "never-married" women they were less likely to receive poor relief, as both Natasha Korda and Amy Froide

---

[9]   Scot, *A Discoverie of Witchcraft*, 30.

[10]   See Jonathan Barry, Marianne Hester, and Gareth Roberts (eds.), *Witchcraft in Early Modern Europe* (Cambridge: Cambridge University Press, 1996) and Diane Purkiss, *The Witch in History* (London: Routledge, 1996), 59–88.

[11]   Holmes, "Women: Witnesses and Witches," *Past and Present* 140 (1993): 52–3 and Willis, *Malevolent Nurture: Witch-Hunting and Maternal Power in Early Modern England* (Ithaca: Cornell University Press, 1995), 41–3.

[12]   Gregory, "Witchcraft, Politics, and 'Good Neighborhood' in Early Seventeenth-Century Rye," *Past and Present* 133 (1991): 62 and passim.

[13]   Thomas, *Religion and the Decline of Magic* (New York and London: Oxford University Press, 1971), 660–74. See esp. 672, where Thomas writes that the Poor Laws "undoubtedly" led to the decline in charity.

[14]   See Paul Slack, *Poverty and Policy in Tudor and Stuart England* (London and New York: Longman, 1988), 113–37 and passim.

indicate.[15] These laws, along with the Statute of Artificers and the Act for the Punishment of Vagabonds, further attempted to ensure that the "idle poor" would be gainfully employed or properly disciplined.[16] While the poor were demonized in some literary and dramatic representations, such portrayals did not correspond to the treatment of the poor in many communities, where charitable giving and values of "good neighborhood" still held sway. Witchcraft accusations were not always directed at the poor, and they did not always stem from neighbors' uncharitable attitudes. As Barry points out, evidence suggests that accusations emerged only after long years of building suspicion; legal prosecution, he suggests, was usually a last resort.[17] The relationship among the secularization of poor relief, a supposed decline in charitable giving, and witchcraft accusations cannot, then, be accurately described as a causal one.

Also problematic is the "charity denied" model's assumption that uncharitable neighbors are actually expressing feelings of guilt over wrongdoing in associating their own ill fortunes with a witch's curse. This theory, while plausible from a psychoanalytic perspective, dismisses early modern people's perception of the witch as a nonworker, or even an *anti-worker*.[18] She was thought to deliberately destroy the products of others' labor or others' means of making a living, for example, by interfering with churning, brewing, and other domestic cookery practices, or by laming livestock. Witches were demonized as anti-workers in similar terms and for the same reasons as other anti-workers, like usurers, rogues, whores, and even players: they were all "caterpillars of the commonwealth" who not only reaped where they did not sow, but also provoked vice and idleness in others. As demonized types represented in performed and printed texts, such "caterpillars," including witches, were frequently blamed for economic hardship, both in local communities and in the nation at large, as several essays in this collection attest.[19]

The relationship between the early modern discourse on magic and the changing economy was thus a fraught one. As we have seen, witches were perceived as

[15] Korda, *Shakespeare's Domestic Economies: Gender and Property in Early Modern England* (Philadelphia: University of Pennsylvania Press, 2002), 176–9 and Froide, *Never Married: Singlewomen in Early Modern England* (Oxford and New York: Oxford University Press, 2005), 34–42.

[16] On secularized poor relief as a mechanism for social regulation, see Slack, *Poverty and Policy in Tudor and Stuart England*, 130–31. On poor relief and the social regulation of women, and on widows versus singlewomen as "deserving poor," see Korda, *Shakespeare's Domestic Economies*, 176–9 and passim, and Froide, *Never Married*, 34–42.

[17] Barry, "Introduction: Keith Thomas and the Problem of Witchcraft," in *Witchcraft in Early Modern Europe*, 13.

[18] Purkiss describes the witch as "anti-housewife" and both Purkiss and Willis conceive of the witch as "anti-mother." Purkiss, *The Witch in History*, 100–112; Willis, *Malevolent Nurture*, 1–81 and passim.

[19] See also Paola Pugliatti, *Beggary and Theatre in Early Modern England* (Aldershot: Ashgate, 2003), 47–51 and Craig Dionne and Steve Mentz (eds.), *Rogues and Early Modern English Culture* (Ann Arbor: University of Michigan Press, 2004).

economic threats and as economic victims; however, other magical practitioners had different relationships to emergent capitalism. Cunning folk protected people and their property by counteracting *maleficia*, healing sick people and animals, finding stolen valuables, and more. Cunning folk thus met specifically socio-economic needs in communities, which may explain why such figures appeared in many locales well into the eighteenth century, long after the firm establishment of the market economy.

Illicit jugglery was, of course, a marginal practice that evolved due to economic hardship as well as the spread of the capitalist ethos of exploitation and self-preservation. But jugglery was not just for cony-catchers and rogues; juggling tricks were disseminated through rogue literature, plays, and instruction manuals. Manuals portray magic as theatrical performance and contribute to increased skepticism among audiences as well as increased agency—people learned how to do it themselves from Samuel Rid, "Hocus Pocus Junior," and Reginald Scot. Jugglery thus became a practice of the literate and the streetwise, the cunning of both city and country.

My reading of Anne Bodenham, Delphia, and Doll Common attends to these nuances of economic engagement. Influenced by feminist historians of women's work and witchcraft, my discussion aims to identify an important bridge between these two fields of inquiry.[20] I argue that through their appropriation of the gendered characteristics of the male magus, Delphia and Bodenham acquire the power culturally ascribed to the magus and denied the witch. In so doing, however, they revise the traditional role of the magician as elite *nonworker*, insofar as the working-class Delphia and Bodenham practice magic to earn a living. Bodenham and Delphia are thus rare serious depictions of the kinds of cultural synthesis and self-fashioning performed by actual cunning folk. *The Alchemist* explores the notion of jugglery as magical work, thus emphasizing a feature of magical labor that is amplified in Jonson's play, namely, that the performance of magic, whether "real" or "fake," is acting, and acting is work. The theatricality of magic was observed by both skeptics and playwrights; yet the focus on performance in Jonson's play reflects a decided engagement with the notion of magical practice as work.

"To use their cunnings"

Anne Bodenham was a cunning woman dwelling in Fisherton Anger, a suburb of Salisbury.[21] When she was accused of witchcraft in 1653, she was eighty years

---

[20]   I have already cited important studies of witchcraft; on women's work, see Marjorie Keniston McIntosh, *Working Women in English Society, 1300–1620* (Cambridge: Cambridge University Press, 2005) and Sara Mendelson and Patricia Crawford, *Women in Early Modern England, 1550–1720* (Oxford: Oxford University Press, 1998).

[21]   Bodenham is subject of two pamphlets and a ballad: Edmond Bower, *Doctor Lamb Revived, or Witchcraft Condemn'd in Anne Bodenham* (London, 1653); James Bower, *Dr Lambe's Darling: Or, Strange and Terrible News from Salisbury* (London, 1653); and *The Salisbury Assizes*, broadside (London, 1653). In addition, she receives mention in Henry More, *Enthusiasmus Triumphatus* (London, 1656); More, *Tetractys Anti-astrologica*

old. She had been practicing magic for decades. Her witch finder and pamphleteer, Edmond Bower, writes that Bodenham "taught divers young Children to read, pretending to get her livelyhood by such an employment."[22] She actually earned a living, he implies, by selling magical services to the community. Bodenham learned her trade through an apprenticeship with the notorious magician John Lambe, sorcerer to George Villiers: "she reading in some of his Books, with his help learnt her Art, by which she said she had gotten many a penny, and done hundreds of people good ... " (27). Bodenham's apprenticeship with Lambe facilitates her professional success; she incorporates characteristics of the male magus into her own magical persona. This borrowing of the magician's characteristics and symbols was not, in itself, unique. According to Davies and Thomas, cunning folk accessed the symbolic capital associated with the learned magician by displaying signs of learning, thereby increasing their own respectability and attracting business.[23] Even if illiterate, they might wield large and impressive, ancient-looking magic books as props, or employ scrying glasses, draw conjurer's circles, write Latin charms (the meanings of which were unknown to them), or incorporate elements of Catholic ritual. Such practices reveal the reliance of cunning folk on performance and outward display in their profession, forms of spectacle in which Anne Bodenham likewise engages.

What is unusual about Bodenham is that she identifies, or is identified, so explicitly with one infamous sorcerer. Having learned from Lambe, boasting that she can best William Lilly, and invoking the Faustian blood pact, Bodenham demonstrates awareness of the power specific to the male magician in the cultural imagination. We can read her as endeavoring to tap the power of that symbolic capital. Bodenham's magical self-fashioning may be understood as a reaction against cultural assumptions about women as receptacles of popular magical practices and beliefs. Unlike Bodenham, many women workers of magic acquired their skills within the household economy. In Renaissance culture, children of accused witches were deeply suspect because, despite arguments of divines and demonologists attributing magical power to the devil, English witchcraft beliefs held that magical power was inherent and passed through bloodlines. More practical-minded writers noted that in the predominantly female domestic sphere, women "witches" passed their practices on to their daughters and granddaughters.[24] In addition to magical practices, women caregivers passed along fairy stories and

---

(London, 1681); Joseph Hall, *The Invisible World Discovered to Spiritual Eyes* (London, 1659); William Drage, *Daimonomageia* (London, 1665); Joseph Glanvill, *Saducismus Triumphatus* (London, 1681); and Increase Mather, *A Further Account of the Trials of the New England Witches* (London, 1693).

[22]   Bower, *Doctor Lamb Revived*, 1. Cited hereafter in text.

[23]   Davies, *Popular Magic*, 69–71; Thomas, *Religion and the Decline of Magic*, 269.

[24]   Clive Holmes, "Popular Culture? Witches, Magistrates, and Divines in Early Modern England" in *Understanding Popular Culture: Europe from the Middle Ages to the Nineteenth Century*, (ed.) Steven L. Kaplan (Berlin; New York; Amsterdam: Mouton Publishers, 1984), 96–7.

"old wives' tales," magical beliefs that were increasingly satirized and demonized. Regina Buccola writes that fairy beliefs were "firmly tied to the domestic, agricultural economy and thus logically fell into disfavor in an increasingly urban, mercantile culture," the latter comprising the primary audience for printed texts and dramatic performances.[25] Citing a particularly degrading passage from Scot's *Discoverie of Witchcraft* that attributes fairy stories to frightening, manipulative women, Wendy Wall similarly writes that "Scot links [fairylore] to lower-class domestic forms of knowledge and, more generally, to behavioral control—the moment when an earlier and vulnerable self was coerced into obedience through mystification."[26] The ascription of fairy stories and magic to mean mothers and diabolical witches, and more generally to uneducated rural female culture, by *both* skeptics like Scot and believers like James, served to demonize women as the bearers of traditional magical beliefs and magical beliefs themselves as ridiculous "old wives' tales."

Bodenham counters such negative representations by styling herself after the fashion of a male wizard and as a professional worker of magic. Diane Purkiss identifies Bodenham as "a kind of occult businesswoman" who attempts to create a master/apprentice relationship and to pass along her magical legacy to Anne Styles, the servant from the Goddard household who pays her several visits on behalf of her employers and who will ultimately, at Edmond Bower's behest, accuse Bodenham of witchcraft.[27] Like Malcolm Gaskill, Purkiss situates Bodenham's "choosing to be a witch" in the context of godly politics.[28] While my understanding of Bodenham as a working woman corresponds to her argument, I find it necessary to clarify terminology. Rather than imagining Bodenham as a "witch" whose adherence to the recusant "old ways" comprises her resistance to the oppressive godly discourse of Edmond Bowers, I understand Bodenham as a woman worker of magic who decidedly rejects being identified as a witch and who plays an integral role in her community. Bodenham certainly did not see herself as a witch and says to Bower that no one ever called her one until Styles accused her (17). Having practiced magic for decades without ever having been accused of witchcraft, Bodenham's case attests to the fact that early modern

[25]   Buccola, *Fairies, Fractious Women, and the Old Faith* (Selinsgrove: Susquehanna University Press, 2006), 118.

[26]   Wall, *Staging Domesticity: Household Work and English Identity in Early Modern Drama* (Cambridge: Cambridge University Press, 2002), 98; see also Mary Ellen Lamb, *The Popular Culture of Shakespeare, Spenser, and Jonson* (London and New York: Routledge, 2006), 45–62.

[27]   See Purkiss, *The Witch in History*, 148–62.

[28]   Gaskill, "Witchcraft, Politics, and Memory in Seventeenth-century England," *The Historical Journal* 50.2 (2007): 289–308. Gaskill situates Bodenham's case in its contemporary political context, but he also shows that that very context is informed by pervasive memories of the recent past that haunt the cultural imagination. Purkiss writes about Bodenham in a chapter entitled, "Self-fashioning by Women: Choosing to be a Witch," in *The Witch in History*, 145–76.

individuals and communities differentiated between types of magical practitioners. Where Purkiss reads Bodenham's self-fashioning in terms of resistance to godly interregnum culture, I understand it in broader terms of a tradition of resistance to the widespread demonization of women practitioners of magic. The denigration of women like Bodenham, and their practices, appeared in the culture at large— among the godly as well as less zealous Protestants, among people who believed that women witches could harness the power of the devil and among skeptics who scoffed at such superstitious nonsense. Situating the Bodenham case in the context of religious and sectarian politics, Purkiss ultimately confirms Bower's own reading of Bodenham as a Catholic, royalist, unruly woman whose supposed lust for drink on the way to the gallows is her way of thumbing her nose at the godly who oppose drinking and traditional festivities. But Bodenham was also a literate, professional woman; she was married, and she was known in her community. We are confronted here by the same problem that arises in so many witchcraft narratives: we tend to come away with more information about the aims and politics of the accuser than we do of the accused. In the Bodenham case in particular, a focus on sectarian politics tells us more about Bower than it does about Bodenham.

So, what *can* we know about Bodenham, really, or about any "witches"? In this case, we learn at the very least that Bodenham was a learned, cunning woman whose position in the community was stable until a godly outsider came along. We learn how much money she made, as Bower carefully accounts for the coins changing hands in each transaction—if these were the going rates, Bodenham did moderately well for herself.[29] We see in Bodenham a woman steeped in knowledge of contemporary representations of magicians who puts that knowledge to use in creating her own spectacular magic scenes. Bodenham also appears as a mature woman concerned about the welfare of a younger woman who is in danger. Bower's own description of Bodenham offering to take Styles in after she has been let go by her employers undercuts his aim of depicting Bodenham as a maleficent witch. Bodenham "earnestly desired the Maid to live with her, and told her, that if she would do, she would teach her to do as she did, and that she would never be taken [arrested]" (10).[30] Bodenham's endeavor to create a feminocentric master/apprentice relationship and practice, and her efforts not only to take on the role of magician for herself but to pass this role along to another woman, suggest that we read Bodenham's character as resistant to learned—and not just godly—culture's denigration of female magical culture and as an example of female agency in appropriating literary, dramatic, and intellectual elements of the male magician type in the fashioning of a professional identity.

The depiction of a professional woman magician looking after a younger woman also appears in Fletcher and Massinger's *The Prophetess*, and just as

---

[29] From the several visits from Styles on behalf of the Goddards, Bodenham might have made as much as £2.

[30] Styles was rightly afraid of being arrested as she was implicated in a plot to poison one of her former employers. Bower, *Doctor Lamb Revived*, 9.

Bower's description of Bodenham conjures a number of contemporary magician figures, so Fletcher and Massinger's Delphia recalls a number of dramatic magical predecessors. When we meet Delphia in the beginning of *The Prophetess*, she is assuring her niece, Drusilla, that the latter's love-interest, Diocles, will indeed become emperor of Rome.[31] Delphia has prophesied that Diocles will become emperor after killing the "fatal boar." Hunting wild boars day after day, Diocles has yet to realize that the "fatal" boar is a man, Volutius Aper, who has assassinated the current emperor, Numerianus. Learning of the assassination of their brother, Charinus and Aurelia take out a proscription on Aper's life, promising that whoever kills Aper will rule as co-emperor with Charinus and will wed Aurelia. Diocles then realizes the meaning of Delphia's prophecy. He kills Aper and becomes emperor, but also breaks his engagement to Drusilla in favor of Aurelia's offer of marriage. Delphia spends the remainder of the play teaching Diocles, or rather prompting him to realize on his own, that a life with the chaste and fair Drusilla in the pastoral seat of his humble country grange is preferable to life at court, where even good people are turned sour by ambition and focus on outward appearances. Diocles learns his lesson, marries Drusilla, turns the throne over to his nephew, Maximinian, and retires to the grange to live the good life. Maximinian marries Aurelia and, suspicious that his uncle may one day wish to return as emperor, decides he must kill Diocles. Accompanied by an army, Maximinian marches on the grange, where Diocles's and Drusilla's marriage masque is in progress. Maximinian's murder attempt is halted when Delphia calls forth the hand of a god carrying a thunderbolt. Rather than punishing Maximinian, however, Diocles merely tells him to "learn to deserve" the position of emperor, and in the end, the play promises a humble but hearty feast for the entire group.

Gordon McMullan describes Delphia as a "curiously feminized Prospero," for him, a thoroughly ambivalent character in whom he finds echoes of Faustus, Prospero, Clorin of *The Faithful Shepherdess* and Dionyza of *Pericles*.[32] While McMullan reads Delphia as a morally ambivalent character with whom the audience cannot sympathize until the final act of the play, what he calls Delphia's "angry strategizing" can be better understood as a reaction to the treachery of male characters who endeavor to demonize her in terms borrowed explicitly from the discourse on witchcraft. Though not a witch, neither is Delphia only a prophetess. In constructing her character, Fletcher and Massinger incorporated essential characteristics of the male magician figure. Descendant of Prospero and Faustus, Delphia's powers surpass theirs: she commands deities, not simple daemons. She performs rites to Hecate and Ceres; from the latter she "force[s] her winged

---

[31]   I am aware of only two critical discussions of the play: Gordon McMullan, *The Politics of Unease in the Plays of John Fletcher* (Amherst: University of Massachusetts Press, 1994), 183–96; and Jean-Pierre Teissedou, "*The Prophetess* de John Fletcher (1579–1625): Puissance de la Magie ou Magie de la Puissance?" in *La Magie et ses Langages*, (ed.) Margaret Jones-Davies (Lille: Universitè de Lille, 1980), 83–93.

[32]   McMullan, *The Politics of Unease,* 183–5.

dragons"[33] and flies, in a bit of spectacular stage magic, over the action of the play with her niece, Drusilla (2.3.341). The moon, an emblem for Hecate, hides when Delphia crosses the sky, afraid that Delphia will "force her from her sphere," just as she forced Ceres's dragons into submission (2.3.341). Delphia raises a she-devil for the fool, Geta, in a humorous echo of Marlowe's play (3.3.354–5). In a scene that would be evoked in Milton's *Maske Performed at Ludlow Castle*, Delphia raises a spirit from a crystal well (5.3.385).[34] She engages the services of Ceres and Pan for a marriage masque, recalling Prospero's marriage masque featuring Ceres, Iris, and Juno (5.3.386); she calls forth the angry hand of a god armed with a thunderbolt (5.3.388), perhaps an echo of the moment in which Faustus cowers before an angry god who "Stretcheth out his arms and bends his ireful brows!"[35]

Delphia is thus a formidable magician, meant both to invoke and to best her predecessors in displays of power. Unlike other plays in the Fletcher canon, in which "apparently magical events turn out to have been orchestrated and fabricated by ordinary mortals," *The Prophetess* displays actual, effective magic.[36] More significantly in the present context, Delphia's spectacular magic, while evocative of other significant contemporary representations, is portrayed as *work*. Without an Ariel or a Mephistopheles to perform tasks on her behalf, Delphia works her own magic in order to earn a living. In a play largely concerned with questions of work, virtue, and social mobility, the attention that Fletcher and Massinger devote to the representation of Delphia as a working woman ought not be overlooked.

In the beginning of the play, Diocles's faith in Delphia's magical abilities is presented in contrast with the skeptical view of Maximinian, whose derisively misogynistic comments about Delphia typify contemporary views on women who practice witchcraft from both sides of the demonological debate. His claims reflect the arguments of skeptics like Reginald Scot and Johann Weyer, as well as those of believers like Jean Bodin and James I.[37] Maximinian's remarks reveal how both skeptics and believers emphasize the powerlessness of the female witch. If the skeptic believes that the witch is a delusional melancholic incapable of performing the acts attributed to her, the credulous demonologist argues that the witch's acts are performed by the devil. From both sides, the argument is not about women's agency or power, but about their pathology or subjection to the devil.

[33] John Fletcher and Philip Massinger, *The Prophetess*, vol. 5 of *The Works of Francis Beaumont and John Fletcher*, (ed.) A.R. Waller (Cambridge: Cambridge University Press, 1907), 2.1, 336. This edition does not include line numbers, so act, scene, and page numbers are cited in the text hereafter.

[34] See McMullan, *The Politics of Unease*, 194–6.

[35] Christopher Marlowe, *Doctor Faustus*, in *English Renaissance Drama*, (ed.) David Bevington (New York: Norton, 2002), 5.2.80.

[36] McMullan, *The Politics of Unease*, 183.

[37] Weyer, *De Praestigiis Daemonum*, (ed.) John Shea (1563; repr., Binghampton: Center for Medieval and Renaissance Studies, 1991); Bodin, *On the Demon-Mania of Witches*, trans. Randy A. Scott (1580; repr., Toronto: Centre for Renaissance and Reformation Studies, 1995).

Maximinian deeply resents the fact that he, Diocles, and Geta "provide [Delphia] daily, / and bring in Feasts while she sits farting at us, / and blowing out her Prophecies at both ends" (1.3.327). He satirizes the otherworldly phenomenon of prophecy by relocating it in the bodily one of flatulence. Maximinian's tactics here are reminiscent of those employed by Samuel Harsnett in the possession controversy at the end of the sixteenth century.[38] As Katharine Maus notes, Harsnett discredits both the possessed and the dispossessor through satire, which "from time immemorial has operated by uncovering a 'base'—that is, bodily, this-worldly, self-interested, and local—explanation for behaviors that pretend to be spiritual, transcendent, altruistic, or universal."[39] Here, Delphia's prophecies are reduced to the scatological. As the "transcendent" prophecy takes the form of a specific bodily function, Delphia becomes another example of the woman as a "leaky vessel."[40] Maximinian further implies that it is Delphia's excessive consumption of food and wine that reveals her to be a fraud.

> Twould make a fool prophesie to be fed continually
> What do you get? your labour and your danger;
> Whilst she sits bathing in her larded fury,
> Inspir'd with full deep Cups, who cannot prophesie? (1.3.328)

True prophets did not eat or drink to excess; just the opposite: they fasted.

Maximinian does not stop there; he further demonizes Delphia in terms strongly influenced by continental demonological theory and espoused by James I:

> I would have [malice]
> Against these purblind Prophets; for look ye, Sir,
> Old women lie monstrously; so will the Devil,
> Or else he has had much wrong; upon my knowledge,
> Old women are malicious; so is he;
> They are proud and covetous, revengeful, lecherous;
> All which are excellent attributes of the Devil;
> They would at least seem holy; so would he;
> And to vail over these villainies, they would prophesie;
> He gives them leave now and then to use their cunnings,
> Which is, to kill a Cow, or blast a Harvest,
> Make young Pigs pipe themselves to death, choak poultry,

---

[38] See Philip Almond (ed.), *Demonic Possession and Exorcism in Early Modern England* (Cambridge: Cambridge University Press, 2004); F.W. Brownlow, *Shakespeare, Harsnett, and the Devils of Denham* (Newark: University of Delaware Press, 1993); and Stephen Greenblatt, "Shakespeare and the Exorcists," in *Shakespearean Negotiations* (Berkeley and Los Angeles: University of California Press, 1988), 94–128.

[39] Katharine Eisaman Maus, "Sorcery and Subjectivity in Early Modern Discourses of Witchcraft," in *Historicism, Psychoanalysis, and Early Modern Culture*, (eds.) Carla Mazzio and Douglas Trevor (New York and London: Routledge, 2000), 336.

[40] See Gail Kern Paster, *The Body Embarrassed* (Ithaca: Cornell University Press, 1993).

...
But when he makes these Agents to raise Emperors,
When he disposes Fortune as his Servant,
And tyes her to old wives tails [*sic*]—(1.3.328)

Here, Maximinian is interrupted by Diocles, but it seems he would finish by saying something like, "that'll be the day"—even Satan himself would not permit slavish "witches" to "raise Emperors," or let "old wives tails" dictate fate. The derisive tone is amplified by the misspelling of "tale"; the popular notion that witches' relations with the devil or with demon familiars was sexual is neatly encapsulated in the bawdy pun.

Subsequently, Diocles accuses Delphia not of fraud but rather of not eating her bread in the sweat of her brow—of not working for a living and of delaying the fulfillment of the prophecy in order to gain more from Diocles:

... you are cunning, Mother;
And with that Cunning, and the faith I give you,
Ye lead me blindly to no end, no honour;
You find ye are daily fed, you take no labour;
Your family at ease, they know no market,
And therefore to maintain this, you speak darkly,
As darkly still ye nourish it, whilst I,
Being a credulous and obsequious Coxcomb,
Hunt daily, and sweat hourly, to find out
To clear your mystery; kill Boar on Boar,
And make your Spits and Pots bow with my Bounties;
Yet I still poorer, further still—(1.3.330)

Though Diocles accuses Delphia of "tak[ing] no labour" and "know[ing] no market," he also twice employs the word "cunning," a word that also appears in Maximinian's preceding speech. Fletcher and Massinger thus invoke the figure of the cunning person, inviting us to conceive of Delphia not just as stage magician in the Neoplatonic tradition, but as a working woman who exchanges magical services for payment in kind. Having already revised the magician figure in gendered terms, the playwrights further complicate the figure by incorporating elements of cunning folks' popular magic and occupational labor—just as, in real life, as we see with Anne Bodenham, cunning folk incorporated identifying characteristics of the elite male magician. Delphia practices magic in order to put food on the table, rather than for any of the reasons detailed in demonological treatises (e.g., curiosity, acquisitiveness, revenge). In his discussion of cunning people, Davies writes, "There are a number of reasons why people may have wanted to become cunning folk. The desire for money, power, or social prestige, and even to do good, all undoubtedly played their part ... [but] it has been suggested that cunning folk were primarily motivated by the desire for prestige rather than payment."[41] In contrast, Delphia does not seem to care about prestige: "I am a poor weak woman,

---

[41] Davies, *Popular Magic*, 84.

to me no worship," she tells Maximinian and Diocles, once they become convinced of her power (1.2.332). Parts cunning person, magician, and prophetess—and also worker, singlewoman, and maternal guardian—Delphia is vindicated in the remaining four acts of the play. She is, after all, an agent who raises emperors, and also one who leads them to realize that being an emperor is not as desirable as it may seem. Fletcher and Massinger create a world where social climbing, but also social stepping down are possible: retreat from the world of the court is depicted as a wise choice for Diocles. McMullan reads Delphia as "at best a figure of moral ambivalence" and at worst a character whose "moral compromises ... cannot have sustained the sympathy of the audience."[42] This reading, however, does not account for the fact that Delphia, though wronged by others, seeks revenge not on her own account, but on behalf of her niece. She is a protective aunt, and her "revenge" teaches rather than punishes. Delphia is a benevolent character who imparts values of loyalty, mercy, and gratitude to characters steeped in vice, particularly ambition and willingness to betray others. Through Delphia, these positive values are developed in Diocles, who passes them along to Maximinian, and so forth, in a great chain of reform and redemption.

"Labour kindly in the common work"

The skeptical view of magical practice sought, in part, to deprive magical practitioners of any real power that was attributed to them. Reginald Scot's *Discoverie*, for example, includes a lengthy catalogue of the "juggling tricks" that might be mistaken for magic. Prior to this section of his book, however, Scot apologizes to those who might make their living through such practices. He is

> sorie that it falleth out to [his] lot, to laie open the secrets of this mysterie, to the hinderance of such poore men as live thereby: whose doings herein are not onlie tolerable, but greatlie commendable, so they abuse not the name of God, nor make the people attribute unto them his power.[43]

Scot demystifies magical performance and reveals it to be work. Such unveiling of magical performance as work occurs in other expressions of culture. Mountebanks, itinerant performers peddling their medicinal wares with the help of juggling acts, attracted audiences through staged magic and then astonished them with the powers of their tonics and tinctures. Mountebanks worked with confederates, people in the audience who were in on the trick, who might, for example, have fake teeth in their mouths, which the mountebanks would pull with the greatest of ease. Theatricality was an integral aspect of the mountebank's profession.[44]

---

[42]   McMullan, *The Politics of Unease*, 184–5.

[43]   Scot, *Discoverie*, 268–9.

[44]   See M.A. Katritzky, *Women, Medicine, and Theatre, 1500–1750: Literary Moutebanks and Performing Quacks* (Aldershot: Ashgate, 2007) and Bella Mirabella,

Texts such as Robert Greene's and Thomas Dekker's rogue pamphlets chronicled tricksters' sly performances and their successful duping of naïve gulls. Scot's *Discoverie* and Greene's and Dekker's pamphlets might have been perceived as manuals, both for citizens wishing to avoid being tricked, and for literate tricksters, wishing to pick up new skills.[45] Real manuals followed shortly thereafter. In 1612, Samuel Rid's *The Art of Jugling or Legerdemaine* instructed readers on how convincingly to perform juggling tricks, suggesting, "You must also have your words of Arte, [so] you may induce the minde, to conceive, and suppose that you deale with Spirits."[46] With a first edition in 1634, and numerous subsequent editions, the enormously popular "Hocus Pocus Junior's" *Anatomie of Legerdemaine* was published "so that an ignorant person may thereby learne the full perfection of the same, after a little practice," according to the title page.

On the stage, jugglers were nowhere better represented than in Ben Jonson's *The Alchemist*. While Reginald Scot explicitly acknowledges that some "jugglers" may work their magic tricks for a living, Jonson's play shares with the texts of Greene and Dekker the paradoxical feature of demonizing as idle and vicious the very characters it reveals to be working subjects, a point that is illuminated in Elizabeth Rivlin's essay in this volume. Adjuring Face and Subtle to "labour kindly in the common work,"[47] Doll Common performs a wide range of magical roles: she becomes a fairy queen, a radical prophetess, and a witch promising a demon familiar. She is also ostensibly a "common" whore who is strangely able to quote from Broughton and to imitate, with ease, a member of the elite. Like Delphia and Bodenham, Doll appropriates and deploys elements from a variety of discourses; she incorporates into her "act" pieces of identities that are supposedly unable to be performed (witchcraft inheres in the physical body, the inspiration of the radical prophetess is an expression of divine presence, and the fairy queen is a non-human supernatural being). "A kind of modern happiness to have / Doll Common for a great lady" (4.1.123–4), Face says, suggesting that the milieu of burgeoning capitalism in London allows for this sort of self-fashioning, this modern happiness of becoming what had seemed inaccessible. That *The Alchemist* ends unhappily for Subtle and Doll does not mean that we cannot read them as successful workers of magic. In their illicit jugglery, Doll, Face, and Subtle labor extensively for their pay. The "indenture tripartite" (5.4.315) as Face calls it later in the play, demystifies the notion that rogues were idle, sturdy beggars. In *The Alchemist*, the labor of magical performance is commodified, sold by the venture

---

"'Quacking Delilahs': Female Mountebanks in Early Modern England and Italy," in *Women Players in England, 1500–1660: Beyond the All–Male Stage*, (eds.) Pamela Allen Brown and Peter Parolin (Aldershot: Ashgate, 2008), 89–107.

[45] See Craig Dionne, "Fashioning Outlaws: The Early Modern Rogue and Urban Culture," in *Rogues and Early Modern English Culture*, 33–61.

[46] Rid, *The Art of Jugling or Legerdemaine* (London, 1612), B4.

[47] Jonson, *The Alchemist*, in *English Renaissance Drama*, (ed.) David Bevington (New York: Norton, 2002), 1.1.156. Cited hereafter in text.

tripartite, and purchased by eager buyers. While Jonson satirizes these characters, he also explicitly and emphatically portrays magic as theatrical performance, and theatrical performance as work.

Readers who see Doll, Face, and Subtle as fraudulent workers of magic miss out on seeing the play within what was obviously a popular element of Renaissance magical discourse, and, what is more, on seeing Doll specifically as a female worker of magic. Our understanding of women practitioners of magic as workers depends on our reading such characters as Doll, Delphia, and Anne Bodenham against the dominant discourse, which demonized them as witches, idle women, and so forth. In order to understand Doll as a working woman, we must read beyond the signifiers that identify her as an idle whore, or as a rogue's "doxy," in contemporary thieves' cant. Fletcher and Massinger make the project of understanding Delphia as a woman worker of magic somewhat easier for us, and so, in a way, does Jonson. A performance of *The Alchemist* would clearly show the main characters constantly on the move, preparing for their next client, negotiating identities, slipping into one and then another, spouting terms from the discourse of witchcraft, from erudite alchemical science, from radical religion, and so on. This obviously required practice; as performers of jugglery, Doll, Face, and Subtle were professionals.

Such professionalism displayed by these workers of magic allows us to see how the trend of demonizing practices specific to women, including traditional magical practices and women's domestic labor was, occasionally, problematized. It is not easy to identify early modern women practitioners of magic as workers, whether in dramatic representations, literary texts, or the accounts found in pamphlets and treatises; but if one concern of feminist literary scholars and historians is to continue to seek out cultural spaces where subject positions for women were articulated, rather than elided—even if that articulation is shadowy and even if those spaces are liminal—then this is certainly an area of study worth pursuing. Cunning women and women jugglers were working subjects. Paradoxically, this is sometimes revealed in the very treatments that would ostensibly efface the possibility of seeing women workers of magic as such. The texts I have examined here reveal a range of perspectives: Delphia's status as worker and as powerful magician is emphasized by Fletcher and Massinger throughout *The Prophetess*. Jonson's skeptical and satirical comedy portrays its jugglers, including a woman worker of magic, as the hardest workers of all the play's dramatis personae. *Doctor Lamb Revived* portrays a cunning woman as a witch, but also figures her as a working woman, describing her apprenticeship in her trade, her magical practices, the business end of her trade, and even her success within the community. We find women to be working subjects, in this case women workers of magic, in rather unexpected places when we look for them.

Chapter 11
Raising Mephistopheles:
Performative Representation and
Alienated Labor in *The Tempest*

David Hawkes

Labor omnia vincit

I

Virgil's famous aphorism contains a much-debated ambiguity. It means that human labor has conquered the world, re-shaping nature according to the patterns of culture and bending man's objective environment to his subjective will. Labor, in the general sense of human subjective interaction with the external environment, has effected a re-creation, and the world constructed through human labor has occluded the world of nature in itself. Yet the phrase can also mean that labor conquers man's subjective experience, changing the nature of his activity, making it appear external and hostile to himself, and thrusting him into the condition of alienation.[1] The conflict is between labor as human activity in general and labor as specifically burdensome, unpleasant activity. The disturbing suggestion borne by this ambiguity is that these two meanings of labor are inseparable, that the price we pay for the right to inhabit a world of our own creation is the fetishistic, antagonistic autonomy of our own activity. A great deal of recent scholarship has called attention to the many Virgilian echoes in *The Tempest*, and I would suggest that these extend to the play's treatment of alienated labor.[2] The people of early modern England recognized usury, the independent growth of financial signs, as

---

[1]   See Anthony Low, *The Georgic Revolution* (Princeton University Press, 1985) and Susan Scheinberg Kristol, *Labor and Fortuna in Virgil's Aeneid* (New York: Garland Publishing, 1990). In "Sacerdotal Vestiges in *The Tempest*," Robert L. Reid makes an instructive connection between Ariel's song, "Where the bee sucks there suck I" (5.1.88), and Virgil's description of bees as "happy workers" (*Comparative Drama* 41.4 (2007): 513n60).

[2]   See Donna B. Hamilton, *Virgil and The Tempest: The Politics of Imitation* (Columbus: Ohio State University Press, 1990); Margaret Tudeau-Clayton, *Jonson, Shakespeare, and Early Modern Virgil* (Cambridge: Cambridge University Press, 1998); Barbara J. Bono, *Literary Transvaluation: From Vergilian Epic to Shakespearean Tragicomedy* (Berkeley: University of California Press, 1984), 220–24 and David Scott Wilson–Okamura, "Virgilian Models of Colonization in Shakespeare's *The Tempest*," *ELH* 70.3 (2003): 709–37.

the alienated form of human activity. Usurers were constantly said to evade the curse God laid on Adam by living on "the sweat of other men's brows" rather than their own. Henry Smith's *The Examination of Usury* (1591) comments that:

> When God set *Adam* his worke, he sayd, *In the sweate of thy browes shalt thou live*: not in the sweate of his browes, but in the sweate of thy browes; but the Usurer liveth in the sweat of his browes, & her browes: that is, by the paines and cares, and labours of another …

And yet the same assumption occurs in the period's most highly specialist texts on trade, such as Gerard Malynes's *The Maintenance of Free Trade* (1622). Malynes condemns the "biting Usury" practiced by pawnbrokers "which feedeth upon the sweat & blood of the meere merchanicall poore" (40). John Milton, who followed his father into the family business of usury, imagines a future critic reproaching him for idleness despite the fact that "ease and leasure was given thee for thy retired thoughts out of the sweat of other men."[3] The idea that money is stored-up labor-power, that it is a performative sign, a symbol that can do things, is a basic assumption of the early political economy that developed in the mid-seventeenth century. Thomas Hobbes observed that "[a] man's Labour also, is a commodity exchangeable for benefit, as well as any other thing."[4] Exchange-value represents labor-power in symbolic form so that "[t]he Value, or Worth of a man is, as of all other things, the Price; that is to say, so much as would be given for the use of his Power" (151). A human being's "power" can be used by somebody else if it is represented in the form of money. Money is transferable power, congealed human activity, the force of which can be stored and released because it has been encapsulated in symbolic form. It was this kind of power that magicians aspired to exercise, for magic also works by the manipulation of efficacious signs.

This essay attempts to show how Shakespeare's *The Tempest* treats the issue of labor and its relationship to magical and financial representation. Shakespeare was especially well-placed to make such an analysis, being both the son of a professional usurer (his father was prosecuted for criminal usury) and himself a practitioner of money-lending. He was in a peculiarly advantageous position to survey the rise of autonomous financial representation, and to consider its implications for representation in general. Indeed, the theaters of early modern London provided a particularly apt venue for exploring the notion of alienated labor. The actions performed on stage were already alienated, in the sense that they did not belong to the person who performed them, but to the character he played. The plays were themselves commodities, purchased for the price of admission, and they also engaged in detailed analyses of commodification's religious and political effects. As John Parker puts it: "What people saw on stage was the money they had paid, incarnate now in costume, stage-properties, high rhetoric, even the actors'

---

[3]   Milton, *The Reason of Church-government*, in *Complete Prose Works*, (ed.) Don M. Wolfe (Yale University Press, 1953), 1:804.

[4]   Hobbes, *Leviathan*, (ed.) C.B. MacPherson (London: Penguin Books, 1985), 295. Subsequent references will be to this edition.

bodies, which the price of admission fed."[5] Plays frequently raised the questions of how an action can be separated from its actor, and of how labor-power can remain powerful after having been separated from its performance.[6] My argument here is that the early modern analysis of alienated labor took place, in large part, through the medium of the contemporary debate about witchcraft and magic. Magic and money both depend on the power of performative symbols, and this led the people of early modern England to treat them as aspects of a single, over-arching process: the growth in the autonomous power of representation.

The Tempest examines the dramatic change in the ethical status of magic that was already underway as Shakespeare wrote, although it would not finally achieve unchallenged orthodoxy until the end of the seventeenth century. People did not cease to believe in magic because magic had disappeared. On the contrary, it was the ubiquity of magic that brought about the shift in its moral evaluation, so that it ceased to be regarded as evil. Just as alchemy disappeared because its aim of creating financial value out of nothing was finally realized when money was allowed to breed, so magic ceased to be a crime because the performative power of symbols became a necessary and universal assumption in economic activity.[7] When everyone is a magician, magic can no longer be regarded as Satanic. In Thomas Dekker's *The Witch of Edmonton*, Elizabeth Sawyer uses this argument to defend herself against charges of witchcraft. "A witch!" she exclaims, "who is not?"

> These by enchantments can whole lordships change
> To trunks of rich attire, turn ploughs and teams
> To Flanders mares and coaches, and huge trains
> Of servitors to a French butterfly.
> Have you not city-witches who can turn
> Their husband's wares, whole standing shops of wares,
> To sumptuous tables, gardens of stolen sin;
> In one year wasting what scarce twenty win?
> Are not these witches?[8]

---

5   Parker, "What a Piece of Work is Man: Shakespearean Drama as Marxian Fetish," *Journal of Medieval and Early Modern Studies* 34.3 (2004): 646. See also David Hawkes, "Idolatry and Commodity Fetishism in the Antitheatrical Controversy," *SEL* 39.2 (1999): 255–73; Richard Halpern, "Marlowe's Theater of Night: *Doctor Faustus* and Capital," *ELH* 71.2 (2004): 455–95; and Graham Hammill, "Faustus's Fortunes: Commodification, Exchange and the Form of Literary Subjectivity," *ELH* 63.2 (1996): 309–36.

6   Richard Halpern demonstrates how the early modern theater negotiated the relationship between productive and unproductive labor in "Eclipse of Action: *Hamlet* and the Political Economy of Playing," *Shakespeare Quarterly* 59.4 (2008): 450–82.

7   On the concept of "performative" representation, see especially J.L. Austin, *How To Do Things With Words* (Oxford: Clarendon, 1962) and Judith Butler's expansion of Austin's ideas in *Excitable Speech: A Politics of the Performative* (New York: Routledge, 1997).

8   Dekker, John Ford, and William Rowley, *The Witch of Edmonton*, (ed.) Arthur Kinney (London: Bloomsbury Press, 2009). On performative speech and representations of early modern witchcraft see Kirilka Stavreva, "Fighting Words: Witch-Speak in Late Elizabeth Docu-fiction," *Journal of Medieval and Early Modern Studies* 30.2 (2000): 309–38.

Like magic, the immaterial operations of the market transform substantial objects and aristocratic titles into frivolous commodities, turning substantial use-values into symbolic exchange-values. Everyone in a market society believes in the objective power of autonomous representation. Everybody accepts that money, a supernatural symbol containing congealed labor-power, is efficacious. Everybody therefore practices what had previously been conceived as witchcraft on a daily basis. Shakespeare's society established capitalism's most basic preconditions: the legalization of usury and the predominance of wage labor. This process raised intransigent ideological difficulties, and the commercial theaters of early modern London provided an ideal medium through which they could be explored.

Sixteenth-century England identified certain types of labor as alienated on the basis of natural teleology. Labor was hostile, irksome and alien only when it was directed towards an improper end. When directed towards its proper end, labor involved the imposition of rational direction on the chaotic flux of fortune. It thus served as the means of manufacturing virtue, as the Stoics had argued, using Hercules as the ultimate exemplar of unalienated labor.[9] Since the pursuit of virtue was the *telos* of a human being, this kind of labor could be considered an end in itself. Aristotle condemns labor performed for the purpose of making money as "chrematistic," while labor that is carried out for its own sake is "autotelic." The former is degraded and servile, while the latter is exalted and free:

> ... if some activities are necessary and desirable for the sake of something else, while others are so in themselves, evidently happiness must be placed among those desirable in themselves, not among those desirable for the sake of something else; for happiness does not lack anything, but is self-sufficient. Now those activities are desirable in themselves from which nothing is sought beyond the activity.[10]

In the Aristotelian tradition, unalienated labor was directed to the fulfillment of one's own potential, identified with the rational "activity of the soul in accordance with virtue." In Christian Europe, the pursuit of virtue became a means to the ultimate end of salvation. The specific content of the labor was irrelevant to its ethical status; labor was defined by its end. For George Herbert, this was "the elixir" that "makes drudgery divine." Herbert appeals to God to force him to act like a rational creature: "[n]ot rudely, as a beast/ To run into action."[11] Unlike the acts of an animal, human labor can mean something, it can take on a higher significance.

---

[9]   See Scott Goins, 'Two Aspects of Virgil's Use of Labor in the *Aeneid*," *The Classical Journal* 88.4 (1993): 375–84.

[10]   Aristotle, *Nicomachean Ethics*, in *Works*, vol. 9, trans. W.D. Ross (Oxford: Clarendon, 1908), 1176b 1–5.

[11]   Herbert, "The Elixir," in *The Complete English Poems*, (ed.) John Tobin (London: Penguin Books, 1991).

Yet human action can also be degraded below the level of bestial behavior, when it is directed towards an alien purpose. When labor was not performed as a means towards the realization of one's proper *telos*, it became humiliating and irksome, regardless of the activities it involved. Aristotle, and also the people of Renaissance Europe, identified such alienated activity with slavery. In Aristotle, a slave is a person whose actions serve the purposes of somebody else, a person whose own activity is alien to him, because it belongs to another. By serving the purposes of another a slave ceases to belong to himself, he becomes an attribute, a "property," of the other person. Adherents of the Aristotelian tradition believed that many, perhaps most people, are naturally inclined towards slavery.[12] It is easy to dismiss the concept of natural slavery as a piece of self-interested fiction. Obviously the ruling class in a slave-owning society will need to believe that slaves are naturally suited to their condition. Yet Aristotle was well aware that legally enslaved people are not necessarily natural slaves, and that many natural slaves are not legally enslaved. The Aristotelian argument describes the intrinsic nature of slavery, not the empirical characteristics of slaves.

We might think that slavery was rare in early modern England, but in fact it was well on the way to becoming universal. Anyone who works for a salary enters into a servile condition. Any wage worker sells his life piecemeal, serving the purposes of his employer for a given amount of time. Wage labor is not necessarily unpleasant, and it can even be highly lucrative, but it is nevertheless piecemeal slavery because it involves the alienation of activity. Peasants can produce the means of their own subsistence and, however lowly their lifestyle, they therefore retain a degree of independence. A peasant is basically a free person. Over the course of the sixteenth and seventeenth centuries, however, most English peasants were driven off their ancestral lands by fraud or force. They found their land "enclosed" within the estates of larger landowners, and lacked the legal documents or skills to challenge this process, which would be repeated throughout the world in the eighteenth and nineteenth centuries. Many newly wealthy landowners looked to invest their surplus fortunes as capital. Most dispossessed peasants became proletarians: people who lived by exchanging their labor-power for money. These processes, known to economic historians as the "primitive accumulation of capital" and the "proletarianization of the peasantry," gathered pace rapidly over the sixteenth and seventeenth centuries, and the literature of the period often reflects on their social and psychological implications.[13]

---

[12]   See Aristotle, *Politics* (ed.) Trevor Saunders, trans. T.A. Sinclair (London: Penguin, 1981), book one, chapters 4–5.

[13]   For a detailed history of enclosures in England see J.A. Yelling, *Common Field and Enclosures in England, 1450–1850* (Hamdon, CT: Archon Books, 1977). Marx discusses "primitive accumulation" in *Capital: A Critique of Political Economy*, vol. 1, trans. Ben Fowkes (London: Penguin Books, 1992), part 7, chapter 26. For an illuminating analysis of the influence of England's history of enclosures on the thought of Marx, see William Lazonick, "Marx and Enclosures in England," *Review of Radical Political Economics* 6 (1974): 1–59.

The establishment of a market in labor involves the reduction of labor to a commodity, but it also involves the elevation of the universal commodity to the status of labor: it puts money to work. Labor is translated into financial form so that it can be alienated, separated from the person who performs it, and allowed to reproduce in an apparently independent fashion. In early modern England this independent reproduction of alienated labor was known as "usury," and at the time of *The Tempest*'s composition it still carried a heavy moral stigma. Shakespeare's oeuvre shows a consistent engagement with the issue of usury, not only in his overt, detailed treatments of the subject in *The Merchant of Venice, Timon of Athens* and the Sonnets, but also covertly, in his analysis of matters like magic, which the modern mind does not immediately recognize as having economic implications. *The Tempest* presents the new autonomy of representation, and the concomitant growth of wage labor, as the universalization of magic: a process which abolishes the traditional conception of magic as a particular, discrete, ethically culpable activity practiced only by specialists. When Prospero doffs his cape and burns his books, he indicates that the age of specialized professional magicians is over, for we are all magicians now.

II

The autonomous reproduction of financial value is one prerequisite of a capitalist market economy. The other is the commodification of labor. These conditions are mutually dependent mirror-images: usury involves the subjectification of the object, as financial value comes alive, while wage labor involves the objectification of the subject, as human activity is translated into money. The legalization of usury and the creation of a proletariat are parts of the same process, whereby labor takes on an alien form in which it is allowed to reproduce. Both aspects of this process were subjected to sharp ethical criticism in early modern Europe, and much of that criticism came from the stage. The moralistic objections to usury are well known, as are the plays that rehearse them. The ethical critique of wage labor is less familiar because, in the theater at least, it was usually couched in a form that the modern mind does not recognize as economic.

In the early sixteenth century, Europeans grew convinced that magical power was spreading throughout the world. People became aware of an invisible, supernatural, and yet strongly efficacious force moving among them, and they spent a great deal of effort debating that force's nature and identity. This was the era of the witch-craze. The vital question at issue in the witch trials is posed by Marlowe's Doctor Faustus to Mephistopheles: "Did not my conjuring speeches raise thee?"[14] Faustus asks whether magic is efficacious: can the signs and rituals employed by magicians achieve practical, objective effects in the real world? The devil's reply, "That was the cause, but yet *per accidens*" (1.1.46), gives some idea

---

[14] Christopher Marlowe, *Doctor Faustus and Other Plays*, (eds.) David Bevington and Eric Rasmussen (Oxford University Press, 1995), 1.3.45.

of the issue's complexity. In scholastic thought, *per accidens* was the opposite of *per se*. Something that happened *per accidens* was due to a cause that was extrinsic, external, alien, to the object effected. In Aquinas, sensation *per se* is empirical, while sensation *per accidens* is conceptual. *Per se*, we experience a yellow, feathery, twittering creature; *per accidens* we experience a bird. The *per se* is inherent in the object, while the *per accidens* is imposed upon it.[15] The autonomous reproduction of financial value is the liberation of the *per accidens* from the *per se*. Use-value is inherent in an object, but exchange-value is imposed on the object, and in usury exchange-value takes on a life of its own. Mephistopheles, and Satanic power in general, inhabits this realm of autonomous images. His currency is the performative sign, and it is he who truly performs the apparent effects of Faustus's magic. The question of whether the devil or the magician caused the magical effects lay at the heart of legal and dramatic witchcraft discourse. Legally, if Satan was responsible for the effects of a witch's magic, it could be argued that the witch was innocent, and so both the witch-trials themselves and the plays that present them in dramatic form considered the question of how magic works. How can magical signs possess efficacious power or "virtue"? Is that power necessarily evil? Could there be a species of performative sign that was ethically neutral? Could money be such a sign?[16]

Hobbes and his successors use terminology that is recognizable to modern economists but, lacking our notion of the economy as a separate field of activity, sixteenth-century accounts of alienated labor recognize its effects in every sphere of experience. As a result, they tend to be more overtly moralistic. As the English economy monetarized over the sixteenth century, and as inflations and debasements of the coinage distinguished financial value from its material incarnation in *specie*, it became obvious that financial reproduction was not literal or material. As one pamphlet pointed out: "the mighty sommes imployed by the waye of Usurye ... are thought to be soe hudge, that if all the money of England were layd on one heape and every Usurer should clayme his parte there would not be coyne sufficient to pay them."[17] If money bred, it did so only in the mind. Our modern world is so accustomed to this idea that money has lost the magical aura it retained

---

[15] For accounts of Aquinas on the *per se* and the *per accidens*, see Jan Aertsen, *Nature and Creature: Thomas Aquinas's Way of Thought* (New York: E.J. Brill, 1988), 58–67 and Robert Pasnau, *Thomas Aquinas on Human Nature: A Philosophical Study of Summa Theologiae 1a 75–89* (Cambridge University Press, 2002), 270–78.

[16] Much recent anthropological work has focused on the association between capitalism and magic in the postcolonial world. The basic premise of such research is summarized by Jean and John Comaroff: "Occult economies, then, are a response to a world gone awry, yet again: a world in which the only way to create real wealth seems to lie in forms of power/knowledge that transgress the conventional, the rational, the moral—thus to multiply available techniques of producing value, fair or foul." "Millenial Capitalism: First Thoughts on a Second Coming," *Public Culture* 12.2 (2000): 316.

[17] Cited in Lloyd Kermode, introduction to *Three Renaissance Usury Plays* (Manchester University Press, 2008), 2.

in the early modern period, having been relegated to the prosaic, dismal science of economics. However, the concept of the economy as a distinct area of human activity did not emerge until the Restoration, and it emerged precisely as a means of separating financial representation from the ethical strictures that remained in place against magic.

The witch-hunters of the sixteenth and seventeenth centuries were generally not concerned with the deeds perpetrated by the witch, but with the means by which she had effected them. Because images were not naturally efficacious, any more than money is naturally fertile, any attempt to use images for objective effects was a violation of nature and thus Satanic. William Perkins, one of the most respected authorities on witchcraft in early modern England, declared that:

> Of witches there be two sorts: The bad Witch, and the good witch: for so they are commonly called … howsoever both of these be evil, yet of the two, the more horrible & detestable Monster is the good witch … the healing and harmlesse witch must die … though he kill not, onely for covenant made with Satan. For this must always be remembered, as a conclusion, that by Witches we understand not those onely, which kill and torment: but all Diviners, Charmers, Jugglers, all Wizzards, commonly called wise men and women.[18]

The witch's crime was not any material harm, or *maleficia*, she might have done through her magic. Magic was a crime even if its effects were benign. The witch's crime was to believe in the efficacious power of performative representation. That is also the crime that legalized usury forces upon humanity. In order for capitalism to function, belief in performative representation must be discredited: we must cease to "believe in magic." The phrase itself is odd, for everyone believes that magic exists, in the sense that there are people who practice it. Our knowledge of the psychosomatic also allows the modern mind to accept that, under certain circumstances, magic can "work." What the people of the modern world absolutely cannot believe, however, is that magic works through the intervention of Satan. That is the major difference between the early modern mind and our own. We do not conceive of the autonomous power of representation as a metaphysically evil phenomenon, and they did.

The process by which they ceased to believe this was remarkably swift for such a seismic shift in consciousness; it took place over the course of the seventeenth century. This rapidity would not have been possible had not the minds of English people been prepared for it by a course of ideological indoctrination, and the theater was an important part of that curriculum. The theater was often described as a "school of abuse," a place where people learned erroneous ways of thinking and feeling. Above all, the theater trained people to disregard the distinction between sign and reality: in order to enjoy a play, the audience must assume that the actor actually is the character he represents. Theater depends on, and therefore

---

    [18]   Perkins, *Discourse of the Damned Art of Witchcraft*, in *English Witchcraft 1560–1736*, vol. 1, (ed.) James Sharpe (London: Pickering and Chatto, 2003), 289–90.

also inculcates, our ability to take signs for reality, to occlude essence beneath appearance: in short, to commodify experience.

At the beginning of our period the usurious, liturgical and magical modes of autonomous representation were not fully distinguished from each other. The drama of the early sixteenth century often explicitly connects them, pointing out that they are all forms of alienated labor. In John Bale's *Comedy Concernynge Thre Lawes* (1538) we hear that the character named Idololatria can perform labor by means of both pagan and Papist magic. She

> can by saying her Ave Marye
> And by other charmes of sorcerye,
> Ease men of tot hake [tooth ache] by and bye,
> Yea, and fatche the devyll from hell.
> She can mylke the cowe and hunte the foxe,
> And helpe men of the ague and poxe,
> So they brynge moneye to the boxe.[19]

Idolatry, Satanic magic, and commodification are parts of a single wider enterprise. Idololatria announces her capacity to perform all sorts of labor by magic. She embodies the objective force of congealed subjective labor-power. She can also make objects come alive: she represents the autonomous, subjective power of commodities. Her speech illustrates the interdependence of the two aspects of labor's alienation: the objectification of the subject, and the subjectification of the object:

> I can make stoles to daunce,
> And earthen pottes to praunce,
> That non shall them enhaunce,
> And do but cast my glove.
> I have charmes for the plowgh,
> And also for the cowgh;
> She shall geve mylke ynowgh,
> So longe as I am pleased.
> Apace the mylle shall go,
> So shall the credle do,
> And the musterde querne also ...

Idololatria claims to perform her magic alone, but in fact she does so by the aid of Satan. This anticipates the vital question in the witch trials of the subsequent century: were the accused acting alone, in which case their magic could not work and they would be innocent, or had they made a pact with the devil, which permitted him to carry out the magical effects? This question of agency was often stated in terms of hierarchy: was the magician the master or the slave of Satan? The Clown in *The Fair Maid of the Inn* expresses the popular opinion on the subject: "a Conjurer is

---

[19]   Bale, *Comedy Concernynge Thre Lawes* (London: Tudor Facsimile Series, 1908).

the Devills Master, and commands him; whereas a witch is the Devills Prentice and obeys him" (1.1.5–6).[20] Learned sorcerers claimed to be able to control the dark powers, but a concerted propaganda campaign, in which the story of Faustus figured prominently, was designed to refute such proud assertions.[21] Anyone who practiced magic, it was claimed, was a slave of the devil, although Satan might encourage the magician to form the opposite impression. That is exactly what happens to Marlowe's Faustus. At first he believes that "the spirits are enforced to rise" (1.1.13) by his magic. He assumes that his magical signs are efficacious in themselves, that they contain magical power: "I see there's virtue in my heavenly words" (1.1.28). And of course Mephistopheles is happy to encourage him in this delusion: "I will be thy slave, and wait on thee" (2.1.46). In a pattern that would be repeated in hundreds of witch plays and pamphlets, Faustus is gradually brought to the dreadful realization that he has been tricked. He serves the ends of the devil, not the other way around. He is the slave, and Satan the master.

III

In her contribution to this volume, Meredith Molly Hand correctly remarks that "early modern representations of magic as work are rare," and that magical efficacy is usually attributed either to the devil or to fraud in sixteenth- and seventeenth-century literature. Shakespeare's *The Tempest* is a notable exception to this rule, however, as the question of alienated labor drives its entire plot. The play's opening scene depicts the traditional conception of labor. When the ship's microcosmic society is under the power of natural forces in the shape of the storm, possession of labor-power reverts to those who perform it, as is natural. The humble boatswain dismisses the aristocrats with the injunction "you mar our labour" (1.1.12). He mockingly asks whether they are capable of affecting the objective world by mere words, and sarcastically suggests that his physical, natural labor might be displaced by the performative power of lordly command: "You are a counselor," he tells Gonzalo, "if you can command these elements to silence, and work the peace of the present, we will not hand a rope more" (l. 18). When Sebastian arrogantly tries to interfere the Boatswain dismisses him: "Work you, then" (l. 52).

On the ship, the use-value of labor has displaced the symbolic power of words. We soon learn, however, that the apparently natural storm has been artificially manufactured by Prospero's magically efficacious spells, which give him control of Ariel's supernatural labor-power. Prospero's "art" consists in his ability to command the labor-power of others: the magical tricks of Ariel, the physical work of Caliban and the temporary enslavement of Ferdinand. Labor and magic, the

---

[20]   Fredson Bowers (ed.), *The Dramatic Works in the Beaumont and Fletcher Canon*, vol. 10 (Cambridge University Press, 1996).

[21]   See David Hawkes, *The Faust Myth: Religion and the Rise of Representation* (New York: Palgrave, 2007).

natural and the supernatural, blend seamlessly throughout the play, as when Ariel lays the crew asleep "with a charm join'd to their suffer'd labour" (1.2.231).

In an incisive recent analysis, James Kearney demonstrates that *The Tempest* represents magic as alienated labor through the fetish of Prospero's book, which "is a mystified reification of the island's social relations, a reification in which the alienated labor of Caliban, Ariel, and the spirits appears before them as the 'magical' property of this material object."[22] Yet the play also distinguishes between the labor of Ariel and Caliban, using these figures of Ariel and Caliban to forge a distinction between wage labor and slavery. Shakespeare wants to solve the ideological dilemma posed by the fact that, according to the traditional Aristotelian standard, wage labor *was* slavery. This opinion could not be allowed to stand in a society where wage laborers were fast becoming the most numerous class. We first encounter both Ariel and Caliban in the act of bemoaning Prospero's extraction of surplus-value from their labor-power. "There's wood enough within" (1.2.460) are Caliban's opening words, while Ariel complains "Is there more toil?" (1.2.242) on his first appearance. The difference between the labor of Ariel and that of Caliban serves to assimilate alienated labor into the traditional moral economy. While the labor of both characters is alienated, they are associated with different aspects of alienated labor. Caliban embodies labor as slavery, while Ariel bears the intangible efficacy of autonomous exchange-value.

In Act 1, scene 2, Prospero's constant demands that Miranda pay attention to his lengthy and detailed account of how he lost his Dukedom—"I pray thee, mark me" (l. 68), "Dost thou attend me?" (l. 78), "'Thou attendst not?'" (l. 87), "Dost thou hear?" (l. 105)—are also directed towards the audience. They force our attention onto what we might otherwise have missed: his developing understanding of value. He describes his life in Milan, locked away in his library, "neglecting worldly ends, all dedicated/ To closeness and the bettering of my mind/ With that which, but by being so retired,/ O'er-prized all popular rate" (ll. 89–92). These lines are richly ambiguous. They suggest that, simply because they were secret, Prospero's studies surpassed the popular mode of evaluation. Yet they can also be read as meaning that, had his studies *not* been secret, they would have surpassed the popular mode of evaluation; or that, due to the fact that they were secret, the true value of Prospero's studies was not appreciated by the people; or that, if it had not been "retired," Prospero's knowledge would have been more valuable, more powerful, than the esteem of the people.

These readings can stand together without contradiction only if we accept that Shakespeare is describing two different kinds of value. The magical kind of value with which Prospero is bettering his mind is distinct from, and opposed to, the "popular rate" because it is "retired," hidden from popular view, not understood by the people. Had it not been so hidden, had the people been aware of that with which Prospero was bettering his mind, their mode of evaluation would have been

---

[22] James Kearney, "The Book and the Fetish: the Materiality of Prospero's Text," *Journal of Medieval and Early Modern Studies* 32.3 (2002): 433–68.

surpassed by his, because the esoteric nature of his studies made those studies inherently superior to everyday evaluation. Popular knowledge of his magic would translate its theoretical superiority into practice. Magic offers a new, alternative source of value, one which has yet to be appreciated by the people, but which possesses infinite potential once it attains popular esteem. This is the lesson that Prospero has learned as a result of Antonio's usurpation, and *The Tempest* shows him regaining his lost power through the practical application of this lesson. Whereas in Milan his devotion to magic had isolated him and deprived him of power, he has now learned to use magic to practical, instrumental ends: as a means to power rather than an escape from it.

It was the disjunction between the "popular rate" and Prospero's magical studies that allowed Antonio to usurp his political power. Like King Lear, Prospero made the mistake of transferring actual power to a deputy, under the illusion that he could retain what Lear calls "the name, and all th'addition" (1.1.136) of a ruler. He describes Antonio as "being thus lorded,/ Not only with what my revenue yielded,/ But what my power might else exact" (1.2.97–9). There is another significant ambiguity here. Antonio is made into a ruler by the financial power of Prospero's ordinary "revenue," combined with additional money that he exacts by fully exploiting the "power" of the Dukedom. Yet the lines also distinguish between financial revenue and a different kind of power, which together make Antonio lord. If we read "else" as meaning "otherwise," Prospero is saying that Antonio was "lorded" by the combination of revenue and Prospero's failure to "exact" what his power was capable of exacting. If Prospero had used the kind of power he has come to possess through study, if he had applied his magical knowledge to practical effect, then Antonio could not have usurped his position. Having grasped this fact during his exile, Prospero now puts his magic into practice, to devastating effect. *The Tempest* foretells the conquest of the world by magic by presenting it in microcosmic form.

Prospero describes Antonio's usurpation as the triumph of appearance over essence. Because he looks and behaves like a ruler, "executing the outward face of royalty" (1.2.104), Antonio comes to "believe/ He was indeed the duke" (ll. 102–3). Shakespeare's image alludes to the financial value hidden within a coin, which displays the face of the king. Antonio brings this subterranean value to the surface, becoming a Duke in reality because his "outward face" is that of a Duke, just as the purely symbolic, financial value represented by a coin achieves an objective, independent efficacy when it is treated as capital. He refuses to acknowledge the Aristotelian distinction between accident and substance. Like an actor in naturalistic drama, Antonio cannot tolerate any mediation between himself and the role he plays: "To have no screen between this part he play'd/ And him he play'd it for, he needs will be/ Absolute Milan" (ll. 107–9). The person "for" whom Antonio played his part was simultaneously himself, the private man temporarily assuming the role of Duke, and Prospero, at whose instigation he has adopted the role, and whose person he represents while playing it. By making himself "Absolute Milan," Antonio abolishes the distinction, tearing down the "screen" between Prospero and himself, and so transforming himself into what Prospero is: the Duke of Milan.

In his island exile, Prospero learns how to beat Antonio at his own game. His magic can turn appearance into reality, producing hallucinations that exercise objective power in the material world. His magic gives him control of Caliban's physical, useful labor: "he does make our fire,/ Fetch in our wood and serves in offices/ That profit us" (1.2.314–16). As Caliban admits, Propsero's "art is of such power,/ It would control my dam's god, Setebos,/ And make a vassal of him" (ll. 375–7). Prospero and Miranda impose the power of representation upon Caliban's material efficacy, teaching him language in order to transform his physical activity into symbolic form. As Miranda tells him: "I endow'd thy purposes/ With words that made them known" (ll. 360–61). Caliban's labor is mediated through representation in order to facilitate its expropriation. His natural impulse towards sexual reproduction is suppressed, and replaced by the artificial breeding of magic and money. To Stephano and Trinculo, Caliban's value does not reside in his useful labor but in his "marketable" (5.1.265) price, and Shakespeare depicts the development of market value into the "popular rate" of evaluation through the clowns' plots to exchange the visual spectacle of the "monster" for cash. Stephano gives demotic expression to the emergent form of value with his consistent response to the new discoveries on the island, "What things are these ... Will money buy 'em?" (ll. 263–4).

In contrast to Caliban's physical, useful labor, Ariel's efficacy is supernatural, and works by the manipulation of appearances. Caliban is constantly called "earth," while Ariel is an "apparition," an immaterial sign with no material essence, yet possessing immense objective power. This distinction is reflected in the different kinds of labor that they embody. Where Caliban is a slave, Ariel is a wage laborer. His servitude is temporary and measured by the clock, as Prospero reveals when he tells Ariel that "[t]he time 'twixt six and now/ Must by us both be spent most preciously" (1.2.240–41). Ariel's initial reluctance indicates that his labor is alien to him, owned by another, and directed towards Prospero's purposes rather than his own. Yet the temporary nature of his bondage transforms his attitude towards it, making his "drudgery divine," as George Herbert put it. Prospero reminds him of the distinction between permanent and temporary servitude, recalling his subjection to the tyranny of the witch Sycorax: "Thou, my slave,/ As thou report'st thyself, wast then her servant" (ll. 270–71). He recalls that Sycorax commanded Ariel to perform earthy, material labor, but that he refused, being "a spirit too delicate" (l. 273). Ariel achieves practical effects by magical, symbolic means rather than through material labor of the kind performed by Caliban. With this distinction in mind, Ariel is happy to be Prospero's "industrious servant," the living embodiment of the power exercised by "my potent master" (4.1.35).

Shakespeare conducts a second, subsidiary debate about the nature of labor through the figure of Ferdinand. The force of sexual attraction was often connected to both slavery and magic: erotic sympathy was an irrational appetite that attempted, frequently with success, to usurp the reign of reason over the will. Prospero redeems sexual appetite from its magical taint by making it the product of labor, "lest too light winning/ Make the prize light" (1.2.451–2). The love of

Miranda must be Ferdinand's wages, it must not be gained by the quasi-magical force of sex. The value of his "prize" arises from his labor:

> There be some sports are painful, and their labour
> Delight in them sets off: some kinds of baseness
> Are nobly undergone and most poor matters
> Point to rich ends. This my mean task
> Would be as heavy to me as odious, but
> The mistress which I serve quickens what's dead
> And makes my labours pleasures. (3.1.1–7)

Ferdinand's labor is not autotelic, in Aristotle's terms; it is not performed as an end in itself. Yet neither is it chrematistic; it is not performed for money. Shakespeare offers a third term, a secularized version of George Herbert's Christian teleology that we mentioned earlier. The romantic remuneration he will receive makes Ferdinand's drudgery divine. The fact that he is Miranda's "slave" transforms the nature of his "wooden slavery" (3.1.54). This is Shakespeare's answer to Gonzalo's utopian proposal to abolish labor altogether, so that "[a]ll things in common nature should produce/ Without sweat or endeavour" (2.1.158). Labor *per se* is good; the point is not to avoid it but to redeem it from its alienated condition. Ferdinand's predicament alludes to the Biblical story of Jacob, who earned the hand of Rebecca by performing seven years' labor. However, while Jacob's labor remained servile and irksome to him, the prospective reward transforms Ferdinand's attitude to his work itself.[23] Shakespeare is redeeming wage labor from its traditional association with servility.

At the same time, he is attempting to redeem magic in general from its association with the Satanic. Like William Perkins, he denies the distinction between "white" and "black" magic, but reverses Perkins's conclusion in suggesting that all magic is "white": harmless, ethically neutral, or even good. By the standards of the witch-hunters, the magic Prospero practices is black (or as he puts it "rough" [5.1.50]), not benign or white. He commands the labor, not only of Ariel, Caliban and Ferdinand, but also of the "elves" and "demi-puppets" (5.1.36) who manufacture "green sour ringlets" (l. 37) and "midnight mushrooms" (l. 39). He practices necromancy: "graves at my command/ Have waked their sleepers, oped, and let 'em forth/ By my so potent art" (ll. 48–50). By the standards of the early seventeenth century, Prospero is unequivocally a sorcerer, and his real-life counterparts would be subjected to criminal prosecution for many years after Shakespeare's death. *The Tempest,* however, directs the attention of its audience towards the future, holding out the prospect of a new, different evaluation of practical magic.

What Prospero calls his "prescience" (1.2.180) involves knowledge of the future. But his magic is also the knowledge of the future in the sense that the performative

---

[23]   A point made in a different context by William Rockett in "Labor and Virtue in *The Tempest*," *Shakespeare Quarterly* 24.1 (1973): 77–84.

efficacy of autonomous representation would, over the century following the composition of *The Tempest*, grow into the world's dominant power. Those with knowledge of that power, those able to manipulate financial representation to their own benefit (as Shakespeare and his father did in real life), will control the world of the future just as Prospero controls events on the little world of his island, and by the same means. The dominance that autonomous representation would soon achieve freed it from moral taint, and the era of European witch-hunts would draw to a close within the lifetime of the youngest among *The Tempest*'s first audiences. As a result of exchange-value's triumph over use-value, people would soon stop noticing the reality lurking beneath representation. They would, in other words, cease to "believe in magic," as Prospero predicts when he discards his cape and books. As generations of political economists have pointed out, however, exchange-value is merely a sign of alienated labor. Financial value is labor-power in symbolic form. This awkward fact is forgotten and ignored as far as possible in the interest of the market economy's smooth functioning, but it will not go away. Shakespeare prophesied as much when, in the midst of Prospero's exultant triumph over his enemies, the magician turns to his slave and admits, with as much foreboding as resignation, "this thing of darkness I/ Acknowledge mine" (5.1.275–6).

Chapter 12
Custom, Debt, and the Valuation of Service Within and Without Early Modern England

Amanda Bailey

> Let there be freedoms from custom till the plantation be of strength: and not only freedom from custom, but freedom to carry their commodities where they make their best of them.
>
> —Francis Bacon, "Of Plantations," 1621.[1]

The Custom of the Colony

Although colonial servitude has long been regarded as an extension rather than an aberration of English apprenticeship, recent scholarship has suggested that New World labor practices marked a significant break with Old World ones.[2] According to Edmund Morgan, "servitude in Virginia's tobacco fields approached closer to slavery than anything known at the time in England."[3] Planters, as Hilary McD. Beckles stresses, as a matter of course "freely bought, sold, gambled away, mortgaged, taxed as property, and alienated in wills their indentured servants."[4]

---

[1]   Francis Bacon, "Of Plantations," in *The Genesis of the United States*, 2 vols., (ed.) Alexander Brown (New York: Russell & Russell, 1964), 2:801.

[2]   Revisionist scholarship on the relation between indentured service and slavery includes, Leonie Archer (ed.), *Slavery and Other Forms of Unfree Labour* (New York: Routledge, 1988); James Walvin, *Questioning Slavery* (New York: Routledge, 1996); Robin Blackburn, *The Making of New World Slavery: From the Baroque to the Modern, 1492– 1800* (London: Verso, 1998); Tommy L. Lott (ed.), *Subjugation and Bondage: Critical Essays on Slavery and Social Philosophy* (Boulder, CO: Rowman and Littlefield, 1998); Ira Berlin, *Many Thousands Gone: The First Two Centuries of Slavery in North America* (Cambridge, MA: Harvard University Press, 1998); David Turley, *Slavery* (Oxford: Blackwell, 2000); Kevin Bales, *Understanding Global Slavery: A Reader* (Berkeley: University of California Press, 2005); and Susan Dwyer Amussen, *Caribbean Exchanges: Slavery and the Transformation of English Society, 1640–1700* (Chapel Hill: University of North Carolina Press, 2007).

[3]   Morgan, *American Slavery, American Freedom: The Ordeal of Colonial Virginia* (New York: W.W. Norton & Co., 1975), 296.

[4]   Beckles, "The Concept of 'White Slavery' in the English Caribbean during the Early Seventeenth Century," in *Early Modern Conceptions of Property*, (eds.) John Brewer and Susan Staves (New York: Routledge, 1996), 575.

Indentured servants could be used as stakes in card games and seized as property by colonial magistrates to satisfy their masters' unpaid debts.[5] Agents of the Virginia Company were among the worst offenders of good labor practices, as demonstrated by reports sent back to England. In a June 8, 1617 letter to Edwin Sandys, John Rolfe describes Virginia's servants as men who "cheerfully labour … their harts and hands not ceasing from worke, though many have scarce rags to cov[e]r their naked bodyes."[6] One servant bound to the treasurer of the colony, George Sandys, writes of his master that: "he maketh us serve him whether wee will or noe and how to helpe yt we doe not knowe for hee beareth all the sway."[7] In a letter to his brother, Thomas Best writes on April 12, 1623, "I am in great danger of Starvinge. My Master Atkins hath sold me for a £150 ster. like a damnd slave as he is for using me so baselie" (*RVC*, 4:235).

John Rolfe, who acknowledged that the "buying and selling of men and boies" was steady business in the colonies, tried to reassure his fellow Englishmen by reminding them that "in England" slavery was "a thing most intolerable."[8] While Englishmen who served in America may not have been slaves technically, in the absence of any established political-legal framework, they remained at the mercy of the custom of the colony. They were subjected to corporal punishment, denied wages, controlled by their masters both during laboring and non-laboring hours, required to obtain a pass to leave the plantation, forced to seek permission to marry, and regarded "primarily as a capital investment."[9] Thus unlike servants who remained in England, whose Oath of Service granted their masters some degree of authority over their lives, New World servants entered into a labor relation in which their masters demonstrated an unprecedented investment in the *bodies* of their charges.

Historians will remain divided as to whether or not indentured servitude was indeed slavery by another name as long as their inquiry privileges labor as an analytic. What has yet to be fully examined, however, is the fact that colonial servants were not only members of an impressive overseas work force but also participants in an elaborate system of credit. For this reason, the most productive frame through which to examine the meaning and purpose of colonial indenture may not be the social traditions of service but the legal implications of debt. The employment conditions of those who crossed the Atlantic were established by the terms of a signed, sealed and witnessed document that bound servants to planters they had never met and advanced them the cost of transport in lieu of

---

[5]   Abbot Emerson Smith, *Colonists in Bondage: White Servitude and Convict Labor in America, 1607–1776* (Chapel Hill: University of North Carolina Press, 1947), 233.

[6]   Susan Myra Kingsbury (ed.), *The Records of the Virginia Company of London, 1607–1626*, 4 vols. (Washington D.C.: United States Government Printing Office, 1906–35), 3:71. Hereafter cited as *RVC* by volume and page number.

[7]   Morgan, *American Slavery*, 121.

[8]   John Smith, *Travels and Works*, 2:542 as quoted in Morgan, *American Slavery*, 128.

[9]   Beckles, "The Concept of 'White Slavery,'" 576.

compensation, either in the form of wages or livery (room, board, and clothing). The indentured servant, as David Galenson explains, "unable to borrow elsewhere the money necessary for the passage fare and provisions, borrowed against the future returns from his labor."[10] Neither daily wage-earners nor live-in servants, colonial workers were unlike their existing counterparts in England insofar as "the mechanism used to secure the investment in their voyage to the colonies had made them into property."[11]

Debt-bondage cast workers into uncharted waters where culturally predominant ideas of ownership and self-ownership no longer obtained. The surety, called the "gage," that the borrower was required to supply the lender upon the signing of a debt bond was usually an object, but human beings were also used as sureties. When an indentured servant put up his person as collateral, he was considered "an animated gage, a hostage delivered over to slavery but subject to redemption."[12] The servant was not incarcerated, but was nonetheless "held" by the planter who rightfully possessed his person until the debt was satisfied. The indenture thus functioned both as a labor contract and a *prima facie* debt bond. Its promissory element was subtended by the logic of *capias ad satisfaciendum*, the writ that allowed for the detention of the body of the borrower in the event of nonpayment.[13]

While the structure of debt underwriting the terms of his indenture identified the New World servant as collateral, the contractual nature of his agreement distinguished him from the foreign captive or penal galley slave. A consideration of the peculiar legal logic of colonial indenture and its conception of the male body as akin to moveable property informs my analysis of Fletcher and Massinger's *The Custom of the Country*. Despite the aspersions of Pepys and Dryden, who deem this play the most obscene ever performed on the English stage, *Custom* was one of the most popular plays of the period, and its 1628 revival outsold *Othello*, *Richard II* and *The Alchemist*.[14] Critics who have examined this underappreciated tragicomedy have considered its Spanish source material and conformity to the chastity play convention. More recently Carolyn Prager has brought into focus

---

[10]   Galenson, *White Servitude in Colonial America: An Economic Analysis* (Cambridge: Cambridge University Press, 1981), 8.

[11]   Ibid, 8. On juridical rulings on property in person in the period, see Sir William Blackstone, *Commentaries on the Laws of England*, 4 vols. (Oxford; Oxford University Press, 1765–69), 1:412–17, 2:440–54, and 3:142 and Duncan Kennedy, "The Structure of Blackstone's *Commentaries*," *Buffalo Law Review* 28 (1979): 205–382.

[12]   Sir Frederick Pollock and Frederic William Maitland, *The History of English Law Before the Time of Edward I*, 2 vols., 2nd ed. (Cambridge: Cambridge University Press, 1968), 2:186.

[13]   Indenture served as a contract as well as a covenant because it provided a legal means by which to pass property that was actionable by writ of debt. See A.W.B. Simpson, *The History of the Common Law of Contract: The Rise of the Action of Assumpsit* (Oxford: Clarendon Press, 1975), 187.

[14]   G. E. Bentley, *The Jacobean and Caroline Stage*, 7 vols. (Oxford: Clarendon Press, 1941–68), 3: 325.

the significance of the play's mercantile paradigm.[15] Building on Prager's analysis of this play's complex interweaving of financial, legal, and emotional bonds, I argue that *Custom* justifies a new psychology of economic obligation insofar as it explores the affective grounds of consensual bondage. By heralding moderation, expressed by the curtailing of appetite, as necessary to the performance of public duty, this play envisions the well-being of the commonwealth as predicated on its members' abilities to work through the antimony of coercion and consent. On the most obvious level, the play participates in the popularization of the neo-Stoic movement gaining influence in late sixteenth-century England, promoted in large part by Thomas Lodge's newly translated works of Seneca. Certainly, *Custom* advances the standard Stoic precept when its characters claim adversity as the spur to virtue. I would, however, like to historicize further the play's championing of self-restraint. By examining how Fletcher and Massinger identify constancy, a pose of self-retention, as the appropriate response to temptation, which threatens to take one away from oneself, I aim to show that the playwrights single out moderation as the quality that one must cultivate in a context in which selves are alienable. Here passion is no longer merely the subject of stoic (or neo-stoic) mediation but a vehicle for participation in economic obligation, and the social bonds it entails, insofar as the process of tempering passion is constitutive of the contractual subject.[16]

Custom presents indebtedness as an ethical alternative to physical bondage. Accordingly, throughout the play arrangements of economic obligation are shown to be the by-products of individuals acting predictably in accordance with their economic interests, producing and reinforcing webs of interdependency that buttress cohesive community. In order to advance this perspective, Fletcher and Massinger exploit the central trope of tragicomic transformation, redemption, as they work through the moral problems produced by new economic geographies. *Custom*'s understanding of redemption as at once a mental and material phenomenon—it is in this play both the ability to liberate oneself from the throes of passion and the experience of being purchased by someone who delivers one from slavery—

---

[15]   *Custom* was entered into the Stationer's Register February 22, 1619 and first performed by the King's Men in 1619–1620. For the stage history, see Bentley, *The Jacobean and Caroline Stage*, 3:324–38. For eighteenth– and nineteenth–century responses to the play, see Lawrence B. Wallis, *Fletcher, Beaumont & Company, Entertainers to the Jacobean Gentry* (New York: Kings Crown Press, 1947): 21–2, 83, 118, and 175. Prager "The Problem of Slavery in *The Custom of the Country*," *SEL* 28.2 (1988): 301–17. On chastity in the play, see Nancy C. Pearse, *John Fletcher's Chastity Plays: Mirrors of Modesty* (Lewisburg: Bucknell University Press, 1973), 210–17. On the play's use of Cervantes, see W. D. Howarth, "Cervantes and Fletcher: A Theme with Variations," *The Modern Language Review* 56.4 (1961): 563–6 and T. L. Darby, "Resistance to Rape in *Persiles y Sigismunda* and *The Custom of the Country*," *The Modern Language Review* 90.2 (1995): 273–84.

[16]   On the role of the passions in forging political obligation, see Victoria Kahn, "'The Duty to Love': Passion and Obligation in Early Modern Political Theory," *Representations* 68 (1999): 84–107.

–remains in keeping with medieval Christian and Reformation exegeses on the debt man owes to God. A New World context also informs the play's notion of redemption, since at the moment of its performance "redemptioner" was the term used by colonial officials for a young man who sold himself for transport to the New World.

Custom is set in Lisbon, which at the end of the sixteenth century was known as the hub of a thriving international slave trade, and the country's associations with piracy and slavery made it a vital topic for the London stage.[17] This play is, however, not merely interested in showcasing the exoticism of trade in the Mediterranean. The troubling custom of Christians enslaving other Christians was not solely a reality of the Mediterranean world, and the play's concerns with issues of possession and self–possession in an exotic milieu have yet to be considered in light of England's Westward expansion. While England remained on the fringes of Eastern trading networks, larger shifts in commerce were beginning to transform it into a nation poised to take advantage of new opportunities to the West. In this period, London became a premier port city known throughout Europe as the hub of an international servant trade.[18] By 1616, London authorities arranged for the exportation of hundreds of orphans, felons, and impoverished youth, and by 1620, a system had been put in place whereby a staggering number of young men were exported on a regular basis, made possible by the Virginia Company's ability to advance these men the cost of passage, setting the stage for servants to become "the most liquid form of capital" in the New World.[19]

There are no explicit references to the Virginia colony in *Custom*; nevertheless, it's guiding conceit—the "custom of the country"—indexes an emerging notion of property in person forged by debt law and solidified by New World indenture. Younger, unskilled servants who arrived at the colony without proper documentation were deemed "custom-of-the-country-servants."[20] Yet the distinction between "custom-of-the-country-servants" and others was negligible since the conditions of servitude for all men, whether or not they arrived with bonds in hand, were

---

[17] Ferdinand Braudel, *The Mediterranean and the Mediterranean World in the Age of Philip II*, 2 vols., trans. Sian Reynolds, rev. 2nd ed. (New York: Harper, 1975), 2:865–91. On the Mediterranean as a popular topic for the London stage, see Daniel Vitkus, "Turks and Jews in *The Jew of Malta*," in *Early Modern English Drama: A Critical Companion*, (eds.) Garrett A. Sullivan, Jr., Patrick Cheney, and Andrew Hadfield (New York: Oxford University Press, 2006), 63.

[18] James Horn and Philip D. Morgan, "Settlers and Slaves: European and African Migrations to Early Modern British America," in *The Creation of the British Atlantic World*, (eds.) Elizabeth Mancke and Carole Shammas (Baltimore: John Hopkins University Press, 2005): 36.

[19] Smith, *Colonists in Bondage*, 227.

[20] Lorena S. Walsh, "Servitude and Opportunity in Charles County, Maryland, 1658–1705," in *Law, Society, and Politics in Early Maryland*, (eds.) Aubrey C. Land et al. (Baltimore: Johns Hopkins University Press, 1977), 112, 129, 131. See also Smith, "Custom of the Country," in *Colonists in Bondage*, 226–52.

ultimately determined neither by English statutory provisions nor by the recommendations of London authorities, but by "the Custom of the Country," the phrase written on *every* indenture.[21] Thus when in 1622 the London Deputy of the Virginia Company admonished stockholders for not upholding the terms of their servants' bonds, company officials had only to point to this phrase on the face of the deed.[22] English law mandated that "all contracts made in *England* betweene the owners of lande ... & Servantes wch they shall send hither" be duly observed in the Americas upon pain of penalty. Nonetheless, even those who arrived with copies of their bond discovered that overseers regarded themselves as answerable only to those laws "suche as might proceed out of every mans private conceit."[23]

The legal ambiguities of custom and the uncertainties to which they gave rise fueled defenses of the Virginia project. In *A True Declaration of the Estate of the Colonie in Virginia*, company official William Barret, for instance, celebrates rather than denies the unstable intermixing of peril and profit that characterized working conditions beyond England. He poses the rhetorical question: "what is there in all this *tragicall comedie* that should discourage us with the impossibilities of the enterprise?"[24] For Barret, the risks of the venture prove worthwhile, since "from ... Calamatie" comes the "abundant and sustaining life" to be found in the New World, a place where all "extremities" are rendered "wholesome and temperate."[25] Barret's description indexes a colonial imaginary attempting to mediate a situation in which the government's stability is, like the wages of the servants on whom it depended, a speculative gambit. Members of an embryonic society that was in essence based upon a provisional economy were vulnerable to engaging in fantastical imaginings of riches at best and resorting to extreme brutality in the face of unprecedented chaos at worst. Treatises like Barret's encouraged readers to construe the love of gain as the rational alternative to love of pleasure.[26] Thus the acquisition of wealth is represented as inspiring temperate conditions, internally and externally, which may serve to calm the turbulent effects of an unpredictable environment and the baser impulses it potentially inspired.

Those who objected to the enterprise did not accept defenses like Barret's, which may be characterized by Valerie Forman's apt phrase "narrative[s] of

---

[21]   See, for example, the 1683 Indenture bond in Galenson, *White Servitude*, 41.

[22]   Smith, *Colonists in Bondage*, 67.

[23]   Ibid, 227.

[24]   William Barret and the Councell of Virginia, *A True Declaration of the Estate of the Colonie in Virginia with a Confutation of Such Scandalous Reports as have Tended to Disgrace so Worthy an Enterprise* (London, 1610), 11.

[25]   Ibid, 12.

[26]   My discussion of the transformation of disruptive passion into something constructive, namely interest in monetary gain, is indebted to Albert O. Hirschmann, *The Passions and the Interests: Political Arguments for Capitalism before its Triumph* (Princeton: Princeton University Press, 1977).

transformative prosperity."[27] Rather than herald the temperate outcome of near-calamity, detractors instead condemned colonial magistrates for *their* intemperance. Francis Bacon, in his essay on New World plantations advises that the colony's government be made up of "temperate" men only—sound advice for maintaining order in a context in which men no longer able to look to a traditional social hierarchy to buttress their standing had to rely on restraint to demonstrate nobility of character.[28] London investors questioned the legitimacy of the colony by accusing planters of using their servants "with more slavery then if they were under the Turke" (*RVC*, 1:334–5). Thomas Dale's implementation of martial law in particular drew protests from those who complained that authorities left unchecked were keeping certain segments of the population in "extreme misery and slavery."[29] The word "slavery," a slippery term in an evolving early seventeenth century discourse of liberty, functioned, as Alison Games stresses, "as a code, a single word conveying horrors no Englishman should have to endure" and was used to refer to any government considered illegitimate or abusive.[30] At the same time, an association of chattel bondage with the Mediterranean abided within early modern English culture, and this conceptual link buttressed the efforts of those who worked to defend themselves against claims that the Virginia colony was instituting de facto slavery. As long as colonists could refer to the Mediterranean as the epicenter of human traffic, slavery would be demarcated as a foreign, specifically Portuguese, institution. Thus, members of the Virginia Company represented plantations with indentured servants as a far cry from the slave markets and galley ships that English emissaries and merchants encountered elsewhere.[31]

In the final analysis, the defense of indentured servitude hinged on its being a contractual arrangement. Colonial indenture hardly stood, however, as a testament to the progression away from custom and towards contract. Rather, in the absence of national or civic jurisdictional definitions and boundaries, custom and contract were one in the same. In recommending temperance as the necessary disposition for participation in economic and legal bonds put under pressure by global expansion, *Custom* stages the dilemma posed by labor relations that exposed the limits of an English notion of liberty founded on self–ownership. In

---

[27] Forman, *Tragicomic Redemptions: Global Economies and the Early Modern English Stage* (Philadelphia: University of Pennsylvania Press, 2008), 6.

[28] Bacon, "Of Plantations," 2:801.

[29] *A Brief Declaration of the Plantation of Virginia* (London 1624), as quoted in Alison Games, *The Web of Empire: English Cosmopolitans in an Age of Expansion, 1560–1660* (Oxford: Oxford University Press, 2008), 145.

[30] Ibid, 145.

[31] See Robin Blackburn, "The Old World Background to European Colonial Slavery," *William and Mary Quarterly* 54.1 (1997): 65–102 and John Michael Archer, *Old Worlds: Egypt, Southwest Asia, India, and Russia in Early Modern English Writing* (Stanford: Stanford University Press, 2001).

a functionally unstable credit economy, in which all one owned was the promise of a future return, the bodies of dependents took on unprecedented value as one of the only secure possessions. The conversion of passion into interest, a word that in seventeenth-century philosophical discourse served as the generic term for that which trumped destructive human impulses, was necessary for participation in an uncertain market structure and unregulated labor system.[32]

Redeeming the Male Body

One of many early seventeenth-century dramatizations of hapless Christians adrift in a foreign culture, *Custom*'s particular preoccupation with bridal rape and prostitution points to its general interest in corporal violation. Insofar as to be an alien means to be vulnerable to alienation, the play's concern with sexual purity speaks to its notion of self-possession as a triumph of the rational mind, whose superiority ensures the preservation of bodily integrity. Moreover, those who fight to protect their chastity show themselves to be free of self-doubt and divided consciousness. Their steadfastness and single-mindedness offer an idealized image of the self as unalterable and indivisible, and hence these characters stand in opposition to the uncertain selves populating the play whose insatiable desires and fluctuating extremes of emotion make for labile and violent interactions. Constancy on the part of inferiors is heralded as the correct response to threats posed by intemperate rulers, but the play is also careful to demonstrate that immoderate masters create the conditions for a slave society. Here the play's perspective on the social dangers of extreme passion remains in keeping with an Aristotelian notion of immoderation as inimical to civil order.[33] Aristotle advises those who occupy positions of authority to guard against "disproportionate excess" because their lapses create the conditions for those beneath them to slide into a state of "slavery."[34] This prescription for temperate mastery is taken up by a variety of seventeenth-century commentaries in which "a monarch who abuses property rights is described in ways that define him as passionate ("lustful") rather than reasonable, self-indulgent ("sensuall") rather than disciplined, and governed by a desire for 'goodes' rather than a commitment to the good of his people."[35] While unrestrained passion in this play stands as an obstacle to achieving liberation—whether literal or spiritual—

[32]   Hirschmann, *The Passions and the Interests*, 28.

[33]   Aristotle, *Nicomachean Ethics*, 2nd ed., trans. and intro. Terence Irwin (Indianapolis: Hackett Publishing Company, 1999), "Justice in Exchange" Book 5, Chapter 5, 74–6. On the implications of Aristotle's theories of justice for economic theory, see Scott Meikle, *Aristotle's Economic Thought* (Oxford: Oxford University Press, 1995).

[34]   Aristotle, *Nicomachean Ethics*, Book 5, Chapter 5, 74.

[35]   Constance Jordan, "'Eating the Mother': Property and Propriety in *Pericles*," in *Creative Imitation: New Essays on Renaissance Literature in Honor of Thomas M. Greene*, (eds.) David Quint et al. (Binghamton, New York: Medieval and Renaissance Texts & Studies, 1992), 336.

for masters and servants alike, intemperance is at the same time identified as the necessary precondition for the production of the consensual subject, who through the act of tempering his appetite uses passion as the means to attain self-mastery. This process of tempering is associated in the play with redemption, whereby characters agree to the binding terms of economic obligation that at first appear enslaving but in the end enable civil enfranchisement.

The play begins with the crisis precipitated by the Roman governor's misuse of custom to satisfy his appetite for virgins, by which he asserts first–night rites (whereby a bride on her wedding night is deflowered by her husband's kinsmen), a custom that, as one character proclaims, "this wretched country hath wrought into a law."[36] Critics have assumed that *Custom*'s title refers only to first-night rites as described within late sixteenth-century travelers' accounts of the Canary Islands, Peru and Cuba.[37] The assertion of *ius primae noctis* that frames the play is depicted, as in Cervantes's *Persiles y Sigismunda*, as an iniquitous practice that offends social mores. Yet the playwrights curiously substitute the traditional rite, in which defloration is initiated by members of the same class, with the brutal assertion of ownership by a singular tyrannical authority. In *Custom*, the governor of Rome claims rights to the body of a virgin bride whose family desperately tries to satisfy him with monetary compensation. By highlighting the proprietary underpinnings of *ius primae noctis*, Fletcher and Massinger's version of this custom resonates with the English feudal practice involving the payment grooms made to ecclesiastical authorities in order to ensure that the church lift its ban on first-night consummation. The English custom of *mercheta mulierum* became secularized as mandatory payment to the manor lord, because, as W.D. Howarth explains, serfs "were the property of the overlord," and marriage to someone belonging to another manor signaled the loss of service and most importantly, manor property.[38]

English villeinage had long been extinct by the time Fletcher and Massinger's play was performed, but the concept of white slavery remained "unmistakably fossilized in common law."[39] The relation of manor lord to his serf and the sanctioning of bridal rape are linked at the onset of this play as equivalent abuses of authority and means of designating the bodies of others as property. The "custom of the country" thus functions as an overdetermined phrase, freighted by the historical baggage of medieval serfdom and animated by travelers' tales of *ius primae noctis*, but emerging most prominently in recent accounts of colonial

---

[36] John Fletcher and Philip Massinger, *The Custom of the Country* (New York: Routledge Theatre Arts Books, 1999), 12. This edition will hereafter be cited by page number only.

[37] See W.D. Howarth, "'Droit du Seigneur': Fact or Fantasy," *Journal of European Studies* 1 (1971): 295–7.

[38] Howarth, "'Droit du Seigneur,'" 300.

[39] Winthrop D. Jordan, *White over Black: American Attitudes Towards the Negro, 1550–1812* (Chapel Hill: University of North Carolina Press, 1968), 50.

authorities' exploitation of the gray area between English law and local custom. In the acts that follow, the particular "unresistable" custom of bridal rape (8) is implicitly compared with the Portuguese practice of enslaving foreign captives.

The crisis that frames *Custom* is sexual exploitation, but the opening scene establishes erotic enslavement as a metaphor for intemperate relations based upon various forms of corporal coercion. When Count Clodio refuses to take a monetary fine as a substitute for Zenocia's maidenhead, and insists instead on observing the "black and barbarous" custom of *ius primae noctis*, the play links his overweening passion to his irrational refusal of payment (21). Zenocia's husband and brother-in-law stress that the Count intends to subject her to his "intemp'rate, rude and wild embraces" (9). Described as a "maiden-monger" (11), Clodio is "a cannibal that feeds on the heads of maids/ ... / a cat o'mountain" that would make "a town bull" seem a "mere stoic," and "a Spanish jennet a most virtuous gentleman" (11). Even Clodio confesses, "I am hot and fiery/ And my blood beats alarums through my body / And fancy high" (20). For Clodio, "to possess [Zenocia]" (8) is "to enjoy" or consume and use her up. He is thus likened to a slave-driver who "would weary her" (10) and described as a merciless overseer who "breaks young wenches to the saddle and teaches them to stumble ever after" and "whip[s] off [their] heads" (11). Despite repeated offers, he remains resolute that "no money nor prayers shall redeem that [her body]" (18). Zenocia herself begs him to "set [her] own price" (918), and her father later pleads with Clodio to "let [him] pay the ransom" (22). Yet for Clodio only "[Zenocia's] body will content [him]" (18). When bride, groom, and brother-in-law flee Rome, Clodio deems their flight a crime of property, protesting to Zenocia's husband Arnoldo, "thou hast robb'd me, villain, of a treasure" (23).

Once the setting of the play shifts from Rome to Lisbon, the interplay of sexual exploitation and threat of enslavement become even more pronounced as the plight of the virgin bride, who construes the trial of her honor as a test of her "male constancy" (32), is linked to that of the male foreign captive. When Portuguese pirates hijack the ship carrying the wedding party, the bride's husband and his brother leap into the ocean to ensure that they will "never" have to "taste the bread of servitude" (30). Yet when they come ashore, they are described as "disarm'd and ready to be put in fetters" (30). Arnoldo and his brother Rutillio are then subjected to a series of trials that threaten their respective rights of self-ownership.

In staging the careful negotiation of the ever-shifting boundary between voluntary and compulsory service, *Custom* represents the male body as vulnerable to an immoderate authority that seeks to drain it of its prowess. Once on shore, Zenocia is sold to the Portuguese Countess Hippolyta who is determined to "ravish" Zenocia's erstwhile groom Arnoldo (54). The occasion of Arnoldo's capture is the signing of a debt bond, when upon his arrival a Jewish moneylender recognizes the brothers as "poor and strangers" (34) and offers to assist them with a loan. The gold he provides, however, is not as he claims "bounty" that he "give[s]" "freely" (35). Instead, it is the "earnest of that which is to follow," and he explains to Antonio that this is "the bond which you must seal for 'tis your advancement"

(35). Having been granted an advance, Antonio is then expected to work off his debt by servicing the Jew's mistress, the ravenous Hippolyta whose "touches" are described as "fetters" and whose "locks" are "soft chains to bind the arms of princes" (60). Arnoldo only narrowly escapes enslavement, as she declares, "Upon my conscience, I must ravish thee!" and attempts "to bind him" in literal chains (54). Like Clodio, Hippolyta strives to possess Arnoldo so that she may "enjoy [him] indeed" (54). When he flees her court, Hippolyta's exclamations echo that of Clodio, when she deems this as an offense akin to the wrongful seizure of property and has Arnoldo imprisoned for theft (presumably of himself) (55).

Hippolyta, however, undergoes a miraculous transformation after being advised by the Governor of Lisbon that her bondwoman Zenocia cannot be counted as "a lawful prize," because she is "of that country we hold friendship with" (81). Suddenly willing to marshal rather than exhaust her resources, Hippolyta generously decides to "redeem all" (61), as she comes to recognize that "It is in vain / To strive with destiny" (104). The ultimate sign of her conversion occurs when she acknowledges her place in Lisbon's credit economy and, as "recompense" for the suffering she has caused, offers to forgive Lisbon "the hundred thousand crowns the city owes [her]" (104). She summarily "discharge[s]" Zenocia from her bonds (81) and "unloose[s]" the imprisoned Arnoldo from "[his] bonds" as well (65), allowing him to "redeem" himself in exchange for his bride. Although no longer enslaved, her charges remain indebted to her. While Arnoldo has been released from his shackles, he must now "pay dearly for her favour," as one character wryly observes (65). With a kiss, he publicly pledges himself to Hippolyta and asks that she "accept [his] ready service" (66). Formally acknowledging his debt to her, he agrees, "forever to be fetter'd to [her]" (78), so that she may "command [him] through what danger" (78). This time it is with his voluntary submission that she "makes him [her] slave," as he "give[s] [his] freedom" over to her in acknowledgement of his debt (78).

While Arnoldo successfully staves off Hippolyta's advances, his brother Rutillio faces an even more dangerous trial when he agrees to serve in a male brothel. The main function of the play's infamous brothel scene would seem to be the generation of material for a subplot involving the rakish brother of the morally upright protagonist. Yet this scene occupies a more central function in the play than previous scholarship has allowed in that it amplifies the perils of labor in an exotic locale by dramatizing the association of coerced sexual performance and compulsory service. Brothels appear frequently on the early modern English stage, but unlike the majority of plays featuring bawdy houses, *Custom* does not present a tale of female fall and redemption. Fletcher and Massinger instead use the male stews as a means to show the brutal effects of a market economy on the impressed young man. Although the brothel revolves around the laboring male body, in relinquishing rights to both his capacities and the product of his labor, the male sex-worker alienates himself. Undermining the fantasy of the stews as a proving ground for male stamina, here the brothel is a work site determined by the relationship between the dispossessed worker and the intemperate overseer.

Human traffic is initially posited as an alternative to penal bondage. When Rutillio is apprehended for having "wand'r[ed]" into the city's munitions storehouse (57), he is given the choice of either "six years tug[ging] at an oar i'th' galleys" (57) or allowing Sulpitia the brothel madam to purchase him for 600 ducats. He gladly accepts the madam's offer and in return vows to "give her [his] whole self," which she concurs she "has reason to expect ... considering the great sum she pays for it" (58). Rutillio erroneously assumes that his potency will allow him to excel as a he-whore, and he boasts, "I am excellent at it" (58):

> Bring me a hundred of 'em: I'll dispatch 'em.
> I will be none but yours. Should another offer
> Another way to redeem me, I should scorn it.
> What women you shall please: I am monstrous lusty,
> Not to be taken down. Would you have children?
> I'll get you those as fast, and thick as fly-blows. (58)

From the first act of the play Rutillio's enthusiasm for sexual conquest is established as he admits his envy of the Count's plan to enact the "admirable, rare custom" of bridal rape (6). When, however, it becomes evident that he has consigned himself to a life of "tug[ging] in a feather bed" (59), he moderates his passion, wishing to be "honestly married" so that he might be "civilly merry" (87–8). Work in the stews, it turns out, is another form of chattel bondage, since his clientele, the "men-leech[ing]" city women of Lisbon, are relentlessly demanding and never satisfied (86).

Despite the brothel's labor force of able-bodied, young men, demand pushes production to its breaking point. One worker bemoans the grueling conditions and warns the unyielding Madam, "You do so over-labour 'em when you have 'em, / And so dry-founder 'em, they cannot last" (55). Another complains, "the labor [is] so much ... and so few to perform it" (87). They curse the climate, which is described as sultry; the "dampish air" causing "a snuffing in [the] head" (86) and "too warm for [their] complexions" (87). The Danish and German men are broken: one is described as in "fitters," or fragments, and "chin'd" (55), or broken-backed, and another is in hospital and no longer able to "labour like a thresher" (56). The English workers fare no better and are left to "draw their legs like hackneys" (56). In the end, even Rutillio complains bitterly:

> Now do I look as if I were crow-trodden!
> Fie, how my hams shrink under me! Oh, me,
> I am broken-winded too. Is this a life?
>
> ...
>
> I had a body once, a handsome body,
> And wholesome too. Now I appear like a rascal
> That had been hung a year or two in gibbets.
> Fie, how I faint.
>
> ...
>
> Place me before a cannon; 'tis a pleasure.

Stretch me upon a rack.
…
No galleys to be got, nor yet no gallows? (86)

A man who "draw[s] [his] legs after [himself] like a lame dog" and who is "too feeble" to run away (87), Rutillio is outdone at the prospect of pleasing "an old, dead-palsied lady in a litter" (84). He realizes that the brothel cannot serve as an opportunity for adventure and empowerment since value does not inhere in the skills he offers but rather in his body's capacity to endure. Pleasing the women of Lisbon proves more demanding than "labouring in [the] fulling-mills" (88), and he grows wistful at the thought of wage-labor whereby he could lease his person while still retaining proprietorship of himself: "Death, if I had but money, / Or any friends to bring me from this bondage, / I would thresh, … keep hogs / … Thatch for three half-pence a day and think it lordly, / From this base stallion trade" (89).

The Madam's response to Rutillio's request for liberty parodies that of the planter cum slave-owner:

If you be so angry,
Pay back the money I redeem'd you at
And take your course. I can have men enough.
You lost me an hundred crowns since you came hither,
In broths and strength'ning caudles.
Till you do pay me,
If you will eat and live, you shall endeavour.
I'll chain you to't else. (88)

Through the figure of the Madam we are shown the dire results of the gross mismanagement of liquid assets (in this case, of semen rather than cash or tobacco): A demoralized, and potentially rebellious, workforce and an enterprise always hovering on the verge of extinction. Labor performed outside the stable context of the guild or household devolves into a promiscuous arrangement when the worker's performance is compelled by threats of an emasculating authority, misogynistically coded as female.

The moral problem of male prostitution as presented in *Custom* spoke to the most startling example of England's involvement in human traffic in the colonies. The selling off of a servant's contract was not entirely unknown in early seventeenth-century England; with the permission of guild members, a master could sell his apprentice to another company member. But by the time Fletcher and Massinger's play was performed, the binding of an apprentice with the intent to sell him was considered a gross abuse of authority.[40] In a cash-poor colony, however, the bodies of young men, in the words of Virginian planter John Pory, were understood to serve as the colony's "principall wealth" (*RVC*, 3:221). In official reports and personal letters, young men tell of being equated with pounds sterling or pounds of tobacco (*RVC*, 4:235). Despite being recognized as valuable investments, colonial

---

[40]   Jocelyn O. Dunlop, *English Apprenticeship and Child Labour: A History* (New York: MacMillan, 1912), 57–8; 128–9.

masters apparently had no compunction about abusing or wasting their precious assets. Word spread quickly that "divers m[aste]rs. in Virginia doe much neglect and abuse their servants there with intolerablle oppression and hard usage" (*RVC*, 2:442), and that:

> [D]ivers old Planters and others did allure and beguile divers younge p[er]sons and others (ignorant and unskillfull in such matters) to serve them upon intollerable and unchristianlike condicons upon promises of such rewards and recompence, as they were no wayes able to performe nor ever meant. (*RVC*, 2:113)

Rutillio's delusions of unlimited sexual potency mirror the misguided hopes of the beguiled young men who slavishly labored on plantations, clinging to the promise of recompense that would never materialize.

Rutillio's problem is solved, however, not simply by his own change of heart but also by the introduction of yet another economic arrangement. He is released from the "base trade" into which he has been impressed when he is redeemed by the once-hotheaded aristocratic Duarte, who, like Hippolyta, has undergone a miraculous transformation. Juxtaposed both to the lusty he-whore and the greedy Madam, Duarte is the embodiment of temperance, exemplified by his magnanimous offer to pay the Madam the entire balance due, despite the fact that the amount of Rutillio's debt has inexplicably doubled. The character of Duarte represents the process by which passion may be refined, as he comes to obtain an awareness of the virtue of exchange over and above possession. Once his extremities are calmed, Duarte's interest in gain overtakes his unbridled passion for pleasure. He effectively forswears obsessive self-love, exemplified by compulsive boasting and dueling, and in seeking to achieve a temperate existence based on an understanding of the self as embedded within economic and social networks, he demonstrates that appetite may prove to be a socially useful channel for the production of consensual community.

Rutillio is redeemed, but he is not free. He ends his days as Duarte's stepfather when he agrees to marry his creditor's mother, the woman to whom he declares himself bound by "the infinite debt [he] owe[s] [her]" (41). (He has also accepted a loan of 100 crowns from her [44]). Through his financial dependence on both mother and son, Rutillio is inserted into a credit economy that requires him to identify himself as "a creature bound [to them]" (107). In the end, the distinction between degrading labor and economic bondage turns on the temperament of the consenting parties.

In heralding economic obligation as socially restorative, Fletcher and Massinger echo Aristotle who advocates redemption as mediated by considerations of the status and disposition of the participating parties:

> If, for instance, someone has ransomed you from pirates, should you ransom him in return, *no matter who he is*? Or if he does not need to be ransomed, but asks for his money back, should you return it, or should you ransom your father instead? Here it seems that you should ransom your father, rather than even yourself.[41]

---

[41]   Aristotle, *Nicomachean Ethics*, Book 9, Chapter 2, 139.

This example further illustrates Aristotle's discussion of proportionate reciprocity as suited neither to distributive justice, exemplified by the communal dispensation of wealth, nor to retificatory justice, which offers retribution. Conjoining the concerns of social justice and economic obligation in Aristotelian terms, *Custom* rejects exploitation and equality alike demonstrating that only a mutual arrangement devised between a rational superior and an economically beholden, self-possessed inferior buttresses a harmonious social order.[42] In this respect, the play offers a psychological primer for a functional commercial society based on relations of credit. Although a social order founded on the speculative prospect of redeeming one's bonds may inspire speculation, fantasy, and passion, it also creates the conditions in which the subject may transcend his primitive appetites, allowing him to abandon barbarous custom and embrace mutual agreement.

Conclusion

Custom begins with the call to "make with all main speed to th' port" (23), and at its bleakest moments its protagonist muses "my life's so full of various changes that I now despair of any certain port" (65). It ends, however, with "the evening … set clear after a stormy day" (113) and everyone's bark at last "having found a quiet harbour" (114). Certainly by 1620 no harbor was quiet as long as it was part of an oceanic world driven by pursuit of profit. At the moment of *Custom*'s first performance, the financial and legal scaffolding that upheld a thriving credit economy within England tied London to a world of commerce beyond its borders and a new epistemological order that identified certain bodies as viable commodities. Through *Custom*'s dramatization of the ambiguity of the port, insofar as oceanic travel leads to travail, the play speaks to both the unlimited potential of the colonial expansion and the limits of colonial imaginary.

In volume one of *Capital*, Marx argues that the slave can only exist in underdeveloped relations of production in which a person unable to lay claim to his or her own labor may be possessed by others. The difference between the slave and the worker marks a key moment in the evolution of the capitalist mode of production based on the interdependency of wage-labor and primitive accumulation, providing Marx with the theoretical means by which to integrate the history of labor into that of capital.[43] By arguing that only those who exercise the right to buy and sell commodities (including themselves) are free, Marx identifies the market as determinative of the valuation of workers, rather than the quality

---

[42] Meikle in *Aristotle's Economic Thought* makes a convincing case for proportionate reciprocity, exchange premised on inequity, as a distinct kind of justice rather than a species of either corrective or distributive justice, 129–46.

[43] Karl Marx, *Capital: A Critique of Political Economy*, vol. 1, trans. Ben Fowkes (New York: Random House, 1977), 1:272–3.

or quantity of their labor.[44] The Virginia colony put Marx's market valuation theory of labor to the test, since even though the colonial economy determined the value of indentured servants, they were unable to either profit from or trade in their own labor and were far from free. Through its reliance on debt-bondage, indenture proved that capitalist expansion depended upon the coexistence, and even the amalgamation, of unfree and free labor.[45] It also demonstrated that under certain circumstances political relations could be reduced to relations between creditors and debtors, thus potentially allowing for "the despotism of speculative fantasy," whereby the fluctuating value of public stock put politics at the mercy of passion.[46]

As Zachary Lesser has shown, the hybridity of tragicomedy allows for the representation and resolution of otherwise irreconcilable political, economic, and social perspectives.[47] The genre's dialectical logic, or propensity for achieving "paradoxical unity," makes it ideally suited for working through the antimonies of arrangements, like colonial indenture, in which rational subjects agree to bind themselves rather than submit to external coercion. This play's ideal of proportionate reciprocity, which speaks to a particular early Stuart notion of enfranchisement as inequitable entitlement, is figured as the heroic achievement of self-rule in the face of the internal and external chaos potentially unleashed by the unstable mix of slavery and servitude. The play's crude representation of compulsion as chattel bondage allows it to legitimate voluntary bondage as the end point of a process of internal persuasion, thus rendering consent and coercion compatible. Once passion gives way to interest, the play shows, men are constant, and the debt bond, which serves as a mutual agreement between stable subjects, can occupy the place of social contract. The substitution of economic agreement for social contract was crucial in contexts like the early stages of the Virginia colony, in which a cohesive, consistent political order had yet to be firmly established.

----

[44]   At times, Marx refers to wage labor as "economic bondage," and even as a form of "slavery" when extra-economic market constraints render wage-labor compulsory. See Robert Miles, *Capitalism and Unfree Labor: Anomaly or Necessity?* (London: Tavistock Publications, 1987), 24.

[45]   Marx acknowledged that the colonies offered new markets for manufactured commodities and a source of wealth that could be transformed into capital. His interest in colonization, however, did not challenge his assumption that slavery and wage labor are rooted in two distinct social and economic systems. On the limits of Marx's analysis in regard to the colonial system, see Immanuel Wallerstein, *The Modern World System I: Capitalist Agriculture and the Origins of the European World Economy in the Sixteenth Century* (New York: Academic Press, 1974) and Andre Gunder Frank, *ReORIENT: Global Economy in the Asian Age* (Berkeley: University of California Press, 1998).

[46]   J.G.A. Pocock, "The Mobility of Property and the Rise of Eighteenth-Century Sociology," in *Theories of Property: Aristotle to the Present*, (eds.) Anthony Parel and Thomas Flanagan (Waterloo, Ontario: Wilfrid Laurier University Press, 1979), 152.

[47]   Lesser, "Tragical-Comical-Pastoral-Colonial: Economic Sovereignty, Globalization, and the Form of Tragicomedy," *ELH* 74 (2007): 881–908.

Chapter 13
The Comic-Tragedy of Labor: A Global Story

Valerie Forman

The high costs of conducting long-distance overseas trade and the enormous profits that were imagined and at times realized from it made England's increasing participation in a global economy a heated topic of debate.[1] The stage genre of tragicomedy was a participant in this debate about how profit could be made in the face of so much loss. The seventeenth-century English stage's most popular genre, tragicomedy frequently, perhaps even disproportionately, makes global trade and travel its subject precisely because of the relationship between the two genres that constitutes its form.[2] Tragicomedy is the product of a relationship between two potentially opposing genres—one that foregrounds loss, and the other resolution.

---

[1] Dennis Flynn and Arturo Giraldez argue that global trade begins in 1571, the year the city of Manila was founded, and the first time that all "important populated continents began to exchange products continuously ... and in values sufficient to generate crucial impacts on all trading partners." "Born with a 'Silver Spoon': The Origin of World Trade in 1571," in *Metals and Monies in an Emerging Global Economy*, (eds.) Flynn and Giráldez (Brookfield, Vt.: Variorum, 1997), 259–79.

We now call the pamphlet war generated by the concerns over global trade in the early seventeenth century the mercantilists' debate. The primary participants in these debates––Gerald Malynes, a master of assay at the mint; Edward Misselden, a member first of the Merchant Adventurers and later of the English East India Company; and Thomas Mun, a director of the East India Company—would not have considered themselves of the same school of thought, however. On the contrary, they were often in disagreement with one another. At the heart of the debate was the question of whether the wealth of the country depended on keeping money within the kingdom. For insightful discussions of the terms and impact of these debates, see Joyce Appleby, *Economic Thought and Ideology in Seventeenth-Century England* (Princeton, NJ: Princeton University Press, 1978); Mary Poovey, *A History of the Modern Fact: Problems of Knowledge in the Sciences of Wealth and Society* (Chicago: University of Chicago Press, 1998); Andrea Finkelstein, *Harmony and Balance: An Intellectual History of Seventeenth-Century English Economic Thought* (Ann Arbor: University of Michigan Press, 2000); and Jonathan Gil Harris, *Sick Economies: Drama, Mercantilism, and Disease in Shakespeare's England* (Philadelphia: University of Pennsylvania Press, 2004).

[2] For a discussion of tragicomedy's popularity, see the Introduction of *The Politics of Tragicomedy: Shakespeare and After*, (eds.) Gordon McMullan and Jonathan Hope (London: Routledge, 1992).

That relationship is narratively structured by the fortunate fall of Christian redemption in which man's loss in the Fall, through which mankind became indebted to God, is more than regained in the salvation of mankind through Christ's sacrifice. As a result of its narrative basis in this economic logic of redemption, tragicomedy is a genre particularly well suited to negotiate the complexities of England's participation in global trade in the seventeenth century.[3] Tragicomedy's redemptive emphasis on loss *and* return registers and addresses these economic complexities through its reimagining of initial losses as expenditures that return as, and even produce, more prosperous futures.[4]

Yet neither the plays nor the economic theories of the period ever fully illuminate the processes by which potentially tragic losses transform into prosperity. These processes remain mysterious and often some form of the magical takes their place.[5] Reading two tragicomic plays in which the importance of labor to the economy is variably recognized in relation to developing ideas about global trade, I analyze how the valuing or devaluing of labor corresponds both to the generic movements in the plays and to the potential to imagine prosperity as resulting from such trade.[6]

---

[3]   For a book-length study of the relationship between tragicomedy and the beginnings of global trade, see my *Tragicomic Redemptions: Global Economics and the Early Modern English Stage* (Philadelphia: University of Pennsylvania Press, 2008).

[4]   I am here building on Mimi Dixon's formulation of the central paradox of tragicomedy. Emphasizing the importance of recognition and recognition scenes to tragicomedy, Dixon argues that tragicomedy involves a reenvisioning. The moment of recognition results in a redefinition—for example, crucifixion as divine comedy. As a result, pain itself can be creative. I want to make an even stronger case: it is not just that the recognition results in redefinition, but that the tragic component and the conflict that develops from it produce a prosperous return. Dixon, "Tragicomic Recognition: Medieval Miracles and Shakespearean Romance," in *Renaissance Tragicomedy: Explorations in Genre and Politics*, (ed.) Nancy Maguire (New York: AMS Press, 1987), 56. Gordon McMullan recognizes a similar, though not identical, structure in his reading of *The Two Noble Kinsmen*. He says that the character Palamon (when he says that nothing could buy dear love, but the loss of it) recognizes "the paradox that the vehicle of [the new genre's] regenerative teleology is dispersal, dissemination, and loss." In his formulation, however, there is no transformation, only an equivalent return. *The Politics of Unease in the Plays of John Fletcher* (Amherst: University of Massachusetts Press, 1994), 261.

[5]   See David Hawkes's essay in this volume for a discussion of the ways in which the conceptual understanding of new economic practices depended on a paradoxical acceptance of magical practices as part of ordinary life.

[6]   By placing the genre of tragicomedy in relation to contemporary economic texts, my intention is to develop a reading practice that both contextualizes the genre and argues for its role in the newly developing public discourse of economic theory. This essay thus participates in a developing conversation about "historical formalism," which centers on reclaiming form and genre as historical, and on viewing the historicity of texts through the lens of genre. See Mark David Rasmussen (ed.), *Renaissance Literature and Its Formal Engagements* (New York: Palgrave, 2002); Stephen Cohen, "Between Form and Culture: New Historicism and the Promise of a Historical Formalism," in *Renaissance Literature*, 17–41; and Jean Howard, "Shakespeare, Geography and the Work of Genre on the Early Modern Stage," *Modern Language Quarterly* 64 (2003): 299–322.

In particular, the essay focuses on two plays: Fletcher's *The Island Princess* (a play that disavows labor, especially global labor) and Shakespeare's *The Winter's Tale* (a play that attempts to situate domestic labor within global networks of trade), both written during a period in which England began to perceive itself as a significant participant in the emerging arena of global commerce.

My aim in juxtaposing these two plays is to address the following questions: first, why does tragicomedy have so much difficulty providing a straightforward account of labor? In other words, why is labor difficult to incorporate narratively and dramatically, and why is its value difficult to determine? Second, what can the study of English tragicomedy, with its complex and ambivalent accounting of global labor, tell us about the way in which the contributions of labor to profit, capital, and even the moral economy came to be understood in the early part of the seventeenth century? In the essay that follows, I explore how the incorporation of questions about labor's value into tragicomedy's generic requirement that loss produce return provides insight into the ways that early modern England grappled with potentially contradictory imperatives: to allow for new economic practices that would benefit investors and to acknowledge the value of labor.

A severe economic depression marked by high inflation and a shortage of coin and bullion marked the early decades of the seventeenth century. The relatively new English East India trade (the English East India Company conducted its first voyage in 1601) was considered especially to blame for the desperate economic situation of these years, because of the large quantity of coin and bullion being sent out of the country to conduct its trade. The East India Company's ventures were particularly bullion-intensive for two reasons: first, England's primary product—wool cloth—was not particularly vendible in the East Indies, making bullion necessary to buy the spices produced there.[7] Second, conducting overseas trade across such vast distances incurred great costs, much of which was expended on labor: in its first twenty years, the East India Company (EIC) established dozens of trading stations in Asia with over two hundred factors (i.e., agents). In addition, it employed considerable numbers of other workers both at home and abroad, for example, mariners and shipbuilders. The EIC was one of the largest employers in the London area.[8]

Given the bullion-intensive, high cost of overseas trade, the EIC and its defenders had to argue against the idea that sending money out of the country to conduct commerce with the East Indies constituted a loss. Thomas Mun, a director of the EIC and the most influential participant in the economic debate provoked by

---

[7]   For discussions of the East India Company's reliance on imports and re-exports rather than English exports, see K.N. Chaudhuri, *The English East India Company: The Study of an Early Joint-Stock Company, 1600–1640* (New York: August Kelley, 1965) and Robert Brenner, *Merchants and Revolution: Commercial Change, Political Conflict, and London's Overseas Traders, 1550–1653* (Princeton, NJ: Princeton University Press, 1993).

[8]   Chaudhuri, *English East India Company*, 21.

the crisis argues that these commercial outlays are not to be understood as losses, because the outlays undergo transformations:

> For it is in the stock of the Kingdom as in the estates of private men, who having store of wares, doe not therefore say that they will not venture out or trade with their mony (for this were ridiculous) but do also turn that into wares, whereby they multiply their Mony, and so by a continual and orderly change of one into the other grow rich, and when they please turn all their estates into Treasure; for they that have wares cannot want mony.[9]

Wares and money, which are at first represented as equivalents that can be transformed into one another, have the ability to valorize themselves through that very exchange: money is valuable because it can purchase wares, and wares are valuable because they are convertible into money. This argument seems tautological until we recognize that money has value because it can be used to purchase commodities, which can then be sold for more money.[10] Mun imagines economic exchange as a kind of magical process, whereby the transformation of one thing into another through continued circulation produces an excess—a profit by which treasure, even capital, is ultimately accumulated. Accordingly, he concludes, "why should we then doubt that our monys sent out in trade, must not necessarily come back again in treasure; together with the great gains … ?"[11]

Yet this logic begs the questions it seeks to answer: how is profit materially produced? And how is it determined to whom that value accrues? In order to answer these questions, we must understand the way in which the EIC considered wages paid to its employees as categorically separate from profits. Such a division provided the basis for the company's express prohibition against its employees privately venturing any of their own funds on Indian goods. This prohibition comes up repeatedly in the company's agreements with its factors and in the rules and regulations laid out in detail in the commissions for voyages:

> Those who live by our employment should deal with the commodities which we labor to get to produce meanes for payment of their wages and defraying of this our greate and costly voyage.[12]

That directors serve as both laborers and employers in this formulation produces an inversion in which the wages of hired workers are the fruits of the labor of those who employ them. In this passage, those who are receiving wages, while not

---

[9]   Mun, *England's Treasure by Forraign Trade* (1664) (Oxford: Basil Blackwell, 1928), 16. Though published in 1664, the text was written between 1623 and 1628.

[10]   This is in essence a noncritical, early version of Marx's "General Formula for Capital." Karl Marx, *Capital: A Critique of Political Economy*, vol. 1, trans. Ben Fowkes (New York: Vintage, 1976), 247–57.

[11]   Mun, *England's Treasure*, 19.

[12]   George Birdwood and William Foster (eds.), *The First Letter Book of the East India Company, 1600–1619* (London: Bernard Quartich, 1965), 344, March 1610.

receiving charity per se, nonetheless "live" by the good graces of the company, whose members themselves labor. The discourse of charity effectively elides the workers' labor from the formulation. Rather than adding value themselves, they are the company's beneficiaries. By eliminating the addition of value from the purview of the worker, wages are categorically divided from profits.

The value of this labor is further mystified by the company's financial structure. Because it was a joint-stock, the EIC was able to have subscribers who were not merchants, but only investors with no other tie to the work of the company. It is the money of these investors, then, that labors. Thus, the transformation of money into more money and reusable money (i.e., capital) is itself also the product of that initial outlay. In Mun's terms, money sent out comes back enhanced. Such a circular logic enables an economic system in which profit is understood to belong to money, or to be the result of the outlay of money and not to the labor that actually adds value.[13] Indeed, the commercial definition of "to invest" is "the outlay of money in the *expectation* of a profit," a definition coined in the correspondence of the EIC in 1613.[14]

This transformed capital in no way belongs to the mariners, or shipbuilders and other workers whose labor is (at least theoretically) paid for. In the accounting of the EIC, laborers are divided from the means of production and from the profits or value they add to "natural" products. This discounting of labor applied to the native inhabitants of the lands where the EIC traded as well. Indeed, Mun claims that "natural wealth" makes "people careless, proud and given to all excesses"; whereas artificial wealth (which he defines as "manufactures and industrious trading with forraign commodities") "enforceth vigilancy, literature, arts, and policy."[15] Implicit in Mun's distinction is not just potential racial and ethnic stereotyping, but a literal discounting of the labor of the native inhabitants of the lands where the company's products grow. Mun does not even imagine the possibility that the growth of spices is labor-intensive. He also argues that the trade in these products results in more economic profit for England than for the countries where they "naturally appertain."[16] Clearly the two claims are linked. The purchase of goods to be resold at a higher value is more profitable than merely selling things that grow naturally; the former depends on English industriousness (conceived as an abstract virtue, rather than as a specific form of labor), which Mun then contrasts

---

[13]   More than two centuries later, Marx would argue that profit on capitalist investment (i.e., surplus value) is the result of unpaid labor. What we can see here is how the logic that would support denying the value of labor develops.

[14]   *Original Correspondence of the English East India Company*, India Office Records, vol. 2, 102. For an expanded discussion of the significance of the emergence of the commercial usage of "investment," see Forman, *Tragicomic Redemptions*, especially the Introduction and Chapter 5. See also my "Transformations of Value and the Production of 'Investment' in the Early History of the East India Company," *Journal of Medieval and Early Modern Studies* 34 (2004): 611–41.

[15]   Mun, *England's Treasure*, 81–2.

[16]   Ibid., 10.

with the excesses and laziness of those who live in regions where products grow without the need for manufacture.

While Mun is not wrong about for whom the trade is more profitable, he is wrong about the way that spices are grown and harvested. Contrary to Mun's assumptions, the growing of pepper, whose import and re-export was crucial to the success of the EIC, is quite labor intensive: land needs to be cleared, and vines planted. Those vines then need to be kept clear of weeds and trained for four to seven years before they mature. Berries then need to be picked, dried, sifted, and marketed.[17] Pepper does not, as we say, "just grow on trees."

Indeed, The radical expansion of global, overseas trade in black pepper had considerable effects both on those who performed these tasks and on the profits they derived from the sale of pepper. Initially native only to India, black pepper in the sixteenth and seventeenth centuries became a major export of Southeast Asia. The first imported crop of the Indonesian archipelago to move from family gardens to widespread commercial planting, the cultivation of pepper had especially significant effects on the valuing of female labor. Traditionally involved in many aspects of growing and selling pepper, women in Sumatra (the area most well known for its pepper exports) became increasingly marginalized in its merchandizing. This process of marginalization began with the increased demand from Portuguese traders, which resulted in a shift to larger scale plantations and the need to sell product at greater distances from the household. Since women needed to labor closer to home, their participation was greatly diminished. Women were pushed further to the periphery in the seventeenth century when the Dutch and English began to dominate the trade. They attempted to negotiate monopoly contracts with rulers and preferred to trade with men rather than women. The latter were then relegated to more menial tasks, with female slaves sifting and bagging pepper. (Slaves, housed and fed by growers, were often sent by rulers to help with the increased demand.) Because women lost control of the pepper they grew as it went to market, their labor became increasingly alienated, creating surplus value that would accrue primarily to the Dutch and English East India Companies, then to native, male inhabitants. The labor of women of the lower classes was most severely alienated. Some courtly women were able to invest, but most merely labored, some as slaves. Whereas the EIC categorically divided the labor of its employees from its profits, and distinguished between the labor of English and native inhabitants, in actuality further distinctions of gender and among classes of women in the valuing of labor developed as a result of the global trade in spices.

By incorporating questions about labor's value into tragicomedy's generic requirement that loss produce returns, the plays I discuss in the remainder of this essay help to elucidate how and why England's emergent, global commerce depended on this complex accounting for, and discounting of, labor. These plays

---

[17]   Barbara Watson Andaya, "Women and Economic Change: The Pepper Trade in Pre-modern Southeast Asia," *Journal of the Economic and Social History of the Orient* 38 (1995): 165–90. Much of the factual information in the following discussion about labor and gender in the cultivation of pepper in Sumatra is taken from this article.

allow us to see how accounting for indigenous labor may disrupt the fantasy that global trade necessarily produces prosperous English investors, and how that fantasy may be rescued by reintroducing domestic labor into the equation.

I begin with Fletcher's *The Island Princess* (1623–1624), the first English play to be set in the Spice Islands of the East Indies. Taking a familiar romance narrative in which the titular princess is the source of competition among a number of suitors, *The Island Princess* relocates the genre, situating it within the context of the European exploitation of the Spice Islands and the continuing conflicts among the islands themselves. The play thus takes as its context the struggles over the islands' extraordinarily valuable commodities and engages with England's debates over the profitability of these trades and the labor necessary to conduct them. After the play's romance obstacle is overcome, the villainous Governor of one of the play's warring islands introduces tragic potential by poisoning the relationship between the other island and its Portuguese trading partners.[18] (In actuality, these islands often signed exclusive trading agreements with European countries in exchange for defense against other islands as well as for defense against other European nations.)[19] Disguised as a Moorish priest, the Governor recounts the Portuguese involvement in the islands as a shift from friendly traffic to a form of subjection: the Portuguese, he says, "suckt the fat and freedom / Of this most blessed Isle." In general terms, he envisions a "faire fac'd Prologue to a further mischiefe."[20] He thus imagines a counter-tragicomic genre, a comic-tragedy that has the potential to overtake the play.

---

[18] In the play, all of the European characters are Portuguese. Shankar Raman persuasively argues, however, that it is possible to read the play's hero Armusia as representative of the English newcomers. *Framing "India": The Colonial Imaginary in Early Modern Culture* (Stanford: Stanford University Press, 2001). For additional insightful readings of the play's complex negotiations among European nations and the Spice Islands, see Michael Neill, "'Material Flames': The Space of Mercantile Fantasy in John Fletcher's *The Island Princess*," *Renaissance Drama* 27 (1999): 19–31 and Ania Loomba, "'Break Her Will and Bruise No Bone Sir': Colonial and Sexual Mastery in Fletcher's *The Island Princess*," *Journal for Early Modern Cultural Studies* 2 (2001): 68–108.

[19] For example, a letter from the King of Ternate to James expresses his sadness that he cannot allow the English to set up a factory because of a prior treaty with the Dutch in which the Ternatans agreed to trade with the Dutch exclusively in return for help against the Portuguese. They say that they are thus "enforst against [our] liking" to say no. A letter from the island of Tidore, in contrast, asks for help from the English against the Dutch who have sided with Ternata against them, and who "jointly together have overrun and spoyled part of our country … and are determined to destroy both us and our subjects." See Henry Middleton, *The Last East-Indian Voyage Containing Much Varietie of the State of the Severall Kingdomes Where They Have Traded: with the Letters of Three Severall Kings to the Kings Majestie of England, Begun by One of the Voyage: Since Continued out of the Faithfull Observations of Them that are Come Home* (London, 1606), K3v, K4r.

[20] John Fletcher, *The Island Princess,* in *The Dramatic Works in the Beaumont and Fletcher Canon*, vol. 5, (ed.) George Williams (Cambridge: Cambridge University Press, 1966), 4.1.49–50, 60. All further references are cited in the text.

The play, however, never represents this subjection, whether in the form of restrictions on the islanders' choice of trading partners, or of the alienated conditions under which the native inhabitants labor in the production of spices. In order to explore why the play does not account for this labor, or for labor in general, let us consider the one passage in which at least the absence of labor is invoked. These lines are also those that most explicitly refer to spices, the commodities that have made the island a center of global trade and conflict. Ruminating on the island's fecundity—that is, on its "natural" products—the play's Portuguese hero, Armusia, speaks his opening lines:

> The treasure of the Sun dwels here, each tree
> As if it envied the old Paradice,
> Strives to bring forth immortall fruit; the spices
> Renewing nature, though not deifying,
> And when that fals by time, scorning the earth,
> The sullen earth, should taint or sucke their beauties,
> But as we dreamt, for ever so preserve us.
> Nothing we see, but breeds an admiration;
> The very rivers as we floate along,
> Throw up their pearls, and curle their heads to court us. (1.3.19–28)

This passage, especially the section regarding the spices, is difficult (if not impossible) to parse grammatically. To attempt a paraphrase: recalling the trees that strive to imitate those of Eden, the spices have a renewing effect. They scorn the earth's power by not rotting when they fall to it. Borrowing from the rhetoric of wonder so often used in narratives of travel and discovery in the period, Armusia imagines that spices, whose extraordinarily high resale value in Europe was the reason for the establishment of trades to the East Indies, have extraordinary powers.

The spices belong to a postlapserian world, one that would be marked by the introduction not only of mortality, which is invoked by the passage, but also of labor, which is conspicuously not. Although the earth's potential to corrupt and corrode recalls the Fall, the implications of this reference are largely mitigated by the spices' restorative function. If the spices are the referent for "that" preceding falls (although the referent is unclear, no other possibility makes logical sense) and the subject of "preserve," which is likely given the existing association between spices and preservation, the spices end up preserving the Portuguese. Yet the inscrutability of the passage's grammar and logic renders the manner in which the spices preserve the Portuguese unclear. The poetic vehicle and dramatic medium for the spices' effects—dreams and the passage's inscrutability—suggest that a sort of magical transformation, rather than the labor necessary to grow and harvest spices, lends power to falling spices that would otherwise be a sign or source of loss.

The very next lines reinforce and extend the power of natural products to preserve and to profit the Portuguese. These lines bear repeating:

Nothing we see, but breeds an admiration;
The very rivers as we floate along,
Throw up their pearls, and curle their heads to court us.

Whatever uneasiness the play registers regarding the potential for loss invoked by the falling spices disappears in this image. The striving and falling of the earlier lines are reconfigured in the image of pearls that rise. These pearls are not harvested from riverbeds; they are thrown or cast upwards by them. While this image explains how the pearls are free to "circulate" (and thus to be transferred from the possession of the native inhabitants to the Portuguese) it also suggests that the islands' commodities make their way into Portuguese hands through the natural agency of the rivers (the medium of their circulation) rather than through that of human subjects—native or otherwise. The point here is not simply that the objects become possessions of the Portuguese, but that they do so without labor. If the image of the spices raises questions about labor's presence (why are they falling, and is anyone picking them up?) the image of the pearls does away with those questions' necessity.

Similarly, as the passage progresses from spices to pearls, the location of inherent value shifts from the objects themselves to the Portuguese. The spices have a kind of agency; they actively preserve the Portuguese. Reversing cause and effect, the rivers throw up the pearls *because* of the Portuguese nobility, whose presence they sense. Whatever value the spices transfer to the Portuguese appears already inherent in them by the end of the passage, and whatever threats are posed by the fallen and potentially rotting spices in the absence of labor is erased in the final image. Value inheres not only in these "natural" objects, but also in the Portuguese themselves; labor-free circulation guarantees the surplus value accrued by the latter.

The negative effects of the Fall suggested by the image of the fruit trees and fallen spices are transformed into treasure that ultimately accrues to the Portuguese. In tragicomic fashion, the threat of loss—in this case, mortality and the necessity of labor—transforms into something more prosperous. Only the fortunate aspects of the Fall remain intact. Nothing rots, everything yields treasure—and all without labor. Indeed, it is through the disavowal of labor that this passage translates the language of discovery and encounter (which emphasizes plenitude) into that of trade and global capitalism (which emphasizes the transformation of loss into profit). Central to the emerging commercial concept of "investment" was the idea that initial loss not be understood as an isolated and potentially cataclysmic event. Instead, the developing economic theories conceived investment as the transformation of that deficient beginning into a different, more prosperous ending.

The prosperous return in the passage above, essential to the genre of tragicomedy, allows us to glimpse the transfer and transformation of labor's value necessary to the developing logic of global capitalism in which the value of goods seems to belong rightfully to the subjects who trade or invest in them. Indeed, the river, as circulating medium, produces value in a manner analogous to that described by Mun in his defense of the East Indies trade. Yet the river's transformation of potential loss into profit goes even further in that value here accrues directly to the stand-ins for the company itself, whereas in Mun the value accrues to the money invested. By reading this image in relation to the EIC's categorical division of profit from labor, we can see how a class of increasingly endowed merchant-capitalists, who seem not to be dependent on the laborers they employ, can be conceived. Reading this tragicomedy in conversation with early documents pertaining to global trade, we can see how profitable investment and global capitalism are made possible by the simultaneous distinguishing of what we would now call third world workers from those of the industrious first world and the separation of wages from profits in general, which then partially erases the difference between English and East Indian workers, at least in terms of the financial valuing of their labor. The destiny of global workers, that is, of workers who travel the globe or those who work on products that travel the globe is united in what is for them a comic-tragedy.

Nonetheless, *The Island Princess*'s discounting of labor depends on its location in a land far away that has little resemblance to that of home. What happens when the genre tries to imagine more familiar forms of labor that take place in a locale that resembles home? How does the genre of tragicomedy negotiate the effects of global trade on domestic labor? Even more to the point, what happens when global trade and its profits are brought back into contact with the domestic economy? The following section explores how domestic labor is tragicomically transformed by its interdependence on a global economy.

In his prologue to the tragicomic *Mydas*, John Lyly identifies foreign trade as the reason for tragicomedy's existence and as a threat to domestic labor: "Traffic and travel hath woven the nature of all nations into ours, and made this land like arras, full of device, which was broadcloth, full of workmanship ... if we present a mingle-mangle our fault is to be excused, because the whole world is become a hodgepodge."[21] Lyly's concern is that global trade adulterates English culture, threatening the solid workmanship that has provided the foundation of the English economy: the production of sturdy broadcloth is replaced by contrived and superfluous luxury. He connects this economic problem to the aesthetic one of tragicomedy as a mixed genre or generic "hodgepodge," while pointing to the transformative potential of both. The shift from broadcloth to arras suggests a fall from grace, but it also scripts mixed genres in general, and tragicomedy in particular, as the transformation of broadcloth into a higher form of art (an "arras") that develops through intercultural contact and commerce. He thus suggests a tragicomic potential for a domestic economy and its labor that are interdependent on global commerce. Loss can be transformed into profit, and labor that is devalued in one arena has the potential to be revalued elsewhere or in another form.

---

[21]   John Lyly, *Midas*, (ed.) David Bevington (Manchester: Manchester University Press, 2000), Prologue in Paul's (13–15, 20–22). An arras is a tapestry that has a story woven into it.

The Winter's Tale is a tragicomedy that responds to the perceived threat posed by global trade to domestic labor—namely, that the latter will be discounted or made less useful by the former—by imagining the transformation of the domestic economy as a result of global trade. Whereas the transformation of loss into profit in *The Island Princess* cannot accommodate an acknowledgment of labor, Shakespeare's *The Winter's Tale* takes its tragicomic turn just as labor is introduced into the narrative.[22] After three acts consisting of a downward spiral of losses at King Leontes's Sicilian court, the play's third act ends with a shepherd and his son discovering Perdita, the infant daughter King Leontes forced into abandonment, and the box of gold left with her. The next act, which takes place not in the tragic world of Sicilia, but in the seemingly more pastoral world of Bohemia, centers on a sheep-shearing festival—a community celebration of labor and its products.

In his first lines, Autolycus (who might be said to structure the fourth act and the tragicomic resolution of the play as a whole) announces his past and present occupations: "I have served Prince Florizel" and "my traffic is sheets."[23] He is also a thief and peddler of ballads, occupations emphasized throughout the fourth act. The first lines of the shepherd's son (i.e., Perdita's brother) in this scene also invoke labor and traffic. He crosses paths with Autolycus while engaged in the mathematical quandary of trying to ascertain how much wool shorn from his father's flocks will be needed to buy the food to furnish the sheep-shearing festival: "Every 'leven wether tods, every tod yields pound and odd shilling. Fifteen hundred *shorn*, what comes the wool to? … I cannot do't without counters" (4.3.30–32, 34, emphasis added). The shepherd's son is trying to figure how many pounds of wool are gained by the shearing of 1500 sheep and how much money those pounds of wool will bring him. Put another way, he is attempting to account for the value of labor, or at least the profits derived from the sale of labor's products. Yet the son's inability to complete the calculations (at least without the help of counters) suggests that accounting for labor might not be a straightforward affair.

The sheep-shearing scene, which follows this encounter, invites its audience to consider how England's current economic conditions were affecting domestic labor patterns and value. Wool was England's primary domestic product and export, and the decline of wool sales was one of the contributing factors to England's domestic woes. Autolycus, who is about to rob the son, is an itinerant and a thief, a quintessential "masterless man," feared to be at best idle, at worst a vagabond, and either way a threat to the productivity and well-being of the commonwealth. One of the most visible causes of masterlessness in the period was the enclosure

---

[22] See the opening of Michelle Dowd's essay in this volume for the suggestion that imagined female servant labor also helps to effect the generic transition away from tragedy.

[23] All citations of *The Winter's Tale* are from *The Norton Shakespeare: Based on the Oxford Edition*, (eds.) Stephen Greenblatt, et al. (New York: Norton, 1997), 4.3.13, 23. All further references are cited in the text.

of land for the grazing of sheep, necessary to wool production. Enclosures pushed poorer farmers off common land, leaving them to find other means of survival. It is to this problem that Thomas More refers in the *Utopia* when he says that men are being devoured by sheep.[24] Marx likewise refers to the process of enclosure when he argues that primitive accumulation—the divorcing of the worker from the ownership of the conditions for the realization of their labor—is necessary for the creation of a wage labor force.[25] Yet as Michael Bristol points out, sheep-shearing depended on a significant amount of temporary wage labor and, I would add, the very wage laborers that the enclosures produced.[26] Such circularity is reproduced in the son's purchase of foodstuffs as partial payment for the laborers who (according to More's *Utopia*) the sheep themselves devour. Theoretically, these dried fruits and spices would be paid for with the proceeds of the previous sale of wool and thus would be the fruits of prior labor—that is, surplus value (labor that remains un(der)paid)—re-employed as largesse to feed and thus reproduce still more labor for future sheep-shearings in order to generate even more profits that would accumulate from them. As a masterless person who is subject to the forces of the market, on the one hand, and one who steals from laborers, on the other, Autolycus might be read as an allegory of both the production of surplus value and the theft on which it depends. Autolycus in this sense acts as the usurper of his own surplus value. (After all, "Autolycus," from the Greek, means "self wolf.")

Moreover, the exchange of wool for money to buy currants, rice, and spices links England's domestic labor to its participation in global trade. When the shepherd's son gives up on his calculations, he immediately turns his mind to the task his sister assigns him—the purchasing of foodstuffs for the sheep-shearing festival:

> Let me see, what am I to buy for our sheep shearing feast? Three pounds of sugar, five pounds of currants, rice—what will this sister of mine do with rice, but my father has made her mistress of the feast ... I must have saffron to colour the warden pies, mace, dates, none—that's out of my note; nutmegs, seven; a race or two of ginger ... . (4.3.34–7, 41–3)

Though the play does not insist on the connection, one is invited to assume that the proceeds from the sale of the wool will be used to purchase the items on the son's list. Significantly, the products purchased to reproduce these laborers are primarily luxury, imported food products, many of them coming from the West or East Indies (ginger, nutmeg, saffron, rice, sugar) or the Levant (the great demand for currants may have inaugurated England's direct trade there).[27] The domestic

---

[24] Thomas More, *Utopia*, (ed.) Robert M. Adams (New York: Norton, 1975).

[25] Marx, *Capital*, vol. 1, 874–5.

[26] Michael Bristol, "In Search of the Bear: Spatiotemporal Form and the Heterogeneity of Economies in *The Winter's Tale*," *Shakespeare Quarterly* 42 (1991): 145–67.

[27] On the English trade in currants, see J. Theodore Bent, "The English in the Levant," *English Historical Review* 5 (1890): 654–64.

economy is here intricately intertwined with global commerce. The gravitational force of the latter is so powerful that Bohemia, which was actually landlocked, gets pulled to a sea-coast in the world of the play. Domestic labor is thus also global labor here, not in the sense that laborers travel from one country to another to find work (though the increased production of many of the commodities listed above required the movement of laborers, many to be slaves), but because the importation and consumption of foreign products is revealed to be necessary to the reproduction of workers at home—and not just any workers, but those in England's traditional, primary industry.

The pull of the global economy is strong, but the domestic economy puts its effects to good use. Spices not only preserve as they do in *The Island Princess*; they participate in the reproduction of labor that would at least theoretically allow for the purchase of ever more spices. The wealthy shepherd and his son (with the help of Perdita's gold they have grown to an "unspeakable estate") exchange their proceeds from the wool sale for spices and exotic dried fruits, but the result is not waste: it is the reproduction (and entertainment) of their own labor force. Unlike Lyly's arras, which threatens to unravel the fabric of the English commonwealth, what we are served up here is a festival whose function is to strengthen bonds among different classes and to stimulate the domestic economy. In the tragicomic spirit, all of the expenditure on foreign goods is transformed into something seemingly more valuable within England's domestic economy: surplus value is redeployed to produce more workers, who will then produce still more surplus value, in a cycle of increase that mirrors the relationship Mun establishes between wares and money. The tragicomic potential of the loss of Perdita and her wealth reverses the threat Lyly voices, and the play thereby imagines a global economy that preserves the faltering domestic one. The reproduction of labor becomes a vehicle for that vision. It is not so much that labor is valued per se, but that its fortification and reproduction become vehicles for imagining how the global economy can be put in the country's service.[28] The play's fantasy says nothing about what to do about the reduced demand for wool, a problem that gets put aside as the regeneration of the workforce (a topic with more theatrical potential) takes center stage, and the play focuses instead on showing how surplus laborers who are no longer viable in one industry can be put to use in another: the cashiered servant becomes a thief and peddler just as farmers became sheep-shearers. Moreover, in these scenes laborers are useful not so much for the work they do, but as consumers of the products of a global economy.

---

[28] Indeed, as I mentioned above, increased labor was one of the justifications for sending money out of the country: in that case ships and shipbuilding employ the potentially idle poor. R.W.K. Hinton, "The Mercantile System in the Time of Thomas Mun," in *The Early Mercantilists*, (ed.) Mark Blaug (Hants, England: Edward Elger, 1991), 73. See also, Mun, *England's Treasure*, and Edward Misselden, *The Circle of Commerce, or the Balance of Trade, in Defence of Free Trade* (London, 1623).

This wish-fulfillment fantasy is both supported and undermined by the events of the festival and by the play's tragicomic and spectacular conclusion: Autolycus robs the son, who nonetheless seems to have the money to buy all of the things necessary for the festival. Autolycus calls attention to this problem, saying both that the son's "purse is not hot enough to purchase [his] spice" and that he plans to rob him and the sheep-shearers at the festival; he expects "the shearers [will] prove sheep" (4.3.109, 111). Unlike the relationship between spices and those they preserve, or pearls that enhance the value of venturers, sheep-shearers are collapsed into the commodity they produce, but do not sell. Moreover, the other sheep-shearers buy frivolous items and inauthentic ballads from Autolycus, who also uses the mesmerizing effects of his products to distract his audience and pick their pockets. The cycle of reproduction and investment is stalled through theft, and if the festival is supposed to bring different classes together, the focus of this one is the outrage of the king at his son's desire for Perdita, who is believed to be just a shepherd's daughter.

And yet, the old shepherd still has an unspeakable estate, produced in part by his investment in sheep enabled by Leontes's sending of Perdita and a box of gold across the sea. Leontes's action is careless, but the play transforms all of these losses into profitable investment, which is nonetheless also complexly intertwined with theft and particularly theft from those who labor. This complexity is at least partially attributable to the paradox at the heart of accounting for labor in a capitalist economy—a problem with which twenty-first century economists and politicians are still grappling. On the one hand, if we fully account for the value of labor, there is no profit for investors and the cycle of productivity is halted; on the other, discounting labor goes against a principle gaining ground in the early seventeenth century: putting people to work and valuing their labor is fundamental to the wellbeing of the commonwealth. The play calls attention to this paradox through Autolycus's discounting of his own labor, which is nonetheless necessary to the play's prosperous resolution. Though the plot depends on Autolycus's actions to bring all of the characters back to Sicilia, he generously disowns his role in the final discoveries: "But 'tis all one to me, for had I been the finder-out of this secret it would not have relished among my other discredits" (5.2.109–10).

What the play imagines, however, is not the mere elision of Autolycus's labor, but its transformation, so that surplus rematerializes elsewhere. This scene is followed by the play's final one, which centers on the revivification of the supposedly dead Hermione's statue. The statue is at first credited in relation to the value of the labor necessary to produce it. It is "a piece many years in doing and newly performed by that rare Italian master Giulio Romano" (5.2.86–8). Moreover, it is "masterly done," the product of the "carver's excellence" (5.3.65, 30). Yet the value of the statue as statue (that is, as a work of art) gives way to the theatrics of its animation, which is the mixing of art and life—that is, theater, a medium that depends on the laboring bodies of actors and thus the literal embodiment of artistic value. What is important is not the masterfully carved statue, but the performance of the return to life, which stands as emblem of tragicomic theater itself. The theater (or Shakespeare, at least) like Leontes, learns not just that money can be made through the "rational" process of investment, but also that there is profit to be made from spectacle effects. These effects are the surplus value that theater can produce when it transforms art into life, and life into death into life, through its own mystifying labor. Like the reproduction of sheep-shearers through imported foodstuffs, these spectacle effects create surplus value that conceals labor—that of the sculptor and that of the actor—the latter being necessary for magic to achieve its effects. Yet both forms of labor still seep through. Students often insist that the statue really does come to life (quite a laborious feat for an actor or a sculptor to pull off) and others insist that the ending is ambivalent, in that all of the losses, including the stolen labor, remain in the image of a work of art that is subject to the effects of time. (The play makes much of the fact that the statue represents an aged Hermione.)

In the image of the statue, I want to argue, the play struggles with the possibility of simultaneously creating profit and acknowledging labor. Tragicomedies like *The Winter's Tale*, with its (part tongue-in-cheek) attempt simultaneously to acknowledge labor and to imagine the transformability of loss into profit, and *The Island Princess*, with its conspicuous assignation of all value to European trading companies, work to come to terms with this paradox as the economy becomes increasingly global and complex and requires both greater funds of capital and movement of workers and products. The theater companies and their playhouses, many of them organized as joint-stocks like the newer trading companies, provide a potential arena in which to imagine a part for global trade that makes labor something of great account.

Chapter 14
Labor and Travel on the Early Modern Stage: Representing the Travail of Travel in Dekker's *Old Fortunatus* and Shakespeare's *Pericles*

Daniel Vitkus

"What does accursed greed for gold not drive men to do?"

Desire to have, doth make us much indure,
In travaile, toile, and labour voide of reste:
The marchant man is carried with this lure,
Throughe scorching heate, to regions of the easte.
— Geoffrey Whitney, *Emblemes* (1586), 179.

The many travel narratives written in early modern England have received much attention from scholars, but travel plays, as a sub-category of travel literature, have attracted scant critical interest. While there are numerous cultural histories of early modern travel that describe the attitudes expressed and experiences faced by sixteenth- and seventeenth-century voyagers, and there are many monographs and collections of essays on Renaissance travel writing, these existing studies say very little about how long-distance or overseas travel was portrayed in the theater.[1] There

---

[1] Book-length studies or collections of essays on early modern travel include: E.S. Bates, *Touring in 1600: A Study in the Development of Travel as a Means of Education* (Boston: Houghton Mifflin, 1912); Thomas Betteridge (ed.), *Borders and Travelers in Early Modern Europe* (Aldershot and Burlington, VT: Ashgate, 2007); Mary Baine Campbell, *Wonder and Science: Imagining Worlds in Early Modern Europe* (Ithaca: Cornell University Press, 1999); Chloe Chard, *Pleasure and Guilt on the Grand Tour: Travel Writing and Imaginative Geography, 1600–1830* (Manchester: Manchester University Press, 1999); Carmine G. Di Biase (ed.), *Travel and Translation in the Early Modern Period* (Amsterdam: Rodopi, 2006); Andrew Hadfield, *Literature, Travel, and Colonial Writing in the English Renaissance, 1545–1625* (Oxford University Press, 1998); Clare Howard, *English Travelers of the Renaissance* (London: John Lane, 1914); Gerald Maclean, *The Rise of Oriental Travel: English Visitors to the Ottoman Empire, 1580–1720* (New York: Palgrave, 2004); Antoni Maczak, *Travel in Early Modern Europe* (Cambridge, UK: Polity, 1995); Peter C. Mancall (ed.), *Bringing the World to Early Modern Europe: Travel Accounts and Their*

is, however, a discussion of "the dramatic form of journeys in English Renaissance drama" in an essay by Peter Holland, which surveys the journey motif and shows how various travel plays explore "the limitations of the representation of place."[2] Holland comments on a series of plays, reading them through the topos of the psychological journey that links geography, identity and recognition. He defines the stage journey as a formal device that separates characters (like the Antipholi in *The Comedy of Errors*, Viola and Sebastian in *Twelfth Night* or the four sons of the Old Earl of Boloigne in Thomas Heywood's *The Four Prentices of London*) and exposes those characters to a loss and recovery of identity during the course of their wanderings.[3] In this essay, rather than looking at the theatrical representation of travel from Holland's formal and psychological point of view, I will consider instead how the theatrical representation of long-distance travel represses or recognizes the actual toil and trouble that made early modern journeying possible. In doing so, I will show how the staging of travel referred to a set of ideological conflicts surrounding the labor, effort, and investment required to undertake profitable, long-distance enterprise.

As England expanded its global economy, there was a new tendency to glorify and idealize travel, to depict the resourceful traveler as a heroic figure, or at least as an admirable gatherer of both commodities and knowledge. This emergent effort to present the difficulty of travel as a heroic test, or to conceal the harsh labor and the high mortality rate that underpinned the profitability of commercial voyaging, was only partially successful. It was accompanied by voices of objection, protest

---

Audiences (Leiden and Boston: Brill, 2007); Jean-Pierre Maquerlot and Michele Willems (eds.), *Travel and Drama in Shakespeare's Time* (Cambridge: Cambridge University Press, 1996); Justin Stagl, *A History of Curiosity: The Theory of Travel 1550–1800* (Chur, Switzerland: Harwood, 1995); Anna Suranyi, *The Genius of the English Nation: Travel Writing and National Identity in Early Modern England* (Newark: University of Delaware Press, 2008); and Sarah Warneke, *Images of the Educational Traveler in Early Modern England* (Leiden and New York: Brill, 1995). For recent anthologies of Renaissance travel writing, see Andrew Hadfield (ed.), *Amazons, Savages & Machiavels: Travel & Colonial Writing in English, 1550–1630* (Oxford: Oxford University Press, 2001); Peter C. Mancall (ed.), *Travel Narratives from the Age of Discovery: An Anthology* (Oxford: Oxford University Press, 2006); and Kenneth Parker (ed.), *Early Modern Tales of Orient: A Critical Anthology* (New York: Routledge, 1999). On travel drama, see Parr's excellent introduction to *Three Renaissance Travel Plays*, (ed.) Anthony Parr (Manchester: Manchester University Press, 1995); William H. Sherman, "Travel and Trade," in *A Companion to Renaissance Drama*, (ed.) Arthur F. Kinney (Oxford: Blackwell, 2004), 109–20; and Claire Jowitt, *Voyage Drama and Gender Politics, 1589–1642: Real and Imagined Worlds* (Manchester: Manchester University Press, 2003).

[2]   Holland, "'Travelling Hopefully': The Dramatic Form of Journeys in English Renaissance Drama," in *Travel and Drama in Shakespeare's Time*, (eds.) Maquerlot and Willems, 162.

[3]   All quotations from Shakespeare's writings are taken from *The Norton Shakespeare: Based on the Oxford Edition*, (eds.) Stephen Greenblatt et al., 2nd edition (New York: W.W. Norton, 2008).

and denunciation; and we find various moments in voyage drama when the travails of travel (the impressment and exploitation of maritime laborers, the suffering and hunger in failed colonial or commercial outposts, the many dangers facing travelers of all social classes, etc.) erupt in representations of suffering and failure. The theater was an especially conflicted medium of representation in this regard because sometimes it revealed the difficult realities of travel, and at other times it made travel seem heroic, pleasurable or even effortless. After all, experiencing the illusion of travel through time and space was one of the core pleasures of playgoing. Spectators in the London playhouses participated in fantasies of painless travel: for instance, in Marlowe's *Tamburlaine* plays, playgoers watched as Tamburlaine and his conquering armies march across the map, or in Heywood's *The Fair Maid of the West*, the audience looks on as Bess sails from Foy in Cornwall to the Canary Islands and on to Morocco and Italy. In many early modern plays, travel is staged without acknowledging the tremendous time, cost and labor that were necessary in order to transport people to faraway destinations. Playgoers were frequently invited to enjoy the spectacle of spatial or temporal mobility and to participate in an imaginary experience of magical or effortless transportation from one distant "scene" to another, without considering the labor of mariners or the discomfort of travel on the road or the seas. Thus, in *Antony and Cleopatra*, the audience never hears any of the characters complain about the difficult and dangerous conditions of their trans-Mediterranean journeys—the action merely skips back and forth from Alexandria to Rome. Hamlet's encounter with pirates on his sea journey to England reminds the audience of the threat of piracy but in the end represents those pirates as helpful, deferential enablers of Hamlet's return to Denmark: they don't rape or pillage, but act as polite messengers. Some plays employ a Chorus to deliver metatheatrical speeches about travel through time and space, or use dumb shows to inform the audience of how time has passed and distances have been crossed between scenes.

Early modern drama does not always abstract or fetishize travel as a painless stage device or labor-free experience. In some plays, the plot relies on the fortune of the seas or the overland journey to separate characters or test them to their limits, and such plot devices also serve to indicate that real-world travel was laborious and dangerous. However hackneyed they may have been, playwrights' usage of the conventional romance devices of shipwreck or separation at sea (going back to Homer and Plautus), as well as the staging of episodic wanderings that took characters far from home, did point to the real and present danger faced by those who undertook long-distance travel in pre-modern times. Examples include Lear and Gloucester wandering on the heath as they make their way to Dover, and Fletcher and Massinger's *The Sea Voyage*, in which "the furious sea and famine/ Strove which should first devour" (4.1.24–5) a group of castaways stranded on an island off the coast of Brazil.[4] Both plays represent the journey as a severe test of

---

[4]   John Fletcher and Philip Massinger, *The Sea Voyage*, in *Three Renaissance Travel Plays*, (ed.) Parr.

body and spirit, and not as an effortless leap over land and sea. Storms at sea in *Othello* and *The Tempest*, as well as the opening scene of *The Sea Voyage*, work to remind the audience of the kind of terrifying ordeal that could ensue on any long-distance voyage when storms arose without warning.[5]

These divergent modes of representing the journey on stage (as painful ordeal and as fantastic fun) indicate the ideological tensions and contradictions produced under an emergent capitalism in the early modern context. I will argue here that these opposing tendencies—either to occlude or to emphasize the suffering and hardship of travel—partake of a larger crisis involving the new status of labor in a society that was turning toward capitalism as it formed stronger ties with the global maritime economy. By the late sixteenth century, English merchants and investors increasingly exploited the labor power of wage laborers whose surplus labor enabled the primitive accumulation of capital by those who invested in the joint-stock overseas enterprises.[6] The enclosure of common lands, and the appropriation of that land for pasture to support the production of exportable woolen products, helped to create a growing class of "masterless men" who could then be employed as agricultural or maritime wage laborers. I concur with those scholars who have argued that we can trace the origins of our current global economy and its transnational migration of workers back to the early modern expansion of the maritime economy.[7] The "spatial crisis" of post-1492 European expansionism led to the development of a world-wide network of long-distance maritime trade with new forms of mobile labor, a restructured transnational credit matrix, and a huge increase in the overseas transportation and exchange of commodities (including the transportation of indentured servants and slaves described by Amanda Bailey in her essay in this collection.)[8] A gradual change began to take place, from a feudal

---

[5]   On the significance of the storm in the first scene of *The Tempest*, see Hawkes's essay in this volume.

[6]   On primitive accumulation and the role of the merchant classes and the joint-stock companies, see Robert Brenner, *Merchants and Revolution: Commercial Change, Political Conflict, and London's Overseas Traders, 1550–1653* (New York: Verso, 2003) and Ellen Meiksins Wood, *The Origin of Capitalism: A Longer View* (New York: Verso, 2002).

[7]   Bartolovich, Netzloff, Forman, and Balasopolos all offer convincing arguments for a linkage between domestic and overseas commerce during the emergence of capitalism. See Crystal Bartolovich, "Travailing Theory: Global Flows of Labor and the Enclosure of the Subject," in *A Companion to the Global Renaissance: English Literature and Culture in the Era of Expansion*, (ed.) Jyotsna Singh (Oxford: Wiley-Blackwell, 2009); Mark Netzloff, *Internal Colonies: Class, Capital, and the Literature of Early Modern Colonialism* (New York: Palgrave, 2003); Valerie Forman, *Tragicomic Redemptions: Global Economies and the Early Modern English Stage* (Philadelphia: University of Pennsylvania Press, 2008); and Antonis Balasopoulos, "'Suffer a Sea-Change': Spatial Crisis, Maritime Modernity, and the Politics of Utopia," *Cultural Critique* 63 (2006): 122–56.

[8]   Balasopoulos employs the term "oceanic turn" in his article, "'Suffer a Sea-Change.'" See also Dennis Flynn and Arturo Giráldez, "Born with a 'Silver Spoon': The Origin of World Trade in 1571," in *Metals and Monies in an Emerging Global Economy,*

order in which land comprised the primary material basis of political and economic power, to a new order in which control over the sea took on a new importance. The ideological implications of this new maritime activity were enormous, comprising an "oceanic turn," according to Ulrich Kinzel.[9] The London theater was one site of cultural production in which this oceanic turn was represented and tested in travel plays that conveyed both the pleasures and perils of the new maritime mobility and the cross-cultural contact that ensued.

In order to understand the conflicting theatrical representations of travel (the voyage as hard labor versus travel as pleasurable experience), and place them in the context of emergent capitalism, I want to look first at the changing meaning of the word "travel" in the early modern period. Today the word "travel" is frequently associated with leisure and pleasure, but in the sixteenth and seventeenth centuries "travel" had not yet been distinguished in spelling, pronunciation, or meaning from what later came to be spelled "travail" as a distinct word with a different meaning. The original root of the word is the medieval Latin "trepalium," a three-pronged instrument of torture. Various forms of this root passed into the romance languages, and then from Old French into Middle English. In medieval English a variety of spellings of the verb "travail" came to signify "afflict, vex, trouble, harass, weary" and then later, "to toil, work hard, labour" (*OED*, "travail, *v.*," etymology). By the late sixteenth century, three main strands of signification had emerged for the English word "travail" (and its variant spellings): 1) hard work or effort in general, 2) the work and effort required to travel from one place to another, and 3) the pain and "labor" of child-birth (*OED*, "travail, *n.*," I. 1–4 and "travail, *v.*," I. 1–2). All three definitions were considered consequences of the Fall: the forced removal from Eden to wander through a world in which all must labor to earn their bread in the sweat of their brow, and in which women must give

---

(eds.) Flynn and Giráldez (Brookfield, VT: Variorum, 1997), 259–79, and Chloe Houston, "Traveling Nowhere: Global Utopias in the Early Modern Period," in *A Companion to the Global Renaissance*, (ed.) Singh, 82–98. Rediker and Linebaugh have shown how the enclosure of common lands at home produced a newly-uprooted labor force who became available for hire as workers in the port communities and sailing vessels that served merchant capitalism. Marcus Rediker and Peter Linebaugh, *The Many-Headed Hydra: Sailors, Slaves, Commoners, and the Hidden History of the Revolutionary Atlantic* (Boston: Beacon Press, 2000). On the link between "internal" and "external" colonies (i.e., between enclosure and plantation), see Crystal Bartolovich, "Travailing Theory" and Mark Netzloff, *Internal Colonies*.

9   Kinzel, "Orientation as a Paradigm of Maritime Modernity," in *Fictions of the Sea: Critical Perspectives on the Ocean in British Literature and Culture*, (ed.) Bernhard Klein (Burlington, VT: Ashgate, 2002), 28–48. See also Margaret Cohen, "The Chronotopes of the Sea," in *The Novel*, (ed.) Franco Moretti (Princeton: Princeton University Press, 2006), 647–65. Cohen sketches out a taxonomy of spatiality that includes "blue water," "the island," "the shore," and "the ship." The literary texts that she cites are examples of the post–1700 sea novel, but one could come up with historically specific versions of these spatial-narrative categories that would be based on earlier texts and contexts.

birth in pain. Job 5:7 declares, "Man is borne to travaile."[10] "Travel" as a separate word, untainted by the connotation of labor, toil, and suffering, only gradually achieved a distinct sense. For example, when Falstaff says in *2 Henry IV*, "Travel-tainted as I am" (4.3.40), he lies, not only about the distance he claims to have covered, but in asserting that he has been hard at work, or has suffered genuine hardship, on the field of battle.

Throughout the early modern period, the various spellings ("travail," "travayle," "travel," etc.) signified the labor, trouble, discomfort, hardship, and pain associated with travel. To be a "traveler/travailer" was to undertake the difficult and time-consuming work of moving overland on foot, by horse, by wagon or carriage, or over water by riverboat or by sea-going vessel. Even well-heeled travelers had to endure many hardships and dangers—risks of shipwreck, piracy, robbery, fraud, disease, harsh weather, and malnutrition.

As Ann Christensen points out, travel was not only difficult for those who wandered the muddy roads of England or sailed overseas, but also disrupted the "domestic economy" of wives and other dependents who remained in England while their husbands or fathers served as merchants or seaman on long-distance voyages, often resulting in suffering and deprivation.[11] Some sailors never returned, some were gone for years without word of their fate, while others were captured by pirates and held for ransom.[12] In a 1572 book of prayers written by Thomas Achelley, the following prayer was published, to meet the needs of those who traveled by sea:

---

[10]   In his discussion of work and play in Shakespeare's drama, Rutter points out that early modern England experienced a tension between an older notion that manual labor is God's curse, inflicted fully on the common people but mitigated for members of the aristocratic warrior class and priestly class, and a new mentality that asked all people, including the upper classes, to labor industriously in their calling. After the Reformation, he argues, the medieval "three estates" theory weakened as labor was increasingly described as a virtuous activity, and contrasted with "idleness." See Tom Rutter, *Work and Play on the Shakespearean Stage* (Cambridge: Cambridge University Press, 2008), 1–21. Rutter cites a passage from the new "Homily against Idleness," included in the expanded 1563 official *Book of Homilies*, which refers to "man, being born not to ease and rest, but to labour and travaile" (14).

[11]   Christensen, "'Absent, weak, or Unserviceable': The East India Company and the Domestic Economy in *The Launching of the Mary, or The Seaman's Honest Wife*," in *Global Traffic: Discourses and Practices of Trade in English Literature and Culture from 1550 to 1700*, (eds.) Barbara Sebek and Stephen Deng (New York: Palgrave, 2008), 117–36.

[12]   See Nabil Matar's chapter on "Barbary and British Women" in *Britain and Barbary, 1589–1689* (Gainesville: University Press of Florida, 2005). He argues that "Although the captivity of seamen and sailors was chiefly felt among ship owners and trading companies, it was also felt at the family and parochial levels" and especially by the wives of those seamen (76). Matar also discusses the travails of those British women who were taken captive and enslaved in Barbary.

I beseeche thee to be mine aide, and defence, in this daungerous viage, whiche I have presumed to take, reposing mine only trust and confidence in thy mercie, to be delivered and preserved from all maner daungers, and jeopardies, that may happen either upon the sea or on the drye lande. Thou knowest most mercifull Father, that all those that travayle by sea are subject to the hazarde of divers calamities, eyther to be tossed at the pleasure of the winde and waves, either to be dashed violently upon the mayne rockes, or to sticke in the quicke sandes, or to be dispoyled both of lyfe, and goodes, by the tyrannie of Pyrates.[13]

In the case of upper-class travelers like Fynes and Henry Moryson, their long-distance peregrinations were considered so risky that they took advantage of a financial arrangement available to those travelers who could put down a substantial sum of money in London before embarking and, if they returned with proof that they had reached their intended destination (Venice, Constantinople, Jerusalem or the like), they could collect as much as five times the amount they had deposited.[14] If they never returned, the broker kept the money. This practice is mocked in Ben Jonson's *Every Man Out of His Humor*, when the "vainglorious knight" Puntarvolo declares his plan "to travaile: and … I am determined to put forth some five thousand pound, to be paid me, five for one, upon the returne of my self, my wife, and my dog, from the Turkes court in Constantinople" (3.477).[15] It is also alluded to by Gonzalo in *The Tempest* when he refers to how "each putter-out of five for one" (3.3.48) brings back strange but true stories of outlandish wonders and exotic people encountered while traveling. Anne-Julia Zwierlein argues that such practices show how travel, time spent traveling, and human life itself were becoming commodified for the first time by early modern capitalists.[16] We see the labor of travel abstracted as an exchange-value in the marketplace, along with other new forms of investment, risk, hazard, and adventuring that came about as emergent capitalism forged its linkages with markets across the globe.

Long-distance travel was a dangerous, uncomfortable, labor-intensive activity, but for some the risk was worth taking because huge profits could accrue from a successful trip. For merchant investors who stayed at home, the risk of "no

---

[13] Achelley, *The Key of Knowledge Contayning Sundry Godly Prayers and Meditations, Very Necessary to Occupy the Mindes of Well Disposed Persons* (London, 1572), 192–3.

[14] See Moryson's detailed discussion of how he and his brother left considerable sums in London, to be repaid with interest on their return, or forfeited if they failed (as his brother did, who died on the road in Syria). Fynes Moryson, *An Itinerary Containing His Ten Yeeres Travell through the Twelve Dominions of Germany, Bohmerland, Sweitzerland, Netherland, Denmarke, Poland, Italy, Turky, France, England, Scotland & Ireland*, 4 vols. (Glasgow: James MacLehose and Sons, 1907), 1: 425–8.

[15] Jonson, *Every Man Out of His Humor*, in *Ben Jonson*, vol. 3, (eds.) C.H. Herford, Percy Simpson, and Evelyn Simpson (Oxford: The Clarendon Press, 1925–52).

[16] Zwierlein, "Shipwrecks in the City: Commercial Risk as Romance in Early Modern City Comedy," in *Plotting Early Modern London: New Essays on Jacobean City Comedy*, (eds.) Dieter Mehl, Angela Stock, and Anne-Julia Zwierlein (Aldershot and Burlington, VT: Ashgate, 2004), 75–94.

return" was merely a financial one: those who hazarded life and limb were the workers whose surplus labor was the basis of their masters' gain. According to Marx, "surplus labor" is the labor performed in excess of the "necessary labor" that is adequate merely to produce the worker's means of livelihood.[17] It is that extra labor, constituting a "surplus value," that allows the owners of the means of production to live off the labor of others if the owners can systematically seize that extra value. Thus, surplus labor is the fundamental source of the capitalist's profit, and its intensification in the early modern period is closely associated with the growth of commerce and the development of distinct social classes—the proletariat who sell their labor power, and the capitalist class who systematically expropriate the surplus value generated by the travail of the workers. Marx also points out that capitalism originated in the economic activity of buying in order to sell—this was one of the earliest forms of extracting surplus value. It was invented by merchants long before the emergence of capitalism, but it was taken to a new level of sophistication by the investors in the global joint-stock corporations, including companies like the East India Company who dealt in luxury goods and "the carrying trade." At the same time that capitalists extracted surplus value from the direct producers of commodities at home (for example, the laborers who manufactured exportable woolen goods), they also expropriated the surplus value of the work performed by seamen and shipwrights, and thirdly, they gained from exploitation of foreign labor (for instance the Asian workers who toiled in the pepper plantations of southeast Asia). This third form of exploitation is described by Marx in the *Grundrisse*: "not only individual capitalists, but also nations may continually exchange with one another, may even continually repeat the exchange on an ever-expanding scale, *without for that reason necessarily gaining in equal degrees*. One of the nations may continually appropriate for itself a part of the surplus labour of the other, giving back nothing for it in the exchange."[18] This kind of "unequal exchange" is greatly enabled by the system of investment in long-distance trade conducted by monopolistic interests like the East India Company. In his article, "A Multinational Corporation: Foreign Labor in the East India Company," Richmond Barbour shows how Muslim and Hindu workers from South Asia were recruited by the East India Company to aid in the spice trade and to replace the deceased mariners who had manned their ships when they set out from England.[19] Barbour's work on the East India Company helps us to see the layered

---

[17] See Marx's discussion of surplus value in *Capital*, vol. 3, part 1, where he writes, "The only way in which [the capitalist] can convert the value of his advanced variable capital into a greater value is by exchanging it for living labour and exploiting living labour." http://www.marxists.org/archive/marx/works/1894-c3/ch02.htm.

[18] Marx, *Grundrisse*, http://www.marxists.org/archive/marx/works/1857/grundrisse/ch17.htm#p872.

[19] In *A Companion to the Global Renaissance*, (ed.) Singh, 129–48. On the East India Company's early seventeenth-century system for the control of information and the production of profit, see Richmond Barbour, *Before Orientalism: London's Theatre of the East, 1576–1626* (Cambridge: Cambridge University Press, 2003), 156–61.

structure of surplus labor extraction under the joint-stock company: the corporate system pioneered by the Levant Company and East India Company in the late sixteenth and early seventeenth centuries was a system founded on the human suffering of ill-paid seamen. Their under-compensated labor made it possible to cross the vast distances between the "spice islands" and England without added expense for investors, and their great travail brought huge profits to company investors in London. Unlike the mariners and merchants who labored in their far flung trades, the early modern investor in overseas trade was in a position simply to wait and watch, and in that regard was not unlike spectators in the theater, who watched the action of travel unfold on stage. The toil, suffering, sickness, and death of the seamen hired to sail East India Company vessels, for example, could be understood by investors as a loss of effective service or of assets, and these losses were described in narrative "reports" or quantified and abstracted in written financial accounts.[20]

In a variety of plays, travel was enacted by means of the audience's imaginative participation, while various theatrical, imaginative devices were employed, sometimes to indicate, and sometimes to render invisible, the time, labor, and expense necessary to make a long-distance voyage. Although contemporary travel plays often aimed to produce a pleasing fantasy of instant, effortless mobility, they sometimes acknowledged the reliance of travelers on a transcultural, global network of labor. What we see happening during the Elizabethan and Jacobean periods is a tension between the notion of travel as labor or "travail" and, in contrast, an emerging, modern conception of travel's purpose as a satisfying venture, as commercial exchange, commodity acquisition, or knowledge acquisition. In many plays, this tension is resolved when the sacrifices and deprivations of travel are ultimately redeemed by the gains of those who endure and survive the test of travel. As Zachary Lesser and Valerie Forman have demonstrated, this fictional outcome was increasingly given generic form through the rise of the tragicomedy on the early seventeenth-century stage.[21] In the Jacobean theater, then, we see

---

[20] For a discussion of maritime labor that places it in the wider social context of the unsettled, working poor as a growing social class in seventeenth-century Britain, see Patricia Fumerton's chapter titled "Poor Men at Sea: 'Never to be worth one groat afore a beggar'," in *Unsettled: The Culture of Mobility and the Working Poor in Early Modern England* (Chicago: University of Chicago Press, 2006). Cheryl Fury provides a detailed description of the conditions of labor for Elizabethan seamen employed on long-distance voyages in *Tides in the Affairs of Men: The Social History of Elizabethan Seamen, 1580–1603* (Westport, CT: Greenwood, 2002). A list of the official monthly rates for seamen's wages in 1626 is given in M. Oppenheim (ed.), *The Naval Tracts of Sir William Monson*, 6 vols. (London: Navy Records Society, 1913), 3:185–6. According to that source, a common sailor's wages were fifteen shillings a month.

[21] According to Lesser, "The colonial ... tragicomedies of the 1620s functioned as another aesthetic form for naturalizing this counterintuitive imaginary. I am building here on the work of Forman, who has recently argued that the tragicomic transformation of apparent loss (tragedy) into the very engine of a redemptive comic ending mirrors the emergent

an inconsistent or contradictory representation that depicts travel as a painful or frightening experience, but simultaneously asserts a celebratory or redemptive meaning for travels that serve commercial or imperial purposes. Similarly, the editorial projects of Hakluyt and Purchas contained many descriptions of adversity within a larger framework of commercial enterprise and national ambition. Many of the narratives included in Purchas's 1625 compilation included descriptions of shipwreck, storm, piracy, and other difficulties, but Purchas claimed that through his labors readers could enjoy, "at no great charge," all of the intellectual benefits of travel without any of the physical or spiritual dangers.[22] The rhetoric used by Purchas to present his multi-volume collection of travel writings indicates the nationalistic and religious framework that had come, by 1625, to shape English perception of travel.

By 1625, the labor and suffering involved in travel had not become less dangerous or necessary (on the contrary), but the new commercial classes and their expanding system of surplus labor extraction were growing stronger, and so their power instigated and stimulated a discourse that could provide ideological support for their enterprises. As the upper-class merchants' profit increased through exploitation of the lower classes, slaves, and foreigners, the arduous travail of travel was abstracted or presented as an "adventure" on stage, taking fantastic leaps from place to place, but also demonstrating the travails involved in the episodic trials of picaresque or romance.[23] When early modern drama reminds the audience that travel is long and hard, it increasingly does so in a way that makes that hardship a noble or necessary sacrifice. In what follows, I will draw upon a variety of examples in order to explore the tension between theatrical fantasies that concealed the exploitation of maritime labor, on the one hand, and those moments in the plays that reveal the travail of mariners or the dependence of travelers on the labor of others.

As I mentioned above, in the Elizabethan and Jacobean theater, the illusion of travel is often invoked through the old theatrical device of the Chorus or some other allegorical persona who addresses the audience directly, asking them to participate in the dramatic illusion of time-space travel. Perhaps the most famous

---

idea of investment developed by ... the [East India Company]. Just as the ideology of investment transforms the outflow of bullion into the mechanism for increased profits, so too tragicomedy transforms loss into the mechanism for redemption (in both economic and moral terms.)" Zachary Lesser, "Tragical-Comical-Pastoral-Colonial: Economic Sovereignty, Globalization, and the Form of Tragicomedy," *ELH* 74 (2007): 894. Like Lesser, I am indebted to Forman's work on tragicomedy, investment, and redemption in early modern culture. See her recent study, *Tragicomic Redemptions*, as well as her essay in this volume.

[22]   Samuel Purchas, *Purchas his Pilgrimes* (London, 1625), 5.

[23]   See Nerlich's account of how the European literature of adventure changed with the emergence of capitalism in Michael Nerlich, *Ideology of Adventure: Studies in Modern Consciousness, 1100–1750*, 2 vols., trans. Ruth Crowley (Minneapolis: University of Minnesota Press, 1988).

instance of this device occurs in the Prologue to Shakespeare's *Henry V*, where the Chorus admits the inadequacy of the players within the space of the Globe's "wooden O" (Prol. 13) to bring to life the foreign battles of the past with full verisimilitude. The Chorus asks the audience to "work," using their "imaginary forces" (l. 18), to compensate for that lack: "For 'tis your thoughts that now must deck our kings, / Carry them here and there, jumping o'er times" (ll. 28–9). The spectators must labor in their minds to manufacture the dramatic illusion. In the Prologue to Act 2, the playgoers are told that they will travel from London to the port of Southampton and then to France and back, but are jokingly assured that they will not be made seasick in the process:

> There is the playhouse now, there you must sit,
> And thence to France shall we convey you safe,
> And bring you back, charming the narrow seas
> To give you gentle pass—for if we may
> We'll not offend one stomach with our play. (2.0.36–40)

In the play's final act, the Chorus continues to flatter the audience by invoking their power to "place" the king himself, and to "heave him away upon [their] winged thoughts / Athwart the sea" (5.0.8–9) from Calais to Blackheath. The time and effort required to travel is abstracted by the power of imagination and by the labor of the players for which the audience has paid. In this case, the commercial interests at stake in the war with France, and the play's topical references to the contemporary war effort against Spain, work to encourage a nationalistic unity and sacrifice that will redeem suffering with a victory over England's Catholic competitors.

In other plays, time and space are collapsed even further by the employment of magic or supernatural power. In Marlowe's *Faustus*, the magus uses his necromancy to enjoy a Grand Tour from Trier to Paris to the Rhine Valley, to Naples, Venice, Padua, and Rome (7.1–22), after which Mephistophiles returns from Constantinople in an instant to deal with Ralph and Rafe.[24] Faustus brings grapes from the other side of the earth "by means of a swift spirit I have" (11.22–3) to answer the craving of the pregnant Duchess of Vanholt. Not unlike the German magus who uses his art to "journey through the world and air" (Chorus 3.8), in *A Midsummer Night's Dream*, Robin Goodfellow can "put a girdle round about the earth / In forty minutes" (2.1.175–6). In David Hawkes's contribution to this volume, he points out the homology between the magical power of a Puck, a Prospero or a Faustus to create substance and value from "airy nothing" and the power of capitalism to do the same. Magical travel partakes of capitalism's reliance on what Hawkes terms the "efficacious power of performative representation," which in the form of money allows exchange value to conceal the extraction of surplus value from labor-power. According to Hawkes, "Theater depends on, and

---

[24] Christopher Marlowe, *Doctor Faustus*, (ed.) Roma Gill (New York: W. W. Norton, 1989).

therefore also inculcates, our ability to take signs for reality, to occlude essence beneath appearance: in short, to commodify experience" (see above 184–5). The theatrical illusion of instant travel is a sign that conceals the alienated labor that is actually necessary to "journey through the world" in pursuit of pleasure or profit.

The Elizabethan play that offers what is perhaps the most extended fantasy of instantaneous and labor-free travel is Thomas Dekker's *Old Fortunatus* (1599), in which the title character obtains from Fortune a magical purse that provides ten gold coins each time he puts his hand inside.[25] Fortunatus immediately declares his intention to put his endless supply of capital to work to "travell to the Turkish Emperor" (1.2.197) and then to visit other imperial courts. Through Fortunatus, the audience vicariously experiences world travel as a series of encounters with exotic wonders. As in *Henry V*, the audience is asked to assist in the magical transportation by using the power of imagination:

> The world to the circumference of heaven,
> Is as a small point in Geometrie,
> Whose greatnes is so little, that a lesse
> Cannot be made: into that narrow roome,
> Your quicke imaginations we must charme,
> To turne that world: and (turn'd) againe to part it
> Into large kingdoms, and within one moment,
> To carry Fortunatus on the wings
> Of active thought, many a thousand miles.
> Suppose then since you last beheld him here,
> That you have saild with him upon the seas,
> And leapt with him upon the Asian shores ... (2 Chorus.1–12)

As in *Henry V*, the audience is prompted to imagine a transoceanic journey, and this perspective is established by envisioning the world from an imperial point of view, one that makes the globe smaller so that it can be "turn'd ... / Into large kingdoms."

In the scene that follows, the spectators find Fortunatus at the court of the sultan of Babylon, where Fortunatus persuades the sultan to show him his greatest treasure, a "wishing Hat" (2.2.306) about whose magical powers the sultan tells him, "I (onely with a wish) am through the ayre, / Transported in a moment over Seas, / And over lands to any secrete place" (2.1.87–9). Fortunatus steals the magic hat and wishes himself home in Cyprus with his two sons. When he arrives there and reveals to his sons that he possesses the purse and hat, his son Ampedo urges him to remain at home: since he is an old man, reasons Ampedo, "those short lived minutes, / That dribble out your life, must needs be spent, / In peace not travel" (2.2.141–3). Though his virtuous son Ampedo counsels restraint and

---

[25]   Thomas Dekker, *Old Fortunatus*, in *The Dramatic Works of Thomas Dekker*, vol. 1, (ed.) Fredson Bowers (Cambridge University Press, 1953). All subsequent references are to this edition.

dismisses the pleasure of travel as vanity, Old Fortunatus will not be restrained and tells Ampedo, "thy soule is made of lead, too dull, too ponderous to mount up to the incomprehensible glorie, that travel lifts men to" (2.2.159–60). Here the play juxtaposes the contrasting understandings of travel—as the troublesome opposite of "peace" and as a means to "glorie."

Fortunatus's earlier travels, which were enabled by the gold-producing magical purse, are about to be accelerated to the speed of thought by the wishing hat. But before Fortunatus can begin, and just as he finishes declaring "In these two hands doe I gripe all the world" (2.2.218), Fortune and the Parcae visit Fortunatus in his pride to bring on his sudden death. His sons inherit the purse and hat, and with them the troubles that come from attachment to worldly things. Their father's choice of riches over wisdom haunts them as they journey to England, where the play continues to offer the fantasy of travel without travail. Ampedo and his brother Andelocia join an international cast of aristocrats at the English court, where Andelocia falls in love with the vain and greedy princess Agripyne. What at first seems a miraculous boon, like the magical returns or fortunes accrued by successful merchant-travelers, produces an ever more restless activity driven by desire, rather than quiescent satisfaction.

As the play moves toward its moralizing conclusion (Fortune and Vice are ultimately vanquished by Virtue), the folkloric fantasy of limitless riches and boundless travel becomes anchored in a cosmopolitan London where the courtiers consume exotic luxuries and where exchange-value rules the day. "There's nothing in the world, but may for gold be bought in England" (5.1.139–40), declares the rapacious Agripyne, who steals both the purse and hat from Andelocia. Andelocia recovers both by disguising himself, first as an Irish costermonger selling "Damasco apples" (they are really fruit from the Tree of Vice, and once eaten, cause Agripyne to grow horns), and then as a French doctor who says he can cure Agripyne's affliction but first must "buy many costily tings dat grow in Arabia, in Asia, and America" (5.1.137–8) to prepare a medicinal remedy. Once Andelocia has her in his power, he tells her, "Ile teach you to live by the sweate of other mens browes" (5.2.7). The virtuous Ampedo burns the hat, but in the end Andelocia's unwillingness to relinquish the purse leads to the deaths of both brothers.

Old Fortunatus is a text that never quite resolves the tension between travel as a means to pleasure and knowledge acquisition, on the one hand, and as an extreme form of worldly desire that can only result in a fall from pride into woe and death, on the other. It offers the folkloric fantasy of globe-trotting, but ultimately locates that fantasy in an acquisitive English court that prioritizes "riot" and the consumption of luxury goods over wisdom and virtue. The purse becomes a symbol of how social-climbers and ambitious courtiers "live by the sweat of other men's browes." The adventuring, acquisitive model for travel, embodied by Andelocia, is held up for censure, and the play asserts an old-fashioned moral—that those who rise to wealth through the aid of Fortune are equally liable to fall by her hand as well. The play links mobility to wealth, and as in the homiletic message of Whitney's emblem, the "accursed greed for gold" drives men to misfortune (Figure 14.1). At the end of *Old Fortunatus*, a wrathful Fortune holds up the purse, declaring to the English king and courtiers,

> This prodigall purse did Fortunes bounteous hand
> Bestow on them, their ryots made them poore,
> And set these markes of miserable death,
> On all their pride, the famine of base gold
> Hath made your soules to murders hands be sold,
> Onely to be cald rich. But[,] Ideots [,] see
> The vertues to be fled, Fortune hath causd it so,
> Those that will all devowre, must all forgoe. (5.2.210–18)

At the end of the old queen's reign, Dekker compressed what had been two plays into one, creating a popular fantasy play tricked up with allegorical masque elements and a new prologue and epilogue designed to flatter Elizabeth. In the above passage, which was performed during the Christmas season at court in December 1599, Fortune unambiguously denounces the adventuring mode of primitive accumulation and condemns the magical production of riches and the fantasy of effortless, global travel. The play is a curiously grim statement about what the pursuit of riches (as opposed to virtue) might be doing to the English court. And though it was published in 1600 under the title of *The Pleasant Comedie of Old Fortunatus*, the deaths of Fortunatus and his two sons push its generic position into the territory of tragicomedy, that genre that was soon to become so prevalent on the London stage.

Later plays that represent long-distance travel include Heywood's *The Fair Maid of the West, Part I* (1600), *The Travels of the Three English Brothers* by John Day, William Rowley and George Wilkins (1607), Heywood and Rowley's *Fortune by Land and Sea* (1608), Fletcher and Massinger's *The Sea Voyage*, Shakespeare's *Pericles* (ca. 1608) and *The Tempest* (1610), and Robert Daborne's *A Christian Turned Turk* (1612). These plays do not use the device of magical travel (for example, Prospero renounces his magic before embarking for Milan) and rather than glorying in a fantasy of superhuman mobility, instead represent the suffering or humiliation that occur when travelers, no matter how proud, rich or powerful, must take risks with the elements. In these plays, travel is represented as travail rather than a source of no-strings-attached pleasure or an opportunity for leisurely exoticism. When characters are shipwrecked and stranded, the labor and hardship endured by travelers is emphasized—Prospero is set adrift with his infant daughter Miranda, and Pericles washes up on shore in Pentapolis "bereft … of all his fortunes" (5.49).

The storm scene in act 3, scene 1, of Shakespeare's *Pericles*, like the opening scene of *The Tempest*, offers a representation of maritime labor in action. Furthermore, the audience sees another side of maritime labor in the earlier scene in which Pericles, having survived a shipwreck, washes up alone on the seaside in Pentapolis and encounters a group of common fishermen. These poor fishermen embody the lower-class labor that supports and underpins, even as it criticizes, the

Auri ſacra fames quid non? 179

D ESIRE to haue, dothe make vs muche ìndure,
In trauaile, toile, and labour voide of reſte:
The marchant man is caried with this lure,
Throughe ſcorching heate, to.regions of the Eaſte:
  Oh thirſte of goulde, what not? but thou canſt do:
  And make mens hartes for to conſent thereto.

The trauailer poore, when ſhippe doth ſuffer wracke,
Who hopes to ſwimme vnto the wiſhed lande,
Dothe venture life, with fardle on his backe,
That if he ſcape, the ſame in ſteede maye ſtande.
  Thus, hope of life, and loue vnto his goods,
  Houldes vp his chinne, with burthen in the floods.

Horat. lib.1. Epiſt.1.
Impiger extremos curriß
mercator ad Indos,
Per mare pauperiens
fugiens per ſaxa per
ignis.

Z 2   *Verbum*

Fig. 14.1   Geoffrey Whitney, *A Choice of Emblemes* (1586), 179.

wealthy merchant class. Their criticism focuses on social injustice and the unfair advantages given to the "idle rich" over the working poor. After having cited the example of Halicanus, who "stay'd at home / Not to eat honey like a drone / From others' labors" (2 Chorus 1–3), Gower recounts Pericles' attempt to return to Tyre by sea, and the shipwreck that Pericles alone survives. Pericles then appears on stage, "wet," according to the stage direction. After lamenting his victimization at the hands of fate and the elements, he then sees the three fishermen, and overhears one of them complaining: "the great ones eat up the little ones. I can compare our rich misers to nothing so fitly as a whale: a' plays and tumbles, driving the poor fry before him, and at last devours them all at a mouthful" (2.1.28–32). As Pericles eavesdrops on their conversation, another fisherman replies, using an image that reiterates the same homebound/mobile and idle parasite/laborer binaries used by Gower: "We would purge the land of these drones, that rob the bee of her honey" (ll. 46–7). Pericles then comes forward and reveals himself, saying "Peace be at your labor, honest fishermen" (l. 51). He asks for their help, though as a king he tells them he "never us'd to beg" (l. 62). "No friend, cannot you beg?," asks the First Fisherman, and declares, "here's them in our country of Greece gets more with begging than we can do with working" (ll. 63–5). In this scene, seagoing labor is present and speaks for itself in ways that question the expropriation of maritime surplus labor by "rich misers" and privileged "drones" who perform no labor themselves but suck the honey of profit from the toil of underpaid seamen and wage laborers. When the fishermen offer to clothe and feed Pericles, he exclaims, "How well this honest mirth becomes their labor!" (l. 94). In this scene, the fisherman speak truth to power: their presence and their words of protest serve to juxtapose the suffering of a royal traveler at the hands of Fortune with the travails of those who work to make travel possible for "rich misers" and kings.

Travel and travail coincide again in scenes 10 and 11 of *Pericles* when Thaisa dies after giving birth to Marina on board the storm-tossed ship. In that scene, the choric speaker Gower tells the playgoers, "In your imagination hold / This stage the ship, upon whose deck / The sea-tossed Pericles appears … " (10.58–60), by now a conventional invocation of the audience's imaginative participation in the staging of a tempest at sea. Pericles delivers a prayer to Neptune and to Lucina, goddess of childbirth: "make swift the pangs / Of my queen's travails" (11.13–14), he cries to the raging tempest. Working mariners appear on stage to trim the sails. They bravely defy the storm, and their courage seems to give strength to Pericles, who agrees to throw his wife's body overboard in response to their belief that the storm will not abate when a dead body is on board. The next day, more careful labor and skill, that of the physician Cerimon, revives the queen, giving her a second birth after her seeming death in childbirth. The tragicomic dialectic of suffering and redemption continues throughout the play to combine romantic, fateful wandering with real-world scenes of lower-class labor on the sea–shore and in the brothel.

Later, just before Leonine attempts to murder her, Marina recounts the story of her birth:

> My father, as nurse says, did never fear,
> But cried "Good seamen" to the mariners,
> Galling his kingly hands with haling ropes
> And, clasping to the mast, endured a sea
> That almost burst the deck. (15.103–7)

"When was this?" asks the would-be murderer, and she responds, "When I was born. / Never was waves nor wind so violent" (15.108–10). The twining of birth and death revolves, in a repeated pattern, around the determined labor of the "Good seamen," the helping hands of Pericles, whose royalty was humbled by the social class-leveling, natural power of the storm, and even the grim determination of Leonine to do the murderous work that is his sworn "commission" (15.131).

Pericles resumes its travels with another choric request for the audience to proceed by "imagination/From bourn to bourn, region to region" (18.3–4) and thus make "long leagues ... short" (18.1). The play's pattern of birth, death and resurrection is developed by the characters' travels that carry them painfully through a series of labors and (re)births, including the moral regeneration of the Governor Lysimachus, the return to life accomplished by the "sacred physic" (21.63) of Marina's midwife-like efforts to save the regressed "infant" (he no longer speaks) Pericles, and the final rebirths of Marina and Thaisa from servitude and nunnery to their identity of "royal birth." At the final stop in Ephesus, Thaisa and Pericles are reunited, and the recurring language of birth continues until the play's end.

Despite their many differences, what *Old Fortunatus* and *Pericles* share is the notion that the power of imagination and "winged thoughts" will enable their audiences to participate in an abstracted, mock travel mimicked by the "sweating labor" of the actors. While both plays offer a tragicomic journey from one royal court to another, what marks the plays as different is the insistent sense in *Pericles* (typical of the later period) that the travail of long-distance travel will ultimately be compensated: "Although assail'd with fortune fierce and keen / Virtue preserv'd from fell destruction's blast, / Led on by heaven, and crown'd with joy at last" (Epilogue 4–6) is Gower's concluding summary of the plot. In the end, he counsels the audience to show "patience" so that "new joy" will "wait on you" (Epilogue 17–18). Both plays contain messages of warning about those who would pursue riches without consideration for the consequences. The defense of honest labor and the attack on unjust exploitation in *Pericles* exists in tension with the tendency to explain misfortune and travail by referring to an abstract fate or invisible higher power, and to attribute to those higher powers a providential, redemptive purpose. In *Old Fortunatus*, the tragicomedy is darker: the magic purse and wishing hat signify that the fantasy of gaining gold and traveling the world is achieved by arbitrary luck and by trickery, not by patient merit. Those who do no legitimate work themselves and choose instead to hazard all and use magical money-making tricks ("liv[ing] by the sweat of other men's browes") are the enemies of Virtue. And consequently, they become the victims of a fickle Fortune—their (ill-gotten) joy leads to suffering and death without redemption (the opposite of the pattern in *Pericles*).

In the drama of the early seventeenth century, the tension between travel as painful or deadly, on the one hand, and travel as pleasurable or profitable, on the other, will continue, but increasingly that tension is resolved, not as it is in the folkloric and homiletic manner of *Old Fortunatus*, with wailing and gnashing of teeth as Fortune forces pride to fall, but in the manner of traveling tragicomedies like Fletcher's *The Island Princess* (1621), Fletcher and Massinger's *The Sea Voyage*, and Massinger's *The Renegado* (1624). As Valerie Forman has shown, plays like these enact an "investment" of money and effort that leads the plot through loss and suffering to a tragicomic resolution that "redeems" or repays that initial investment.[26] As Gordon McMullan puts it, these tragicomedies exhibit a generic structure in which, paradoxically, "the vehicle of its regenerative teleology is dispersal, dissemination, and loss."[27] As increasing numbers of English workers joined the ranks of maritime labor, the economic momentum of long-distance travel and global mobility gained strength. The extraction of surplus value from the labor of maritime workers was a successful profit-making procedure for those long-distance adventurers whose primitive accumulation helped to engender the capitalist system. The dangers and costs of travel became more familiar, but as the extraction of surplus value from an increasingly global economy brought new power to the English capitalist classes, those familiar sufferings were given meaning within a new class structure. The London theater, like the joint-stock companies that invested in overseas ventures, created wealth through the investment of sharers in a "company" that exploited the surplus labor of its indebted and underpaid workers (actors and playwrights were constantly in debt to theater owners like Philip Henslowe.)[28] When playgoers paid to experience, vicariously and imaginatively, the travels of dramatic characters like Fortunatus or Pericles, they were participating in the same structure of adventuring, hazarding and investing that claimed to create substance out of an airy nothing, while relying on the sweating labor of those whose surplus labor-power made those adventures and profits possible.

---

[26] Forman, *Tragicomic Redemptions*.

[27] McMullan, *The Politics of Unease in the Plays of John Fletcher* (Amherst: University of Massachusetts Press, 1994), 262.

[28] See my article, "'Meaner Ministers': Theatrical Labor, Mastery, and Bondage in *The Tempest*," in *The Blackwell Companion to Shakespeare's Works: The Poems, Problem Comedies and Late Plays*, (eds.) Jean E. Howard and Richard Dutton (Oxford: Blackwell, 2003), 408–26, for a discussion of labor and debt in the London playhouses.

Afterword
Early Modern Work and the Work of Representation

Jean E. Howard

Reading this excellent collection of essays with an eye to the critical trends it exemplifies, I start with its pronounced emphasis on production over consumption. For several decades, a substantial amount of criticism has focused on how the early modern economy made many new goods available for consumption, whether the simple household objects, like pins and pewter plates, explored by Joan Thirsk, or the luxury items, such as oil paintings and exotic foods and textiles, examined by Linda Levy Peck and Lisa Jardine.[1] By contrast, *Working Subjects in Early Modern English Drama* looks at the labor that goes into the production of goods, whether the labor of members of the traditional guilds or the more culturally occluded labor of female magicians or ocean-going seamen.

In fact, in its recurring attention to the labor of commoners and of women, the collection participates in a tradition of early modern scholarship that, at least since the 1980s, has focused on those who are neglected in criticism centered on the court, or in criticism that privileges members of the elite classes. This is, in part, the legacy of feminism and of that considerable fraction of new historical work that took the dispossessed and the lowly as its object, beginning with Stephen Greenblatt's essay, "Murdering Peasants," in the first issue of *Representations*.[2] It is encouraging to me, at least, to see these commitments and interests persist, even as the country at large has trouble deciding if it wants to provide health care for everyone or to alter bank practices that for some time have favored the interests of our own elite over the interests of those who work for a wage. Literary

---

[1]   Thirsk, *Economic Policy and Projects: The Development of a Consumer Society in Early Modern England* (Oxford: Clarendon Press, 1978); Jardine, *Worldly Goods: A New History of the Renaissance* (New York: W.W. Norton, 1996); Peck, *Consuming Splendor: Society and Culture in Seventeenth-Century England* (Cambridge: Cambridge University Press, 2005).

[2]   Greenblatt, "Murdering Peasants: Status, Genre, and the Representation of Rebellion," *Representations* 1 (1983): 1–29. A common critique of New Historicism is that it focused only on male and elite members of society and often on court culture. Like most generalizations, this one is only partially true. In the complex stew of influences that nourished the historical study of literature in the 1980s and 1990s, Marxism, cultural anthropology, and social as well as political history had their place, resulting in a not inconsiderable number of studies that focused on non-elite and female subjects.

criticism does not directly change public policy; it does legitimate certain topics for discussion and analysis with our students and affects what it is possible to see, to say, and to feel. This book provides resources for thinking about work, labor, the social regimes in which they are embedded, and the role of representation in providing the stories that make work intelligible or that conceal its realities.

Working Subjects in Early Modern English Drama also shares with much work of the last two decades a methodological commitment to mixing canonical with much less canonical texts. While Shakespeare never fails to command attention, many of the essays in this collection turn to a much broader archive of dramatic texts to fuel their investigations of how the drama represents working subjects in early modern England. Texts such as Fletcher and Massinger's *Custom of the Country* or Lady Elizabeth Russell's 1592 entertainment at Bisham or Haughton's *Englishmen for My Money* are showcased in some of the collection's most energetic essays. Freed from the stricture to focus on (and to define) literary greatness, the scholars here assembled have seized on what is interesting and culturally revelatory in a refreshingly diverse array of texts.

The book, then, is both a continuation and a departure from other criticism produced during the last two decades, engaging a fresh round of texts and highlighting the world of work and production over that of consumption, but sharing an interest in marginalized subjects and in non-canonical texts with other cultural critics. Perhaps most surprising about the book is its real if non-doctrinaire engagement with Marxist modes of inquiry. Partly this seems a "natural" extension of the book's commitment to investigating work and workers. A considerable part of Marx's oeuvre, after all, focuses on questions of labor: how it becomes alienated and how it is expropriated, how it serves as a basis, or not, for valuing things that are socially produced. Sometimes explicitly and sometimes by indirection, many of the essays in this collection take up the question of how labor "makes the world," but also how labor is frequently erased in cultural representations or its effects attributed to something else—such as magic. Within what I would call a loosely Marxist framework, *Working Subjects in Early Modern English Drama* nonetheless eschews grand narratives about successive modes of production, maybe in part because the essay form does not allow for nuanced exposition of such narratives, but more probably because grand narratives *per se* have become discredited, especially teleological narratives predicated on the eventual collapse of capitalism.

Interestingly, when the contributors to this volume do make historical claims about the proto-capitalist or mercantilist aspects of the period, they do not talk, as did earlier Marxist critics, primarily about enclosures, capitalist agricultural practices, and the process of primitive accumulation by which rural commoners were transformed into wage laborers (although a number of the essays do address these topics from fresh perspectives).[3] Instead, a number of these essays focus on how new forms of long-distance trade both produced and were enabled by

---

[3]   For a good introduction to these topics see Robert DuPlessis, *Transitions to Capitalism in Early Modern Europe* (Cambridge: Cambridge University Press, 1997).

developments in finance, asset accumulation, and the expropriation of the labor of distant peoples, all of which were essential for full-blown capitalism to arise.[4] Bartolovich, Rutter, Bailey, Forman and Vitkus each explore parts of the story of an England increasingly involved in overseas trade and examine the contradictions, occlusions, and new forms of exploitation occasioned by it. This interest in the traffic and trade of the English nation is not in itself new and has arisen at least in part in response to the pressures of the present moment in which every corporation attempts to exploit new "global markets" and each university rushes to put courses on globalization at the center of the curriculum. *Working Subjects in Early Modern England*, however, explicitly links an interest in the early modern global to questions of labor and of whose interests were promoted and whose obliterated in the large-scale historical processes to which the fictions under examination directly or obliquely allude.

The central question hovering over the book, however, is how literature contributes to the analysis of these historical processes or the historical moment in which these altered regimes of labor and work were being instantiated. Put most simply, why read literature to find out anything about early modern work or workers? I think this collection provides several interesting answers to that question, sometimes self-consciously and sometimes simply through the employment of a particular critical practice. In every case, however, the most interesting answers flow from a full reckoning with the complexity of representation: for example, with the conventional nature of representation, with the contradictions often implicit in representational structures, and with the ways in which the means of representation affects the meaning of what is represented. The cultural texts explored in this collection tell us only a limited amount about early modern work *per se*, but they reveal a great deal about the often-conflicting stories told about work at the site of the early modern stage. The contradictions and occlusions of those stories are a window onto the pressure points of a changing social formation. Analyzed in all their complexity, early modern dramatic fictions help us understand the processes through which a culture in transition conceptually and emotionally negotiated its

---

[4] For important considerations of how the expanding networks of long-distance trade helped create the conditions for the development of the capitalist marketplace see Fernand Braudel, *The Wheels of Commerce* and *The Perspective of the World*, vols. 2 and 3 of *Civilization and Capitalism 15th–18th Century*, trans. Sian Reynolds (New York: Harper and Row, 1979 and Berkeley: University of California Press, 1992), and Jean Favier, *Gold and Spices: The Rise of Commerce in the Middle Ages*, trans. Caroline Higgitt (New York: Holmes and Meier, 1998). For a classic account of capitalist agriculture and the growth of integrated large-scale markets, see Immanuel Wallerstein, *The Modern World System*, vol. 1, *Capitalist Agriculture and the Origins of the European World-Economy in the Sixteenth Century* (New York: Academic Press, 1974), and for the expansion of early modern England's overseas trade, see Robert Brenner, *Merchants and Revolution: Commercial Change, Political Conflict, and London's Overseas Traders, 1550–1653* (Princeton: Princeton University Press, 1993), and K.R. Andrews, *Trade, Plunder, and Settlement: Maritime Enterprise and the Genesis of the British Empire, 1480–1630* (Cambridge: Cambridge University Press, 1984).

conflicting engagements with the world of work, revealing both what the culture thought and felt, and also what is only comprehensible from the perspective of a later point in time.

I want briefly to discuss three terms that seem to me helpful in understanding the productive ways in which this collection engages the question of how dramatic fictions illuminate the world of early modern work. The terms are simple ones: genres, structures of feeling, and the means of representation. From first to last *Working Subjects in Early Modern England* explores the complex consequences of genre on representations of work. From a Marxist perspective, genre has long been regarded as one of the representational conventions through which social and economic change is registered and the contradictions of a particular cultural formation revealed.[5] Eschewing a form of analysis that ties particular genres tightly to particular class interests, a number of essays in this collection nonetheless tie popular genres to the imaginative resolution of particular conjunctural crises. In Valerie Forman's essay, for example, she argues that tragicomedy is particularly concerned with the economic and social problems attending long-distance trade in the early modern period. Consequently, she explores the various strategies by which the genre manages the problems surrounding labor that arise as a result of such trade, including, in *The Island Princess*, erasure of indigenous labor in foreign nations and the substitution, instead, of the idea of laborless profits and investments that "work" by themselves to turn loss into gain; or, in *The Winter's Tale*, the incorporation of domestic labor into a global economy. Focusing on larger patterns of loss and recovery that mark the genre, Forman argues that at the largest level it struggles to make risk acceptable, labor expendable, and profit a certainty, even if long delayed. Quite brilliantly, she reveals what literary genres *do*, ideologically, to naturalize new economic and social arrangements for the benefit of some and to the detriment of others.

The opening two essays of the collection focus on a quite different genre, the "citizen play," here represented by *The Shoemaker's Holiday*. It has become a critical truism that "citizen plays" (London histories and London comedies) foreground the world of work, especially the work of artisans and merchants, in a way that other early modern plays do not. But Crystal Bartolovich and John Archer, from quite different perspectives, query and complicate that basic assumption. For Archer, citizen plays affirm and celebrate the right of citizens to work, but he zeros in on the figure of the foreign-born Hans (actually an English aristocrat in disguise) to point up the fact that some workers, especially in the 1590s those from the Low Countries, were *not* welcome into the fraternity of men and women who had the freedom of the city and the right to work within it. In the play Hans is embraced by his English counterparts, but he is not an actual foreign worker and

---

    5   See, for example, Fredric Jameson's *The Political Unconscious: Narrative as a Socially Symbolic Act* (Ithaca: Cornell University Press, 1981) and, in the field of early modern studies, the classic analysis by Walter Cohen of genres as sites for ideological contestations and class struggle, *Drama of a Nation: Public Theater in Renaissance England and Spain* (Ithaca: Cornell University Press, 1985).

is comically and non-threateningly represented; actual foreign workers are not otherwise represented. For Bartolovich, by contrast, not even the most successful of the English guildsmen, in this case Simon Eyre, is elevated socially *because of* his labor. Instead, his rise into the city's merchant and governmental elite comes from the sharp practice by which he profits from selling the cargo of a merchant ship that has fallen into his hands. In her reading of Dekker's play, actual guildsmen, while overtly celebrated, are decisively subordinated to the combined merchant and civic elite.

As a generic formation, the citizen play, then, is a slippery thing. It foregrounds work in a way other dramatic genres do not, but aspects of the play (the peculiar representation of Hans and the quickly-mentioned scam by which Eyre becomes Mayor) can be pressured to reveal the fissures in the play's and the culture's valuation and embrace of work. As Dympna Callaghan has elsewhere argued in regard to women and racialized subjects, it is not always a good thing to be thrust to the representational foreground as if being in the center of the picture means that one's interests are adequately advanced.[6] In *The Shoemaker's Holiday*, not everyone gets to partake of the citizen's freedom *to* work, and the rewards of work are not always what they seem. Not only does Eyre experience social mobility only when he becomes a merchant, but another of Eyre's guildsmen, Ralph, is impressed into service in the French wars and comes back permanently lame. Now there is a reward for work, the catastrophic costs to the laborer papered over only by Ralph's sentimental reclamation of his wife from the clutches of Hammon, a vilified gentleman.

A hard-headed examination of the play's contradictions and fissures does not, however, take away from the fact that *The Shoemaker's Holiday* creates a powerful fiction of the pleasures of guild work. The verbal excesses of Eyre, the camaraderie of the male workers, including their participation in a celebratory morris dance, the drink they convivially consume, the delight taken in identifying a person by the shoes the workers crafted for him or her—all of this creates what Raymond Williams calls a powerful structure of feeling generated by the aural, kinetic, and even olfactory elements of performance.[7] A gap opens between the nostalgic

---

[6]   Callaghan, "Introduction: Cleopatra Had a Way with Her," in *Shakespeare Without Women: Representing Gender and Race on the Renaissance Stage* (London: Routledge, 2000), 1–25.

[7]   In *The Country and the City* (New York: Oxford University Press, 1973), Williams elaborated what was to become one of his key ideas, namely, that a powerful force in culture are those subjectively experienced but culturally determined feelings that evoke one's affiliations with others or one's sense of belonging. Generations inhabit certain structures of feeling, but so do different ethnicities and genders, and they are most sharply elicited and reconstituted by cultural artifacts such as literature, fashion, food, and aspects of the built environment. They can be and were, I argue, evoked in the theater by elements of performance including song, dance, speech patterns, and habits of dress. The Eyre workshop is staged to evoke a sense of familiarity and belonging even as other elements of the play suggest its residual status and the presence of other cultural forces that will overwhelm the guild household.

staging of male guild culture as a site of pleasurable identification and the fleeting acknowledgment not only that many are left out of this culture but that that culture itself is slipping from urban pre-eminence, the route to riches lying somewhere other than in the handicraft work of shoemaking. One sees both the contradictions and fissures in this particular text and also how the stage plays on the potential to set not only the word against the word, but the thought against the emotion. The theater not only uses genre to tell stories that naturalize certain understandings of economic life, including how work is defined and valued, but it does so in fictions whose affective dimensions are a central part of the representational technologies by which cultural fault lines and tensions are given complex expression.

Other essays focus on different genres and structures of feeling. In one of several essays that examine representations of servants and their work, Michelle Dowd looks at how tragedies of the period depict the sexuality of serving women in such a way that their sexual exploitation by masters is hidden or mitigated and their reproductive labor taken from their control. Daniel Vitkus, in his turn, examines how the subgenre of travel plays frequently masks the labor of travel and the expropriation of the labor of seamen and servants by narratives focusing on the magical implements or charms that waft the traveler (Faust and Old Fortunatus, for example) to the courts of Europe or the Ottomans. Magic appears in a number of essays as a device that allows labor to be occluded, as a power greater than the individual allows him or her to accomplish what otherwise would require the labor of many.

This brings me to my third term: the means of representation. What a play or other text means depends, among other things, on the representational mode employed. This collection deals mostly with theatrical entertainments, and most of those are works produced for the commercial stage. Theatrical workers, whether the women who prepared costumes (as Natasha Korda demonstrates) or the male actors who performed scripts, were commoners, and not elite members of society, though a number of playwrights had educations that might, in some circumstances, have offered them considerable social advancement as clergymen or lawyers. Consequently, a potential existed for tension between the erasure of common laborers in some of the scripts being enacted and the sometimes self-consciously underscored deployment of skilled laborers (who sang, danced, fenced, jigged and declaimed) in the actual presentation of the performance. To some degree all early modern theatrical performance celebrated skilled craft labor, though actors had an ambiguous and complicated social standing. Technically servants of a noble patron, frequently members of a guild such as the bricklayers, actors were sometimes also sharers in their companies, taking part in a theatrical industry at once proto-capitalist in its joint-stock arrangements and yet tied to older structures of service and patronage.[8]

---

[8]   For good discussion of the complicated status of the early modern player see William Ingram's *The Business of Playing: The Beginnings of the Adult Professional Theater in Elizabethan London* (Ithaca: Cornell University Press, 1992).

These complexities created many and varied possibilities for the presentational elements of theatrical performance and for an awareness of the actor as worker to impact a play's meaning. As many have argued, in the 1590s skilled clowns like Will Kempe could call attention to their performative prowess in ways that disrupted and eclipsed the performance of the dramatic story of which they were a part, celebrating actorly labor over the mimetic seamlessness of the total play. As Ronda Arab argues, Will Kempe's notoriety as a particularly skilled theatrical performer allowed him, eventually, to take his own show on the road in the sense of becoming the solo performer of a famous London to Norwich morris dance, thereby changing his status from paid member of a theatrical company to an entrepreneur capitalizing on his personal popularity and the exceptional nature of his physical skills.

In the hands of an astute and sardonic playmaker like Ben Jonson, plays themselves often encoded their own running metadramatic commentary on the status of various aspects of theatrical labor. As Elizabeth Rivlin suggests in her essay on *The Alchemist*, Jonson closely imbricated the theatrical and alchemical professions in his depiction of the highly theatrical labor of alchemical concoction and audience seduction. The play is sharply aware of the ambiguous and transitional status of theatrical work. Does it involve service or entrepreneurship? Does it have use-value? Is it productive of anything? By whom can it be expropriated? On the one hand Jonson presents alchemy and theater as producing only vapors and fumes, productive of nothing but fleeting moments of audience pleasure and profit for no one but the owner of the house. On the other hand, theatrical and alchemical work are both depicted as involving intense labor accompanied by equally intense hopes for material gain, though, again, these gains are realized only by Lovewit, the gentleman-owner who does no theatrical work and who quietly appropriates the profits stemming from the labor of his servant. Jonson's attitude toward the parallels he exposes is ambiguous, and, in any case, the impact of the play may well exceed his intentions, since *The Alchemist,* no matter what the playwright's cynicism toward the work of theatrical performance, makes highly attractive the energy and inventiveness of the play's rogues. Despite the technical assertion of legitimate, non-theatrical, and property-based authority at the play's end, *The Alchemist* feels like a defense of actorly rogues or roguish actors and of the value of the messy and not quite quantifiable work of theatrical performance. In this case, the early modern theatrical mode of production is itself under scrutiny in the play, and the continual counterpoint between rogues and actors, alchemy and theater, foregrounds the question of what theatrical labor is, who benefits from it, and what social use it serves.

David Hawkes, by contrast, sees the early modern theatrical mode of production as directly contributing to the seismic and pernicious cultural shift by which abstract symbols came to substitute for actual things both in finance and in regimes of representation. For him, the early modern theater was part of the world of alienation and "magic" in which signs came to be mistaken for things, actors for the roles they play. I would argue that this is only partly true, precisely because the theater was itself a transitional and mixed institution in its own economic and representational practices. Not committed to a regime of seamless realism, it still, as Robert Weimann has convincingly shown, drew on popular performance traditions, such as clowning, jigging, asides, and other *platea* actions that broke the representational frame and reminded the audience of the labor of the actor and the difference between actor and role.[9]

To the extent, then, that the early modern theater anticipated in its practices our modern notions of representational autonomy and the impenetrability of the fourth wall, it does the work Hawkes attributes to it. But that is hardly the whole story of the early modern theater, as Jonson knew and Rivlin argues. This theater's mode of artistic production was mixed, not only in terms of the status of the actor, but also in terms of its commitment to performance conventions that masked the gap between actor and role, fiction and the world outside the fiction. Thinking about the embodied means of representation in the early modern theater remains, then, an essential element in analyzing how that theater contributed to our understanding of early modern working subjects, a project significantly advanced by the present collection, with its energetic reminders of why the world of work, and its representations, matter.

---

[9]   Weimann, *Shakespeare and the Popular Tradition in the Theater: Studies in the Social Dimension of Dramatic Form and Function*, (ed.) Robert Schwartz (Baltimore: The Johns Hopkins University Press, 1978), 151–2, and *Author's Pen and Actor's Voice: Playing and Writing in Shakespeare's Theatre*, (eds.) Helen Higbee and William West (Cambridge: Cambridge University Press, 2000), 180–215.

Selected Bibliography

Aaron, Melissa D. "'Beware at what hands thou receiv'st thy commodity':
   The Alchemist and the King's Men Fleece the Customers, 1610." In *Inside
   Shakespeare: Essays on the Blackfriars Stage*, ed. Paul Menzer, 72–9.
   Selinsgrove, PA: Susquehanna University Press, 2006.
Abbot, George. *An Exposition upon the Prophet Jonah Contained in Certaine
   Sermons*. London, 1600.
Achelley, Thomas. *The Key of Knowledge Contayning Sundry Godly Prayers and
   Meditations*. London, 1572.
Aertsen, Jan. *Nature and Creature: Thomas Aquinas's Way of Thought*. New York:
   E.J. Brill, 1988.
Almond, Philip C., ed. *Demonic Possession and Exorcism in Early Modern
   England: Contemporary Texts and their Cultural Contexts*. Cambridge:
   Cambridge University Press, 2004.
Althusser, Louis. "Ideology and Ideological State Apparatuses." In *Lenin and
   Philosophy, and Other Essays*, trans. Ben Brewster, 121–76. London: New
   Left Books, 1971.
Amussen, Susan Dwyer. *Caribbean Exchanges: Slavery and the Transformation
   of English Society, 1640–1700*. Chapel Hill: University of North Carolina
   Press, 2007.
———. "Punishment, Discipline, and Power: The Social Meanings of Violence in
   Early Modern England." *Journal of British Studies* 34.1 (1995): 1–34.
Andaya, Barbara Watson. "Women and Economic Change: The Pepper Trade in
   Pre-Modern Southeast Asia." *Journal of the Economic and Social History of
   the Orient* 38 (1995): 165–90.
Andrews, K.R. *Trade, Plunder, and Settlement: Maritime Enterprise and the
   Genesis of the British Empire, 1480–1630*. Cambridge: Cambridge University
   Press, 1984.
Appleby, Joyce Oldham. *Economic Thought and Ideology in Seventeenth-Century
   England*. Princeton, NJ: Princeton University Press, 1978.
Arab, Ronda. "Ruthless Power and Ambivalent Glory: The Rebel-Laborer in *2
   Henry VI*." *Journal for Early Modern Cultural Studies* 5.2 (2005): 5–36.
———. "Work, Bodies and Gender in *The Shoemaker's Holiday*." *Medieval and
   Renaissance Drama in England* 13 (2001): 182–212.
Archer, Ian. *The Pursuit of Stability: Social Relations in Elizabethan London*.
   Cambridge: Cambridge University Press, 1991.
Archer, Jayne Elisabeth, Elizabeth Goldring, and Sarah Knight, eds. *The Progresses,
   Pageants, and Entertainments of Queen Elizabeth I*. Oxford: Oxford University
   Press, 2007.
Archer, John Michael. *Citizen Shakespeare: Freemen and Aliens in the Language
   of the Plays*. New York: Palgrave Macmillan, 2005.

————. *Old Worlds: Egypt, Southwest Asia, India, and Russia in Early Modern English Writing*. Stanford: Stanford University Press, 2001.

Archer, Leonie, ed. *Slavery and Other Forms of Unfree Labour*. New York: Routledge, 1988.

Arden of Faversham. Ed. Martin White. London: A & C Black, 1982.

Aristotle. *Nicomachean Ethics*. 2nd ed. Trans. Terence Irwin. Indianapolis: Hackett Publishing Company, 1999.

————. *Nicomachean Ethics*. In *Works*, vol. 9, trans. W.D. Ross. Oxford: Clarendon, 1908.

————. *Politics*. In *The Basic Works of Aristotle*, ed. Richard McKeon. New York: Random House, 1941.

————. *Politics*. Ed. Trevor Saunders. Trans. T.A. Sinclair. London: Penguin, 1981.

Arthur, Liz. *Embroidery 1600–1700 at the Burrell Collection*. Great Britain: Glasgow Museums, 1985.

Austin, J.L. *How To Do Things With Words*. Oxford: Clarendon, 1962.

Bacon, Francis. *The Essayes or Counsels, Civill and Morall*. London, 1625.

————. "Of Plantations." In *The Genesis of the United States*, ed. Alexander Brown. 2 vols., 2:799–802. New York: Russell & Russell, 1964.

Bakhtin, Mikhail. *Rabelais and His World*. Trans. Helene Iswolsky. Bloomington: Indiana University Press, 1984.

Balasopoulos, Antonis. "'Suffer a Sea-Change': Spatial Crisis, Maritime Modernity, and the Politics of Utopia." *Cultural Critique* 63 (2006): 122–56.

Bale, John. *Comedy Concernynge Thre Lawes*. London: Tudor Facsimile Series, 1908.

Bales, Kevin. *Understanding Global Slavery: A Reader*. Berkeley: University of California Press, 2005.

Balibar, Etienne. "Citizen Subject." In *Who Comes After the Subject?*, ed. Eduardo Cadava, Peter Connor, and Jean-Luc Nancy, 33–57. New York: Routledge, 1991.

Barbe, Simon. *The French Perfumer*. London, 1697.

Barbour, Richmond. *Before Orientalism: London's Theatre of the East, 1576–1626*. Cambridge: Cambridge University Press, 2003.

————. "A Multinational Corporation: Foreign Labor in the East India Company." In *A Companion to the Global Renaissance: English Literature and Culture in the Era of Expansion*, ed. Jyotsna Singh, 129–48. Oxford: Wiley-Blackwell, 2009.

Barker, Francis. *Culture of Violence: Shakespeare, Tragedy, History*. Manchester: Manchester University Press, 1993.

Barret, William, and the Councell of Virginia. *A True Declaration of the Estate of the Colonie in Virginia*. London, 1610.

Barry, Gerat. *A Discourse of Military Discipline Devided into Three Boockes*. Brussels, 1634.

Barry, Jonathan, and Christopher Brooks, eds. *The Middling Sort of People: Culture, Society and Politics in England, 1550–1800*. New York: St Martins, 1994.

Barry, Jonathan, Marianne Hester, and Gareth Roberts, eds. *Witchcraft in Early Modern Europe.* Cambridge: Cambridge University Press, 1996.

Bartolovich, Crystal. "History After the End of History: Critical Counterfactualism and Revolution." *New Formations* 59 (2006): 63–80.

———. "Travailing Theory: Global Flows of Labor and the Enclosure of the Subject." In *A Companion to the Global Renaissance: English Literature and Culture in the Era of Expansion,* ed. Jyotsna Singh, 50–66. Oxford: Wiley-Blackwell, 2009.

Bates, E.S. *Touring in 1600: A Study in the Development of Travel as a Means of Education.* Boston: Houghton Mifflin, 1912.

Beckles, Hilary. "The Concept of 'White Slavery' in the English Caribbean During the Early Seventeenth Century." In *Early Modern Conceptions of Property,* eds. John Brewer and Susan Staves, 572–85. New York: Routledge, 1996.

Beier, A.L. *Masterless Men: The Vagrancy Problem in England 1560–1640.* London: Methuen, 1985.

Ben-Amos, Ilana Krausman. *Adolescence and Youth in Early Modern England.* New Haven, CT: Yale University Press, 1994.

Bennett, Judith M., and Amy M. Froide. "A Singular Past." In *Singlewomen in the European Past, 1250–1800,* eds. Bennett and Froide, 1–37. Philadelphia: University of Pennsylvania Press, 1999.

Bent, J. Theodore. "The English in the Levant." *English Historical Review* 5 (1890): 654–64.

Bentley, G.E. *The Jacobean and Caroline Stage.* 7 vols. Clarendon: Oxford University Press, 1941–68.

Bergeron, David. *English Civic Pageantry, 1558–1642.* Columbia: University of South Carolina Press, 1971.

Berlin, Ira. *Many Thousands Gone: The First Two Centuries of Slavery in North America.* Cambridge, MA: Harvard University Press, 1998.

Betteridge, Thomas, ed. *Borders and Travellers in Early Modern Europe.* Burlington, VT: Ashgate, 2007.

Bevington, David, ed. *The Complete Works of Shakespeare.* New York: Longman, 2003.

Bindoff, S.T. "The Making of the Statute of Artificers." In *Elizabethan Government and Society: Essays Presented to Sir John Neale,* eds. Bindoff et al., 56–95. London: The Athlone Press, 1961.

Birdwood, George, and William Foster, eds. *The First Letter Book of the East India Company, 1600–1619.* London: Bernard Quartich, 1965.

Blackburn, Robin. *The Making of New World Slavery: From the Baroque to the Modern, 1492–1800.* London: Verso, 1998.

———. "The Old World Background to European Colonial Slavery." *William and Mary Quarterly* 54.1 (1997): 65–102.

Blackstone, Sir William. *Commentaries on the Laws of England.* 4 vols. Oxford: Oxford University Press, 1765–9.

Blomefield, Francis. *The History of the City and County of Norwich.* Norwich, 1745.

Bodin, Jean. *On the Demon-Mania of Witches.* 1580. Trans. Randy A. Scott. Toronto: Centre for Renaissance and Reformation Studies, 1995.

Bonavita, Helen Vella. "Maids, Wives and Widows: Multiple Meaning and Marriage in *The Witch of Edmonton.*" *Parergon* 23.2 (2006): 73–95.

Bono, Barbara J. *Literary Transvaluation: From Vergilian Epic to Shakespearean Tragicomedy.* Berkeley: University of California Press, 1984.

Bower, Edmond. *Dr Lamb Revived, or Witchcraft Condemn'd in Anne Bodenham.* London, 1653.

Bower, James. *Dr Lamb's Darling: Or, Strange and Terrible News from Salisbury.* London, 1653.

Bowers, Fredson, ed. *The Dramatic Works in the Beaumont and Fletcher Canon*, vol. 10. Cambridge: Cambridge University Press, 1996.

Brathwaite, Richard. *The Captive Captain, or, The Restrain'd Cavalier.* London, 1665.

———. *The English Gentleman.* London, 1630. Norwood, NJ: Walter J. Johnson, 1975.

Braudel, Fernand. *Civilization and Capitalism 15th–18th Century*, vols, 2 and 3. Trans. Sian Reynolds. New York: Harper and Row, 1979. Berkeley: University of California Press, 1992.

———. *The Mediterranean and the Mediterranean World in the Age of Philip II.* 2nd ed. Trans. Sian Reynolds. 2 vols. New York: Harper & Row, 1975.

Breitenberg, Mark. *Anxious Masculinity in Early Modern England.* Cambridge: Cambridge University Press, 1996.

Brenner, Robert. *Merchants and Revolution: Commercial Change, Political Conflict, and London's Overseas Traders, 1550–1653.* Princeton: Princeton University Press, 1993.

Brewer, John, and Roy Porter, eds. *Consumption and the World of Goods.* London and New York: Routledge, 1993.

Bristol, Michael. "In Search of the Bear: Spatiotemporal Form and the Heterogeneity of Economies in *The Winter's Tale.*" *Shakespeare Quarterly* 42 (1991): 145–67.

Brown, Cedric. *John Milton's Aristocratic Entertainments.* Cambridge: Cambridge University Press, 1985.

Brown, Pamela Allen, and Peter Parolin, eds. *Women Players in England, 1500–1660.* Burlington, VT: Ashgate, 2008.

Brown, Thomas. *A Collection of Miscellany Poems, Letters, &c. by Mr Brown, &c.* London, 1699.

Browne, John. *The Marchants Avizo.* London, 1589.

Brownlow, F.W. *Shakespeare, Harsnett, and the Devils of Denham.* Newark: University of Delaware Press, 1993.

Bruster, Douglas. *Drama and the Market in the Age of Shakespeare.* Cambridge: Cambridge University Press, 1992.

Buccola, Regina. *Fairies, Fractious Women, and the Old Faith: Fairy Lore in Early Modern British Drama and Culture.* Selinsgrove, PA: Susquehanna University Press, 2006.

Burn, John S. *The History of the French, Walloon, Dutch and Other Foreign Protestant Communities Settled in England.* London: Longman, Brown, 1846.

Burnett, Mark Thornton. "*The Changeling* and Masters and Servants." In *Early Modern English Drama: A Critical Companion*, eds. Garrett A. Sullivan, Jr, Patrick Cheney, and Andrew Hadfield, 298–308. New York: Oxford University Press, 2006.

————. *Masters and Servants in English Renaissance Drama and Culture: Authority and Obedience.* New York: St Martin's Press, 1997.

Butler, Judith. *Excitable Speech: A Politics of the Performative.* London: Routledge, 1997.

Butterworth, Philip. *Magic on the Early English Stage.* Cambridge: Cambridge University Press, 2005.

Callaghan, Dympna. "Looking Well into Linens: Women and Cultural Production in *Othello* and Shakespeare's England." In *Marxist Shakespeares*, eds. Jean E. Howard and Scott Cutler Shershow, 53–82. London and New York: Routledge, 2001.

————. *Shakespeare Without Women: Representing Gender and Race on the Renaissance Stage.* London: Routledge, 2000.

Camp, Charles W. *The Artisan in Elizabethan Literature.* New York: Columbia University Press, 1923.

Campbell, Mary Baine. *Wonder and Science: Imagining Worlds in Early Modern Europe.* Ithaca, NY: Cornell University Press, 1999.

Carroll, William. *Fat King, Lean Beggar: Representations of Poverty in the Age of Shakespeare.* Ithaca: Cornell University Press, 1996.

Cerasano, S.P. "The Chamberlain's-King's Men." In *A Companion to Shakespeare*, ed. David Scott Kastan. Malden, MA: Blackwell Publishers, 1999.

Chard, Chloe. *Pleasure and Guilt on the Grand Tour: Travel Writing and Imaginative Geography, 1600–1830.* Manchester: Manchester University Press, 1999.

Chapman, Alison. "Whose Saint Crispin's Day is it?" *Renaissance Quarterly* 54.4 (2001): 1467–94.

Chapman, George. *Sir Gyles Goosecappe Knight A Comedie Presented by the Children of the Chappell.* London, 1606.

Chaudhuri, K.N. *The English East India Company: The Study of an Early Joint-Stock Company, 1600–1640.* New York: August Kelley, 1965.

Christensen, Ann. "'Absent, weak, or Unserviceable': The East India Company and the Domestic Economy in *The Launching of the Mary, or The Seaman's Honest Wife*." In *Global Traffic: Discourses and Practices of Trade in English Literature and Culture from 1550–1700*, eds. Barbara Sebek and Stephen Deng, 117–36. New York: Palgrave, 2008.

Chitty, C.W. "Aliens in England in the Sixteenth Century." *Race* 8 (1966–1967): 129–45.

Clark, Peter, and Paul Slack. *English Towns in Transition 1500–1700.* London: Oxford University Press, 1976.

Cogan, Thomas. *Haven of Health*. London, 1596.

Cohen, Margaret. "The Chronotopes of the Sea." In *The Novel*, ed. Franco Moretti, 647–65. Princeton, NJ: Princeton University Press, 2006.

Cohen, Stephen. "Between Form and Culture: New Historicism and the Promise of a Historical Formalism." In *Renaissance Literature and Its Formal Engagements*, ed. Mark David Rasmussen, 17–41. New York: Palgrave, 2002.

Cohen, Walter. *Drama of a Nation: Public Theater in Renaissance England and Spain*. Ithaca, NY: Cornell University Press, 1985.

Cole, Mary Hill. *The Portable Queen: Elizabeth I and the Politics of Ceremony*. Amherst: University of Massachusetts Press, 1999.

Comaroff, Jean, and John Comaroff. "Millenial Capitalism: First Thoughts on a Second Coming." *Public Culture* 12.2 (2000): 291–343.

Consitt, Frances. *The London Weavers' Company*, vol. 1. Oxford: Clarendon, 1933.

Cooper, Helen. "Location and Meaning in Masque, Morality, and Royal Entertainment." In *The Court Masque*, ed. David Lindley, 135–48. Manchester: Manchester University Press, 1984.

Craik, T.W. "The Political Interpretation of Two Tudor Interludes: *Temperance and Humility* and *Wealth and Health*." *Review of English Studies* n.s. 4 (1953): 98–108.

Darby, T.L. "Resistance to Rape in *Persiles y Sigismunda* and *The Custom of the Country*." *The Modern Language Review* 90.2 (1995): 273–84.

Darell, Walter. *A Short Discourse of the Life of Servingmen*. London, 1578.

Davies, Owen. *Popular Magic: Cunning-Folk in English History*. London: Hambledon and London, 2003.

Dekker, Thomas. *The Dramatic Works of Thomas Dekker*. Ed. Fredson Bowers. 4 vols. Cambridge: Cambridge University Press, 1953–61.

———. *The Shoemaker's Holiday*. Eds, R.L. Smallwood and Stanley Wells. Manchester: Manchester University Press, 1999.

Dekker, Thomas, John Ford, and William Rowley. *The Witch of Edmonton*. Ed. Arthur F. Kinney. London: A & C Black, 1998.

Deloney, Thomas. *The Gentle Craft*. London, 1637.

———. *The Gentle Craft*. In *The Works of Thomas Deloney*, ed. Francis Oscar Mann. Oxford: Clarendon, 1967.

———. *Jack of Newberry*. London, 1597.

———. *The Novels of Thomas Deloney*. Ed. Merrit E. Lawlis. Bloomington: Indiana University Press, 1961.

———. *Shorter Novels*, vol. 1. London: J.M. Dent & E.P. Dutton, 1929.

Di Biase, Carmine G., ed. *Travel and Translation in the Early Modern Period*. Amsterdam: Rodopi, 2006.

Dionne, Craig. "Fashioning Outlaws: The Early Modern Rogue and Urban Culture." In *Rogues and Early Modern English Culture*, eds. Dionne and Mentz, 33–61. Ann Arbor: University of Michigan Press, 2004.

Dionne, Craig, and Steve Mentz, eds. *Rogues and Early Modern English Culture.* Ann Arbor: University of Michigan Press, 2004.

Dixon, Mimi. "Tragicomic Recognition: Medieval Miracles and Shakespearean Romance." In *Renaissance Tragicomedy,* ed. Nancy Maguire. New York: AMS Press, 1987.

Dolan, Frances E. *Dangerous Familiars: Representations of Domestic Crime in England 1550–1700.* Ithaca, NY: Cornell University Press, 1993.

———. *Whores of Babylon: Catholicism, Gender and Seventeenth-Century Print Culture.* Ithaca, NY: Cornell University Press, 1999.

Donaldson, Ian. "Looking Sideways: Jonson, Shakespeare, and the Myths of Envy." *Ben Jonson Journal* 8 (2001): 1–22.

Dove, Linda. "Mary Wroth and the Politics of the Household in 'Pamphilia to Amphilanthus'." In *Women, Writing, and the Reproduction of Culture in Tudor and Stuart Britain,* eds. Mary E. Burke, Jane Donawerth, Linda L. Dove, and Karen Nelson, 141–56. New York: Syracuse University Press, 2000.

Dowd, Michelle M. "Labors of Love: Women, Marriage, and Service in *Twelfth Night* and *The Compleat Servant-Maid.*" *Shakespearean International Yearbook* 5 (2005): 103–26.

———. *Women's Work in Early Modern English Literature and Culture.* New York: Palgrave Macmillan, 2009.

Dugan, Holly. "Ephemeral History of Perfume." PhD diss., University of Michigan, 2005.

Dunlop, Jocelyn O. *English Apprenticeship and Child Labour: A History.* New York: MacMillan, 1912.

DuPlessis, Robert. *Transitions to Capitalism in Early Modern Europe.* Cambridge: Cambridge University Press, 1997.

Elyot, Thomas. *Boke Named the Governour.* London, 1537.

———. *The Castel of Health.* London, 1539.

An Enterlude of Welth and Helth. Ed. F. Holthausen. Heidelberg: Carl Winters Universitatsbuchhandlung, 1922.

Erler, Mary. "'Chaste Sports, Juste Prayses, & All Softe Delight': Harefield 1602 and Ashby 1607, Two Female Entertainments." *The Elizabethan Theatre* 14 (1996): 1–25.

Esser, Raingard. "Immigrant Cultures in Tudor and Stuart England." In *Immigrants in Tudor and Early Stuart England,* eds. Nigel Goose and Lien Luu, 161–74. Brighton: Sussex Academic Press, 2005.

Favier, Jean. *Gold and Spices: The Rise of Commerce in the Middle Ages.* Trans. Caroline Higgitt. New York: Holmes and Meier, 1998.

Ferguson, Arthur. *Clio Unbound: Perception of the Social and Cultural Past in Renaissance England.* Durham, NC: Duke University Press, 1979.

Ferguson, Niall. "Virtual History: Towards a 'Chaotic' Theory of the Past." In *Virtual History: Alternatives and Counterfactuals,* ed. Ferguson, 1–90. New York: Basic Books, 1997.

Findlay, Alison. *Playing Spaces in Early Women's Drama*. Cambridge: Cambridge University Press, 2006.

Finkelstein, Andrea. *Harmony and Balance: An Intellectual History of Seventeenth-Century English Economic Thought*. Ann Arbor: University of Michigan Press, 2000.

Fisher, Will. *Materializing Gender in Early Modern Literature and Culture*. Cambridge: Cambridge University Press, 2006.

Fleck, Andrew. "Marking Difference and National Identity in Dekker's *The Shoemaker's Holiday*." *SEL* 46 (2006): 349–70.

Fletcher, John, and Philip Massinger. *The Custom of the Country*. New York: Routledge Theatre Arts Books, 1999.

———. *The Prophetess*. 1622. In *The Works of Francis Beaumont and John Fletcher*, vol. 5, ed. A.R. Waller. Cambridge: Cambridge University Press, 1907.

Flynn, Dennis, and Arturo Giráldez. "Born with a 'Silver Spoon': The Origin of World Trade in 1571." In *Metals and Monies in an Emerging Global Economy*, eds. Flynn and Giráldez, 259–79. Brookfield, VT: Variorum, 1997.

Fogle, French R. "'Such a Rural Queen': The Countess Dowager of Derby as Patron." In *Patronage in Late Renaissance England: Papers Read at Clark Library Seminar 14 May 1977*, 3–28. Los Angeles: William Clark Memorial Library, 1983.

Forman, Valerie. *Tragicomic Redemptions: Global Economies and the Early Modern English Stage*. Philadelphia: University of Pennsylvania Press, 2008.

———. "Transformations of Value and the Production of 'Investment' in the Early History of the English East India Company." *Journal of Medieval and Early Modern Studies* 34 (2004): 611–41.

Foyster, Elizabeth A. *Manhood in Early Modern England: Honour, Sex and Marriage*. New York: Longman, 1999.

Frank, Andre Gunder. *ReORIENT: Global Economy in the Asian Age*. Berkeley: University of California Press, 1998.

Franits, Wayne E. *Paragons of Virtue: Women and Domesticity in Seventeenth-Century Dutch Art*. Cambridge: Cambridge University Press, 1993.

Freeman, Arthur. "Marlowe, Kyd, and the Dutch Church Libel." *English Literary Renaissance* 3 (1973): 50–51.

Friedman, Albert. "'When Adam Delved ... ': Contexts of an Historic Proverb." In *The Learned and the Lewed: Studies in Chaucer and Medieval Literature*, ed. Larry Benson, 213–30. Cambridge: Harvard University Press, 1974.

Friedman, Alice. "Architecture, Authority, and the Female Gaze: Planning and Representation in the Early Modern Country House." *Assemblage* 18 (1992): 40–61.

Froide, Amy M. *Never Married: Singlewomen in Early Modern England*. Oxford: Oxford University Press, 2005.

Fulwell, Ulpian. *The Dramatic Works*. Ed. John S. Farmer. London: 1906. Reprint, New York: Barnes & Noble, 1966.

Fumerton, Patricia. *Unsettled: The Culture of Mobility and the Working Poor in Early Modern England*. Chicago: University of Chicago Press, 2006.

Fury, Cheryl. *Tides in the Affairs of Men: The Social History of Elizabethan Seamen, 1580–1603*. Westport, CT: Greenwood, 2002.

G., B. *The Joyfull Receyving of the Queenes Most Excellent Majestie into hir Highnesse Citie of Norwich*. London, 1578.

Galenson, David W. *White Servitude in Colonial America: An Economic Analysis*. Cambridge: Cambridge University Press, 1981.

Games, Alison. *The Web of Empire: English Cosmopolitans in an Age of Expansion, 1560–1660*. Oxford: Oxford University Press, 2008.

Gaskill, Malcolm. "Witchcraft, Politics, and Memory in Seventeenth-Century England." *The Historical Journal* 50.2 (2007): 289–308.

Geckle, George. *John Marston's Drama: Themes, Images, Sources*. Madison, NJ: Fairleigh Dickinson University Press, 1980.

Gibbons, Brian. *Jacobean City Comedy: A Study of Satiric Plays by Jonson, Marston and Middleton*. 1968. 2nd ed. London: Methuen, 1980.

Goins, Scott. "Two Aspects of Virgil's Use of Labor in the *Aeneid*." *The Classical Journal* 88.4 (1993): 375–84.

Goodich, Michael. "*Ancilla Dei:* The Servant as Saint in the Late Middle Ages." In *Women of the Medieval World: Essays in Honor of John H. Mundy*, eds. Julius Kirshner and Suzanne F. Wemple, 119–36. Oxford: Basil Blackwell, 1985.

Gosson, Stephen. *Playes Confuted in Five Actions*. London, 1582.

———. *The Schoole of Abuse*. London, 1579.

Goose, Nigel, and Lien Luu, eds. *Immigrants in Tudor and Stuart England*. Brighton: Sussex Academic Press, 2005.

Gowing, Laura. *Common Bodies: Women, Touch and Power in Seventeenth-Century England*. New Haven, CT: Yale University Press, 2003.

Grant, Teresa, and Barbara Ravelhofer, eds. *English Historical Drama*. New York: Palgrave, 2008.

Greenblatt, Stephen. "Murdering Peasants: Status, Genre, and the Representation of Rebellion." *Representations* 1 (1983): 1–29.

———. *Shakespearean Negotiations: The Circulation of Social Energy in Renaissance England*. Berkeley: University of California Press, 1988.

Greene, Robert. *Scottish History*. In *Plays and Poems of Robert Greene*, vol. 2, ed. J. Chruton Collins. Oxford: Clarendon, 1905.

Gregory, Annabel. "Witchcraft, Politics, and 'Good Neighborhood' in Early Seventeenth-Century Rye." *Past and Present* 133 (1991): 31–66.

Grell, Ole Peter. *Calvinist Exiles in Tudor and Stuart England*. Aldershot, UK: Scolar Press, 1996.

Griffiths, Paul. *Youth and Authority: Formative Experiences in England 1560–1640*. Oxford: Clarendon Press, 1996.

Gurr, Andrew. *Playgoing in Shakespeare's London*. 2nd ed. Cambridge: Cambridge University Press, 1996.

————. "Prologue: Who is Lovewit? What is he?" In *Ben Jonson and Theatre: Performance, Practice and Theory*, eds. Richard Cave, Elizabeth Schafer and Brian Woolland, 5–19. London and New York: Routledge, 1999.

————. *The Shakespeare Company, 1594–1642*. Cambridge: Cambridge University Press, 2004.

————. *The Shakespearean Stage, 1574–1642*. Cambridge: Cambridge University Press, 1992.

Gwynn, Robin D. *Huguenot Heritage: The History and Contribution of the Huguenots in Britain*. Boston: Routledge and Kegan Paul, 1985.

Haber, Judith. "'I(t) could not choose but follow': Erotic Logic in *The Changeling*." *Representations* 81 (2003): 79–98.

Hadfield, Andrew. *Literature, Travel, and Colonial Writing in the English Renaissance, 1545–1625*. Oxford University Press, 1998.

————, ed. *Amazons, Savages & Machiavels: Travel & Colonial Writing in English, 1550–1630*. Oxford: Oxford University Press, 2001.

Hall, Kim F. *Things of Darkness: Economies of Race and Gender in Early Modern England*. Ithaca, NY: Cornell University Press, 1995.

Halpern, Richard. "Marlowe's Theater of Night: *Doctor Faustus* and Capital." *ELH* 71.2 (2004): 455–95.

————. "Eclipse of Action: *Hamlet* and the Political Economy of Playing" *Shakespeare Quarterly* 59.4 (2008): 450–82.

Hammill, Graham. "Faustus's Fortunes: Commodification, Exchange and the Form of Literary Subjectivity." *ELH* 63.2 (1996): 309–36.

Hamilton, Donna B. *Virgil and The Tempest: The Politics of Imitation*. Columbus: Ohio State University Press, 1990.

Harman, Thomas. *A Caveat for Common Cursitors, Vulgarly Called Vagabonds*. In *Rogues, Vagabonds, & Sturdy Beggars*, ed. Arthur F. Kinney. 103–53. Amherst: The University of Massachusetts Press, 1990.

Harris, Jonathan Gil. *Sick Economies: Drama, Mercantilism, and Disease in Shakespeare's England*. Philadelphia: University of Pennsylvania Press, 2004.

————. "The Smell of Macbeth." *Shakespeare Quarterly* 58.4 (2008): 465–86.

Harris, Jonathan Gil, and Natasha Korda, eds. *Staged Properties in Early Modern English Drama*. Cambridge: Cambridge University Press, 2002.

Haughton, William. *Englishmen for My Money*. In *Three Renaissance Usury Plays*, ed. Lloyd Edward Kermode. Manchester: Manchester University Press, 2009.

Hawkes, David. "Idolatry and Commodity Fetishism in the Antitheatrical Controversy." *SEL* 39.2 (1999): 255–73.

————. *The Faust Myth: Religion and the Rise of Representation*. New York: Palgrave, 2007.

Haynes, Jonathan. "Representing the Underworld: *The Alchemist*," *Studies in Philology* 86 (1989): 18–41.

Heal, Felicity. *Hospitality in Early Modern England*. Oxford: Clarendon, 1990.

————. "Reputation and Honour in Court and Society." *Transactions of the Royal Historical Society* 6 (1996): 161–78.

Heal, Felicity, and Clive Holmes. *The Gentry in England and Wales, 1500–1700.* Stanford: Stanford University Press, 1994.

Helgerson, Richard. *Forms of Nationhood: The Elizabethan Writing of England.* Chicago: University of Chicago Press, 1992.

Herbert, George. *The Complete English Poems.* Ed. John Tobin. London: Penguin Books, 1991.

Heywood, Thomas. *If You Know Not Me You Know Nobody Part II.* Ed. Madeleine Doran. Oxford: Malone Society, 1935.

Hill, Christopher. *Liberty Against the Law: Some Seventeenth-Century Controversies.* London: Allen Lane; The Penguin Press, 1996.

Hinds, Allen. B., ed. *Calendar of State Papers and Manuscripts Relating to English Affairs Existing in the Archives and Collections of Venice and in Other Libraries of Northern Italy: 1619–1621,* vol. 16. London: H.M. Stationery Office, 1947.

Hinton, R.W.K. "The Mercantile System in the Time of Thomas Mun." In *The Early Mercantilists,* ed. Mark Blaug. Hants, England: Edward Elger, 1991.

Hirschmann, Albert O. *The Passions and the Interests: Political Arguments for Capitalism before its Triumph.* Princeton, NJ: Princeton University Press, 1977.

Hobbes, Thomas. *Leviathan.* Ed. C.B. MacPherson. London: Penguin Books, 1985.

Hoenselaars, A.J. *Images of Englishmen and Foreigners in the Drama of Shakespeare and His Contemporaries: A Study of Stage Characters and National Identity in English Renaissance Drama, 1558–1642.* Rutherford, NJ: Fairleigh Dickinson University Press, 1992.

Hoenselaars, Ton, and Holger Klein, eds. *Shakespeare and the Low Countries.* In *The Shakespeare Yearbook,* vol. 15. Lewiston: The Edwin Mellon Press, 2005.

Holderness, B.A. "The Reception and Distribution of the New Draperies in England." In *The New Draperies in the Low Countries and England, 1300–1800,* ed. N.B. Harte, 217–44. Oxford: Oxford University Press, 1997.

Holinshed, Raphael. *Chronicles.* London, 1587.

Holland, Peter. "'Travelling Hopefully': The Dramatic Form of Journeys in English Renaissance Drama." In *Travel and Drama in Shakespeare's Time,* eds. Jean–Pierre Maquerlot and Michèle Willems, 160–78. Cambridge: Cambridge University Press, 1996.

Holmes, Clive. "Popular Culture? Witches, Magistrates, and Divines in Early Modern England." In *Understanding Popular Culture: Europe from the Middle Ages to the Nineteenth Century,* ed. Steven L. Kaplan, 85–112. New York: Mouton Publishers, 1984.

———. "Women: Witnesses and Witches." *Past and Present* 140 (1993): 45–78.

Honigmann, E.A.J. "Shakespeare and London's Immigrant Community." In *Elizabethan and Modern Studies: Presented to Professor Willem Schrickx on the Occasion of His Retirement,* ed. J.P. Vander Motten, 143–51. Gent, Belgium: Seminarie voor Engelse en Amerikaanse Literatuur, R.U.G., 1985.

Hood, Gervase. "A Netherlandic Triumphal Arch for James I." In *Across the Narrow Seas: Studies in the History and Bibliography of Britain and the Low Countries: Presented to Anna E. C. Simoni*, ed. Susan Roach, 67–82. London: British Library, 1991.

Hopkins, Lisa. "Ladies' Trials: Women and the Law in Three Plays of John Ford." *Cahiers Elisabéthains* 56 (1999): 49–64.

Horn, James, and Philip D. Morgan. "Settlers and Slaves: European and African Migrations to Early Modern British America." In *The Creation of the British Atlantic World*, eds. Elizabeth Mancke and Carole Shammas, 19–45. Baltimore, MD: John Hopkins University Press, 2005.

Houston, Chloe. "Traveling Nowhere: Global Utopias in the Early Modern Period." In *A Companion to the Global Renaissance: English Literature and Culture in the Era of Expansion*, ed. Jyotsna Singh, 82–98. Oxford: Wiley-Blackwell, 2009.

Howard, Clare. *English Travelers of the Renaissance*. London: John Lane, 1914.

Howard, Jean. "Sex and the Early Modern City: Staging the Bawdy Houses of London." In *The Impact of Feminism in English Renaissance Studies*, ed. Dympna Callaghan, 117–36. Basingstoke, UK: Palgrave Macmillan, 2007.

———. "Shakespeare, Geography and the Work of Genre on the Early Modern Stage." *Modern Language Quarterly* 64 (2003): 299–322.

———. *The Stage and Social Struggle in Early Modern England*. London: Routledge, 1994.

———. *Theater of a City: The Places of London Comedy, 1598–1642*. Philadelphia: University of Pennsylvania Press, 2007.

Howard, Jean E., and Phyllis Rackin. *Engendering a Nation: A Feminist Account of Shakespeare's English Histories*. London: Routledge, 1997.

Howarth, W.D. "'Droit du Seigneur': Fact or Fantasy." *Journal of European Studies* 1 (1971): 291–312.

———. "Cervantes and Fletcher: A Theme with Variations." *The Modern Language Review* 56.4 (1961): 563–6.

Hoy, Cyrus. *Introductions, Notes, and Commentaries to Texts in "The Dramatic Works of Thomas Dekker."* Ed. Fredson Bowers, vol. 2. Cambridge: Cambridge University Press, 1979.

Ingram, Martin. *Church Courts, Sex and Marriage in England, 1570–1640*. Cambridge: Cambridge University Press, 1987.

Ingram, William. *The Business of Playing: The Beginnings of the Adult Professional Theater in Elizabethan London*. Ithaca, NY: Cornell University Press, 1992.

James VI (I). *Daemonologie*. 1597. Ed. G.B. Harrison. Oxford: Bodley Head, 1924.

Jameson, Fredric. *Political Unconscious: Narrative as a Socially Symbolic Act*. Ithaca, NY: Cornell University Press, 1981.

Jardine, Lisa. *Worldly Goods: A New History of the Renaissance*. New York: W.W. Norton, 1996.

Johnson, Mark Albert. "Bearded Women in Early Modern England." *SEL* 47.1 (2007): 1–28.

Johnson, Richard. *Crowne Garland of Goulden Roses*. London, 1612.

Johnston, Alexandra. "The 'Lady of the Farme': The Context of Lady Russell's Entertainment of Elizabeth at Bisham." *Early Theatre* 5.2 (2002): 71–85.

Jones, Ann Rosalind, and Peter Stallybrass. *Renaissance Clothing and the Materials of Memory*. Cambridge: Cambridge University Press, 2000.

Jonson, Ben. *The Alchemist*. 1610. In *English Renaissance Drama: A Norton Anthology*, ed. David Bevington. New York: Norton, 2002.

——. *The Alchemist*. Ed. Elizabeth Cook. London and New York: A & C Black and W.W. Norton, 1991.

——. "Cynthia Revells." In *The Workes of Benjamin Jonson,* ed. William Hole. London, 1616.

——. *Every Man Out of His Humor*. In *Ben Jonson*, vol. 3, eds. C.H. Herford, Percy Simpson, and Evelyn Simpson. Oxford: The Clarendon Press, 1925–52.

——. *Five Plays*. Ed. G.A. Wilkes. Oxford: Oxford University Press, 1988.

Jonson, Ben, George Chapman, and John Marston. *Eastward Ho!* Ed. C.G. Petter. London: Benn, 1973. London: A & C Black, 1994.

Jordan, Constance. "'Eating the Mother': Property and Propriety in *Pericles*." In *Creative Imitation: New Essays on Renaissance Literature in Honor of Thomas M. Greene*, eds. David Quint et al., 331–53. Binghamton, New York: Medieval and Renaissance Texts & Studies, 1992.

Jordan, Winthrop D. *White over Black: American Attitudes Towards the Negro, 1550–1812*. Chapel Hill: University of North Carolina Press, 1968.

Jowitt, Claire. *Voyage Drama and Gender Politics, 1589–1642: Real and Imagined Worlds*. Manchester: Manchester University Press, 2003.

Kahn, Coppélia. *Man's Estate: Masculine Identity in Shakespeare*. Berkeley: University of California Press, 1981.

——. *Roman Shakespeare: Warriors, Wounds, and Women*. New York: Routledge, 1997.

Kahn, Victoria. "'The Duty to Love': Passion and Obligation in Early Modern Political Theory," *Representations* 68 (1999): 84–107.

Kamps, Ivo, ed. *Materialist Shakespeare: A History*. London and New York: Verso, 1995.

Kastan, David Scott. "Is There a Class in this (Shakespearean) Text?" *Renaissance Drama* 24 (1993): 101–21.

——. "'Shewes of Honour and Gladnes': Dissonance and Display in Mary and Philip's Entry into London." *Research Opportunities in Renaissance Drama* 33 (1994): 1–15.

——. "Workshop and/as Playhouse: Comedy and Commerce in *The Shoemaker's Holiday*." *Studies in Philology* 84.3 (1987): 324–37.

——. "Workshop and/as Playhouse." In *Staging the Renaissance: Reinterpretations of Elizabethan and Jacobean Drama*, eds. David Kastan and Peter Stallybrass, 151–63. New York: Routledge, 1991.

Kathman, David. "Grocers, Goldsmiths, and Drapers: Freeman and Apprentices in the Elizabethan Theater." *Shakespeare Quarterly* 55.1 (2004): 1–49.

Katritzky, M.A. *Women, Medicine, and Theatre, 1500–1750: Literary Mountebanks and Performing Quacks*. Aldershot, UK: Ashgate, Burlington: VT: 2007.

Kearney, James. "The Book and the Fetish: the Materiality of Prospero's Text." *Journal of Medieval and Early Modern Studies* 32.3 (2002): 433–68.

Kempe, Will. *Nine Daies Wonder*. London, 1600.

Kennedy, Duncan. "The Structure of Blackstone's *Commentaries*." *Buffalo Law Review* 28 (1979): 205–382.

Kermode, Lloyd Edward. "After Shylock: The 'Judaiser' in England." *Renaissance and Reformation* 20.4 (1996): 5–26.

———. *Aliens and Englishness in Elizabethan Drama*. Cambridge: Cambridge University Press, 2009.

———, ed. *Three Renaissance Usury Plays*. Manchester: Manchester University Press, 2009.

King, Thomas. *The Gendering of Men, 1600–1750: The English Phallus*. Madison: The University of Wisconsin Press, 2004.

Kinzel, Ulrich. "Orientation as a Paradigm of Maritime Modernity." In *Fictions of the Sea: Critical Perspectives on the Ocean in British Literature and Culture*, ed. Bernhard Klein, 28–48. Burlington: VT: Ashgate, 2002.

Kingsbury, Susan Myra, ed. *The Records of the Virginia Company of London, 1607–1626*. 4 vols. Washington D.C.: United States Government Printing Office, 1906–35.

Kirk, R.E.G., and Ernest F. Kirk, eds. *Returns of Aliens Dwelling in the City and Suburbs of London from the Reign of Henry VIII to that of James I*, vol. 10. Aberdeen, UK: University Press, 1900.

Knights, L.C. *Drama and Society in the Age of Jonson*. London: Chatto and Windus, 1937.

Knutson, Roslyn Lander. *Playing Companies and Commerce in Shakespeare's Time*. Cambridge: Cambridge University Press, 2001.

———. *The Repertory of Shakespeare's Company 1594–1613*. Fayetteville: University of Arkansas Press, 1991.

Korda, Natasha. "Froes, Rebatoes and Other 'Outlandish Comodityes': Weaving Alien Women's Work into the Fabric of Early Modern Material Culture." In *Everyday Objects: Medieval and Early Modern Material Culture and Its Meanings*, eds. Tara Hamling and Catherine Richardson, 95–106. Burlington, VT: Ashgate, 2010.

———. "Labors Lost: Women's Work and Early Modern Theatrical Commerce." In *From Script to Stage in Early Modern England*, eds. Peter Holland and Stephen Orgel, 195–230. Houndmills, UK and New York: Palgrave, 2004.

———. "Women's Theatrical Properties." In *Staged Properties in Early Modern English Drama*, eds. Jonathan Gil Harris and Natasha Korda, 202–29. Cambridge: Cambridge University Press, 2002.

———. *Shakespeare's Domestic Economies: Gender and Property in Early Modern England*. Philadelphia: University of Pennsylvania Press, 2002.

Kristol, Susan Scheinberg. *Labor and Fortuna in Virgil's Aeneid*. New York: Garland Publishing, 1990.

Kussmaul, Ann. *Servants in Husbandry in Early Modern England*. Cambridge: Cambridge University Press, 1981.

Lamb, Mary Ellen. "The Cooke Sisters: Attitudes Toward Learned Women in the Renaissance." In *Silent But for the Word: Tudor Women as Patrons, Translators, and Writers of Religious Works*, ed. Margaret Patterson Hannay, 107–25. Kent: Kent State University Press, 1985.

———. *The Popular Culture of Shakespeare, Spenser, and Jonson*. London; New York: Routledge, 2006.

———. "Tracing a Heterosexual Erotics of Service in *Twelfth Night* and the Autobiographical Writings of Thomas Whythorne and Anne Clifford." *Criticism* 40.1 (1998): 1–25.

Laroque, Francois. "'Blue Apron Culture,': La culture Populaire dans 2 *Henry IV* et *The Shoemaker's Holiday* de Thomas Dekker." *RANAM* 39 (2006): 57–70.

Larwood, Jacob, and John Camden Hotten. *The History of Signboards*. London: John Camden Hotten, 1866.

Laurence, Anne. *Women in England 1500-1760: A Social History*. London: Phoenix Giant, 1994.

Lazonick, William. "Marx and Enclosures in England." *Review of Radical Political Economics* 6 (1974): 1–59.

Leahy, William. *Elizabethan Triumphal Processions*. Aldershot: Ashgate, 2005.

Lefebvre, Henri. *The Production of Space*. Trans. Donald Nicholson-Smith. Oxford: Blackwell, 2007.

Leggatt, Alexander. *Citizen Comedy in the Age of Shakespeare*. Toronto: University of Toronto Press, 1973.

Leinwand, Theodore B. *The City Staged: Jacobean Comedy, 1603–1613*. Madison: University of Wisconsin Press, 1986.

———. *Theatre, Finance and Society in Early Modern England*. Cambridge: Cambridge University Press, 1999.

Leslie, Michael. "'Something nasty in the wilderness': Entertaining Queen Elizabeth on her Progresses." *Medieval and Renaissance Drama in England* 10 (1998): 47–72.

Lesser, Zachery. "Tragical-Comical-Pastoral-Colonial: Economic Sovereignty, Globalization, and the Form of Tragicomedy." *ELH* 74 (2007): 881–908.

Levi-Strauss, Claude. "The Structural Study of Myth." In *Myth: A Symposium*, ed. Thomas A. Sebeok, 50–66. Philadelphia: American Folklore Society, 1955.

Loomba, Ania. "'Break Her Will and Bruise No Bone Sir': Colonial and Sexual Mastery in Fletcher's *The Island Princess*." *Journal for Early Modern Cultural Studies* 2 (2001): 68–108.

Lott, Tommy L., ed. *Subjugation and Bondage: Critical Essays on Slavery and Social Philosophy*. Boulder, CO: Rowman and Littlefield, 1998.

Low, Anthony. *The Georgic Revolution*. Princeton, NJ: Princeton University Press, 1985.

Luu, Lien Bich. *Immigrants and the Industries of London, 1500–1700*. Burlington, VT: Ashgate, 2005.

Lyly, John. *Midas*. Ed. David Bevington. Manchester: Manchester University Press, 2000.

M., I. *A Health to the Gentlemanly Profession of Servingmen*. London, 1598.

Maclean, Gerald. *The Rise of Oriental Travel: English Visitors to the Ottoman Empire, 1580–1720*. New York: Palgrave, 2004.

Maczak, Antoni. *Travel in Early Modern Europe*. Cambridge, UK: Polity, 1995.

Mancall, Peter C., ed. *Bringing the World to Early Modern Europe: Travel Accounts and Their Audiences*. Boston: Brill, 2007.

———. *Travel Narratives from the Age of Discovery: An Anthology*. Oxford: Oxford University Press, 2006.

Mander, C.H. Waterland. *A Descriptive and Historical Account of the Guild of Cordwainers of the City of London*. London: Williams, Lea & Company, 1931.

Manley, Lawrence. *Literature and Culture in Early Modern London*. Cambridge: Cambridge University Press, 1995.

Manning, Roger B. *Village Revolts: Social Protest and Popular Disturbances in England, 1509–1640*. Oxford: Clarendon Press, 1988.

Maquerlot, Jean-Pierre, and Michele Willems, eds. *Travel and Drama in Shakespeare's Time*. Cambridge: Cambridge University Press, 1996.

Marlowe, Christopher. *Doctor Faustus*. Ed. Roma Gill. New York: W.W. Norton, 1989.

———. *Doctor Faustus*. In *English Renaissance Drama: A Norton Anthology*, ed. David Bevington. New York: Norton, 2002.

———. *Doctor Faustus and Other Plays*. Eds. David Bevington and Eric Rasmussen. Oxford: Oxford University Press, 1995.

Marston, John. *The Dutch Courtesan*. Ed. M.L. Wine. Lincoln: University of Nebraska Press, 1965.

———. *Jacke Drums Entertainment*. London, 1601.

Martin, Catherine Gimelli. "Angels, Alchemists and Exchange: Commercial Ideology in Court and City Comedy, 1596–1610." In *The Witness of Times: Manifestations of Ideology in Seventeenth-Century England*, eds. Katherine Z. Keller and Gerald J. Schiffhorst, 121–47. Pittsburgh: Duquesne University Press, 1993.

Marvell, Andrew. *Poems on Affairs of State, 1660–1714*, ed. George deForest Lord. New Haven, CT: Yale University Press, 1963.

Marx, Karl. *Capital: A Critique of Political Economy*, vol. 1. Trans. Ben Fowkes. New York: Vintage, 1976.

———. *Writings of the Young Karl Marx on Philosophy and Society*. Trans. Lloyd D. Easton and Kurt H. Guddat. New York: Doubleday, 1967.

Matar, Nabil. *Britain and Barbary, 1589–1689*. Gainesville: University Press of Florida, 2005.

Matthews, Leslie Gerard. *The Royal Apothecaries*. London: Wellcome Historical Institute, 1967.

Maus, Katharine Eisaman. "Sorcery and Subjectivity in Early Modern Discourses of Witchcraft." In *Historicism, Psychoanalysis, and Early Modern Culture*, eds. Carla Mazzio and Douglas Trevor, 325–48. New York; London: Routledge, 2000.

Maynard, Stephen. "Feasting on Eyre: Community, Consumption, and Communion in *The Shoemaker's Holiday*." *Comparative Drama* 32.3 (1998): 327–46.

McBride, Kari Boyd. *Country House Discourse in Early Modern England: A Cultural Study of Landscape and Legitimacy*. Aldershot: Ashgate, 2001.

McCluskey, Peter M. "'Shall I Betray My Brother?' Anti-Alien Satire and its Subversion in *The Shoemaker's Holiday*." *Tennessee Philological Bulletin* 37 (2000): 43–54.

McIntosh, Marjorie Keniston. "Servants and the Household Unit in an Elizabethan English Community." *Journal of Family History* 9.1 (1984): 3–23.

————. *Working Women in English Society, 1300–1620*. Cambridge: Cambridge University Press, 2005.

McManus, Claire. *Women on the Renaissance Stage: Anna of Denmark and Female Masquing in the Stuart Court, 1590–1619*. Manchester: Manchester University Press, 2002.

McMullan, Gordon. *The Politics of Unease in the Plays of John Fletcher*. Amherst: University of Massachusetts Press, 1994.

McMullan, Gordon, and Jonathan Hope, eds. *The Politics of Tragicomedy: Shakespeare and After*. London: Routledge, 1992.

McRae, Andrew. "Husbandry Manuals and the Language of Agrarian Improvement." In *Culture and Cultivation in Early Modern England: Writing the Land*, eds. Michael Leslie and Timothy Raylor, 35–62. Leicester and London: Leicester University Press, 1992.

Mebane, John. "Renaissance Magic and the Return of the Golden Age: Utopianism and Religious Enthusiasm in *The Alchemist*." *Renaissance Drama* 10 (1977): 117–39.

Meikle, Scott. *Aristotle's Economic Thought*. Oxford: Oxford University Press, 1995.

Meldrum, Tim. "London Domestic Servants from Depositional Evidence, 1660–1750: Servant-Employer Sexuality in the Patriarchal Household." In *Chronicling Poverty: The Voices and Strategies of the English Poor, 1640–1840*, eds. Tim Hitchcock, Peter King, and Pamela Sharpe, 47–69. New York: St Martin's Press, 1997.

Mendelson, Sara, and Patricia Crawford. *Women in Early Modern England, 1550–1720*. Oxford: Oxford University Press, 1998.

Merrit, J.F. *The Social World of Early Modern Westminster: Abbey, Court, and Community*. Manchester: University of Manchester Press, 2005.

Middleton, Henry. *The Last East-Indian Voyage Containing Much Varietie of the State of the Severall Kingdomes*. London, 1606.

Middleton, Thomas. *Thomas Middleton: The Collected Works*. Eds. Gary Taylor and John Lavagnino. Oxford: Clarendon, 2007.

Miles, Robert. *Capitalism and Unfree Labor: Anomaly or Necessity?* London: Tavistock Publications, 1987.

Miller, Marla. *The Needle's Eye: Women and Work in the Age of Revolution*. Amherst: University of Massachusetts Press, 2006.

Milton, John. *The Reason of Church-government.* In *Complete Prose Works*, vol. 1., ed. Don M. Wolfe. New Haven, CT: Yale University Press, 1953.

Mirabella, Bella. "'Quacking Delilahs': Female Mountebanks in Early Modern England and Italy." In *Women Players in England, 1500–1660: Beyond the All-Male Stage*, eds. Pamela Allen Brown and Peter Parolin, 89–107. Aldershot, UK: Burlington, VT: Ashgate, 2008.

Misselden, Edward. *The Circle of Commerce, or the Balance of Trade.* London, 1623.

More, Thomas. *Utopia.* Ed. Robert M. Adams. New York: Norton, 1975.

Morgan, Edmund S. *American Slavery, American Freedom: The Ordeal of Colonial Virginia.* New York: W.W. Norton & Co., 1975.

Moryson, Fynes. *An Itinerary Containing His Ten Yeeres Travell through the Twelve Dominions of Germany, Bohmerland, Sweitzerland, Netherland, Denmarke, Poland, Italy, Turky, France, England, Scotland & Ireland.* 4 vols. Glasgow, UK: James MacLehose and Sons, 1907.

Mouffe, Chantal. "Democratic Citizenship and the Political Community." In *Dimensions of Radical Democracy*, ed. Mouffe, 225–39. London: Verso, 1992.

———. "Preface: Democratic Politics Today." In *Dimensions of Radical Democracy*, ed. Mouffe, 1–16. London: Verso, 1992.

Mukerji, Chandra. *From Graven Images: Patterns of Modern Materialism.* New York: Columbia University Press, 1983.

Mun, Thomas. *England's Treasure by Forraign Trade.* Oxford: Basil Blackwell, 1928.

Murray, John J. *Flanders and England: A Cultural Bridge: The Influence of the Low Countries on Tudor-Stuart England.* Antwerp, Belgium: Fonds Mercator, 1985.

Nashe, Thomas. *Pierce Penilesse.* London, 1592.

Neill, Michael. "'Material Flames': The Space of Mercantile Fantasy in John Fletcher's *The Island Princess*." *Renaissance Drama* 27 (1999): 19–31.

———. *Putting History to the Question: Power, Politics, and Society in English Renaissance Drama.* New York: Columbia University Press, 2000.

———. "'A woman's service': Gender, Subordination, and the Erotics of Rank in the Drama of Shakespeare and his Contemporaries." *The Shakespearean International Yearbook* 5 (2005): 127–44.

Nerlich, Michael. *Ideology of Adventure: Studies in Modern Consciousness, 1100–1750.* 2 vols. Trans. Ruth Crowley. Minneapolis: University of Minnesota Press, 1988.

Netzloff, Mark. *Internal Colonies: Class, Capital, and the Literature of Early Modern Colonialism.* New York: Palgrave, 2003.

Newman, Karen. "Women and Commodification in Jonson's *Epicoene*." *ELH* 56 (1989): 503–18.

Nichols, John, ed. *The Progresses, Processions, and Magnificent Festivities of King James the First.* 4 vols. London: J.B. Nichols, 1828.

Oppenheim, M., ed. *The Naval Tracts of Sir William Monson.* 6 vols. London: Navy Records Society, 1913.

Orgel, Stephen. *Impersonations: The Performance of Gender in Shakespeare's England.* Cambridge: Cambridge University Press, 1996.

Orlin, Lena Cowen. *Private Matters and Public Culture in Post-Reformation England.* Ithaca, NY: Cornell University Press, 1994.

———. "Three Ways to be Invisible in the Renaissance: Sex, Reputation, and Stitchery." In *Renaissance Culture and the Everyday*, eds. Patricia Fumerton and Simon Hunt, 183–203. Philadelphia: University of Pennsylvania Press, 1999.

Ouellette, Anthony J. "*The Alchemist* and the Emerging Adult Private Playhouse." *SEL* 45 (205): 375–99.

Parker, John. "What a Piece of Work is Man: Shakespearean Drama as Marxian Fetish." *Journal of Medieval and Early Modern Studies* 34.3 (2004): 643–72.

Parker, Kenneth, ed. *Early Modern Tales of Orient: A Critical Anthology.* New York: Routledge, 1999.

Parker, Rozsika. *The Subversive Stitch: Embroidering and the Making of the Feminine.* London and New York: Routledge, 1989.

Parr, Anthony, ed. *Three Renaissance Travel Plays.* Manchester: Manchester University Press, 1995.

Pasnau, Robert. *Thomas Aquinas on Human Nature: A Philosophical Study of Summa Theologiae 1a 75–89.* Cambridge: Cambridge University Press, 2002.

Paster, Gail Kern. *The Body Embarrassed: Drama and the Disciplines of Shame in Early Modern England.* Ithaca, NY: Cornell University Press, 1993.

———. *The Idea of the City in the Age of Shakespeare.* Athens: University of Georgia Press, 1985.

Patterson, Annabel. *Shakespeare and the Popular Voice.* Cambridge: Blackwell, 1989.

Pearse, Nancy C. *John Fletcher's Chastity Plays: Mirrors of Modesty.* Lewisburg: Bucknell University Press, 1973.

Peck, Linda Levy. *Consuming Splendor: Society and Culture in Seventeenth-Century England.* Cambridge: Cambridge University Press, 2005.

Perkins, William. *A Discourse of the Damned Art of Witchcraft.* Cambridge, 1610.

———. *Discourse of the Damned Art of Witchcraft.* In *English Witchcraft, 1560–1736*, ed. James Sharpe. London: Pickering and Chatto, 2003.

Pettegree, Andrew. *Foreign Protestant Communities in Sixteenth-Century London* Oxford: Clarendon Press, 1986.

Plat, Hugh. *The Garden of Eden.* London, 1659.

Plummer, Alfred. *The London Weavers' Company, 1600–1970.* Boston: Routledge and Kegan Paul, 1972.

Pocock, J.G.A. "The Mobility of Property and the Rise of Eighteenth-Century Sociology." In *Theories of Property: Aristotle to the Present*, eds. Anthony Parel and Thomas Flanagan, 141–67. Waterloo, Ontario: Wilfrid Laurier University Press, 1979.

Pollock, Sir Frederick, and Frederic William Maitland. *The History of English Law Before the Time of Edward I.* 2nd ed. 2 vols. Cambridge: Cambridge University Press, 1968.

Poovey, Mary. *A History of the Modern Fact: Problems of Knowledge in the Sciences of Wealth and Society.* Chicago: University of Chicago Press, 1998.

Prager, Carolyn. "The Problem of Slavery in *The Custom of the Country.*" *SEL* 28.2 (1988): 301–17.

Proctor, Thomas. *Of the Knowledge and Conduct of Warres.* London, 1578.

Pugliatti, Paola. *Beggary and Theatre in Early Modern England.* Burlington, VT: Ashgate, 2003.

Purchas, Samuel. *Purchas his Pilgrimes.* London, 1625.

Purkiss, Diane. *The Witch in History: Early Modern and Twentieth-Century Representations.* London: Routledge, 1996.

Rabb, Theodore K. *Enterprise and Empire: Merchant and Gentry Investment in the Expansion of England, 1575–1630.* Cambridge, MA: Harvard University Press, 1967.

Raithby, John, ed. *Statutes of the Realm.* London: G. Eyre and A. Strahan, 1819.

Raman, Shankar. *Framing "India": The Colonial Imaginary in Early Modern Culture.* Stanford: Stanford University Press, 2001.

Ransome, David R. "Wives for Virginia, 1621." *The William and Mary Quarterly* 48.1 (1991): 3–18.

Rappaport, Steve. *Worlds Within Worlds: Structures of Life in Sixteenth-Century London.* Cambridge: Cambridge University Press, 1989.

Rasmussen, Mark David, ed. *Renaissance Literature and Its Formal Engagements.* New York: Palgrave, 2002.

Rediker, Marcus, and Peter Linebaugh. *The Many-Headed Hydra: Sailors, Slaves, Commoners, and the Hidden History of the Revolutionary Atlantic.* Boston: Beacon Press, 2000.

Rid, Samuel. *The Art of Jugling or Legerdemaine.* London, 1612.

Reid, Robert L. "Sacerdotal Vestiges in *The Tempest.*" *Comparative Drama* 41.4 (2007): 493–513.

Riddell, James A. "Some Actors in Jonson's Plays." *Shakespeare Studies* 5 (1969): 285–98.

Rockett, William. "Labor and Virtue in *The Tempest.*" *Shakespeare Quarterly* 24.1 (1973): 77–84.

Rutter, Tom. *Work and Play on the Shakespearean Stage.* Cambridge: Cambridge University Press, 2008.

The Salisbury Assizes. London, 1653.

Schafer, Elizabeth. "William Haughton's *Englishmen for My Money*: A Critical Note." *Review of English Studies* 41.164 (1990): 536–8.

Schalkwyk, David. *Shakespeare, Love and Service.* Cambridge: Cambridge University Press, 2008.

Schama, Simon. *The Embarrassment of Riches: An Interpretation of Dutch Culture in the Golden Age.* New York: Knopf, 1987.

————. "Wives and Wantons: Versions of Womanhood in Seventeenth-Century Dutch Art." *Oxford Art Journal* 3 (1980): 5–13.

Schilling, Heinz. "Innovation Through Migration: The Settlements of Calvinistic Netherlands in Sixteenth- and Seventeenth-Century Central and Western Europe." *Histoire Sociale* 16 (1983): 7–33.

Schrickx, Willem. "Elizabethan Drama and Anglo-Dutch Relations." In *Reclamations of Shakespeare*, ed. A.J. Hoenselaars, 21–32. Amsterdam: Rodopi, 1994.

Scot, Reginald. *A Discoverie of Witchcraft.* 1584. Carbondale: Southern Illinois University Press, 1964.

Scott, James. *Weapons of the Weak: Everyday Forms of Peasant Resistance.* New Haven: Yale University Press, 1985.

Scouloudi, Irene. *Returns of Strangers in the Metropolis, 1593, 1627, 1635, 1639.* London: Hueguenot Society of London, 1985.

Scoville, Warren C. "The Huguenots and the Diffusion of Technology, Part 1." *The Journal of Political Economy* 60: 4 (1952): 294–311.

Sebek, Barbara, and Stephen Deng, eds. *Global Traffic: Discourses and Practices of Trade in English Literature and Culture from 1550–1700.* New York: Palgrave, 2008.

Shakespeare, William. *The Arden Shakespeare.* Eds. W.J. Craig and R.H. Case, et. al. New York: Routledge, 1990.

————. *Coriolanus.* Ed. Philip Brockbank. New York: Routledge, 1996.

————. *Henry IV, Part 1.* Ed. A.R. Humphreys. London: Methuen & Co. Ltd., 1960.

————. *Henry V.* Ed. J.H. Walter. London and New York: Routledge, 1990.

————. *Much Ado About Nothing.* Ed. A.R. Humphreys. London: Methuen, 1981.

————. *The Norton Shakespeare.* Eds. Stephen Greenblatt et al. New York: W.W. Norton, 1997.

————. *The Riverside Shakespeare.* 2nd ed. Ed. G. Blakemore Evans. Boston: Houghton Mifflin, 1997.

————. *The Second Part of King Henry VI.* Ed. Andrew S. Cairncross. New York: Routledge, 1988.

Sharp, Buchanan. *In Contempt of All Authority: Rural Artisans and Riot in the West of England, 1586–1660.* Berkeley: University of California Press, 1980.

Shepard, Alexandra. "Manhood, Credit and Patriarchy in Early Modern England c.1580–1640." *Past and Present* 167.1 (2000): 75–106.

————. *Meanings of Manhood in Early Modern England.* Oxford: Oxford University Press, 2003.

Sherman, William H. "'Gold is the Strength, the Sinnewes of the World': Thomas Dekker's *Old Fortunatus* and England's Golden Age." *Medieval and Renaissance Drama in England* 6 (1993): 85–102.

————. "Travel and Trade." In *A Companion to Renaissance Drama*, ed. Arthur F. Kinney, 109–20. Oxford: Blackwell, 2004.

Simpson, A.W.B. *The History of the Common Law of Contract: The Rise of the Action of Assumpsit.* Oxford: Clarendon Press, 1975.

Slack, Paul. *Poverty and Policy in Tudor and Stuart England.* New York: Longman, 1988.

Smith, Abbot Emerson. *Colonists in Bondage: White Servitude and Convict Labor in America, 1607–1776.* Chapel Hill: University of North Carolina Press, 1947.

Smith, Bruce. *Shakespeare and Masculinity.* Oxford: Oxford University Press, 2000.

Smith, Emma. "'So Much English by the Mother': Gender, Foreigners, and the Mother Tongue in William Haughton's *Englishmen for My Money.*" *Medieval and Renaissance Drama in England* 13 (2000): 165–81.

Smith, Thomas. *De Republica Anglorum.* London, 1583.

———. *De Republica Anglorum.* Ed. Mary Dewar. Cambridge: Cambridge University Press, 1982.

Stagl, Justin. *A History of Curiosity: The Theory of Travel 1550–1800.* Chur, Switzerland: Harwood, 1995.

Staniland, Kay. "Thomas Deane's Shop in the Royal Exchange." In *The Royal Exchange*, ed. Ann Saunders, 59–67. London: London Topographical Society, 1997.

Stavreva, Kirilka. "Fighting Words: Witch-Speak in Late Elizabeth Docu-fiction." *Journal of Medieval and Early Modern Studies* 30.2 (2000): 309–38.

Stevenson, Laura. *Praise and Paradox: Merchants and Craftsmen in Elizabethan Popular Literature.* Cambridge: Cambridge University Press, 1984.

Stow, John. *Stow's Survey of London.* London: Dent, 1965.

Suranyi, Anna. *The Genius of the English Nation: Travel Writing and National Identity in Early Modern England.* Newark: University of Delaware Press, 2008.

Sullivan, Garrett A., Jr. *The Drama of Landscape: Land, Property, and Social Relations on the Early Modern Stage.* Stanford: Stanford University Press, 1998.

Sutcliffe, Matthew. *The Practice, Proceeding, and Lawes of Armes.* London, 1593.

Sutton, James. *Materializing Space at an Early Modern Prodigy House: The Cecils at Theobalds, 1564–1607.* Aldershot: Ashgate, 2004.

Suzuki, Mihoko. *Subordinate Subjects: Gender, the Political Nation, and Literary Form in England, 1588–1688.* Burlington, VT: Ashgate, 2003.

Tawney, R.H., and Eileen Power, eds. *Tudor Economic Documents: Being Select Documents Illustrating the Economic and Social History of Tudor England.* 3 vols. London: Longmans, Green and Co., 1924.

Teissedou, Jean-Pierre. "*The Prophetess* de John Fletcher (1579–1625): Puissance de la Magie ou Magie de la Puissance?" In *La Magie et ses langages*, ed. Margaret Jones-Davies, 83–93. Lille: Universitè de Lille, 1980.

Thirsk, Joan. *Agrarian History of England and Wales*, vol. 4. Cambridge University Press, 1967.

———. *Economic Policy and Projects: The Development of a Consumer Society in Early Modern England.* Oxford: Clarendon Press, 1978.

Thomas, Keith. *Religion and the Decline of Magic: Studies in Popular Belief in Sixteenth and Seventeenth Century England.* New York: Oxford University Press, 1971.

Thomson, Leslie. "'As Proper a Woman as Any in Cheap': Women in Shops on the Early Modern Stage." *Medieval and Renaissance Drama in England* 16 (2003): 145–61.

Traister, Barbara Howard. *Heavenly Necromancers: The Magician in English Renaissance Drama.* Columbia: University of Missouri Press, 1984.

Tudeau-Clayton, Margaret. *Jonson, Shakespeare, and Early Modern Virgil.* Cambridge: Cambridge University Press, 1998.

Turley, David. *Slavery.* Oxford: Blackwell, 2000.

Vitkus, Daniel. "'Meaner Ministers': Theatrical Labor, Mastery, and Bondage in The Tempest." In *The Blackwell Companion to Shakespeare's Works: The Poems, Problem Comedies and Late Plays,* eds. Jean E. Howard and Richard Dutton, 408–26. Oxford: Blackwell, 2003.

———. "Turks and Jews in *The Jew of Malta.*" In *Early Modern English Drama: A Critical Companion,* eds. Garrett A. Sullivan, Jr., Patrick Cheney, and Andrew Hadfield, 61–73. New York: Oxford University Press, 2006.

Wales, Tim. "Poverty, Poor Relief and the Life Cycle: Some Evidence from Seventeenth-Century Norfolk." In *Land, Kinship, and Life Cycle,* ed. R.M. Smith. Cambridge: Cambridge University Press, 1984.

Walker, D.P. *Spiritual and Demonic Magic from Ficino to Campanella.* London: Warburg Institute, 1958.

Walker, Garthine. "Rereading Rape and Sexual Violence in Early Modern England," *Gender and History* 10.1 (1998): 1–25.

Wall, Wendy. *Staging Domesticity: Household Work and English Identity in Early Modern Drama.* Cambridge: Cambridge University Press, 2002.

Wallerstein, Immanuel. *The Modern World System I: Capitalist Agriculture and the Origins of the European World Economy in the Sixteenth Century.* New York: Academic Press, 1974.

Wallis, Lawrence B. *Fletcher, Beaumont & Company, Entertainers to the Jacobean Gentry.* New York: Kings Crown Press, 1947.

Walsh, Brian. "Performing Historicity in Dekker's *The Shoemaker's Holiday,*" *SEL* 46.2 (2006): 323–48.

Walsh, Lorena S. "Servitude and Opportunity in Charles County, Maryland, 1658–1705." In *Law, Society, and Politics in Early Maryland,* eds. Aubrey C. Land et al., Baltimore, MD: John Hopkins University Press, 1977. 111–33.

Walvin, James. *Questioning Slavery.* New York: Routledge, 1996.

Warneke, Sarah. *Images of the Educational Traveller in Early Modern England.* New York: Brill, 1995.

Warner, William Beatty. *Licensing Entertainment: The Elevation of Novel Reading in Britain, 1684–1750.* Berkeley: University of California Press, 1998.

Weil, Judith. *Service and Dependency in Shakespeare's Plays.* Cambridge: Cambridge University Press, 2005.

Weimann, Robert. *Author's Pen and Actor's Voice: Playing and Writing in Shakespeare's Theatre*. Eds. Helen Higbee and William West. Cambridge: Cambridge University Press, 2000.

———. *Shakespeare and the Popular Tradition in the Theater: Studies in the Social Dimension of Dramatic Form and Function*. Ed. Robert Schwartz. Baltimore, MD: The Johns Hopkins University Press, 1978.

Weyer, Johan. *De Praestigiis Daemonum*. 1563. Ed. John Shea. Binghamton, NY: Center for Medieval and Renaissance Studies, 1991.

Williams, Raymond. *The Country and the City*. New York: Oxford University Press, 1973.

———. *Marxism and Literature*. Oxford: Oxford University Press, 1977.

Willis, Deborah. *Malevolent Nurture: Witch-Hunting and Maternal Power in Early Modern England*. Ithaca, NY: Cornell University Press, 1995.

Wilson, Eric. "Abel Drugger's Sign and the Fetishes of Material Culture." In *Historicism, Psychoanalysis, and Early Modern Culture*, eds. Carla Mazzio and Douglas Trevor, 110–34. New York: Routledge, 2000.

Wilson, Jean. *Entertainments for Elizabeth I*. Woodbridge and Totawa: D.S. Brewer, 1980.

Wilson, Thomas. "State of England, anno com. 1600." In *Camden Miscellany*, vol. 16. London: Camden Society, 1845.

Wilson-Okamura, David Scott. "Virgilian Models of Colonization in Shakespeare's *The Tempest*." *ELH* 70.3 (2003): 709–37.

Wood, Andy. "'Poore men woll speke one daye': Plebian Languages of Deference and Defiance in England, c. 1520–1640." In *The Politics of the Excluded, c. 1500–1850*, ed. Tim Harris, 67–98. New York: Palgrave, 2001.

Wood, Ellen Meiksins. *The Origin of Capitalism: A Longer View*. New York: Verso, 2002.

Woodbridge, Linda, ed. *Money and the Age of Shakespeare: Essays in New Economic Criticism*. New York: Palgrave, 2003.

Woodbridge, Linda. "The Peddler and the Pawn: Why Did Tudor England Consider Peddlers to Be Rogues?" In *Rogues and Early Modern English Culture,* eds. Craig Dionne and Steve Mentz, 143–71. Ann Arbor: University of Michigan Press, 2004.

———. *Vagrancy, Homelessness, and English Renaissance Literature*. Urbana: University of Illinois Press, 2001.

Woolley, Hannah. *The Compleat Servant-Maid; Or, The Young Maidens Tutor*. London, 1677.

Worden, Thomas. "Idols in the Early Modern Material World (1599)." *Exemplaria* 11.2 (1999): 437–71.

Wright, Louis B. *Middle-Class Culture in Elizabethan England*. Chapel Hill: University of North Carolina Press, 1935.

Wrightson, Keith. *Earthly Necessities: Economic Lives in Early Modern Britain*. New Haven, CT: Yale University Press, 2002.

Yachnin, Paul. "'The Perfection of Ten': Populuxe Art and Artisanal Value in *Troilus and Cressida.*" *Shakespeare Quarterly.* 56.3 (2005): 306–27.

Yates, Frances. *Giordano Bruno and the Hermetic Tradition.* Chicago: University of Chicago Press, 1991.

Yelling, J.A. *Common Field and Enclosures in England, 1450–1850.* Hamden, CT: Archon Books, 1977.

Yungblut, Laura Hunt. *Strangers Settled Here Amongst Us: Policies, Perceptions and the Presence of Aliens in Elizabethan England.* London: Routledge, 1996.

Zizek, Slavoj. "Eastern Europe's Republics of Gilead," in *Dimensions of Radical Democracy*, ed. Chantal Mouffe, 193–207. London: Verso, 1992.

Zwierlein, Anne-Julia. "Shipwrecks in the City: Commercial Risk as Romance in Early Modern City Comedy." In *Plotting Early Modern London: New Essays on Jacobean City Comedy*, eds. Dieter Mehl, Angela Stock, and Anne-Julia Zwierlein, 75–94. Burlington, VT: Ashgate, 2004.

Index

spectators, 128
speculation, 120n15
Spenser, Edmund, 149
spice trade, 214–16, 220, 221, 232–3
spinners, 63
stage-furniture, 1, 3
stage journeys, 226
Stallybrass, Peter, 55
Stanley family, 149
status, 19–32, 36
Statute of Artificers, 133, 165
Stevenson, Laura, 23
"St Hugh's bones," 46
Stoics, 180
storax, 72, 73, 74
storms, 15–16
Stow, John, 20, 20n13, 33, 111
the Strand, 75, 77
Stuart period, 14
Styles, Anne, 168, 169, 169n29
subjectivity, 1–2, 6, 39, 51–2
   citizenship and, 8–9, 38, 39
   female, 12, 49–50
   forms of, 3
   labor and, 116–17
   male, 101–13
   of perfumers, 80–85
   sexualized, 12
   temperance and, 200–201
sustenance, 121
Sutcliffe, Mathew, 106

Taylor, Joseph, 128
Temple Bar, 78
Ternate, 215n19
textile trades, 9–10, 40, 53–68, 60n32. *See also* clothing trades
theater, 94–5. *See also specific works and genres*
   alienated labor and, 178–9, 179n6
   aristocracy and, 128
   children in, 94–5
   distinguished from labor, 94–5
   Elizabethan period, 16, 53–68, 80, 233, 235–6
   ideological indoctrination and, 184–5
   Jacobean period, 16, 53–68, 131–43, 233–5
   labor and, 104, 104n6, 104–5n7, 178–9, 179n6, 248, 249, 250

   perfumers in, 80–85
   production of surplus value by, 223
   professionalization of, 128
   Stuart period, 14, 80
   trade companies and, 104–5n7
   as transformative, 223
   Tudor period, 14, 41
theater companies, 94–5, 102, 116, 126, 126n25, 126n26, 128. *See also specific companies*
   as capitalist ventures, 126, 128–9
   children in, 95
   class and, 127
   craftsmen in, 128n36
   tradesmen in, 128n36
theaters
   commercial, 7
   public, 1, 3
theater workers, 116–17, 248, 249, 250
   economic subject positions of, 127–8
   guild system and, 104–5n7
theatrical cultures, 10
theatricality, 13–14, 166, 174
theft, 222
Thirsk, Joan, 61–2, 117, 243
Thomas, Keith, 167
   Religion and the Decline of Magic, 164
Thorius, Raphael, 67n55
tobacco, 78
toleration, 46
trade, global networks of, 6, 14–16, 35, 43–4, 121, 209–23, 209n1, 215n19, 228–9, 228n7, 242, 244–6
trade companies, 104–5n7
tradesmen, 21–2n17, 46, 47, 111. *See also* merchants
tragedy, 2–3, 12, 209–10. *See also* tragicomedy
   female servants in, 131–43
   Jacobean, 12, 132
tragicomedy, 7, 15, 132, 196, 208, 209–23, 210n4, 210n6, 233, 233–4n21, 238, 241, 246
transformation, 198–9, 198n26, 200, 212, 213–14, 217–18, 223. *See also* redemption
transition, 26
travel, 15–16, 230–231
   capitalism and, 228